Review Copy - InTer p.

Old Testament Criticism
in the Nineteenth Century
ENGLAND AND GERMANY

W. M. L. de Wette

Old Testament Criticism
in the Nineteenth Century

ENGLAND AND GERMANY

John Rogerson

*Published in the United Kingdom
by the Society for Promoting Christian Knowledge
London, England*

Copyright © 1984 by John W. Rogerson

First Fortress Press edition 1985

Library of Congress Cataloging in Publication Data

Rogerson, J. W. (John William), 1935–

    Old Testament criticism in the nineteenth century.

    Bibliography: p.
    Includes index.
    1. Bible. O.T.—Criticism, interpretation, etc.—
History—19th century. I. Title.
BS1160.R6   1985   221.6'09'034   84–47933
ISBN 0–8006–0737–6

K977d84   Printed in the United Kingdom   1–737

To the Memory of

William Gordon Fallows
Principal of Ripon Hall, Oxford, 1959–68
Bishop of Pontefract, 1968–71
Bishop of Sheffield, 1971–9

Liberal Churchman
Historian
Father in God

Contents

Preface   ix

Abbreviations   xi

Author's Note   xiii

Introduction   1

PART ONE
Germany 1800 – 60

1   The Results of Old Testament Criticism in Germany prior to 1800   15

2   W. M. L. de Wette   28

3   In the Footsteps of de Wette: Gesenius, Gramberg and George   50

4   Vatke's 'Biblical Theology'   69

5   Confessional Opposition to the Critical Method   79

6   Heinrich Ewald   91

7   Hofmann and Delitzsch: Confessional Scholars with a Difference   104

8   Christian Carl Josias von Bunsen: Diplomat and Scholar   121

9   Various Critical Scholars: Bleek, Hupfeld, Hitzig and Umbreit   130

10   Conclusions to Part One   138

Appendix: Table of Old Testament Professors in Protestant Faculties in Germany 1800 – 1900   141

PART TWO
England 1800 – 80

11   English Critical Old Testament Scholarship prior to 1800   147

12   German Old Testament Criticism in England 1790–1859   158

13   English Critical Old Testament Scholarship 1800–57   180

14   Samuel Davidson and his Dismissal in 1857   197

15   *Essays and Reviews* 1860   209

16   John William Colenso   220

17   English Critical Old Testament Scholarship 1864–80   238
18   Conclusions to Part Two   249

PART THREE
England from 1880 and Germany from 1860:
The Streams Converge

19   Germany from 1860: the Path to Wellhausen   257
20   England from 1880: the Triumph of Wellhausen   273

Conclusion   291
Bibliography   294
Index of Biblical References   310
Index of Modern Authors   314
Index of Subjects and Biblical Names   318

Preface

This book is not a history of Old Testament scholarship in the nineteenth century. It is not even a history of *British* Old Testament scholarship in the nineteenth century; for as the title implies and the introduction makes clear, the main concern of the book is with Germany and England, and although there are important references to Scottish and Irish scholars, the discussion concentrates upon the reception of biblical criticism among English (some reviewers might want to add Anglican) Old Testament experts.

The deliberate lack of reference to Dutch, French and American scholarship, not to mention Scottish, Irish and Welsh scholarship, is not meant in any way as a slight on the achievements or importance of these countries' scholars. When I began to write the text of this book, I fully expected that, before I had completed it, the centenary project of the [American] Society for Biblical Literature would be so well advanced, that there would have appeared a number of monographs on the history of American critical scholarship. In the event, less has been published than I had expected, but I did not want in any way to compete with the project. Again, there already exist monographs on aspects of the history of Dutch and French criticism, and I did not want to try to duplicate these.

In fact, as originally conceived and executed, the book is an attempt to deal with two specific questions: how did the critical method arise in Germany in the nineteenth century, and how was its reception into England affected by the theological and philosophical climate prevalent in England in the nineteenth century? These questions have been investigated before but not, I believe, in the detail that is presented here. Indeed, in spite of the areas that I have not covered through lack of expertise, I think that I can claim that there is no book in English which discusses the German material as fully as is done here, and that there is no book in any language that attempts to trace in such detail the effect of German critical Old Testament scholarship upon England.

My reason for investigating these two questions is that I have long wanted to explore some of the implications of the fact that although the critical method is the basis of academic Old Testament studies in Britain today, the *home* of the method and still the place of its most creative use, is Protestant Germany (although German Catholic scholarship is equally creative since its wholehearted acceptance of the critical method). This fact affects any

ix

attempt to teach Old Testament studies in a British university. Although we are presenting to our students results that ought simply to be evaluated on intellectual grounds available to anyone of the requisite intelligence, we are in fact presenting results that originate from a theological and philosophical climate different from our own. The reluctance of some students to come to grips with the critical method is partly born of an unwillingness or an inability to bridge a small, but important cultural gap. In spite of the fact that the book concentrates on Protestant Germany and England, I hope that it will be a contribution both to aspects of the history of Old Testament scholarship, and to the history of ideas.

Among the people who have assisted me in the preparation of the book over the past eight years, I should like to thank the staffs of the libraries of the Universities of Durham and Sheffield, and especially the inter-library loan section in Sheffield. Much of the work on the German material was done at the library of the Eberhard-Karls-Universität, Tübingen, the Niedersächsische Staats- und Universitätsbibliothek, Göttingen, and the Staatsbibliothek Preussischer Kulturbesitz, West Berlin, to whose staffs I offer my thanks for their assistance and courtesy. My Sheffield colleagues, Mr David J. A. Clines and Dr David M. Gunn, have kindly lent me books on a long-term basis, my wife has spent countless hours in producing a typescript from my longhand, and a graduate of the Sheffield Department of Biblical Studies, Mr Mark Satterly, has produced the bibliography from my footnotes.

My most grateful thanks I reserve for Professor Rudolf Smend of Göttingen, who is the greatest living expert on nineteenth century Old Testament scholarship in Germany. From his own library he has made me many gifts of early nineteenth century German material, he has taken a close interest in the present project, and together with his wife, he has been my host on many occasions. It has been a great privilege to be able to discuss so many ideas with a German scholar, whose own family has had such close contacts with some of the greatest names in German academic life.

J. W. ROGERSON
Sheffield, 1983.

Abbreviations

ADB	Allgemeine Deutsche Biographie
AGTL	Arbeiten zur Geschichte und Theologie des Luthertums
AKZ	Allgemeine Kirchenzeitung
BER	Biblisch-Exegetisches Repertorium
BEvTh	Beiträge zur evangelischen Theologie
BFChTh	Beiträge zur Förderung christlicher Theologie
BGBE	Beiträge zur Geschichte der biblischen Exegese
BZAW	Beihefte zur Zeitschrift für die alttestamentliche Wissenschaft
BZRGG	Beihefte der Zeitschrift für Religions- und Geistesgeschichte
DZCW	Deutsche Zeitschrift für christliche Wissenchaft und christliches Leben
EKZ	Evangelische Kirchenzeitung, Berlin
ET	Expository Times
FGLP	Forschungen zur Geschichte und Lehre des Protestantismus
FKDG	Forschungen zur Kirchen- und Dogmengeschichte
FRLANT	Forschungen zur Religion und Literatur des Alten und Neuen Testaments
FSThR	Forschungen zur systematischen Theologie und Religionsphilosophie
GGA	Göttingische gelehrte Anzeigen
HTIBS	Historic Texts and Interpreters in Biblical Scholarship
JR	Journal of Religion
KEH	Kurzgefasstes exegetisches Handbuch zum Alten Testament
NND	Neuer Nekrolog der Deutschen
SVT	Supplements to Vetus Testamentum
TB	Theologische Bücherei
ThLZ	Theologische Literatur Zeitung
TRE	Theologische Realenzyklopädie
TSK	Theologische Studien und Kritiken

TZS	*Theologische Zeitschrift* (ed. Schleiermacher, de Wette, Lücke)
TZTh	*Tübinger Zeitschrift für Theologie*
ZKM	*Zeitschrift für die Kunde des Morgenlandes*
ZThK	*Zeitschrift für Theologie und Kirche*

Author's Note

I have left untranslated the terms *Privatdozent* and *ausserordentlicher* Professor. A *Privatdozent* is a recognized teacher in a theological (or any other) faculty of a particular university. To become a *Privatdozent* in the nineteenth century in Germany, it was necessary at the very least to have gained a doctorate by thesis. In most universities it was also necessary to have submitted an additional thesis (*Habilitationsschrift*) or to have gained by further study a Licentiate in Theology. A *Privatdozent* had the right to give public lectures in the faculty which recognized him. He received no salary, but the students who attended his classes would pay him tuition fees.

An *ausserordentlicher* Professor in the nineteenth century was a university teacher appointed by the Minister for Education in the state or *Land* where the university was situated. He received a salary, but did not occupy an established chair.

Introduction

In 1869, Ludwig Diestel published his 'History of the Old Testament in the Christian Church'.[1] This work of over eight hundred pages is never likely to be surpassed by one scholar working alone. It remains an indispensable source book for anyone studying the history of Old Testament scholarship, and it is a tribute to its abiding value that plans to reprint it have been made on more than one occasion in recent years, culminating in a reprint in 1981.

In his preface, Diestel wrote that there could be no true writing of history without decisions that affected the selection and mode of presentation of the material. He recognized the complexities that made each individual scholar both subject to the burning issues and concerns of his day, and yet a unique and creative person within the general drift of scholarship. Diestel revealed something of the difficulties that he had experienced in deciding how to order and to evaluate his material, and he realistically acknowledged that the subjective element was bound to enter into the writing of a history of interpretation. Other scholars would, perhaps, evaluate differently from him, or see particular aspects of scholarship in a different light. When it came to making judgements about scholarships, Diestel declared that he would be lenient towards those who had worked at times which were not congenial to scientific scholarship, such as the first five centuries, and that he would refrain from harsh judgements upon scholars of his own generation. Where he felt that judgement could be severe was in cases where scholars followed directions which had already been shown in history to be false, and which went against what had been justifiably established as a consensus in theological scholarship.[2]

No such realism, or reluctance to make harsh judgements can be found in Thomas Kelly Cheyne's *Founders of Old Testament Criticism* (1893).[3] This book remains one of the few British contributions to the history of Old Testament scholarship in the nineteenth century, and it is distinguished by the thoroughness with which the author worked on his primary sources, especially those dealing with German scholars such as de Wette and Ewald. However, the net result is that nineteenth-century Old Testament scholarship

[1] Ludwig Diestel, *Geschichte des Alten Testamentes in der christlichen Kirche*, Jena 1869, reprint Leipzig 1981.
[2] Diestel, pp. vii–viii.
[3] T. K. Cheyne, *Founders of Old Testament Criticism*, London, 1893.

1

is depicted in terms of black and white. Those who contributed to the rise of the critical method are praised, those who are judged to have obstructed it are condemned, and those who, in Cheyne's view, should have done more than they actually did for the critical cause receive only qualified approval.

Cheyne's book is clearly apologetic, but the apologetic tone can perhaps be forgiven on the grounds that it was written at a time when both in Britain and Germany, scholars were bitterly divided over the presentation of the history of Israelite religion contained in Wellhausen's *Prolegomena*. Cheyne was a champion of the critical method, and he felt that the cause could be furthered by a history of nineteenth-century Old Testament scholarship in which the founders of criticism were the heroes. His book, however, was an extreme example of a type of 'history of scholarship', in which the criterion for judgement was the point that had been reached by the scholarship that the author himself accepted. This point was seen as the culmination of a process; as a vantage point from which the true stream of scholarly progress could be distinguished from tributaries or backwaters that went nowhere, or even tried to flow uphill. In spite of containing valuable material, it was in some ways no different from books that have been written from a conservative point of view, in which the critical method is 'exposed' as based upon human philosophies, or as yielding contradictory results.

In his 'History of the historical-critical study of the Old Testament since the Reformation', Hans-Joachim Kraus took a <u>modified version</u> of Cheyne's stance. Complaining that recent studies of the history of Old Testament scholarship had not sufficiently distinguished between differing tendencies in interpretation, he stressed the need for the confusion to be sorted out. Among the important questions were: at what points in the past has scholarship followed by-ways or even false paths? In what ways are the results of taking these false paths still with us? Towards what goals is the historical-critical method striving?[4] We note here a greater self-confidence compared with Diestel's intention to judge only scholarship that was moving against the consensus established by 'history'. We seem to have a model of the scholarly enterprise in which progress is broadly unilinear, with an ever greater approximation to the 'truth', such that from the vantage point of the present, true, false and blind paths taken in the past can be distinguished.

It is not only in Old Testament studies that such a model of the history of scholarship is to be found. In Thomas S. Kuhn's famous *The Structure of Scientific Revolutions*,[5] it is argued that historians of science have wrongly seen the development of science as the accumulation of scientific knowledge and technique:

[4] Hans-Joachim Kraus, *Geschichte der historisch-kritischen Erforschung des Alten Testaments*, Neukirchen-Vluyn 1956, 1969², 1982³, pp. 1–2.
[5] Thomas S. Kuhn, *The Structure of Scientific Revolutions*, Chicago 1962, 1970².

Concerned with scientific development, the historian ... appears to have two main tasks. On the one hand, he must determine by what man and at what point in time each contemporary scientific fact, law, and theory was discovered or invented. On the other hand, he must describe and explain the congeries of error, myth, and superstition that have inhibited the more rapid accumulation of the constituents of the modern science text. Much research has been directed to these ends, and some still is.[6]

Kuhn – paradigm shifts

The main positive argument in Kuhn's book is that scientific progress is much more haphazard than might be supposed, and that it takes place essentially by means of paradigm shifts. A paradigm shift occurs when a new theory gains sufficient support from people who matter, to displace the previous prevailing viewpoint. The shift will have been preceded by a period in which attempts to prove a prevailing theory have subjected that theory to increasing modification and qualification.

Popper:

As is well known, Kuhn's viewpoint has received strong criticism from *hypotheses* Karl Popper, who has argued that in the sciences, explanatory hypotheses *do become more* become progressively more adequate formulations about what is the case.[7] *adequate* It is not intended here to comment in detail upon the Kuhn–Popper controversy, which is not an argument about the history of Old Testament scholarship. As applied to Old Testament scholarship, however, some points from the debate can be made.

There IS progress in OT.

First, there is no doubt that there is progress in Old Testament scholarship *scholarship,* whereby explanations more adequately describe what is the case. Discoveries *but not* in the fields of the chronology of the history of Israel in relation to the *nec. progress* history of the ancient Near East, discoveries about the topography of ancient *toward the* Israel, and about the religion of Israel's neighbours guarantee that many *TRUTH* theories about these matters found in earlier scholarship have been superseded once and for all. There is an irreversibility about progress in Old Testament scholarship. However, it does not follow from this that progress in Old Testament scholarship is inevitable progress towards 'the truth' about what is the case, unless we suppose that Old Testament scholarship is being providentially guided towards an ultimate goal. All Old Testament scholars are engaged in the search for truth, but they cannot be sure that they find anything more than the truth for their situation, granted the limits of the evidence available.

OT progress

Secondly, there is no doubt that progress in research can be at times *has been* haphazard. Some of the archaeological discoveries that have profoundly *dependent* altered the course of scholarship have been 'accidental'. Again, Old Testament *on accident-* scholarship has been deeply affected by movements in other disciplines. In *al finds* *or new* *areas* *opp. coming*

---

[6] Kuhn, p. 2.
[7] See, for example, K. Popper, 'Normal Science and its Dangers' in I. Lavatos and A. Musgrave (eds.), *Criticism and the Growth of Knowledge*, Cambridge 1970, pp. 51–8.

Scholarly schools of thought depend on the human factor (pre-mature death; not getting a position, etc.)

our own time, structuralist or synchronic ways of approaching language, social anthropology and literary interpretation have had significant effects upon Old Testament scholarship.

Thirdly, there is the fact that scholarship is often guided by personalities or 'schools', and that scholars who might have made significant contributions die young or cannot gain positions from which they can exert influence through their writings. In the 1830s in Germany, this was the fate of two young scholars whose works will be considered later in this book. Carl Peter Wilhelm Gramberg died in Oldenburg in 1830 at the age of 32. Shortly before his death he had published two parts of a *Critical History of the Religious Ideas of the Old Testament*. Parts 3 and 4 were never completed, neither was his detailed commentary on the Pentateuch. Gramberg's book on the religious ideas of the Old Testament, including a detailed study of sacrifice and the cult, anticipated much of what was later to be found in Wellhausen. The same is true of the book on Jewish festivals by Johann Friedrich Ludwig George, published in 1835. George did not die young, but spent many years as a schoolmaster and was unable to play any significant role in Old Testament scholarship. He gained a chair of philosophy at Greifswald eventually in 1858 and was still at Greifswald when the young Wellhausen arrived there in 1872. An example from the English side concerns the death in 1828, at the age of 35, of Alexander Nicoll, Regius Professor of Hebrew at Oxford. Upon Nicoll's death, E. B. Pusey was appointed to the chair at the age of 28, occupying this position until 1882.

It is idle, although interesting, to speculate about what might have been. Suppose that Gramberg had lived, and that both he and George had obtained chairs of Old Testament. Suppose, further, that the letter of sympathy written by de Wette to the mother of Karl Ludwig Sand had never been intercepted by the Prussian secret police, that de Wette had not been dismissed from Berlin in 1819, and that the conservative Hengstenberg had not eventually filled de Wette's chair. How different German Old Testament scholarship might have been! The theories of the history of Israelite religion presented so brilliantly by Wellhausen in 1878 might have been established 40 years earlier, and the conservative counter-attack against the critical method mounted by Hengstenberg from 1830 to 1860 might never have taken off. In England, if Nicoll had died in 1858 instead of 1828, would Pusey have been able to exert the influence that he did against the critical method in England?

All these questions must remain unanswered; but they serve to underline the point made about the haphazard way in which scholarship is affected by deaths and appointments. Diestel's observation is correct. Although Old Testament scholarship can never separate itself from the ebb and flow of the 'spirit of the age', it is nonetheless also affected by the individualism of the scholars who happen to be influential at any given time.

But there is another vital factor; and one which does not usually receive the attention that it demands in histories of Old Testament scholarship, the national or (in the case of Germany) the regional factor. From Cheyne's book on the rise of the critical method, one gets no hint that there might be a national factor in the way that a method may develop in one country and make little headway in another. This is not meant as a criticism of Cheyne; after all, if something can be demonstrated to be the case, the demonstration should be convincing to people of any nationality. Where we are dealing, however, not so much with the demonstrable hypotheses of physical sciences, but with theories that challenge traditional beliefs about the Old Testament, however well these new theories can be supported by plausible arguments, we are on less firm ground; and it is a fact that in the nineteenth and twentieth centuries, the critical method was pioneered in Germany and received only reluctantly in England. It is the case that to this day, Germany is much more creative in the field of critical scholarship than Britain, and that British expertise lies in the fields of textual criticism and philology, rather than in the profundities of form criticism and redaction criticism.

[handwritten margin note: German vis-à-vis Britain today]

This question must now occupy us for some pages, because one of the main aims of this present work is to trace the interrelationship between German and English scholarship during the rise of the critical method in the nineteenth century. The word English is used deliberately; it is not an expression of the arrogance of an Englishman who uses the word England when he means Britain. It is not a failure to recognize the existence of Old Testament scholarship in Scotland, Wales and Ireland. In one or two instances, non-English scholars from the British Isles will be mentioned. For example, Samuel Davidson was born and educated in Ireland; and it would be impossible to avoid reference to the Scot, William Robertson Smith, who was given refuge in Cambridge after his dismissal from his chair in Aberdeen. However, the countries of Scotland, Wales and Ireland have their own histories, and the rise of critical scholarship in those places cannot be divorced from their histories or their ecclesiastical politics. If the present book concentrates upon England, this is primarily because the author knows sufficient about England to attempt to describe Old Testament scholarship there. He does not have sufficient familiarity with Scotland, Wales or Ireland to attempt the task in the cases of those countries; indeed, he has spent far more time in Germany than in Scotland or Wales, and has never visited Ireland!

That there is a difference between England and Germany when it comes to intellectual pursuits has long been commented upon. In Heinrich Ewald's *Jahrbücher der biblischen Wissenschaft* (1848–65) there are frequent allusions to the superficiality of English Old Testament scholarship in comparison with what was going on in Germany, criticisms which were entirely justified.[8] Hegel went so far as to characterize the English as a nation concerned only with the material things of everyday life, to the exclusion of what had to do with philosophical reflection upon deeper experience.[9] On the other side, F. D. Maurice in an often-quoted letter of 1848 characterized the difference between the English and Germans as follows: 'We, naturally, [start] from that which is above and speaks to us; they, naturally, from that which is within them and which seeks for some object above itself.'[10] Towards the end of the nineteenth century Otto Pfleiderer published his book *The Development of Theology in Germany since Kant, and its Progress in Great Britain since 1825*. Pfleiderer concluded that in England in the nineteenth century no philosophy had penetrated the educated classes or exercised a determining influence on their thought, and he gave this as the reason for 'the remarkable fact that the church life of England . . . has remained almost untouched by the vast progress of scientific thought of the educated classes, and that wherever the two came into contact, such a violent collision is the consequence that popular feeling is shocked, and not a few despair of the possibility of any mutual understanding.[11]

Attempts to play down the differences between English and German intellectual endeavour only appear to prove that there is a difference,

[8] Heinrich Ewald, *Jahrbücher der biblischen Wissenschaft*, 1–12, Göttingen, 1848–65. The following comments are typical: 'Einige andre Aufsätze in Englischen Blättern zur Erläuterung biblischer Alterthümer sind kaum der Erwähnung wert' (2 (1849), p. 34). On J. S. Thrupp's *Ancient Jerusalem* (1855): 'wir vermissen. . . bei ihm wie bei den meisten seinen heutigen gelehrten Landsmänner eine ächte biblische Wissenschaft' (8 (1856), p. 143). On E. Auberlen's works on Daniel: 'Wenn diese aller Wissenschaft ebenso wie allen wahren Christenthume zum Troze noch immer fortgetriebene Gleissnerei und Schwindelei vorzüglich vielen Engländern sehr wohl gefallen hat, so ist das nicht Wunder; die Engländer sind jetzt ihren eignen bessern Vorfahren immer unähnlicher geworden, und schon stehen sich dort Leute wie Pusey und der Bonapartische Palmerston wie unendlich verschieden sonst doch an Gewissenlosigkeit völlig gleich' (10, (1859–60), p. 211).

[9] G. W. F. Hegel, *Vorlesungen über die Geschichte der Philosophie* 3, Stuttgart 1929, 19, pp. 253, 297, 300.

[10] Frederick Maurice (ed.), *The Life of Frederick Denison Maurice*, London 1884, 1, p. 468. S. W. Sykes 'Germany and England: an attempt at theological Diplomacy' in S. W. Sykes ed., *England and Germany: Studies in Theological Diplomacy*, Frankfurt/M, and Bern 1982, p. 150, rejects Maurice's observation on the grounds that 'Maurice is, of course, too individual a thinker to be a reliable guide to the relations of nations, particularly since his knowledge of German was defective, on his own admission'. It is not clear why being an individual thinker should make a person an unreliable guide on this, or any subject. Maurice's observation seems to express well a difference between German and English scholarship for which the present author argues in an essay in the same volume in which Sykes's article appears: 'Philosophy and the Rise of Biblical Criticism: England and Germany', pp. 63–79.

[11] Otto Pfleiderer, *The Development of Theology in Germany since Kant, and its Progress in Great Britain since 1825*, London 1890, p. 307.

however accounted for. This is particularly true of two studies by Klaus Dockhorn, *German historicism in England* (1950), and *The German Spirit and Anglo-Saxon History of Mind* (1954).[12] Dockhorn's books contain valuable summaries of attempts to characterize the different nature of the English *Geist* as opposed to the German *Geist*. These include the view of Troeltsch that German thought is to be seen as secularized Lutheranism while that of England is secularized Calvinism;[13] or there is Barth's distinction between two-dimensional Anglo-Saxon theology and three-dimensional Continental theology.[14] Dockhorn's conclusion is that 'in German and English thought we are not faced with two quite alien world views which, beginning from differing theological teachings have developed into alternative secularized forms which run along parallel and never converging lines'.[15] He prefers to see England and Germany progressing in the same stream of development of Western thought, with Germany travelling faster than England towards new ways of thinking.

Much of Dockhorn's attempt to minimize the difference between German and English thought rests upon his own researches into the influence of German thought upon English thought in the nineteenth century. The purpose of this is to show that because English thought owed much to German thought in the nineteenth century, it is wrong to characterize them as two entirely different things. However, three observations must be made. First, the fact that German thought influenced English thought but hardly vice versa in the nineteenth century is surely significant, since it suggests a much greater creativity in Germany than in England. Second, it does not follow that because thought is received in one country from another, it is going to be understood or to have the same effects on the recipient country as in the donor country. The present book will try to indicate that the critical method received from Germany in Old Testament studies had different effects in England compared with Germany. Third, it must be pointed out that Dockhorn's case rests upon claims, some of which are quite exaggerated, if what is to be presented later in this book is correct.

An example of what the present writer considers to be Dockhorn's exaggerations can be found in the treatment of Bishop Colenso. Colenso is said to have

'. . . studied German criticism and to have reached a radical rejection of the chronology contained in the Bible. The various results of German scholarship,

[12] Klaus Dockhorn, *Der deutsche Historismus in England. Ein Beitrag zur Englischen Geistesgeschichte des 19. Jahrhunderts*, Göttingen 1950; *Deutscher Geist und angelsächsische Geistesgeschichte. Ein Versuch der Deutung ihres Verhältnisses*, Göttinger Bausteine zur Geschichtswissenschaft, 17, Göttingen, Frankfurt/M and Berlin 1954.

[13] Dockhorn, *Deutscher Geist*, p. 12.

[14] ibid., p. 17.

[15] ibid., pp. 70–1 (my translation).

especially those of Ewald and Bleek in the fields of language and literary criticism, and those of de Wette and Hupfeld in the fields of the history of the cult and of [Israelite] religion, provide the foundation for a new view of the chronological order of the books of the Old Testament canon'.[16]

According to Colenso himself, the whole of his stock of German theology while he was writing the substance of Part 1 of his book was Ewald's *History of Israel* (in German), Kurtz's *History of the Old Covenant* (in English translation—a book defending the Mosaic origin and historical accuracy of the Pentateuch), and Hengstenberg's *Psalms* and *Christology of the Old Testament*. Subsequently, while revising the work for publication Colenso read the *Introductions* by de Wette and Bleek and two books by the conservatives Hävernick and Hengstenberg.[17] But it can hardly be claimed that Colenso had absorbed the methods of de Wette, Bleek and Hupfeld. In his review of Colenso in the *Göttingschen Gelehrte Anzeigen* of 1863, Ewald complained:

> if one looks closely at the proof brought by the author [for the unhistorical nature of the Pentateuch], it is as though we have gone a hundred years backwards to the times of the first glimmering of the Enlightenment in Germany or even further back to the time of the English Deists. . . .[18]

The fact is that almost alone of British churchmen of his day, Colenso adopted a theological position that left him free to take German criticism seriously. This did not come about because Colenso 'absorbed the German methods.' It can also be noted that Dockhorn is wide of the mark when he describes Frederick Temple's essay on the 'Education of the World' in *Essays and Reviews* as Hegelian, and when he characterizes A. P. Stanley's *Lectures on the History of the Jewish Church* as following Ewald's view of the history of the Jewish religion and its various stages of Mosaic religion, prophecy and poetry.[19]

Dockhorn's attempt to minimize the differences between English and German thought does not succeed on the evidence that he adduces. Granted a difference, how is it to be explained? A recent discussion of the problem by S. W. Sykes reaches a conclusion from the side of systematic theology which the present author has reached independently from research into Old Testament scholarship, and which forms one of the basic premises of this book. This conclusion is that in England, as opposed to Germany, there has been a reluctance to use 'philosophy in the task of radically reconstructing

---

[16] Dockhorn, *Historismus*, pp. 101–2 (my translation).

[17] J. W. Colenso, *The Pentateuch and the Book of Joshua critically examined*, 1, London 1862², p. xv.

[18] Heinrich Ewald, review of Colenso, *The Pentateuch* Part 1 in *GGA*, 1863, p. 35 (my translation).

[19] Dockhorn, *Historismus*, pp. 102–4.

and re-expressing Christian doctrine'.[20] The important word here is *radically*. It will be shown later that English Old Testament scholarship in the nineteenth century was influenced by philosophical views deriving from German idealism. However, this did not produce a *radical* reconstruction of either Christian doctrine or of theories of Israelite religion in England. As Sykes further points out, when, in the 1870s, a British form of Hegelianism was established in Oxford, it was used rather to re-express what was stated in the Catholic creeds than to indulge in any radical reconstruction of Christian theology.[21] In the area of Old Testament scholarship, it can be said that in the nineteenth century, German scholars adopted philosophically orientated views of religion and theology that led them to propose radical reconstructions of the history of Israelite religion based upon source criticism. In England, much less radical views of religion and theology were adopted, with the result that even when German critical scholarship was accepted, this acceptance did not have radical effects.[22]

This point about the radical results of German Old Testament criticism in the nineteenth century must be borne in mind as we consider another aspect of the relationship between English and German scholarship: the fact that in the eighteenth century, it was English Deism that influenced some of the founding fathers of German criticism, Reimarus, Michaelis and Semler. The publication in 1741 of a German translation of Tindal's *Christianity as Old as the Creation* marked the beginnings of the publication of German translations of a number of Deist and apologetic works. Their most direct effect was upon Reimarus, who drew upon them considerably in the famous fragments that were published by Lessing in 1774–8. But so far as the world at large was concerned, by the time the fragments were published there had been in Germany a change in mood and method, with the result that the viewpoints in the fragments were largely rejected by critical German scholars as well as by the orthodox.

In pioneering studies of the history of English Old Testament scholarship from the Reformation to the Deist controversy, and of the indebtedness of Reimarus to the Deists, Henning Graf Reventlow, has characterized the common ground between the Deists and Reimarus as follows: that they both accepted rationalism and metaphysical objectivism, which saw the content of religion in doctrine, in supernatural or natural truths or in

---

[20] Sykes, op. cit. (n. 10 above), p. 157.
[21] ibid., p. 158.
[22] See Sykes's comments, op. cit., p. 11; 'No one studying the theological history of the seventeenth, eighteenth or nineteenth centuries in England or Germany can avoid the impact of ideas from the other country. Yet the reception of these ideas invariably entailed their transformation, consciously or unconsciously ... it appears that the activity of biblical criticism in each country manifests the signs of these divergences.'

universally valid ethical maxims.[23] Graf Reventlow shows how, throughout the period from the Reformation to the Enlightenment in England, the thought of biblical scholars was grounded in a scholasticism, inherited from the humanism of Erasmus and his forebears, and kept alive by the interest in classical Greek and Latin philosophy at the two English universities. This had the double effect of regarding Christianity as revealed 'truths' and of stressing the importance of reason in approving those 'truths'. The Deist attacks on the Bible, especially upon the Old Testament, derived philosophically from a growth in the primacy of reason over revelation (Graf Reventlow brilliantly adduces many additional political and ecclesiastical factors).[24] However, the important thing about these attacks on the Bible is that ultimately, they did not amount to the sort of radical reconstruction of the history of Israelite religion with the help of source criticism that was central to nineteenth-century Old Testament criticism. The Deist attacks poured scorn upon the rituals, superstitions and miracles of the Bible; but they attempted no radical reconstruction of biblical religion, for the simple reason that they already had what they regarded as the perfect religion. The Bible was merely to be conformed to that religion, and to be ridiculed where it could not be conformed. In the nineteenth century, German and English scholarship took somewhat differing paths because in Germany, idealist philosophies exerted sufficiently powerful influence upon Old Testament scholars in the first half of that century to encourage them to engage in radical reconstruction of Israelite religion. In England, the influence of idealist philosophy was much milder, and used to support a much more traditional view of the history of Israelite religion.

Sufficient has now been written in this introduction for it to be stated what the aims of the present book are. They can be stated under several headings. The first, and main, aim is to present the history of critical Old Testament scholarship in the nineteenth century as accurately as possible. Second, this will not be attempted on the assumption that we can or should make judgements upon scholars depending on whether they did, or did not, advance the critical cause. The attempt will be made to see the contribution of each scholar in the light of the circumstances and problems in which he worked, and in terms of the resources available to him.[25] Third, the book

[23] Henning Graf Reventlow, 'Das Arsenal der Bibelkritik des Reimarus: Die Auslegung der Bibel, insbesondere des Alten Testaments, bei den englischen Deisten' in *Hermann Samuel Reimarus 1694–1768. Ein bekannter Unbekannter der Aufklärung*, Göttingen 1973, p. 50.

[24] See his *Bibelautorität und Geist der Moderne. Die Bedeutung des Bibelverständnisses für die geistesgeschichte und politische Entwicklung in England von der Reformation bis zur Aufklärung*, FKDG 30, Göttingen 1980.

[25] cf. Kuhn (op. cit. n5 above), p. 3; 'Historians of science have begun to ask new sorts of questions and to trace different, and often less than cumulative, developmental lines for the science.... They ask, for example, not about the relation of Galileo's views to those of modern science, but rather about the relationship between his views and those of his groups, i.e., his teachers, contemporaries, and immediate successors in the sciences. Furthermore, they insist upon studying the opinions of that group and other similar ones

3) That although HCM in principle is objective method, national boundaries have an effect.

will try to show that although, in principle, the critical method ought to be an objective method, whose findings can be endorsed by reason regardless of the 'national factor', in fact this had not been the case. The differences between Germany and England will be noted, with particular reference to philosophical and other factors that affected the critical method. Fourth, the book will hope to create a new self-awareness on the part of scholars working today. The view that a discipline takes of its past functions like a 'mythology', commending and justifying the stance that scholarship takes up. For those on the conservative side, it is comforting to have a view of the past in which there was no critical scholarship until after Darwin's *Origin of Species*, what there was being blighted by Hegelianism. On the critical side, it is comforting to see the 'founders of Old Testament criticism' as heroes of great integrity, battling against prejudice and obscurantism. Of course, these descriptions of the conservative and of the critical scholar are parodies; but they contain more than an element of truth. If we can take a less polarized view of our past, we may be able to learn much from past Old Testament scholars of various shades of opinion; and we may be able to identify aspects of past scholarship that have been neglected and which deserve fresh consideration.

4) To provide a new self-awareness for scholars

There must be a final word of warning. Any attempt to place Old Testament scholars and their work in their historical setting must come up against the fact that in most cases, we do not have easy access to relevant, biographical material, if it exists at all. The bulk of the letters utilized by Wiegand in his 1879 biography of de Wette cannot be traced.[26] The bulk of the letters written by Wellhausen has only recently been collected together, and they are not yet published. The nineteenth-century 'Acts' of the universities that were always, or which during the course of the century came, under Prussian administration are at the central archives of the German Democratic Republic at Merseburg. Access to them is not easy. In addition, scholarship does not always agree about the extent or manner of influences upon individual scholars, with the result that secondary literature can develop about the proper interpretation of the life work of a given scholar.

Taking these limitations into account, it has to be acknowledged that at the end of one's labours, the final result can only be provisional, and open to correction in the light of subsequent investigation. Yet it is to be hoped that the present work will represent an advance in some areas of our understanding of the critical method in the nineteenth century, and that it will contribute to a deeper understanding of the tasks facing contemporary scholarship.

---

from the viewpoint usually very different from that of modern science—that gives those opinions the maximum internal coherence and the closest possible fit to nature.'

[26] See E. Staehelin, *Dewettiana. Forschungen und Texte zu Wilhelm Martin Leberecht de Wettes Leben und Werk*, Studien zur Geschichte der Wissenschaften in Basel 2, Basel 1956, p. 9, n3.

Part One
Germany 1800–60

1

The Results of
Old Testament Criticism
in Germany prior to 1800

As the eighteenth century ended and the nineteenth century began, there was no reason to think that a new era in the history of Old Testament criticism was about to dawn. It is true that in the first fifteen years or so of the new century, particularly in the aftermath of the Napoleonic wars, there was an upheaval which led to the closure of some German universities and their theological faculties, and to the opening of several new institutions. Thus, seven Protestant faculties disappeared: Altdorf (1807), Rinteln and Helmstedt (1809), Frankfurt/Oder (1811), Erfurt (1816), Wittenberg (1817), and Duisburg (1818). Of these, Wittenberg was merged with Halle, Frankfurt/Oder's Protestant faculty became part of the new foundation of Breslau (1811), and Altdorf and Helmstedt were not considered to be viable in view of their proximity to Erlangen and Göttingen respectively.[1] New foundations included Berlin (1810) and Bonn (1818), and at Heidelberg, a united Catholic-Lutheran-Reformed Faculty was established in 1803, the Catholics withdrawing to Freiburg in 1807.[2]

In spite of these upheavals, many leading Old Testament scholars who occupied chairs in 1799, and who had been trained in the second half of the eighteenth century, remained in their posts until well into the new century. This was true of J. G. Eichhorn, professor of oriental languages at Göttingen 1788–1827, of J. G. Rosenmüller, professor at Leipzig, 1786–1815, and of J. S. Vater, professor at Halle, 1799–1809 and again, 1820–6, after a spell at Königsberg, 1809–20. J. P. Gabler was professor at Altdorf, 1785–1804, (his departure from Altdorf hastened its closure) and at Jena, 1804–26,

---

[1] See *Universität Breslau. Festschrift zur Feier des hundertjährigen Bestehens, 1, Geschichte der Universität Breslau 1811–1911*, Breslau 1911, pp. 8–20; Charles E. McClelland, *State, Society, and University in Germany 1700–1914*, Cambridge 1980, pp. 101–2.

[2] For Berlin, see Max Lenz, *Geschichte der königlichen Friedrich-Wilhelms-Universität zu Berlin*, 1, Halle 1910; Walter Elliger, *150 Jahre Theologische Fakultät Berlin*, Berlin 1960. For Bonn see O. Ritschl, *Die Evangelisch-Theologische Fakultät zu Bonn in dem ersten Jahrhundert ihrer Geschichte, 1819–1919*, Bonn 1919, pp. 1–4. For Heidelberg, see Heinrich Bornkamm, 'Die theologische Fakultät Heidelberg' in *Ruperto-Carola. Aus der Geschichte der Universität Heidelberg und ihrer Fakultäten*, Heidelberg 1961, pp. 144–5.

while H. E. G. Paulus was a professor for no fewer than 62 years, at Jena, 1789–93 (oriental languages) and 1793–1804 (theology), Würzburg, 1804–11 and Heidelberg, 1811–51. Other scholars who spanned the turn of the century were Arnoldi (Marburg 1789–1835), Staeudlin (Göttingen 1790–1826) and Hezel (Giessen 1786–1801, Dorpat 1802–20).

The majority of the Old Testament professors at the turn of the century were either Neologists or Rationalists, the difference between the two not being very great.[3] The founders of Neologism in the second half of the eighteenth century had been J. S. Semler at Halle and J. D. Michaelis at Göttingen.[4] Both had been brought up as Pietists, and both had moved away from Pietism under the influence of English Deism, and of the results of the biblical criticism of scholars such as the French Catholic Richard Simon and the Jewish philosopher Benedict Spinoza.[5] It is a remarkable fact that Protestant German Old Testament scholarship, which was to dominate the Old Testament scene from the second half of the sixteenth century to the present day, had achieved practically nothing by way of biblical criticism before 1750. On the other hand, Britain and France, who had achieved far more than Germany up to 1750, were to be left far behind Germany in the achievements of critical scholarship in the nineteenth century.

The Neologist approach to the Old Testament was based upon exact grammatical and philological exegesis of the text. Exegesis was not subject to constraints imposed by traditional Christian doctrines, and the doctrinal formularies of the Church were not considered to be sacrosanct. In the nineteenth century, orthodox Lutherans blamed the Neologist attitude to the formularies on to the fact that the Pietists also treated the formularies lightly, and that the first Neologists had been brought up as Pietists.[6]

[3] Klaus Leder, *Universität Altdorf. Zur Theologie der Aufklärung in Franken*, Nuremberg 1965, pp. 157–61, distinguishes several phases in Neology, of which the second phase absorbed something of the rationalism that stemmed from Kant's philosophy, and of which the third phase fought against Rationalism, Supranaturalism and idealist philosophy. A. O. Dyson, 'Theological Legacies of the Enlightenment: England and Germany' in S. W. Sykes, *England and Germany*, pp. 56–7 provides a useful outline of the main positions of the Neologists. He sees their distinctive standpoint as a desire to affirm religious truth as 'historically manifested' and 'appropriable but not discoverable by reason'.

[4] For Semler, see Gottfried Hornig, *Die Anfänge der historisch-kritischen Methode FSThR*, 8, Göttingen 1961. No equivalent monograph exists on Michaelis, to my knowledge, although he is treated in the standard histories of German theology of Hirsch, Franck, etc.

[5] For Simon see Jean Steinmann, *Richard Simon et les origines de l'exégèse biblique*, Bruges 1960. J. G. Herder wrote of Simon, 'Richard Simon ist der Vater der Kritik A. and N.T. in den neuen Zeiten', *Briefe, das Studium der Theologie betreffend*, letter 1, in Bernhard Suphan (ed.), *Herder Sämmtliche Werke*, vol. 10, Berlin 1879, p. 11. Spinoza's influential work was his *Tractatus theologico-politicus* of 1670.

[6] So August (F.A.G.) Tholuck, *Geschichte des Rationalismus 1, Geschichte des Pietismus und des ersten Stadiums der Aufklärung*, Berlin 1865, pp. 48ff.

Since the formularies were not allowed to dictate in advance the results of grammatical and philological exegesis, the context of exegesis was a knowledge of the ancient world in which the Old Testament had been written. A careful study was made of the customs and institutions of the Old Testament, as they were illumined by classical Greek and Latin authors, by reports of travellers to the East, and by Jewish, Arabic and Syriac literature, not to mention the antiquities of Egypt.

The early Neologists, such as Semler, firmly rejected the theory of the verbal inspiration of the Bible. Semler himself distinguished between the Bible and the word of God, and understood by the latter those parts of the Bible that spoke to him of salvation through Jesus Christ.[7] This resulted in dividing the content of the Bible, especially the Old Testament, into two categories: that which witnessed to salvation in Christ, and that which did not. Much of the Old Testament came into this second category, and was regarded as Jewish national history.

At the same time Semler retained a high view of the value of the Bible. Where the Bible was in conflict with the findings of natural science, the Bible was not dismissed out of hand. God was the author of both the Bible and the discoveries of natural science, and there was no conflict in principle between the two. In the case of the Bible, it reflected the scientific understanding of the various times at which its authors lived. This was true not only where narratives reflected a pre-scientific world-view; it was true also in the anthropomorphic language by which God was described. Here, Semler was taking up and extending the ancient principle of *accommodation*.[8]

The later Neologists, especially Eichhorn and Gabler, took the idea of accommodation one step further in their researches upon the primitive or oriental mentality which they believed the biblical authors to possess.[9] These researches were helped, on the one hand, by the Göttingen classicist, C. G. Heyne, who used the then available knowledge of contemporary 'barbaric' peoples, such as North American Indians, in order to interpret ancient Greek texts. On the other hand, J. G. Herder, who had close contact with the Göttingen faculty during his time at Bückeburg (1771–6) and Weimar (from 1776), stressed the importance of entering into the soul (*Geist*) of ancient people if their literature was to be fully understood.[10]

Eichhorn and Gabler developed what came to be called a 'mythical' approach to the Old Testament, by means of which they were able to treat, for example, the opening chapters of Genesis, as authentic records of the experiences of the earliest human beings, once allowance was made for the

[7] Hornig, pp. 85ff.
[8] Hornig, pp. 219ff.
[9] See J. W. Rogerson, *Myth in Old Testament Interpretation, BZAW* 34, Berlin 1974, ch. 1.
[10] See, for example, Herder's *Vom Geist der Ebräischen Poesie* (1782–3) in Suphan's edn, 11 (1874), pp. 213–466, 12 (1880), pp. 1–302.

primitive or oriental thought forms in which the narrative was expressed. What lay behind Genesis 2—3 was the experience of a human couple who had become aware of their sexual differences as the result of eating slightly poisonous fruit from a tree. They had been driven in fright from their oasis by a thunderstorm, which to them indicated divine judgement. The language of the extant form of Genesis 2—3, describing a talking serpent and a God who walked in the garden was the result of the primitive and oriental manner in which alone earliest mankind could conceptualise and narrate events.

As the eighteenth century ended, Neologism was replaced by Rationalism and Supranaturalism, although neologists such as Gabler and Eichhorn lived into the third decade of the nineteenth century.[11] Rationalism and Supranaturalism were responses to the critical philosophy of Kant, which increasingly penetrated most of the theological faculties in the 1790s. The main differences between Neologists and Rationalists seems to have been the acceptance by the former of the necessity for miracles as related in the New Testament as a demonstration of the authority and work of Christ. The Rationalists were inclined to see morality as the highest manifestation of religion, and they used reason in order to give natural explanations to the miracles, including the resurrection. Supranaturalists fastened on to that part of the Kantian system that taught that human knowledge is restricted by the limitations of the perceiving subject. They were thus ready to accept those parts of the Bible that described things beyond the grasp of human understanding. Yet even this position was maintained with the help of mild rationalizing, in which some of the miracles were regarded as having occurred in dreams.

Within the limits of Neologism and Rationalism as sketched briefly here, German scholarship from 1780 devoted itself increasingly to the critical questions of authorship of Old Testament books, and of sources that underlay these books. In some cases, the results did not advance or even improve upon suggestions made in earlier centuries by, for example, Richard Simon or Spinoza. The important point, however, is that they were not the findings of individual scholars which immediately provoked opposition or neglect. They were the beginning of a type of critical scholarship which began to be carried out not only in fifteen or more theological faculties, but also in learned circles outside universities. Yet even so, they did not foreshadow the radical results of Old Testament criticism that were to be achieved in the nineteenth century, although these latter results would have been impossible without the foundation, laid in the late eighteenth century. What some of those results were will now be briefly indicated.

---

[11] On Rationalism and Supranaturalism, see Emanuel Hirsch, *Geschichte der neueren evangelischen Theologie*, 5, Gütersloh 1954, ch. 48.

(a) The Pentateuch

In the first edition of Eichhorn's 'Introduction to the Old Testament' of 1780–83, we find the foundations of the later Documentary Hypothesis already well laid.[12] The pioneering work had been done in France in 1753 by Jean Astruc, when he had divided Genesis into two main sources.[13] Eichhorn, while recognizing Astruc as a pioneer, undertook the work afresh, and divided Genesis into a Jehova and an Elohim source. For Genesis 1—11 his results were as follows:[14]

	ELOHIM SOURCE	JEHOVA SOURCE
Genesis	1.1—2.3	
		4.1–26
	5.1–28	
		5.29
	5.30–32	
	6.1–2	
		6.3
	6.4	
		6.5–8
	6.9–22	
	7.11–16 (omitting: and the LORD shut him in)	7.16 (the LORD shut him in)
		7.10
		7.17
	7.18 (–19)	
	7.20–2	
		7.23
	7.24	
	8.1–19	
		8.20–2
	9.1–17	

[12] J. G. Eichhorn, *Einleitung ins Alte Testament*, Leipzig, 1780–3.
[13] J. Astruc, *Conjectures sur les mémoires originaux dont il paroît que Moyse se servit pour composer le livre de la Genèse*, Brussels 1753.
[14] Eichhorn, *Einleitung*, 2, pp. 349ff.

ELOHIM SOURCE	JEHOVA SOURCE
	9.18–27
9.28–9	
	10.1–32
	11.1–9
11.10–26	
11.27–32	

Chapters 2.4—3.24 were regarded as a self-contained piece, belonging to neither of the two sources because of its unique divine name, but closer in affinity to the Jehova than to the Elohim source.

If Eichhorn's results for Genesis 1—11 are compared with the results of those who accepted the Documentary Hypothesis in its classical formulation by Wellhausen, a high level of agreement can be recognized. The results presented in S. R. Driver's *Introduction to the Literature of the Old Testament* for Genesis 1—11 show an agreement of 87 per cent with Eichhorn's proposals, excluding 2.4—3.24.[15]

In 1798, K. D. Ilgen attempted to reconstruct the documents in the Jerusalem archives, which he believed to underlie the Pentateuch and other historical books.[16] In the course of this, he proposed a division of the Elohim source into E_1 and E_2. Again, in some respects, his results anticipated those of the later Documentary Hypothesis. Here is his analysis of the beginning of the Joseph story:[17]

	E_1	E_2
Genesis	37.1–2	
		37.3–11
		12–13
	37.14	37.14 (and he sent him
	(remainder)	and he came to Shechem)
		37.15–17
	37.18	37.18 (and they saw him
	(remainder)	from afar)
		37.19–20
	37.21–2	

[15] S. R. Driver, *An Introduction to the Literature of the Old Testament*, Edinburgh 1913⁹, p. 14.
[16] Karl David Ilgen, *Die Urkunden des Jerusalemischen Tempelarchivs in ihrer Urgestalt als Beytrag zur Berichtigung der Geschichte der Religion und Politik*, Halle 1798.
[17] ibid. pp. 272ff.

E_1	E_2
37.24–5	
	37.25 (from: and they lifted up their eyes)
	37.26–7
	37.23
37.28 (remainder)	37.28 (from: and they sold him, to: twenty pieces of silver)
37.29–31	
	37.32–3
37.34	
	37.35
37.36	

It is more difficult to compare these results meaningfully with the results achieved by supporters of the Classical Documentary Hypothesis, because these latter results are often quite divergent. However, it is noteworthy that in 1798, Ilgen had already split 37.28 into two sources because of the names Midianites and Ishmaelites, and that in 39.1 he had assigned the words 'Potiphar, an officer of Pharaoh, captain of the guard' to a redactor (*Sammler*). This division of 37.28 into two sources, and the ascription of part of 39.1 to a redactor was common ground for the exponents of the Documentary Hypothesis whatever their disagreements about other details of the analysis. The criteria employed by Ilgen in his source division were headings marking breaks in the material, repetitions, differences of style based upon philological and linguistic considerations, and differences of content and outlook.[18]

The source-critical theories of the late eighteenth century did not lead to any radical theories about the history of Israelite religion. The Mosaic authorship of the Pentateuch had been denied on many occasions prior to Eichhorn's 'Introduction'. Eichhorn himself defended the Mosaic authorship of the Pentateuch especially in the light of his belief in the antiquity of its narratives, for example, about the 'Fall'. In composing Genesis, Moses had used ancient sources. This result gave scholars access to *two* accounts of the earliest history of mankind and of the Israelites. Thus their grasp upon this

[18] ibid. pp. 351ff.

history was more secure, and some of the difficulties of the final form of the text were removed when the sources were disentangled.[19]

(b) The books of Chronicles

The overlap of material between the books of Chronicles and the books of Samuel and Kings received careful attention in Eichhorn's 'Introduction'. Here the results of his first three editions will be presented. Not only do they indicate the position at the end of the eighteenth century; the fourth edition of 1823 received modifications in a conservative direction as a response to de Wette's work on Chronicles.[20]

In view of the lateness of the orthography of Chronicles, its figure of Satan in 1 Chron. 21.1 and its developed angelology in 1 Chron. 21 as compared with 2 Samuel 24, Eichhorn dated the compilation of Chronicles after the Babylonian Exile. Only in this period had the Jews begun to have a developed view of Satan and angels, thanks to Persian influences. However, Eichhorn rejected the view that the author of Chronicles had utilized Samuel and Kings as a source. For the lives of David and Solomon, the author of Chronicles had used not the accounts in 2 Samuel and 1 Kings, but had independently used a version of the source upon which 2 Samuel and 1 Kings depended. By the time that this source reached the author of Chronicles, it had undergone various modifications, and had suffered losses of material. It was these modifications and losses sustained by the common source that accounted for the differences between the presentation of the lives of David in Samuel and Kings on the one hand, and Chronicles on the other. Thus the books of Chronicles, while late in their final form, were composed from early sources, which could be used alongside those in Samuel and Kings.[21]

(c) The prophetic literature

The general approach to the prophetic literature in later eighteenth century German scholarship was deeply affected by Robert Lowth's 1753 *Lectures on the Sacred Poetry of the Hebrews*, a British work whose influence upon the German Old Testament scholarship of its day has probably never been equalled.[22] Lowth illustrated the many poetic and rhetorical devices in

---

[19] Eichhorn, *Einleitung*, 2, pp. 342–4. A most thorough account of the history of Pentateuchal criticism is given by C. Houtman, *Inleiding in de Pentateuch*, Kampen 1980. For Astruc, see pp. 51–7, for Ilgen, pp. 60–2, for Eichhorn, pp. 57–60.

[20] The history of the interpretation of the books of Chronicles is outlined in Thomas Willi, *Die Chronik als Auslegung*, FRLANT 106, Göttingen 1972, pp. 12–47.

[21] Eichhorn, *Einleitung*, 2, pp. 630ff. See also Willi, pp. 31–2.

[22] Robert Lowth, *De sacra poesi hebraeorum*, Oxford 1753.

Hebrew poetry with special reference to Greek and Latin authors. As a result of this, the prophets came to be regarded as literary artists. Further, if they had used literary devices in order to convey their message, it was likely that they were primarily addressing their contemporaries. To suppose that their poetry was employed merely to describe events that would not happen for many hundreds of years seemed absurd. Consequently, appreciation of the poetry of the prophetic material went hand in hand with the attempt to see it in its historical context. Passages traditionally regarded as looking forward to the birth of Jesus, were given an historical interpretation in terms of the situation when the prophet wrote.[23]

It was in a German edition of Lowth's translation of Isaiah that a Göttingen professor, J. B. Koppe, argued in 1780 that Isaiah 40—66 had been written during the Babylonian Exile,[24] This suggestion was quickly taken up by other scholars,[25] and in the third volume of his 'Introduction' (1783), Eichhorn declared that it was possible that Isaiah contained sections from a variety of prophets of differing periods.[26]

In 1793, E. F. K. Rosenmüller suggested in his *Scholia* that Isaiah 42.1–7, 49.1–5, 50.4–10 and 52.13—53.12 should be regarded as pieces belonging together, since they dealt with the prophet and his office (*Amt*).[27] (It was almost a hundred years later, in 1892, that Duhm designated these passages, together with others, as 'Servant Songs'.) These four passages had been added to the book by the exilic author, 53.2–12 being the work of a later poet after the Exile. In 1799, Rosenmüller suggested that 42.1–7 and 49.1–9 dealt with prophetic groups (*Orden*), while 50.4–10 referred to the author of chapters 40—66 himself.[28] Other parts of Isaiah that were thought not to be by the eighth-century prophet of that name included chapters 24—7.

The book of Zechariah was another prophetic book where unity was seriously questioned in the period under discussion, although a late post-exilic dating for chapters 9—14 was not widely accepted until after 1881.[29]

---

[23] See, for example, Leder's brief account of J. C. Döderlein's work on Isaiah in *Universität Altdorf*, pp. 170–3.

[24] According to Leder, op. cit. pp. 171–2, Döderlein had already spoken of ch. 40—66 as Deutero-Isaiah in his *Esaias. Ex recensione textus Hebraei* . . . Altdorf 1775, not obtained by me. For the references to Koppe and Rosenmüller, see further Eberhard Ruprecht, *Die Auslegungsgeschichte zu den sogenannten Gottesknechtslieder im Buch Deuterojesaia unter methodischen Gesichtspunkten bis zu Bernhard Duhm*, Diss. Heidelberg 1972. J. B. Koppe's work is *D. Robert Lowth's Jesaias übersetzt mit einer Einleitung und critischen philologischen und erläuternden Anmerkungen*. See vol. 3, Leipzig 1780, p. 206.

[25] See Ruprecht for references to L. J. C. Justi, H. E. G. Paulus, C. G. Schuster and G. L. Bauer.

[26] Eichhorn, *Einleitung*, 3, 1783, pp. 85ff., 96–7.

[27] E. F. C. Rosenmüller, *Scholia in Vetus Testamentum*, pt 3, Jesajae vaticinia complectentis, sect. 2, Leipzig 1793. See Ruprecht, op. cit., pp. 128–9.

[28] Ruprecht, p. 129.

[29] The history of criticism of Zechariah 9—14 is given by Benedikt Otzen, *Studien über Deuterosacharya*, Acta Theologica Danica, 6, Copenhagen 1964, pp. 11–34.

The usual critical view at the close of the eighteenth century, and well into the nineteenth century, was that chapters 9—14 of Zechariah were pre-exilic, and thus *earlier* than chapters 1—8. Part of the reason for this was that Zechariah 11–13 was attributed to Jeremiah in Matthew 27.9-10; but other alleged pre-exilic references could be adduced, for example, the reference to Assyria in 10.10–11. In 1784, B. G. Flügge anonymously published a translation with critical comments on Zechariah 9—14, in which it was argued that chapters 9—14 consisted of nine separate fragments. Of these, some were earlier than the fall of Samaria (722?), one (containing the verse attributed in Matthew 27.9 to Jeremiah) was from the time of Jeremiah, and of several others it could be said only that they hardly dated from after the Exile.[30] In the first three editions of his *Introduction*, Eichhorn discussed the differences between Zechariah 1—8 and 9—14, but came down on the side of the unity of the book. The fourth edition, of 1823–4, was to advocate a late post-exilic date for chapters 9—14.[31]

Although not strictly speaking a prophetic book, the book of Daniel became the object of critical attention in the second half of the eighteenth century.[32] Its unity, and its setting in the Babylonian Exile had, of course, been assailed long before that time.[33] J. D. Michaelis regarded chapters 3—6 as a later insertion into the book. Eichhorn, in the eighteenth century editions of his *Introduction*, ascribed chapters 7—12 to Daniel, and chapters 2.4—6.28 to a different author. Chapters 1.1—2.3 were an added introduction.[34] This view reflected the fact that chapters 2.4b—7.28 are written in Aramaic, while the remainder of the book is in Hebrew. By the close of the century, no agreement had been reached on the matter of the composition of Daniel. Corrodi, for example, denied the Danielic authorship of the last six chapters of the book. However, the problems of the unity of the book had been clearly recognized.

(d) The History of Israel

By the close of the eighteenth century, no history of Israel had been written which presented the course of events in a fashion radically different from what is implied in the Old Testament. There had, of course, been attacks on the credibility of particular incidents as they were described in the Old

---

[30] Benedikt Gilbert Flügge, *Die Weissagungen welche den Schriften des Propheten Zacharias beygebogen sind, übersetzt und critisch erläutert, nebst einigen Abhandlungen*, Hamburg 1784. See Otzen, pp. 17–18.

[31] Eichhorn, *Einleitung*[1], 3, p. 415.

[32] In general, see H. H. Rowley, 'The Unity of the Book of Daniel' in *The Servant of the Lord and other Essays on the Old Testament*, Oxford 1965[2], pp. 247–80.

[33] As early as the third century AD, the pagan philosopher Porphory argued for a Maccabean dating (i.e., second century BC) for Daniel.

[34] Eichhorn, *Einleitung*[3], 3, pp. 387–443.

Testament; but usually, ways could be found to salvage an historical core from the Old Testament presentation.[35]

One of the most famous attacks upon the credibility of an incident was that by S. H. Reimarus on the account of the crossing of the Red Sea. It was published posthumously by G. E. Lessing in 1777 as a fragment from the papers of an anonymous scholar.[36] Setting out from the statement in Exodus 12.37 that the number of Israelites leaving Egypt was 600,000 men, the women, children, cattle, flocks and herds being in addition to that number, Reimarus showed that however one supposed the Israelites to have organized the crowd, it was quite impossible for such numbers to have crossed the sea in the few hours implied in Exodus 14.21–9. He estimated that the total number of Israelites would have been over three million, needing six thousand carts; also, there would be one hundred thousand horses, three hundred thousand oxen and six hundred thousand sheep. One of the numerous estimates of the length of such a caravan, the estimates varying depending on how many people abreast there might have been, put the length at 180 German miles (a German mile being 7,500 metres, or 4.7 English miles). A discussion of the nature of the bed of the Red Sea indicated that carts were likely to be stuck in sand and that feet could suffer wounds from corals.

As Lessing himself remarked,[37] although such an attack on this incident had often been answered, nobody had succeeded in making the attack in such a sustained and detailed manner as the anonymous 'fragmentist'. For his own part, Lessing preferred to solve the matter simply, by assuming that the figure of six hundred thousand was a mistake or an exaggeration.

Attacks on individual miraculous or incredulous incidents did not lead, then, in late eighteenth-century German scholarship, to any desire to rewrite Old Testament history. The earliest chapters of Genesis were still held to contain authentic accounts of the experiences of earliest mankind, and the story of the Israelites taken as a whole could be seen as an educative process in which divine providence led the Israelites to the truths of religion prized above all in the Enlightenment: the unity of God and the immortality of the soul. In Lessing's *Education of the human race*, of which the first 53 paragraphs appeared in 1777 in connection with his observations upon the Reimarus fragments, and the full 100 paragraphs were published in 1780, the Old Testament account of Israelite history was alluded to as though it

---

[35] See above n8 and p. 17.
[36] *Gotthold Ephraim Lessings sämmtliche Schriften*, ed. Karl Lachmann, bk 12, Leipzig 1897³, pp. 359–68.
[37] ibid., p. 439

could be regarded as a reliable history, including miracles and prophecies, through which providence has guided and educated the people.[38]

The same basic trust in the Old Testament account can also be seen in Herder's treatment of Israelite history in the first twelve of his letters concerning the study of theology (first edition 1780),[39] and in the third part of the twelfth book of his *Reflections on the Philosophy of the History of Mankind* (1787).[40] In the twelfth letter, Herder considers the question whether the history of the Israelites is true, by which he means, did such a people exist? He answers that no one can prove the falsity of the tradition according to which, beginning with Abraham, God brought into being a people which passed through many vicissitudes including those of exile and restoration.[41] In the *Reflections*, he is equally forthright: 'I scruple not ... to take the history of the Hebrews, as related by themselves, for my groundwork'.[42]

The presentation of Israelite history in the *Reflections* is noteworthy, because it contains a hint of that view of the post-exilic period, according to which the restoration was really a time of degeneration compared with the pre-exilic period. This view of the restoration will receive considerable attention later in this book. Herder wrote of the post-exilic period:

> When the Jews, set at liberty by Cyrus, returned from bondage, much diminished in number, they had learned many other things, but no genuine political constitution. Their sentiments fluctuated between monarchical and sacerdotal government: they built a temple, as if this would have revived the times of Moses and Solomon: their religion was pharisaical; their learning, a minute nibbling at syllables ... their patriotism, a slavish attachment to ancient laws misunderstood. . . .[43]

Herder's immanent view of the reason for the downfall of the Hebrew kingdoms was that they lacked a proper constitution:

> ... two things diametrically opposite, the refined nomocracy, on which Moses had settled the constitution, and a sort of theocratic monarchy, such as prevailed among all the nations of this region of despotism, contended together: and thus

---

[38] *Lessings sämmtliche Schriften*, 13, pp. 416–36, ET, in Henry Chadwick (ed.), *Lessing's Theological Writings*, London 1956.

[39] J. G. Herder, *Briefe, das Studium der Theologie betreffend* 1–12, in Suphan, 10.

[40] Herder, *Ideen zur Geschichte der Philosophie der Menschheit*, in Suphan, vol. 14; ET, T. O. Churchill, *Reflections on the Philosophy of the History of Mankind* (London 1800), repr. Chicago 1968.

[41] *Briefe*, no. 12, in Suphan, 10, p. 139.

[42] *Ideen*, bk 12, ch. 3, Suphan, 14, p. 59; ET, p. 136.

[43] ibid. p. 62; ET, p. 139.

the law of Moses became a law of bondage to a people to whom it was intended to have been a law of political liberty.[44]

However, at the transcendent level, Christianity arose out of the heart of Judaism, introduced the books of the Jews to all nations that accepted Christianity, and thereby much good was done to the nations of the world.

Looking back over the contents of this chapter, it can be said that by the close of the eighteenth century, critical German scholarship had already achieved much. It had gained the freedom to investigate questions of authorship of books, unity of books, and sources underlying books, without the restraints imposed by traditional opinions on these matters deriving from narrow views of the nature of inspiration. It had begun to look at prophetic literature in its original and historic setting. It had devised ways of seeeking the historic realities that were expressed in 'mythical' or 'primitive' modes of thought. Yet, arguably, it had not achieved the breakthrough that was to constitute the fundamental difference between critical scholarship in the nineteenth as opposed to the eighteenth century. That breakthrough was, however, only a few years away as the eighteenth century came to an end.

[44] ibid., p. 62.

2

W. M. L. de Wette[1]

(a) The 'Contributions' of 1806–7

To claim on behalf of any particular scholar, or of any particular work by a scholar, that he or the work initiates a new era in a discipline, is to do something rash. Such a claim must be to some extent subjective, and it may suggest a way of looking back upon events which is different from how the events were perceived by those most closely involved. Further, since no work of scholarship exists without indebtedness to what has gone before, it may not be easy to draw a line which marks in a hard and fast way a before and after.

However, bearing in mind the risks of making such a claim, the aim of the present chapter is to argue that the work of W. M. L. de Wette (1780–1849) inaugurated a new era in critical Old Testament scholarship, and that his two-volume *Contributions to Old Testament Introduction* (Halle 1806–7) was his most significant contribution to this end.[2] Inevitably, the *Contributions* owed something to the work of older scholars, and in some respects it was anticipated by J. S. Vater's *Commentary on the Pentateuch* which appeared in three parts between 1802 and 1805.[3] The relationship between the *Contributions* and Vater's *Pentateuch* will be considered below.

---

[1] The standard biography of de Wette is that by Adelbert (Friedrich Julius) Wiegand, *W. M. L. de Wette (1780–1849). Eine Säkularschrift*, Erfurt 1879. It can hardly be described as a scholarly work, but remains valuable because the author had access to some 470 letters of de Wette, few, if any, of which are known to survive. The important biographical source is Ernst Staehelin, *Dewettiana*, Basel 1956. For the most detailed examination of de Wette's work as a biblical scholar see Rudolf Smend, *Wilhelm Martin Leberecht de Wettes Arbeit am Alten und am Neuen Testament*, Basel 1958. The presentation offered here, however, differs from that of Smend in regard to the extent of the influence of J. F. Fries on the young de Wette.

[2] *Beiträge zur Einleitung in das Alte Testament*, 2 vols, Halle 1806–7; 1, *Kritischer Versuch über die Glaubwürdigkeit der Bücher der Chronik mit Hinsicht auf die Geschichte der Mosaischen Bücher und Gesetzgebung. Ein Nachtrag zu den Vaterschen Untersuchungen über den Pentateuch*; 2, *Kritik der Israelitischen Geschichte. Erster Theil, Kritik der Mosaischen Geschichte*.

[3] Johann Severin Vater, *Commentar über den Pentateuch, mit Einleitungen zu den einzelnen Abschnitten, der eingeschalteten Uebersetzung von Dr. Alexander Geddes's merkwürdigeren critischen und exegetischen Anmerkungen, und einer Abhandlung über Moses und die Verfasser des Pentateuchs*, 1–3 Halle 1802–5.

For the moment, the main point of the originality of the *Contributions* will be stated, and because of the fundamental importance of the book, its argument will be presented in some detail.

De Wette's *Contributions* is the first work of Old Testament scholarship to use the critical method in order to present a view of the history of Israelite religion that is radically at variance with the view implied in the Old Testament itself. According to the Old Testament, Moses gave to the Israelites a fully-fledged legal system, sacrificial cult, and priesthood. According to de Wette, Moses did nothing of the sort. It is difficult, according to de Wette, to know in detail what Moses gave to the people;[4] what is certain is that the developed legal, sacrificial and hierarchic systems are much later than the time of Moses, and that the ascription of these mature systems to Moses is anachronistic, or 'mythical' in the sense of mythical to be decribed later. De Wette was not the first to argue that some of the laws and sacrifices ascribed to Moses were introduced much later than the time of Moses. J. C. K. Nachtigall had done this under the name of Othmar in articles in 1794 and 1796, as had F. V. Fulda in 1791.[5] Also, the same view was strongly argued by Vater in his *Pentateuch*.[6] De Wette's originality lay in setting out from the books of Chronicles, and in showing that the picture which they presented, namely, a picture of a Mosaic-Levitical religion practised from the time of David, was an anachronism, and a back-projection of the state of affairs after the Exile. Having disposed of Chronicles, de Wette was able to concentrate upon the picture of Israelite religion implied in the books of Samuel and Kings, and he was able to show how much this was at variance with the Mosaic-Levitical religion of Chronicles and parts of the Pentateuch.

In attacking the authenticity of Chronicles de Wette was, of course, taking on the view defended by Eichhorn in his *Introduction* (see above p. 22) that Chronicles depended upon early sources even if its final form showed signs of lateness. De Wette disposed of Eichhorn's position with the following main points:

1   Eichhorn's assumption that Samuel and Kings on the one hand, and Chronicles on the other hand, had used a common ancient source for the lives of David and Solomon was a hypothesis for which there was no evidence. In fact, if the sources were reconstructed from the material common to Samuel/Kings and Chronicles, they hardly amounted to

---

[4] This is de Wette's view in the *Contributions*. Possibly, the Tent of Meeting and the Ark of the Covenant come down from Mosaic times. See *Beiträge* 1, pp. 260ff.

[5] J. C. K. Nachtigall, *ps.* Othmar, 'Fragmente über die allmählige Bildung der den Israeliten heiligen Schriften' in Henke's *Magazin für Religionsphilosophie, Exegese und Kirchenges-chichte*, 2, Helmstädt 1794, pp. 433ff; 4, 1796, pp. 1–36, 329–370; F. C. Fulda in Paulus's *Neues Repertorium*, 1791.

[6] Vater, op. cit., 3, pp. 676ff.

credible 'lives' since they lacked so many important details. Further, the necessary assumption that Chronicles had used a damaged version of the lives of David and Solomon added a second, unnecessary hypothesis.[7]

2 Eichhorn's theory assumed that the writer of 2 Samuel had inserted very large sections of material into the common source. For example, if 1 Chron. 20.1–3, David's conquest of Rabbah, was cited from the 'life' of David, then the writer of 2 Samuel had interpolated between what we have in 1 Chron. 20.1 and what we have in 1 Chron. 20.2–3 the whole story of David's adultery with Bathsheba, and the killing of Uriah. Yet 2 Sam. 11–12 was an integrated whole with no sign of interpolations.[8]

3 Eichhorn's theory did not explain the quite staggering differences in outlook between Samuel/Kings and Chronicles. The latter said nothing about the attempt of Adonijah to succeed David, neither did it mention Solomon's love of foreign women, and the setbacks to Solomon's rule in the form of revolts against him by Edom and other parts of his empire. In the account of the dedication of the temple, Chronicles contained material not to be found in 1 Kings that made the celebrations and the Levitical ministrations explicitly 'Mosaic'. In the account of the divided monarchy, the books of Kings dealt with Israel and Judah. Chronicles mentioned Israel only when absolutely necessary to its preoccupation with Judah. Such differences required far more explanation than Eichhorn's assumption that Chronicles had utilized a defective version of the common source.[9]

Having shown Eichhorn's theory of the independent use of common ancient sources by Samuel/Kings and Chronicles to be untenable, de Wette proceeded to a detailed examination of the books in question in order to show the lateness of Chronicles, and their dependence upon Samuel and Kings. Among the arguments deployed, de Wette pointed to passages in which Chronicles had heightened the supernatural or mythical elements, a sure sign, for de Wette, of the belief of a later age. Examples included 1 Chron. 21.1, where Satan incites David to hold a census, whereas in 2 Sam. 24.1 the anger of God is responsible.[10] De Wette regarded the emphasis of Chronicles upon the Levites as a sign of lateness, since he held it to be unlikely that Samuel and Kings would have omitted all references to Levites had they in fact been active as described in Chronicles.[11] In some cases, the obsession with proper religious practice in Chronicles led to absurdities. Thus, the statement in 2 Chron. 1.3 (not found in 1 Kings 3.4)

[7] *Beiträge* 1, pp. 14–17, 23–4.
[8] ibid., 1, pp. 18–21.
[9] ibid., 1, pp. 119–20, 53ff, 126–32.
[10] ibid., 1, pp. 50–1.
[11] ibid., 1, pp. 80–102.

that the tent of meeting was at Gibeon raised the question as to why it was not housing the ark in Jerusalem, and by what authority David had pitched another tent for the ark in Jerusalem (2 Chron. 1.4).[12] In de Wette's view, the Chronicles treatment was an unhistorical attempt to vindicate Solomon from the charge of worshipping at the high place at Gibeon.

A conspicuous example of a quite contradictory presentation of an event was the treatment in 2 Chron. 23.1–11 of the accession of Joash, compared with the account in 2 Kings 11.4–12. In the latter account, Joash's accession is the result of a plan thought up by Jehoiada the priest and executed by the Carites (probably foreign mercenaries) and guards (lit. 'runners'), whereby Jehoash was to be proclaimed king in defiance of queen Athaliah. In the account in Chronicles, the conspiracy has reached gigantic proportions. All the Levites from all the cities of Judah are assembled, together with all the heads of fathers' houses. Those who execute the coup are not, as in Kings, the guards, but are the priests and Levites, and it is the Levites who surround and guard the King, not his bodyguard.[13] De Wette's case is that the Kings version is credible whereas the version in Chronicles has projected a later Levitical domination into the incident, surely an unassailable argument.

De Wette has thus exorcised the ghost of the antiquity of the religion attested in Chronicles, and wishes to read Joshua–Kings in order to discover the true course of the development of the religion of Israel. Before he does this, however, it is necessary to show that there is in fact practically no reference to the Pentateuch in the books of Samuel and Kings, nor in the Psalms, and that only in the books of Ezra and Nehemiah can the existence of the Pentateuch be discerned.[14] Much attention is paid to the account of the discovery of the book of the Law in the reign of Josiah (2 Kings 22), with de Wette insisting that it was the discovery of something *that had not been previously known*. How it got into the temple could not be said for lack of historical evidence.[15] What it contained was equally uncertain, although similarities with parts of Deuteronomy are noted. The conclusion is drawn: 'that until Josiah, there is no trace of the existence of the Pentateuch. Thereafter, especially after the Exile, there are the most frequent and definite traces'.[16] De Wette (following Nachtigall (Othmar)) also cites Jeremiah 7.25 in favour of the view that the Israelites had no cult of sacrifices and burnt offerings in the wilderness.[17]

The remaining obstacle before de Wette can reconstruct the history of

---

[12] ibid., 1, pp. 108–12.
[13] ibid., 1, pp. 91–8.
[14] ibid., 1, pp. 135–88.
[15] ibid., 1, pp. 175–9.
[16] ibid., 1, p. 182: 'bis Josia keine Spur von dem Daseyn des Pentateuchs, nachher, besonders nach dem Exil, die häufigsten und deutlichsten.'
[17] ibid., 1, pp. 184–5.

the religion of Israel is the argument from the Samaritan Pentateuch. Eichhorn[18] presented the standard argument that supported the relative antiquity of the Pentateuch. This held that because of the enmity between Israel and Judah after the division of the kingdom (940), it was unlikely that the Samaritans (descended from the Northern kingdom Israel) would take over the Pentateuch from Judah. Thus the Pentateuch must have existed by the time of the division of the kingdom. In reply,[19] de Wette pointed to the many occasions in the book of Kings on which Israel and Judah had contact and co-operated. He denied that there was enmity between the kingdoms, and pointed out that false religion and idolatry flourished in both. After the Exile, representatives of the Samaritans had asked to join in rebuilding the Jerusalem temple, an indication that the Samaritans had no fixed and established cult. Further, the anti-Samaritan sentiments of the book of Nehemiah probably presented in a false light the desire of many Samaritans to be on good terms with Judah, something that many in Judah also wished (cf. Neh. 6.17–19). It was the building of the Samaritan temple on Mt Gerizim that brought about real enmity between the two communities, but it would be wrong to read these late poor relationships into earlier times. The Samaritans first adopted a religious constitution after the Exile, as a result of which they separated from the Jews. This act of separation gave the lower ceiling for the possessing of the Pentateuch by the Samaritans, and in no way ruled out a late date for the Pentateuch to come into existence.

At last de Wette is able to describe the development of Israelite religion, freed from belief in the antiquity of the sources of Chronicles, and in the light of a belief in the late composition of the Pentateuch.[20] He draws attention to the multiplicity of sanctuaries in the books of Judges and 2 Samuel. Shiloh, Bethel, Gilgal, Shechem and Mizpah all figure in the narrative, and speak against the unity of the cult at one place. There is also a sanctuary at Nob (1 Sam. 21) with shewbread, at the very time when the tent of meeting is at Shiloh and the ark is at Kiriath-jearim.

Just as there is no evidence for unity of the cult, so there is no developed priesthood in the early period. At the transfer of the ark to Jerusalem by David, there are no Levites to carry the ark, and David himself wears a priestly garment, blesses the people, and sacrifices (or causes sacrifices to be offered). De Wette summarizes the nature of the cult in the early period as follows:

'There is a complete freedom of worship. As among the Patriarchs and the Homeric Greeks, God's open heaven was his temple, each meal a sacrifice, each

[18] Eichhorn, *Einleitung* 2, pp. 131ff, pp. 251ff.
[19] *Beiträge*, 1, pp. 188–223.
[20] ibid., 1, pp. 223–99.

festive and important event a festival, and each prophet, king and father of a household was without further qualifications a priest'.[21]

Although David and Solomon built the Temple and instituted its worship, the freedom of the people to worship where they wished continued to the time of Josiah. The priests were unable to enforce any uniformity upon the people, and they possessed no power. It was Hezekiah who first sought to restrict the freedom of the people to worship where they wished, a process furthered by Josiah with the help of the lawbook found in the temple.

So far as the Mosaic religion was concerned, little could be known about it. The ark and the tables of the ten commandments could be from the time of Moses, and Moses could have ordered a tent to be used, although the description of the tent in Exodus possibly owed something to the tent erected by David. Since cult becomes more, not less complex, as time passes, Moses can hardly have instituted a coherent system of sacrifices; neither could he have designed the tribe of Levi to be a priestly tribe. Part 1 of the *Contributions* ends with a recapitulation of the arguments presented in de Wette's 1805 doctoral dissertation, in which he maintained that Deuteronomy was later than the other books of the Pentateuch.

The second volume of the *Contributions* can be summarized very briefly. It is an attempt to show that much of the material in Genesis—Numbers is 'mythical'.[22] By 'mythical', de Wette certainly meant unhistorical, and although he also understood a good deal more than this by 'mythical', we shall concentrate for the moment on the equation: mythical = unhistorical. Whereas Neologists such as Eichhorn and Gabler had used the concept of myth in order to salvage scraps of historicity from supernatural biblical narratives, de Wette's aim was to deny that any firm historical information could be obtained from most of Genesis—Numbers. The narratives had originated in various ways. In some cases, they were based upon etymological puns on names.[23] In other cases, they reflected later political relationships between the Israelites and their neighbours.[24] Another factor in the genesis of mythical traditions was the ascription of laws and practices to a great figure of the past, especially Moses.[25] Such ascription was, of course, strictly speaking false. The traditions of Genesis—Numbers were therefore not evidence for the early history of Israel and her forebears; they were evidence

---

[21] ibid., 1, p. 255: 'in der frühern Periode eine gänzliche Freiheit des Gottesdienstes herrschte. Wie bey den Patriarchen und homerischen Griechen, war Gottes freier Himmel sein Tempel, jede Mahlzeit ein Opfer, jede feierliche und merkwürdige Gelegenheit ein Fest, und jeder Prophet, König und Hausvater ohne weitere Umstände Priester.'

[22] See my *Myth in Old Testament Interpretation, BZAW* 134, Berlin 1974, ch. 2.

[23] See, for example, *Beiträge* 2, pp. 124ff. on Gen. 29—32.

[24] ibid., 2, pp. 75–6, on Gen. 9.18–27.

[25] ibid., 2, pp. 267ff.

for the religious spirit of the Israelites from the period of the monarchy onwards. The proper way to interpret them was not to demythologize them in order to discover scraps of historical information. The task was to appreciate the traditions for what they were, authentic expressions of the religious intuitions of the Hebrew people.

The *Contributions* finish without a summary that brings all their results together. Perhaps their young author was in a hurry to get his work published, for fear of being beaten to the press by someone who would present the same arguments.[26] However, readers who bothered to tie up the ends, and who summarized the *Contributions* into a coherent whole, would have obtained results roughly as follows:

1   The books of Chronicles are late in composition, and provide no reliable evidence for the religion of Israel in the pre-exilic period.

2   The Pentateuch in its final form is a late compilation. The first clear evidence for existence of part of it is in Josiah's reign, when the idea of an authoritative 'book of the law' is quite a new idea.

3   The traditions in the Pentateuch do not provide information about the history of Israel in the pre-settlement period. In many cases they are mythical, that is, unhistorical free and poetical compositions expressing the spirit of Hebrew religion in the monarchic and later periods.

4   The history of Israelite religion was quite different from that implied in the Old Testament read uncritically. In the period down to Josiah (seventh century), there was no fixed central sanctuary, no precise regulations about the 'how' of sacrifice, and no priesthood established so as to regulate the worship of the people strictly. In the Old Testament as we have it, there is a reading-back into the earliest periods of Israelite religion as it later came to be.

In arguing the above points, de Wette raised all of the main questions that were to be of central concern in nineteenth-century Old Testament scholarship, and he also gave many of the answers that were to be adopted, rightly or wrongly, after the triumph of the critical method. Only on one crucial point does he seem to have shown any uncertainty, with detriment to his general argumentation.

In his doctoral dissertation published in 1805, de Wette argued that Deuteronomy was later than the other books of the Pentateuch.[27] The

---

[26] De Wette's Jena teacher, Griesbach, describes in the preface to the *Contributions* (p.v) de Wette's reactions on seeing Part 3 of Vater's *Pentateuch*. De Wette was 'bestürzt—halb erfreut, und halb erschrocken'.

[27] *Dissertatio critica qua a prioribus Deuteronomium Pentateuchi libris diversum, alius cuiusdam recentioris auctoris opus esse monstratur 1805,* repr. in *Opuscula Theologica*, Berlin 1839, pp. 151–68.

reason for this assertion will be explained shortly. Yet it was Deuteronomy that showed the similarities with Josiah's reform. How, then, could it be maintained that the Pentateuch was a post-exilic composition, that Deuteronomy was closest to Josiah's 'book of the law', and that Deuteronomy was later than the other books of the Pentateuch? De Wette's answer would appear to be that Deuteronomy is made up of various fragments,[28] that at best, only part of it would be Josiah's law book, and that Deuteronomy in its final form is later than the other books of the Pentateuch in their final form.[29] That this was not a totally satisfactory answer, even in terms of de Wette's own research, meant that the door was left open for more radical conclusions than those of the *Contributions*.[30] However, all in all, the *Contributions* were more far-reaching in their implications than Vater's *Pentateuch* which seemed in so many ways to anticipate de Wette's *Contributions*.

Vater's main intention was to advance the fragmentary hypothesis of the origin of the Pentateuch in opposition to the documentary hypothesis favoured by Eichhorn and Ilgen.[31] He also championed a late date for the final compilation of the Pentateuch, in opposition to Eichhorn's defence of its Mosaic composition. Vater and de Wette were united in arguing that: (a) many laws in the Pentateuch reflected situations later than the time of Moses; (b) there were few, if any, allusions to the Pentateuch in the historical books of the Old Testament prior to the time of Josiah; (c) the Pentateuch as we know it can hardly have existed before the Exile.[32]

The two scholars appear to have differed over Deuteronomy. Vater already recognized what today are regarded as Deuteronomic glosses of passages in the historical books of the Old Testament and concluded that Deuteronomy, or part of it, had existed from the time of Solomon because of what he regarded as allusions to it in the historical books.[33] Against de Wette, he envisaged that parts of Deuteronomy existed before other parts of the Pentateuch were collected together.

[28] *Beiträge*, 1, pp. 265–6.
[29] In *Beiträge*, 1, p. 175, de Wette notes that Lev. 26, like Deut. 27—28 contains blessings and cursings. On p. 176 he says that Josiah's lawbook corresponds with the main tendency (*Haupteindruck*) of Deuteronomy. However, probably *more* than (fragments of?) Deuteronomy was found, but it was (parts of?) Deuteronomy that received attention and made the chief impression: 'so glaube ich annehmen zu müssen, dass dieses (Deuteronomy), wo nicht allein gefunden wurde, so doch vorzüglich in Sprache kam und Sensation erregte' (p. 176).
[30] I mean the conclusion, to be drawn by George (see below p. 64) that parts of Exodus—Numbers were *later* than Deuteronomy.
[31] At the end of part three of his *Pentateuch*, pp. 700–24, Vater plays Astruc, Eichhorn and Ilgen off against each other, by showing their disagreement about the way in which the documents are to be reconstructed from the final form of the text.
[32] Vater, *Pentateuch* 3, pp. 676–80.
[33] ibid., p. 680.

What is completely lacking in Vater is any treatment of Chronicles, any wholesale attempt to designate the origin of traditions as 'mythical', and any attempt to reconstruct the history of Israelite religion in a radical fashion. Although a most important contribution to Old Testament criticism, it does not represent the breakthrough that de Wette's *Contributions* does, precisely because it does not raise in an acute form the questions that were to be central to the nineteenth-century critical debate.[34]

(b) De Wette's other early work and its philosophical assumptions

At first sight, de Wette's *Contributions* is the product of brilliant critical insights fuelled by a negative or sceptical disposition. Surely, only somebody sceptically disposed would sustain his attempt to prove the historical untrustworthiness of the books of Chronicles, and of the traditions of the Pentateuch. Indeed, de Wette has often been presented as a young radical critic who mellowed in his later years as he became influenced by the philosophy of Fries and Schleiermacher. This understanding of de Wette, it will now be argued, is incorrect. In fact, de Wette was motivated by what to him was a very positive form of religious conviction, and he honestly thought that his treatment of Chronicles and of the Pentateuch was a *positive* contribution to theology.

When de Wette entered the University of Jena in 1799 as a student of philosophy and theology, he soon seems to have lost the boyhood belief mediated by his schooling and his upbringing in the family of a Lutheran pastor. A decisive point in his life was his attendance, probably in the summer semester 1801, at lectures on ethics given by Jakob Friedrich Fries (1773–1843), and the life-long friendship with Fries that ensued.[35] In his

---

[34] See also the account of Vater's *Pentateuch* in relation to de Wette's *Beiträge* in Smend, op. cit. pp. 36–40, 1n.

[35] The long obituary of de Wette by his nephew, Gustav Adolf Thöllden, in *NND*, 27. Jahrgang 1849, Weimar 1851, pp. 427–55, says nothing about de Wette's study of philosophy at Jena, and does not mention the influence of J. F. Fries until de Wette's Berlin period. Wiegand, op. cit. (n1) pp. 11–12 speaks of a close friendship with Fries from de Wette's student days in Jena: 'mit wahrer Begeisterung aber finden wir ihm emsig und eifrig in den College von Fries . . .. In dem Fries' schen Hause an Nonnenplan wird bald die Bekanntschaft Freundschaft, und einander sich zum Spaziergange abholend, tauschen sie oft ihre philosophischen Gedanken aus.' R. Smend, op. cit. (n1) makes only three passing references to Fries, on pp. 85, 88 and 90. In his article, 'De Wette und das Verhältnis zwischen historischer Bibelkritik und philosophischem System in 19. Jahrhundert', *ThLZ* 14, 1958, pp. 107–19, Smend sees the decisive influence of Fries as occurring in de Wette's Berlin period, 1811–19. T. K. Cheyne, *Founders of Old Testament Criticism*, in one of the most thorough treatments of de Wette by a British scholar, sees de Wette as a young, radical critic who did not live up to his promise. Staehelin, op. cit. (n1), p. 180 quotes from a letter of de Wette written on the occasion of Fries's death in 1843. This recounts how

semi-autobiographical novel *Theodore, or the Doubter's Ordination* (1821), de Wette described this turning-point as follows:

> Along with these biblical lectures, Theodore heard at the same time some lectures on morals from a Kantian philosopher, through which a completely new world was opened up to him. The notions of the self-sufficiency of reason in its law-giving, of the freedom of the will through which he was elevated above nature and fate, of the altruism of virtue which was its own justification and sought no reward, of pure obedience to the self-given moral law: all these notions gripped him powerfully, and filled him with a high self-awareness. Those shadowy ideas about the love of God and of Christ, about the new birth, about the rule of God's grace in the human mind, all of which he still carried from the instruction of his schoolmaster, these he translated now into this new philosophical language, and so they appeared to him clearer and more certain.[36]

One of the immediate fruits of this experience was an essay written by de Wette in the summer of 1801 and entitled *An Idea about the Study of Theology*.[37] The essay appears to have been given by de Wette to Fries, and from the latter's literary remains it passed eventually to Adolf Stieren, who published it in 1850.[38]

In order to understand the importance of Fries's philosophy for de Wette's

---

Fries described his system to de Wette while they were colleagues at Heidelberg (1807–10) during walks along the banks of the Neckar. De Wette claims, however, that Fries's philosophy merely enabled him to bring to systematic expression what he had worked out for himself.

The view underlying what follows in this chapter is that there were several phases in de Wette's relationship with Fries. The first was during his student days at Jena, when de Wette heard Fries lecture on ethics, and when, according to Wiegand, he began his friendship with Fries. This first phase influenced de Wette's early work on the Old Testament. At Heidelberg (1807–10), Fries's influence was extended, as the two colleagues discussed the Friesian system. To this period may correspond the section in de Wette's novel *Theodor, oder des Zweiflers Weihe*, Weimar 1828[2] where the hero attends the lectures of an unnamed Professor A. This professor is introduced in vol 1, p. 83, in terms that identify him clearly with Fries. The result of this period was that de Wette extended his use of the Friesian system to systematic, dogmatic and biblical theology. In Berlin, de Wette had time to study carefully Fries's three-volume *Neue Kritik der Vernunft* (1807). See his letter to Fries of 15 June 1812 published most fully in Ernst Ludwig Theodor Henke, *Jakob Friedrich Fries. Aus seinem handschriftlichen Nachlasse dargestellt*, Leipzig 1867, pp. 349–50.

[36] *Theodor*, 1, p. 21 (my translation). In the novel this professor is different from the Professor A., whom Theodore later hears, but Fries is meant in both cases.

[37] *Eine Idee über das Studium der Theologie*, ed. Adolph Stieren, Leipzig 1850.

[38] Stieren in the preface to *Eine Idee*, pp. 5–6. Wiegand, op. cit. p. 13, quotes from the *Idee* (p. 11), 'Eine unvergessliche, äussere Veranlassung bewirkte die glücklichste Revolution in meinem Innern und schenkte mir die verlorene Ruhe wieder', and interpolates the phrase, with what authority is not clear, 'es geschah dies in den Vorträgen über die Sittenlehre bei Fries.'

early critical work, it is necessary to outline several elements of the Friesian position.[39] Fries was a strict follower of Kant, and differed from Kant only where he believed that he could complete the Kantian system in a more satisfactory manner than the master himself had achieved. In particular, Fries eschewed the transcendental proofs by which Kant tried to secure the a priori ideas, ideas which were the necessary conditions for human experience and for reflection upon that experience. According to Fries, human intuitions of purpose, value, unity and harmony were true intuitions of 'something real', and did not require proof by way of transcendental logic. Given the limitations of human understanding, however, it was not possible to know what were the 'real things' to which intuitions of purpose, value, etc., pointed. To use an analogy of one of Fries's later exponents,[40] if a person sees a landscape covered by mist, he sees something real, albeit under the limitations imposed by the mist. He also knows what mist is, and how it hampers him as he perceives the landscape. Similarly, when someone perceives purpose, value, unity, etc., he is perceiving something real, albeit limited by the subjectivity which conditions his knowledge. But faced with intuitions of what can never be fully known, the human personality (*Geist*) has one more facility, which can be described in the most original and distinctive word of the Friesian system, in *Ahndung*.[41]

The verb *ahnen* in German, which is related to *Ahndung*, means to have a premonition of something, a presentiment of something to come. This takes us in the direction of the meaning of *Ahndung*, which is the possibility of sensing 'eternal ideas' in such a way that the attempt can be made to express them in symbolic ways. The expression can take the form of mythology, drama, poetry, architecture, forms of religion. None can be an exact reproduction of an 'eternal idea', and their adequacy of expression of the 'idea' must vary greatly. According to Fries, critical philosophy provides, through self-reflection, the most adequate understanding of the nature of the 'ideas', and it also provides the critical tools by means of which to test the adequacy of attempts to express an 'idea' through *Ahndung*. According to this interpretation of mythology, myths are not primarily misunderstood scraps of history, nor pre-scientific failures to understand the ordinary. Myths are attempts of the human spirit to express intuitions of external 'ideas'.[42]

[39] See Rudolf Otto, *Kantisch-Fries'sche Religionsphilosophie und ihre Anwendung auf die Theologie. Zur Einleitung in die Glaubenslehre für Studenten der Theologie*, Tübingen 1909; ET E. B. Dicker, *The Philosophy of Religion based on Kant and Fries*, London 1931.
[40] See Otto, p. 50; English, p. 67. See also J. F. Fries, *Neue oder anthropologische Kritik der Vernunft*, 2, Heidelberg 1831², repr. Aachen 1967, pp. 169ff.
[41] J. F. Fries, *Wissen, Glaube und Ahndung*, Jena 1805, n. ed. Leonard Nelson, Göttingen 1905. *Ahndung* is treated on pp. 171–327.
[42] J. F. Fries, *Neue Kritik*, 3, pp. 368ff. The third volume of the *Neue Kritik* was published in 1807, but much of the material had been prepared by 1798–9.

The young de Wette seems to have been attracted to Fries's ideas, because they provided an alternative to the rationalism which demythologized the Old Testament in order to discover historical or factual 'cores', and to the supranaturalism, which depended on a sort of literalist reading of supernatural narratives.[43] Attracted by the rationalist approach intellectually but repelled by it aesthetically, de Wette saw in Fries's teaching something which used the critical method in order to discover something worthwhile—expressions of deeply-felt religious experience in the Old Testament books.

The Friesian influence is plain in the 1801 essay 'An idea about the study of theology'. De Wette explains how his religious doubts had brought him to the point where he had reduced religion to morality, at which point he felt alone in the world and without purpose.[44] However, an unforgettable occurrence—according to de Wette's biographer his attendance at Fries's lectures on morals[45]—changed all this, and reawakened in his heart new life and faith. This brought the conviction that religion can be properly studied only by those who understand what religion is, and whose own hearts have been warmed by their faith.[46] In language full of Friesian ideas, de Wette described how, for him, the arts (*Kunst*) intimated to him the beauty and harmony of reality, themselves an intimation of the divine and heavenly which could not be found or grasped in the endless universe.[47] Thus, filled with certainty about the divine, de Wette was also able to recognize it in the natural world and in human history. But the study of theology provided for him a veritable temple for contemplation, in the form of the traditions of the Old and New Testaments. He found himself refreshed by the many different witnesses to religion in the Old Testament, from the friendly picture of the patriarchal period, through the patience of Job, the inspiration of the psalmists, the figures of the prophets, to the religion of the ordinary people of the Old Testament.[48]

Friesian ideas and language can be found in the three other principal works of de Wette on the Old Testament of this period: the *Invitation to the Study of Hebrew Language and Literature* (1805), the *Contribution to the Characteristic Features of Hebrew Religion* (1807), and his doctoral dissertation on Deuteronomy (1805).

---

[43] See *Theodor*, 1, pp. 174ff, for de Wette's views on Rationalists and Supranaturalists. Also, see his *Ueber Religion und Theologie. Erläuterungen zu seinem Lehrbuche der Dogmatik*, Berlin 1815, p.v., where he writes about the 'Verstand' party and the 'Glaube' party: 'Der Verstand ohne Glauben wird zum Unglauben und zur leeren Täuschung, und der Glaube ohne Verstand wird zum Aberglauben und zur Schwärmerei.'

[44] *Idee*, p. 10.

[45] See n38 above.

[46] *Idee*, p. 13.

[47] ibid., p. 20. See the section 'Vom Erhabenen der Kunst' in Fries, *Neue Kritik*, 3, pp. 335ff.

[48] *Idee*, p. 23.

In the *Invitation*,[49] published in connection with the beginning of de Wette's work as a lecturer, the author addresses himself to those who doubt the value of Old Testament study in theology. He repeats his point from the *Idea*, that only those who know the nature and meaning of religion should study theology, and he asserts that the best preparation to this end is the study of philosophy and the arts (*Kunst*):

> In contemplation of all that is beautiful and great, and in deep and quiet examination of himself and nature, his heart will go out for what is the highest; the value and meaning of religion will appear to him, and he will grasp (*ahnden*) what it is to believe in God. Whoever succeeds to mount to this point, and to grasp the intuition (*Ahnung*) of the highest: he alone is called and dedicated to the study of theology.[50]

A person thus initiated into true religion will benefit greatly from studying the history of religion, where will be found many manifestations of religion, in the context of a development from fetishism to systematic unity. Each religion will have its peculiarity, but this will contribute a rich harvest for study. In the case of the Jewish religion, a development to monotheism can be seen. There is also a veritable treasure of the remains of Hebrew literature which afford a rich view of Hebrew religious life in the various periods.[51]

A closer study of the characteristics of Hebrew religion is given in the *Characteristic Features*, which will be outlined in a moment. Otherwise, the *Invitation* stresses the importance of the religion of the Old Testament for understanding Christianity, argues that a knowledge of Hebrew is a sure entry into the spirit of Hebrew religion and has some sharp criticism to make against those who do not study the Old Testament as a collection of *religious* literature. In a passage which obviously has in mind scholars such as Eichhorn, whose handling of the Old Testament is so sharply criticized by implication in the second volume of the *Contributions* de Wette says:

> The historical way of handling the Old Testament in the way in which many have sought to employ it in recent times seems to me to be contrary to the spirit of theology and to the true study of religion, as well as illicit and unproductive. The Bible is a religious book, given to us as such, and because we are theologians we ought to seek for religion in it, not secular history, politics or jurisprudence.[52]

He goes on to say that a proper use of the critical method will indicate that we have in the Old Testament very little by way of authentic *historical*

---

[49] *Auffoderung zum Studium der Hebräischen Sprache und Litteratur*, Jena and Leipzig 1805.

[50] *Auffoderung*, p. 9. (translation mine). De Wette tends to use the variant *Ahnung* for *Ahndung*.

[51] *Auffoderung*, pp. 14–17.

[52] *Auffoderung*, pp. 26–7.

sources.[53] The Old Testament was not written with modern historians in view. On the other hand, the *religion* of the Old Testament is of universal importance and it will be possible to reconstruct from the inner character of the documents a history of Hebrew religion in which what is early will be distinguished from what is late.[54] The programme of the *Contributions* of 1806–7 is thus clearly stated.

In the *Characteristic Features* of 1807, more evidence of de Wette's use of Friesian ideas is to be found.[55] The work is mostly a discussion of the Psalms, Job and Ecclesiastes, and in the handling of the Psalms, there is an anticipation of de Wette's type-criticism of the Psalms of his 1811 commentary.[56] However, the main point of the work is that Judaism is a religion of misfortune (*Unglück*).[57] This seems to be a surprising thing to say about the religion of the Old Testament; but it is less surprising when we know that Fries, in the third volume of his *New Critique of Reason* correlated differing types of artistic and literary expression with particular experiences of life.[58] Tragedy and comedy, for example, were two ways of expressing the contradiction experienced between apparent purposelessness in nature and life, and the inner awareness of human freedom. In tragedy or elegy were expressed the misfortune (*Unglück*) that occurred to individuals or nations, and which was in conflict with the inner conviction of individual freedom unaffected by outside constraints.[59] By describing the religion of the Old Testament as one of misfortune (*Unglück*) de Wette meant that throughout the history of Israel there was an unresolved tension between Israel's sense of purpose as the People of God, and the constant threats to Israel's existence from her external enemies. There was also misfortune (*Unglück*) at the individual level, where pious individuals were threatened by personal enemies, and where a discrepancy was perceived between the sufferings of the righteous and the prosperity of the wicked.

The unresolved tensions that were a feature of life in Old Testament

[53] *Auffoderung*, p. 28. '. . . eine vollkommene, durchgreifende Kritik aber wird zeigen, dass kein einziges von den geschichtlichen Werken des A.T. geschichtlichen Werth hat, und alle mehr oder weniger Mythen und Traditionen enthalten, und dass wir unter allen Büchern des A.T. keine eigentlichen geschichtlichen Zeugen haben, als einige Propheten, die aber wenig geschichtliche Ausbeute geben dürften.'
[54] *Auffoderung*, p. 31.
[55] 'Beytrag zur Charakteristik des Hebraismus' in C. Daub and F. Creuzer (eds), *Studien*, 3, 2, Heidelberg 1807, pp. 241–312.
[56] 'Beytrag', pp. 253–77.
[57] 'Beytrag', p. 245, 'Das Judenthum ist das Unglück, das Christenthum der Trost dafür'.
[58] Fries, *Neue Kritik*, 3, pp. 357ff.
[59] See Fries, op. cit., p. 357. 'Es gibt eine eigne tragische oder elegische Weltansicht, welche auf dem Interesse der Trauer und des Unglücks beruht, deren Freude Thränen und deren Ideale Heimweh und die unendliche Sehnsucht nach dem ewigen, überirdischen sind . . .' See also pp. 360–1, 'Das Tragisch-Erhabene und die elegischen Ideale der unendlichen Sehnsucht gehen von dem *für mich zweckwidrigen* in der Natur, vom Unglück aus . . .'.

times gave to Israelite religion a quality of inwardness. According to de Wette, the Hebrew nation was like a child that had never been young, and that spent its life in self-reflection. It was no accident that Old Testament prophecy was directed towards criticism of the national life. Old Testament religion exhibited features that were to be taken on into Christianity: a concern for inwardness, for morality; a tendency to pietism and to mysticism.[60]

The misfortune (*Unglück*) characteristic of Hebrew religion found fullest expression in the psalter, the lyrical anthology of the Hebrews. More than half of the psalms are about misfortune (*Unglück*), suffering, anxiety and danger. But the books of Job and Ecclesiastes were also expressions of this outlook on life.

In the case of Job, the Hebrew poet had become convinced of the futility of any sort of belief in order and justice. After the manifestation of the majesty of God in the awesome sublimity of nature (the notion of the sublime (*Erhaben*) is important in Kantian and Friesian aesthetics)[61] the poet of Job found that his doubts had been removed. God had not been cleared of the charges brought against him by Job, but he had been seen to belong to a realm where human justification was irrelevant. Job was reconciled to God by becoming aware of his own utter powerlessness and nothingness.[62] The writer in Ecclesiastes had become convinced—against the intuitions of *Ahndung*—that there could be nothing of value or of purpose in life. Yet it was not lack of religion that led him to expound his scepticism. An unrecognized God was enthroned in his inner being, and occasioned the sublime pronouncements to be found in Ecclesiastes.[63]

De Wette's famous doctoral dissertation of 1805 on the book of Deuteronomy gave six main grounds for concluding that Deuteronomy was by different authors from those who compiled the other books of the Pentateuch, and was later than the others. Some of the grounds involved pointing out discrepancies between Deuteronomy and the other books. The fourth ground, however, involved a contrast between what de Wette saw as the simple, naive and unselfconscious content of Genesis—Numbers and the more complex, subtle, mystical and superstitious content of Deuteronomy.[64] For example, in Exodus, the miracle of the manna was related

(margin note: Pss express / Unglück ?!)

---

[60] 'Beytrag', p. 251.
[61] I. Kant, *Kritik der Urtheilskraft* (1790), 23–9 'Analytik des Erhabenen' (in Akademie Textausgabe of *Kants Werke* 1902, repr. Berlin 1968), 5, pp. 244–66; Fries, *Neue Kritik*, 3, pp. 322–40, 'Von der Erhabenheit oder Ästhetisch idealen Ansicht der Dinge'.
[62] 'Beytrag', pp. 278–86.
[63] ibid., pp. 288–303.
[64] *Dissertatio*, quoted from *Opuscula Theologica*, p. 161: 'Quae priores libri [Gen.—Num.] simplicia, nativa atque inculta habent, ea noster [Deut.] ornata, subtiliora, corrupta exhibet Mythologiam, quam in illis simplicem atque talem invenimus, qualis a maioribus tradita erat, noster mysticismos quodam et doctrina frigida, subtili, superstitiosa temperatam exhibet'.

without comment. In Deuteronomy, it was the basis of a piece of theologizing designed to teach the Israelites that man could not live by bread alone, but by every word that proceeded out of the mouth of God. Deuteronomy had taken a miracle story that was an unselfconsious creation of *Ahndung* expressing simple Israelite trust in God, and had used it to introduce the sophisticated notion of a word from God that could sustain the people.[65] This movement from unselfconscious narrative to reflective use of narrative was again part of the Friesian system, expounded in part three of the *New Critique*.[66]

When de Wette's *Contributions* of 1806–7 are read in the light of his other important youthful works, and in the context of Friesian philosophy, it is possible to grasp the totality of the position for which the young scholar was arguing. He had arrived at a comprehensive understanding of the nature of religion, of the way in which religious narratives, symbols and worship grasped and expressed 'eternal ideas', of the way in which religion developed from spontaneous to self-conscious forms. He was concerned with the manner in which external circumstances of national and individual life affected the characteristics of a particular religion, and how distinctive literary forms such as tragic drama or lyric poetry expressed certain of these characteristics. He had brought all these elements of his comprehensive understanding to bear upon his study of the Old Testament, and with the help of the critical method, he sought to bring to light the history of Old Testament religion, the distinctive characteristics of Old Testament religion and the way in which these characteristics were expressed in the traditions of the Old Testament. Judged by the criterion that the truth of Old Testament narratives is their *historical* truth, de Wette's *Contributions* of 1806–7 looked very negative indeed. Judged by his own criterion, that theology is concerned to study *religion*, the *Contributions* were meant to be positive.

De Wette's youthful works achieved a breakthrough in critical studies because they shifted attention away from preoccupation with the authorship of the Old Testament books and the sources or fragments used in the compilations. They raised the question 'is the Old Testament read uncritically a true guide to the history of Israelite religion?' His resounding answer of 'no' to this question was born not only of critical acumen, but of his own

---

[65] *Dissertatio*, p. 162.
[66] *Neue Kritik*, 3, p. 371: 'In Rücksicht dieser metaphysischen Mythologie müssen wir endlich zum Letztenmale der mythologischen Religionsphilosophie entgegentreten, in deren Geheimnisse man uns neuerdings wieder einzuweihen sucht. Wir begreifen hier wohl, woher sie das Interessante ihrer geheimnissvollen Sprache entlehnt, sie täuscht mit tiefer Weisheit, indem sie uns Allegorien für Wahrheit unterschiebt, Symbolik für Wissenschaft, wie alle Priester-Kasten und Mystagogen der Vorzeit.'

(Friesian) understanding of religion. His question was to be the central preoccupation of critical nineteenth-century scholarship.

(c) De Wette's later work

De Wette's chief contribution to critical Old Testament scholarship lay in the new questions raised by his early works. His later works were basically a working out of his youthful position in greater detail. Thus, his psalms commentary of 1811 elaborated the type-criticism of the psalms already sketched in the *Characteristic Features* (1807), and his *Introduction to the Old Testament* (1817) restated his views on the Pentateuch and Chronicles, adding his critical opinions upon other books of the Old Testament. In his *Biblical Dogmatics* (1813) to be outlined shortly, he treated the religion of the Old Testament systematically, on the basis of his philosophical position.

The influence of de Wette upon contemporary scholarship was not great. Rather, as we shall see, younger scholars such as Gramberg and George took up the questions that de Wette had raised, and tried to carry them further by means of critical arguments rather than in the context of Friesian philosophy. Indeed, de Wette's adherence to the Friesian system was a hindrance to his influence, mainly because Fries was overshadowed by the speculative philosophy of Schelling and Hegel. Also, in theology, the position of Schleiermacher seemed to be able to achieve what de Wette was aiming to do, without committing one to so overtly a philosophical stance.[67] From 1819, both Fries and de Wette suffered from political victimization. Fries was later forbidden to teach philosophy because he had attended the student rally at the Wartburg, near Eisenach, in 1817. For the rest of his life, he was a professor of physics and mathematics at Jena. De Wette was dismissed from his chair in Berlin in 1819 for writing a letter of sympathy to the mother of the theological student, Karl Ludwig Sand, after Sand had murdered the diplomat, August Kotzebue.[68] In 1822, de Wette obtained a chair of theology in Basel, where he remained until his death in 1849. Even so, he was not free from political harassment, and the Prussian authorities in 1824 forbade any student whose home was in Prussia to study at Basel.[69]

[67] Friedrich Lücke, 'Zur freundschaftlichen Erinnerung an D. Wilhelm Martin Leberecht de Wette' in *TSK* 1850, describes how his initial enthusiasm for de Wette's position was abandoned in favour of that of Schleiermacher.

[68] See the detailed treatment by Max Lenz, 'Zur Entlassung de Wettes', in *Philotesia. Paul Kleinert zum LXX Geburtstag dargebracht von Adolf Harnack u.a.,* Berlin 1907, pp. 337–88.

[69] See Johannes Bachmann, *Ernst Wilhelm Hengstenberg. Sein Leben und Wirken,* Gütersloh, 1, 1879, p. 148, for information on the cabinet order of 21 May 1824, and how it affected Hengstenberg. It is possible that August Twesten refers to this ban in a letter to Schleiermacher of 10 April 1826: 'Es ist sehr zu bedauern, dass de Wette von akademischer Wirksamkeit so gut wie gänzlich ausgeschlossen ist' in *D. August Twesten nach Tagebüchern und Briefen* von C. J. Georg Heinrici, Berlin 1889, p. 409; The editor's explanation (n2), 'Er [de Wette] lebte bis zur Berufung nach Basel in Weimar', is nonsense, since de Wette had already been in Basel for over three years by 1826.

Of de Wette's later works (he also wrote extensively on the New Testament and on the history of ethics) brief reference will be made to three. The *Commentary on the Psalms* was essentially a working out of what was stated in the early works, especially the *Characteristic Features* of 1807. Already in 1807, de Wette had classified the psalms into *four* main types:[70] (1) individual laments (*Unglückspsalmen*); (2) national laments; (3) meditations on the success of evil in the world; (4) theodicy psalms (esp. psalms 37, 73). In the *Contributions* he had even argued that the dates of psalms could be determined by their aesthetic quality. The aesthetic critic could look for the inner value of each of the many-coloured flowers that made up the collection of psalms, so as to recognize the place of each in the garland of Hebrew poetry. He would recognize what was original and what was a copy, what carried the colours of early spring and what carried the colours of late autumn. If a psalm breathed the inner spirit of the earlier centuries, then its comparative age was established.[71]

In the *Commentary*, de Wette classified the psalms differently from in his earlier work, no doubt because here, he was not arguing about the characteristic features of Hebrew religion but was addressing himself to the psalter as a whole.[72] His main classes of psalms in the commentary were: (1) Hymns in praise of God; (2) National psalms concerned with the history of Israel as the people of God (78, 105, 106, 114); (3) Sion and temple psalms (15, 24, 68, 81, 87, 132, 134, 135); (4) Royal psalms (2, 20, 21, 45, 72, 110); (5) Laments, of which there were six sub-types including individual and national laments; (6) A general class of religious and moral psalms, including those expressing trust (23).[73]

His approach to the exegesis of the individual psalms had perforce to take account of the predominant historical exegesis of his day, which sought to set each psalm in its 'original' historical setting. Yet even here, de Wette remained true to his convictions that historical certainty was not as easy to come by as many supposed, and that the first duty of the commentator was to appreciate the psalm as a poetic whole, expressing a particular religious experience or intuition. Further, if the historical hypothesis advanced to account for the psalm did not accord with the psalm's 'character', then the

[70] 'Beytrag', pp. 253–77.
[71] *Beiträge*, 1, pp. 158–9: 'Die einzige Kritik, die über die Psalmen möglich ist, die uns aber auch vollkommen hinreichend seyn kann, ist die des Aesthetikers. Dieser mag der vorhandene bunte Blumenlese der Psalmen sichten, und nach ihren *innern Werthe* ihre Rangordnung in dem Kranze hebräischer Poesie bestimmen . . . wenn nur der innere Geist die Jugend früherer Jahrhunderte athmet, so ist für ihn das frühe Alter entschieden'.
[72] Reference is made here to the second edition of the *Commentar über die Psalmen*, Heidelberg 1823.
[73] *Psalmen*, pp. 3ff.

hypothesis was insecure.[74] Read superficially, the Psalms commentary
appears to be negative because time and again, de Wette argues for the
uncertainty of the historical interpretations advanced in the contemporary
scholarly literature. At the same time, his detailed comments on individual
verses often do not succeed in conveying the mood or aesthetic quality of
the psalm under discussion.

In the *Biblical Dogmatics,* on the other hand, de Wette makes his intentions
much more clear.[75] Forty-one pages are devoted to an exposition of the
nature of religion in Friesian terms,[76] before a brief outline of the history of
Hebrew and Jewish religion leads to a systematic treatment of the leading
ideas of the Old Testament.[77] This systematic treatment sees at the heart of
Old Testament religion a polarity between universalism and particularism;
between belief in a universal God, and belief that the universal God had
established a particular theocracy with the people of Israel.[78]

In the historical traditions of the Old Testament, the universal/particular
polarity was expressed in the conviction that although these traditions were
those about a *particular* nation, the destinies of that nation were controlled
by the power of the universal God.[79] A similar grasping of the ideas of the
universality and freedom of God was expressed in the miracle stories, where
God was sovereign over the natural process.[80] The distinctive Israelite name
of God, Jahwe, was a national name denoting the one, true God. The Old
Testament saw him as the ground of being, the omnipotent, the omniscient,
the omnipresent, the eternal and the unchangeable.[81] In the Wisdom
traditions (e.g., Ps. 104.24; Job 12.13; 38; Prov. 8.22–31.) were expressed
the idea of the purposefulness of all things. The relationship of God to the
created order is expressed in the creation stories of Gen. 1.1—2.4, 2.5–9.
Both are saga-like symbolic narratives, expressing the sovereign freedom of
God over nature. There is much to be said for interpreting Gen. 1.1—2.4 as

[74] ibid., pp. 91–4, esp. p. 92, 'Daher scheint es mir besser, keine historische Erklärung zu
geben, als eine unsichere'.
[75] Reference is made here to *Biblische Dogmatik Alten und Neuen Testaments,* Berlin 1831, 3.
[76] Note the reference to Fries's *Neue Kritik* on p. 1.
[77] In his earlier writings, de Wette does not make the distinction between Hebrew religion
and Judaism so clearly as he does in his later writing. See Smend, op. cit., pp. 103, n663.
However, this distinction between Hebrew religion and Judaism, so significant for later
scholarship, is already implicit in his *Dissertatio,* where he sees already in Deuteronomy a
tendency that is to lead to rabbinic Judaism. De Wette claims: 'Diversa plane et a prioribus
libris dissona esse videtur religionis et iuris doctrina, quam liber noster spirat, quippe quae
ad sequiorem Rabbinorum doctrinam aliquo modo accedere videatur'. *Dissertatio,* in
Opuscula Theologica, p. 161.
[78] *Dogmatik,* p. 64, cf. Smend, pp. 77ff.
[79] ibid., p. 169.
[80] ibid., pp. 79–80.
[81] ibid., p. 73.

God bringing order to pre-existent matter by means of the poetic command 'let there be'.[82]

According to de Wette, Hebrew religion lacked a doctrine of immortality because although Moses was familiar with the idea from Egypt, it could not have been taught to the Hebrews without using the sort of mythology that would have been detrimental to Hebrew religion.[83] In its view of the nature of man, Hebrew religion therefore had to find ways of expressing the dignity of man without the aid of the idea of immortality. This it did by speaking of men being in the image of God, a reference to the idea of man being enlivened by the spirit of God. At the same time, man was corrupted as to his moral nature, the myth of the fall seeking to explain the origin of this.[84]

Relationships between God and man were ordered by the theocracy, and its institutions. The polarity between particularism and universalism was expressed in the view that Israel was to be the kingdom of God upon earth. The will of the invisible God was mediated by laws and by the cult, and was supported by observances such as the sabbath, new moon and sabbatical year observances, and celebration of national festivals such as tabernacles, weeks and passover.[85]

Hebrew religion was also capable of deterioration. The 'particular' side of Israel's relationship with the universal God could become selfish patriotism; the theocracy could forget that it was supposed to display the kingship of the universal God. Holiness could degenerate into legalism, symbols could be mistaken for what they pointed to, and sacrifice and rituals could be thought to be ends rather than means. The lack of a doctrine of immortality and the stress on morality led to a mechanical idea that goodness would always be rewarded with prosperity and vice versa. This in turn led to the scepticism and questioning of books of the Old Testament such as Job and Ecclesiastes.[86]

However, Hebrew religion also gave rise to the notion of the *ideal* theocracy or the hope for the Messiah.[87] The presence of a messianic figure was neither necessary nor early in Hebrew hopes. The idea was essentially a

[82] ibid., pp. 76ff.
[83] ibid., pp. 86–7. De Wette derived this idea of Moses banning [Egyptian] mythology from Hebrew religion from Fries, as he states in his letter to Fries of 15 June 1812 (in Henke, pp. 349–50): 'Ihre Ideen über den Mosaismus als Aufhebung aller Mythologie thut mir treffliche Dienste . . .'. See Fries *Neue Kritik*, 3, p. 369, on the Hebrews: 'Ihre Religion ist überreich an heiligen Gebräuchen; aber ihr erstes Dogma: du sollst dir kein Bildniss machen, das Verbot aller Mythologie, und die Idee *eines* Gottes die erste belebende ihrer Andacht.'
[84] *Dogmatik*, pp. 91–2.
[85] ibid., pp. 93ff.
[86] ibid., pp. 101ff.
[87] ibid., pp. 108ff.

moral and religious one expressing hopes for the true reign of God, for the reconciliation of God and his disobedient people and for the rule of justice and truth. Such hopes and longings were expressed in the *elegiac* literature of the people.[88] Post-exilic judaism was an abortive (*verunglückte*) revival of Hebrew religion; a mixture of positive elements of Hebrew religion with foreign mythological doctrines that purported to give metaphysical explanations, for example, of the origin of evil and of the end of the world. Judaism lacked prophets and it was tied to the letter and not the spirit of Old Testament traditions. In short, whereas Hebrew religion was a thing of life and inspiration, Judaism was a matter of concepts (*Begriffe*) and of slavery to the letter (*Buchstabenwesens*).[89] The treatment of Judaism followed the same plan as the systematic treatment of Hebrew religion, deriving most of its material illustrations from Philo, Josephus and apocryphal and pseudoepigraphical books, with occasional references to Chronicles, Daniel and Zechariah. The sections on both Hebrew religion and Judaism refer to many details of institutions, observances and so on, far more numerous than can be indicated here. The *Biblical Dogmatics* remains, however, a work which arouses both antipathy in the modern reader because of its philosophical handling of the Old Testament, and admiration at the unusual combinations of ideas which this peculiar synthesis affords.

De Wette's *Religion* is a series of lectures on comparative religion, and upon the nature of religion as a phenomenon in human culture.[90] It covers 'primitive' religions (such as they were known from the accounts of travellers) and the religions of Egypt, Greece, Rome, Persia and Israel, as well as the history of Christianity. The account is Friesian in emphasis, and is wide-ranging in its treatment of traditions, rites, laws, architecture, art, poems and hymns. The role of institutional religion is examined in relation to individual religion, and the way in which both mutually enrich each other is specified. The whole work is a monument to de Wette's Christian humanism, and to his desire to place biblical studies in the widest possible context of the study of religions, philosophy and culture. He displays a wholeness of approach that is enviable to modern students.

As a final comment on de Wette it must be observed that his philosophical position did not permit him to see history as a process in which divine purpose was being unfolded. Towards the end of his life, as we shall see, this organic and purposive view of history, including Old Testament history, was influential in the work of scholars of differing schools. One of its most influential expressions was in the work of the 'founder' of *Heilsgeschichte* (history of salvation), J. C. K. Hofmann, who saw the Bible as witnessing to

[88] See Fries, *Neue Kritik*, 3, 360–1 for the role of elegy in expressing hopes.
[89] *Dogmatik*, p. 114.
[90] *Die Religion, ihr Wesen und ihre Erscheinungsformen und ihren Einfluss auf das Leben*, Berlin 1827.

a privileged strand of history in which God had chosen to unfold a purpose, and in which a pattern of prophecy and fulfilment could be discerned. Friesian philosophy could not accept this approach to history. To speak about an unfolding divine purpose, an end or climax towards which history was moving was to speak about that which could not be known. At best, we could have an intuition that there was purposefulness, an ultimate harmony of all goodness and value. The study of history could help us to see how the intuition of purposefulness had been understood and expressed symbolically. A *belief* in a purpose such as that held by the Israelites in regard to the destiny of their own nation was, however, only a way of expressing belief in the ultimate harmony of values. Presumably, it was the unwillingness of the Friesian system to allow that history is a purposive process that enabled de Wette to make such radical proposals about the history of Israel; to suggest that there was a radical divergence between the Old Testament story and what could be known about the actual facts. Again, lack of commitment to history as moving towards a goal made it easier for de Wette to see Judaism as such a *degeneration* as compared with Hebrew religion. Thus de Wette not only raised some of the questions that were to be central to critical discussion in the nineteenth-century, his view of history helped to ensure that his particular solution was ignored, at least by the scholarship of the period 1840–60, which must have regarded his notion of history as unattractively static and unproductive.

3

In the Footsteps of de Wette:
Gesenius, Gramberg and George

Although de Wette founded no 'school', the breakthrough contained in his early critical works was taken up by others, and developed along critical lines. Of the scholars to be considered in the present chapter, Gesenius taught many of the results of de Wette's early criticism during his career at Halle (1810–42); Gramberg, in a work published in 1829–30, tried to work out the implications of de Wette's results in a detailed fashion, while George, in a work on Jewish festivals published in 1835, exploited a fundamental ambiguity in de Wette's results, and in so doing, largely anticipated Wellhausen's account of the history of Israelite religion.

(a) Wilhelm Gesenius, 1786–1842[1]

Gesenius is best known in Old Testament scholarship for his work as a grammarian and lexicographer. His lexicon of 1810–12 and his grammar of 1813 passed through many transformations at his own and others' hands, and thus are still widely used.[2] His views on other aspects of Old Testament interpretation do not seem to be so widely known. Diestel and Kraus deal mainly with Gesenius's philological work, and with his outstanding *Commentary on Isaiah* (1820–1).[3] Among his other published works are his

---

[1] There is no biography of Gesenius, a fact lamented by O. Eissfeldt in his *Kleine Schriften* 2, Tübingen 1963, p. 430, n2, 'Auch jetzt wäre eine derartige Biographie des Mannes noch eine lohnende Aufgabe'. Three short articles by Eissfeldt are reprinted in *Kleine Schriften* 2, pp. 430–42. They deal with Gesenius's knowledge of archaeology and the study of Palestine. Rudolf Haym published a valuable essay at Gesenius's death under the initials R.H.S.: *Gesenius. Eine Erinnerung für seine Freunde*, Berlin 1842. There is also a valuable section on Gesenius in Wilhelm Schrader, *Geschichte der Friedrichs-Universität zu Halle*, 2, Berlin 1894, pp. 136–43.

[2] W. Gesenius, *Hebräisch-deutsches Handwörterbuch über die Schriften des Alten Testaments*, 2 vols, Leipzig 1810–12; idem, *Hebräische Grammatik*, 1813.

[3] See the respective indexes to Diestel and Kraus. The Isaiah commentary is *Philologisch-kritischer und historischer Commentar über den Jesaia*, Leipzig 1820–1.

History of the Hebrew Language and Script (1815),[4] articles in the Ersch and Gruber *Encyclopedia*,[5] and many reviews in the *Allgemeine Literaturzeitung*.

Gesenius is often described as having been a rationalist, and this charge was brought against him and his Halle colleague Wegscheider by Hengstenberg in 1830, in the articles that provoked the famous 'hallischer Streit' and a ministerial inquiry.[6] According to Rudolph Haym, if Gesenius was a rationalist he was also instinctively feeling his way towards the Hegelian direction, which some theologians began to take from the 1820s.[7] However, as a review of Haym's memoir pointed out, Haym was probably trying too hard to enlist Gesenius as an incipient Hegelian. The review maintained that Gesenius's religion was a private, thoroughly sincere conviction, known best to his family and those closest to him.[8] According to Schrader, Gesenius was not a convinced Rationalist of a theological kind, but was indifferent to theological matters, possessing no dogmatic views, and guided by a *historical* sense of mistrust of anything miraculous or supernatural.[9]

Whatever Gesenius's religious convictions may have been, he held them together with an acceptance of critical scholarship in such a way that he agreed with, and taught, the results of de Wette's early critical studies. His published works show that he was a scholar of incredible learning and industry. Like his great rival Ewald, he had an insatiable appetite for knowledge, and he probably possessed a sounder instinct for judgement than did Ewald. During his period at Halle, he exercised great influence upon the future of Old Testament studies through his lectures. These concentrated upon fine details, and although unsatisfying to those who merely wished to have their orthodox views endorsed, they attracted many hearers, and showed that theology required the most exacting scholarly dedication.[10]

---

[4] W. Gesenius, *Geschichte der hebräischen Sprache und Schrift*, Leipzig 1815, repr. Hildesheim 1973.

[5] J. S. Ersch und J. G. Gruber, *Allgemeine Encyclopädie der Wissenschaften und Künste*, Leipzig 1819– (not completed).

[6] So Kraus, p. 162, 'Doch stand er sehr stark unter dem Einfluss des Rationalisten Henke'. For an account of the 'hallischer Streit', see J. Bachmann, *Ernst Wilhelm Hengstenberg*, 2, bk 4, ch. 1, with extracts from official documents on pp. 21*–60*.

[7] Haym, p. 31, 'War in dem historisch-kritischen Verfahren Strauss' für Gesenius der nächste Anknüpfungspunkt, so konnte er, der im Grunde frei von jedem positiven Bekenntniss war, ihm auch bis zu der Einsicht folgen, die hier gebotene Idee sei bedeutender, als das, wozu es der Rationalismus bringe . . .'

[8] *Jenaer Allgemeine Literatur-Zeitung*, February 1843, pp. 298–304. See pp. 303–4, 'Wir mögen den Schleier nicht heben, welcher die in stiller Brust zu hegende und nur im Kreise der Familie mehr hervortretende religiöse Denk- und Empfindungsweise verhüllen soll.'

[9] Schrader, pp. 136–43.

[10] For impressions of Gesenius's lectures see Haym, op. cit. Schrader, p. 137, mentions that Gesenius was sometimes frivolous about parts of the Old Testament that were 'Jewish' and

In his *History of the Hebrew language and script*, Gesenius defended on philological grounds what de Wette had argued on philosophical and critical grounds. The lateness of the books of Chronicles was demonstrated by several pages of examples in which it was shown that Chronicles, in using the books of Samuel and Kings, had substituted later words for earlier words, had added grammatical glosses, explanations and supposed improvements, and had gone in for a variety of minor interpretations.[11] Gesenius characterized the books of Chronicles as an unhistorical compilation based upon earlier historical books, composed by priests and expressing their outlook.[12] He noted that his philological conclusions largely ran parallel to the historical conclusions contained in de Wette's *Contributions*.[13]

The view that Deuteronomy is later than the other books of the Pentateuch, and by a different author is also supported by Gesenius. He notes the quite different style compared with Genesis—Numbers, considers that Deuteronomy 28 and 33 are later than Leviticus 26 and Genesis 49 respectively, and shows that there are numerous similarities between Deuteronomy and Jeremiah. Only two works are mentioned in the recommended literature: Vater's *Pentateuch* and de Wette's *Dissertation*.[14]

Regarding the other books of the Pentateuch, Gesenius points out that the language of these books, whether prose or poetry, does not differ essentially from other historical and poetic books of the monarchic period. If the Pentateuch were really by Moses, there would be a time difference of nearly a thousand years between the Pentateuch and other books, from the point of view of composition. In this case, the language would not have altered noticeably during this period—a singular phenomenon! In fact, it was most likely that the Pentateuch was written during the monarchy. Even documents contained in the Pentateuch that might be very ancient (e.g., the Decalogue) had probably been rewritten in later language.[15] Thus, in dealing with the history of the Hebrew language, Gesenius postulated two periods: before the Exile and after the Exile.

---

which did not touch upon the heart of biblical teaching. An obituary in *Der Courier. Hallischer Zeitung für Stadt und Land*, No. 251, 27 October 1842, records that attendances at his lectures were not outstanding, but that he devoted much time to his inner circle of students. A hostile view of Gesenius's lectures is recorded in Bachmann, *Hengstenberg*, 2, p. 218 (apparently Bachmann's own opinion): 'Ueberall nur Kampf, nirgends bleibender Sieg—Das Alte Testament ging nur als ein Nachwerk späterer Priesterweisheit verloren, blieb mir höchstens wichtig als eine Sammlung der ältesten Literatur der Hebräer . . .'

[11] Gesenius, *Geschichte der hebr. Sprache und Schrift*, pp. 38–43.

[12] ibid., p. 26; 'die Chronik . . . ist eine von spätern Priestern und in ihrem Geiste verfasste unkritische Compilation ältere Geschichtswerke.'

[13] ibid., p. 38, 44n; 'Der Charackter dieser philologischen Bearbeitung . . . läuft in mehrerer Rücksicht parallel mit der historischem, wovon de Wette' (*Beyträge zur Einleit. in das A.T.*, pp. 42ff.).

[14] ibid., p. 32.

[15] ibid., pp. 19–21.

In his section on the post-exilic period, Gesenius can be seen to be making the distinction also to be found in de Wette between the outlook of earlier literature and that of later literature, with the latter's inferior taste and its addiction to legends.[16] A section on the Samaritan Pentateuch upholds the lateness of this recension, and suggests that it is to be dated to the time of the establishment of the Samaritan cult in the Gerizim temple in the late fourth century.[17]

The impression given from the *History of the Hebrew Language and Script*, that Gesenius taught the main positions of de Wette's early critical work is confirmed from a study of lecture notes taken down at Gesenius's lectures. Of these, a volume on the Psalms taken down by C. F. Stolz in the Winter Semester of 1826–7 is in the possession of Professor Smend.[18] It is interesting that pages 1–166 contain Gesenius's lectures on selected psalms, and that the remainder of the psalms on pages 167–283, are commented on as a result of the student's private use of the second edition of de Wette's Psalms commentary of 1823.[19] It is tempting to conclude that Gesenius had recommended his students to base their work on de Wette's commentary for the psalms not covered in the lectures.

Other extant lecture notes were taken by Hermann Schrader between 1836 and 1838, and thus show what Gesenius was teaching four years before his death.[20] These lecture notes cover biblical archaeology, the book of Genesis, Old Testament introduction, Old Testament dogmatics, ecclesiastical history, and the book of Psalms. In the lectures on ecclesiastical history, the range covered is enormous, including the Reformation and the modern period. German philosophers such as Kant, Fichte, Schelling and Hegel are dealt with, as are English theologians and philosophers from Hobbes to Hume.[21]

The most interesting set of lectures for present purposes is entitled 'Old Testament dogmatics'.[22] By Old Testament dogmatics, Gesenius understands 'the scientific presentation of the religious concepts of the books of the Old

---

[16] ibid., p. 26; 'die Bücher Daniel, Esther, Jona enthalten Legenden in einem gesunkenen jüdischen Geschmacke.'

[17] ibid., pp. 84ff. See also Gesenius's *de Pentateucho Samaritano, ejusque indole et auctoritate*, Halle 1814.

[18] I am most grateful to Professor Smend for permission to refer to this source.

[19] The heading to pp. 167–283 reads, 'Die von H. Dr Gesenius ausgelassenen Psalmen nach H. Dr de Wette's Commentar, Zt. Afgb'.

[20] These notes are in the Staatsbibliothek Preussicher Kulturbesitz, West Berlin, numbered Ms. Germ. Qu. 1508–15. Nachlass Hermann Schrader, acc. ms 1913, 320. They are used here by permission of the Director of the Staatsbibliothek. Eissfeldt, *Kleine Schriften*, 2, pp. 438–40, gives an outline of Gesenius's lectures on biblical archaeology as noted by Friedrich Bernhard Conrad (matriculated in October 1833).

[21] Ms. Germ Qu. 1515, pp. 184–8 on Kant, etc., and pp. 218–20 on the English philosophers and theologians.

[22] Ms. Germ. Qu. 1509, hereinafter referred to as *Dogmatik*.

Testament in their historical development and in their inner relationship'.[23]
Thus the lectures fall into two main parts, the history of Israelite religion
and the religious concepts of the Old Testament.

The second section, on the religious concepts of the Old Testament is
descriptive and factual.[24] The first main section, on the doctrine of God,
covers the names of God, God's unity in relation to polytheism, physical
and anthropomorphic portrayals of God, and the attributes of God.

The second section deals with God in relation to the world and to nature.
It covers creation, miracles, the spirit of God and various means by which
God reveals himself. There follows, thirdly, the section on God's relationship
to his people, in the context of the theocracy. The doctrine of the messianic
kingdom is followed by a section on angels and demons, and finally, there
is a section on anthropology. This deals with the fall (which is treated as a
symbol, not history), the image of God in mankind, life after death and
immortality.

The opening part, dealing with the history of Israelite religion, takes up
28 pages,[25] and divides the history into nine periods. Concerning the first,
that of the Patriarchs, the problem is whether the sources (Gen. 12—50)
reflect the time of the Patriarchs or the time of the period in which they
were written (eighth century BC).[26] At best, traces of the polytheism of the
Patriarchs and their forefathers can be found, as evidenced in Joshua 24 and
the account of the stealing of the teraphim in Genesis 31.19 and 30. The
period of the sojourn in Egypt suffers from the same problem of lack of
contemporary sources, although Gesenius is able to refer his students to
work in Egyptology that had been undertaken in the late eighteenth and

---

[23] *Dogmatik*, p. 3; 'Unter Dogmatik des A.T. verstehen wir die wissenschaftliche Darstellung
der religiösen Vorstellungen der heil. Schriften des A.T. in ihrer historischen
Zusammenhange.'

[24] ibid., pp. 36–107.

[25] ibid., pp. 7–35. They are (1) the Patriarchs; (2) sojourn in Egypt; (3) period of Moses; (4)
period of the Judges; (5) period of David and Solomon; (6) Kings and prophets of the
divided monarchy; (7) Babylonian exile; (8) influence of Zoroastrian religion on Jewish
[*sic*] theology; (9) Persian period, from Cyrus to Alexander.

[26] See also Gesenius's article 'Abraham' in the Ersch and Gruber *Encyclopädie*, 1, where he
writes: 'Bei der Geschichte und dem Charakter Abrahams sind wir, da bei den neueren
Traditionen und Muthmassungen über denselben . . . an geschichtlichen Gehalt gar nicht
zu denken ist, lediglich auf die Relationen der Genesis beschränkt, welche aber bei ihrer
mythischen Behandlung nur sehr vorsichtig für die Geschichte benutzt werden können
. . . Aus diesem Grund wollen wir auch nicht willkürlich vermuthend den geschichtlichen
Gehalt aus jenem mythischen Erzählungen herausziehen, und hier als Geschichte aufstellen,
sondern die vornehmsten dieser Sagen, so wie sie die Relation gibt, kurz berühren und
beurtheilen. (There is a footnote reference to De Wette's *Kritik der israelitischen Geschichte*,
1, pp. 49ff.)

It is interesting to note that Gesenius was the joint author, with de Wette, of the
following articles in the Ersch and Gruber *Encyclopedia*: Äthiopische Sprache, Schrift und
Literatur; Arabische Sprache, Schrift, Literatur; Bibelübersetzungen; Bibel.

early nineteenth centuries. For the period of Moses, remnants of Egyptian religion can be detected in the worship of the golden calf and the brazen serpent. Moses had given to the people a constitution making them a theocracy, some laws, and the beginnings of an organized priesthood. It was such Mosaic institutions that Samuel, for example, had used against Saul. However, the developed Mosaic legal and religious system did not come from this time.

The occupation of Canaan and the subsequent period of the Judges exposed the people to the religious practices of the Canaanites, and of the invaders against whom the Judges fought. In leaders such as Samson and Samuel, we find a class of Nazirites, and Samuel is also the leader of bands of ecstatic prophets. The main event of the period of David and Solomon was the building of the temple. This introduced Phoenician architecture and culture, and affected the symbolism of Old Testament religion. Solomon instituted sacrifices and appointed priests from the family of Aaron.

The division of the kingdom saw the establishment of the sanctuaries at Bethel and Dan, and the struggle between Baal and Yahweh in the northern kingdom as Elijah and Elisha opposed the dynasty of Omri. But with the reform of Josiah, an important step forward was taken in the development of Old Testament religion and worship. Leviticus 26 is mentioned explicitly in connection with Josiah's reform. The Babylonian exile saw the composition of the historical books of the Old Testament with the exception of Chronicles. An important factor of the period of the rise of Cyrus and of the Persian hegemony over the Israelites was the influence of Zoroastrian religion. This played a large part in establishing the difference between Hebrew religion and the later Judaism of the latest books of the Old Testament and the books of the Apocrypha.

Compared with de Wette's *Biblical Dogmatics*. Gesenius's lectures on the same subject are less philosophical (he does not devote 43 pages to an exposition of the nature of religion!), and more historical (de Wette devotes only a fraction of Gesenius's space to the history of Hebrew and Jewish religion). However, in the treatment of Old Testament religion, the similarities are very great. Both are uncertain about what can be known of the earliest periods. The role of Moses is important, but nothing like what is attributed to him in the Levitical-priestly account of Chronicles and parts of the Pentateuch. The diversity of Israelite religion before the time of Josiah is stressed, as is the importance of his reform for its development. A fundamental difference between Hebrew religion and later Judaism is assumed.

Gesenius seems to have shared with de Wette the view that many of the narratives of the Pentateuch had been 'generated' by mythical processes, and in his lectures on Old Testament Introduction he devoted a section to this matter.[27] He divided myths into the following classes: (a) historical myths, which have a historical event as their basis but which present the happenings in a fanciful and elaborated manner (e.g., the exodus from Egypt); (b) philosophical myths (Here, there are four sub-divisions: (i) myths which explain the origin of customs and institutions such as the sabbath (Gen. 2.2); (ii) etymological myths, which are puns on names, such as Babel (Gen. 11.9), Jacob (Gen. 25.26) and Israel (Gen. 32.29); (iii) myths such as Gen. 49 and Numbers 22—4, which reflect historical relationships between groups, but present them as prophecies; (iv) myths, such as Genesis 11, which are 'mixed' in that they are both etymological and attempts to explain a state of affairs); (c) myths which result from 'floating' traditions being associated with particular persons or incidents, or those which have a catastrophe such as an earthquake as their basis (e.g., the fate of the Korahites in Numbers 16); (d) myths in which the miraculous element is heightened, often by simple mistakes, such as taking the word for the Arabs who fed Elijah in 1 Kings 17.4 to mean 'ravens', or mistaking the word for commander (*âluph*) for that which means thousands (*èleph*), with the result that impossible numbers appear; (e) myths also expressing the 'spirit' of the Hebrew people, such as their religious zeal (e.g., Abraham's readiness to sacrifice Isaac) or their national hate against neighbouring peoples such as Ammon, Moab and Edom.

This review of the mythical processes does not rely upon de Wette alone, of course. De Wette's work had been prepared for by the rationalists and Neologists, and Gesenius referred in his bibliographical paragraph to this section to Eichhorn, Gabler and G. L. Bauer as well as to de Wette's *Contributions*. However, Gesenius's *use* of the notion of myth for historical purposes corresponds to that of de Wette, and not to that of Eichhorn, Gabler and Bauer, all of whom wanted to salvage more history from the historical sections of the Pentateuch than Gesenius or de Wette could allow.

In his lectures upon the psalms,[28] Gesenius, like de Wette, classified the

---

[27] Ms. Germ. Qu. 1510, pp. 47–51. See esp. § 24: Von der mythischen Beschaffenheit der ältern Bücher insbesondere. 1. In der frühesten Zeit der Geschichte wo noch nicht an gleichzeitige schriftliche Aufzeichnung gedacht werden konnte, sind die historischen Relationen mythischer Art. Sie sind aus der Volkssage geschöpft, an der welcher (?) nicht bloss reine Geschichte sondern auch die Individualität und Einkleidung der Erzählungen ihren Antheil hat. Wir haben denn eine Art historischer Poesie vor uns, die sich theils auf die Urgeschichte der Welt und zum (?) Theil auf die älteste Geschichte des hebräischen Volkes bezieht. (Es sind Mythen, darum aber (?) noch nicht Fabeln).

[28] Ms. Germ. Qu. 1513, pp. 8–10. The agreement of content between the lecture notes of Schrader and of Stolz is very high indeed. The German can be extracted as follows: (1) Hymnen auf Gott, also *t^chillim* im engern und eigentlichen Sinne. In diesen Hymnen wird Gott in den verschiedenen Beziehungen besungen und geschildert, in einigen als Naturgott, als Schöpfer und Regierer der Welt . . .; (2) Tempellieder, gedichtet in Bezug auf religiöse Feierlichkeiten, oder überhaupt den Cultus, zum Exempel beim Einzuge der Bundeslade nach einem Kriege Ps. 24. bey der (zweiten(?)) Tempelweihe, Ps. 132. für die Pilger, die

psalms into their types. The classification, although not the order is similar to that of de Wette: (a) Hymns to God (i) as ruler of the world of nature, (ii) as protector of the Hebrew nation, (iii) as protector in general, (iv) about the nature of God in his eternity, omniscience and omnipresence; (b) Temple songs for use in the cult; for example for the bringing up of the ark of the covenant (24), or for pilgrims (122); (c) general religious and moral hymns, including expressions of trust in God, prayers for forgiveness, teaching psalms about the prosperity of the righteous and the misfortune of the ungodly, and psalms for use in worship; (d) laments (*Klagepsalmen*): individual, national, psalms about belief and unbelief, and theodicy psalms justifying God's ways; (e) royal psalms: expressions of good fortune at coronations (e.g., 72), hopes for victory and success in battle (26, 110) and in time of war (2 and 20); (f) historical psalms such as 78, 105 and 106 presenting the history of the people for the purpose of admonition and instruction.

In what has been written here about Gesenius, I hope that I have not exaggerated or overstated the similarities between Gesenius and de Wette. It has not been my intention to suggest that Gesenius was a 'disciple' of de Wette. However, it seems to be an established fact that for over thirty years, Gesenius taught many of the results that are to be found in de Wette's early critical writings, even if he did not share de Wette's Friesian philosophical-theological position. This cannot have been without significance for the future of the critical method in German Old Testament studies.

(b) C. P. W. Gramberg

Carl Peter Wilhelm Gramberg was born near Oldenburg in 1797, studied in Halle under Gesenius and Wegscheider, and was for a time a teacher at a boarding school in Züllichau (now Sulechow in Poland) before his

---

nach Jerusalem zogen, Ps. 122; (3) allgemeine religiös-moralische Lieder, einiger derselben enthalten die dichterische Ausführung religiöse Empfindungen, frommer Vorsätze oder Überzeugungen zum Exempel des Vertrauens auf Gott . . .; (4) Klagepsalmen, Klagelieder, also Elegien unglücklicher verfolgter Frommen nebst Bitte um Hülfe. Diess ist die reichhaltigste Klasse, und umfasst über ein Drittheil aller Gedichte . . .; (5) Die Oden an Könige zum Exempel enthaltend einen Glückwunsch bey einer Thronbesteigung (Salomos) Ps. 72. oder bey der Vermählung Ps. 45. oder nach einem Siege Ps. 21. 110. oder bey einem Kriegszuge gegen (?) Völker Ps. 2. cf. Ps. 20; (6) Historische Lieder, d.i. solche, worin die alte Geschichte des Volkes zur Warnung und Belehrung für die Nachkommen wieder durchgegangen wird. Ps. 78. 105. 106 und 114. Anmerkung. Nicht auf dem ursprünglichen Inhalte sondern auf später dogmatischer und theologischer Anwendung, beruhen die folgenden beyden Klassen von Psalmen, nämlich: (1) messianische Psalmen. So nennt man diejenigen, welche einzelnen Stellen nach von den neutestamentlichen Schriftsteuern oder den jüdischen Auslegern vermöge der damals herrschenden Exegese auf den Messias bezogen worden sind . . .; (2) Busspsalmen [the seven Christian Penitential Psalms].

premature death in Oldenburg in 1830.[29] Before his death, he had published
books on Chronicles and Genesis, and two of four projected volumes
entitled *Critical History of the Religious Ideas of the Old Testament*.[30] He was
also in the process of writing an extensive commentary on the Pentateuch.[31]
The *Critical History*, which will be considered in the present section, is not
mentioned at all in Kraus, and receives the comment in Diestel that its
critical and religious assumptions vitiate its treatment of individual subjects.[32]
Yet it is an important elaboration of de Wette's position, and it paved the
way for George's account of the history of Israelite festivals.

The method of the *Critical History* makes it a difficult book to use. It
amounts to over twelve hundred pages of text, much of which is devoted
to epitomizing the biblical text to the accompaniment of critical
observations. Very short summaries precede each main section, but on the
whole, no attempt is made to present the results systematically. It is thus the
sort of book that either has to be read in full, or ignored.

Its first important feature is that it directly relates the history of the
religious ideas of the Old Testament to the dates of composition of the
various books of the Old Testament. In fact, there is a reciprocal relationship
at work. The dates of some of the books are established on the basis of the
type of religion that they contain; the dating of the books assists the task of
reconstructing the history of the religious ideas.

The *Critical History* distinguishes seven periods in the history of Old
Testament religion.[33] The first, reflected in Genesis, Exodus and Judges, is
the period from David to Joram and Hezekiah. Underlying these books are
written and oral sources, which in some cases, for example the heroic sagas
about the Judges, record memories of actual conditions before the time of
David.[34] The second stage is to be found in the books of Samuel and in Ruth.
Although compiled shortly before the Exile, these books contain written
and oral sources from the time of David. The third stage is represented by
the prophetic books of Isaiah 1—35 (substantial parts), Hosea, Joël, Amos,
Micah, Nahum and Zephaniah. The material contained in these books
originated in the eighth–seventh centuries, but reached its final form
somewhat later. Stage four is the beginning of the Babylonian Exile. It is
represented by Leviticus and Numbers, whose cultic regulations are more

[29] Entry: Gramberg, Karl Peter Wilhelm in *ADB* 9, 1879, pp. 577–8. See also *NND*, 1, 1830, p. 270.
[30] C.P.W. Gramberg, *Die Chronik nach ihrem geschichtlichen Charakter und ihrer Glaubwürdigkeit neu geprüft*, Halle 1823; *Libri Geneseos secundum fontes rite dignoscendos adumbratio nova*, Leipzig 1828; *Kritische Geschichte der Religionsideen des alten Testaments*, 1, Hierarchie und Cultus; 2, Theocratie und Prophetismus, 2 vols, Berlin 1830.
[31] See *ADB* 9, 1879, 2, p. 578.
[32] Diestel, *Geschichte*, p. 715.
[33] Gramberg, *Kritische Geschichte*, 1, pp. xxv–xxvi.
[34] ibid., 2, p. 56.

developed than those in Exodus, and by Jeremiah and Lamentations, Ezekiel, Habakkuk, Obadiah and many Psalms. Leviticus and Numbers contain material from the time of Josiah, while a similarity between Ezekiel and Leviticus on the question of holiness is observed.[35] The fifth stage is represented by the books of Kings, Deuteronomy, Joshua, Isaiah 40—66, Proverbs, Job and Jonah. It is the period of the end of the Exile. The books of Kings are seen to contain earlier material on a par with that found in 1 and 2 Samuel; but the insistence upon the central sanctuary shows that it belongs to the same period as Deuteronomy.[36] Similarly, Joshua implies knowledge of Deuteronomy, as in 8.30–5 where the Deuteronomic regulation about building an altar on Mt Ebal (Deut. 27. 2–8) is observed.[37] The sixth period, that of the return from exile is represented by Ezra, Nehemiah, Haggai, Zechariah, Malachi, Song of Songs, Ecclesiastes, while the books of Chronicles, Esther and Daniel are placed in the seventh period, from the end of Persian domination to the death of Antiochus Epiphanes.

Gramberg acknowledges that this division largely agrees with what de Wette already presented in his *Contributions* and his *Introduction*. He sees his own work as an elaboration of what de Wette has begun.[38] However, at one or two points there are interesting disagreements with de Wette. The most fundamental is about the law book found in the Temple in Josiah's reign. De Wette, as we have seen was not as clear about the law book as one would like.[39] Gramberg is far more definite. He sees clear allusions from 2 Kings 22—3 to Exodus 23.24ff (the command not to worship the gods of the nations in Canaan), and to Exodus 34.12–17 (the command to destroy the altars and pillars of the gods of the nations in Canaan), and he notes that whereas Josiah ordered the passover to be celebrated, it is the festival of passover that is the most prominent festival in Exodus. Thus Gramberg confidently asserts that Exodus or parts of it was found as Josiah's law book, and that for de Wette to admit the possibility that part of Deuteronomy might have been the law book threatens the proper respective dating of the

---

[35] ibid., 1, p. 215.

[36] ibid., 1, pp. 146–7.

[37] ibid., 1, pp. 155–6.

[38] ibid., 1, p. xxvii: 'Ich verhele gar nicht, was dem Kundigen auch auf den ersten Blick einleuchten würde, dass dieser Eintheilung, mit geringen Abweichungen, die Ansicht zum Grunde liegt, welche Hr Dr de Wette in seinem Lehrbuch der historisch-kritischen Einleitung ins A.T. (2te Aufl. Berlin 1822) aufgestellt hat; doch wenn ich mich berufen glaube, auch hier wieder die Idee, welche dieser mit Recht allgemein geachtete Gelehrte in dem genannten Werke und in seinem Beyträgen zur Einleitung ins A.T. angeregt hat, systematisch durchzuführen und von allen Seiten zu vertheidigen, so fürchte ich gar nicht, mit den Namen eines sclavischen Nachbeters zuzuziehen.'

[39] de Wette, *Beiträge*, 1, pp. 175–6 allows that other parts of the Pentateuch apart from Deuteronomy could have caused Josiah's reformation, but concludes that Deuteronomy particularly 'in Sprache kam'.

books.[40] Similarly, Gramberg is disturbed by a remark of de Wette's (not fully worked out) that Jeremiah 50—1 had been taken from 2 Kings.[41] This, again, is an implied threat to the need to date 2 Kings after Jeremiah, and an alternative explanation has to be sought.

On the basis of his seven periods Gramberg treats in volume 1 the priesthood and the cult and in volume 2 the leaders of the theocracy. By theocracy is understood political authority exercised in the name of God. It is clear that Gramberg regards theocratic leadership as a good thing, and priestly leadership as a bad thing, and what emerges from his discussions is that priesthood gradually increased its power in ancient Israel as time went on, until after the Exile the priestly triumph was virtually complete, and it was left to the author of Chronicles to rewrite Old Testament history in order to give the false impression that Israelite religion was dominated by the priests from the outset. The prophets had been the opponents of the increasing power of the priests, and they did not seek that control over the people which was the hallmark of priestly power.[42]

Before the time of David, little can be known for certain about Israelite history.[43] Although the traditions about Abraham and Jacob may rest upon old folk traditions, it is clear that Abraham is deliberately presented as a type of David, and that the two figures are linked by the fact that the promises made by God to Abraham are realized in the reign of David.[44] Precisely what can be known about the exodus is not clear from Gramberg's discussion, since he concentrates upon exposing discrepancies, errors and 'fictions' on the part of the writer of Exodus. Elsewhere, however, he allows that Moses instituted a simple tent for containing the ark, and that he declared his own tribe of Levi to be a holy (but not necessarily priestly) cast.[45] The account of the worship of the golden calf indicates that a bull-

---

[40] Gramberg, op. cit., 1, pp. 307–8.

[41] ibid., 2, p. 185.

[42] ibid., 2, pp. 247–8; 'Um also die Propheten des A.T. hier im Allgemeinen zu charakterisieren, so wollten sie mit eigner Überzeugung Vermittler zwischen Jehova und seinem Volke seyn, aber auf eine ganz andre Art, als die Priester, mit denen sie bald in Opposition treten mussten, weil ihre Zwecke und Mittel so ganz verschieden waren.'

[43] ibid., 2, pp. 7–8 on the patriarchal narratives: 'es wird uns hier Dichtung, nicht Geschichte gegeben, und ob die auftretenden Personen, Abraham, Isaak, Jakob u.s.w. historisch-wirkliche sind, können wir aus diesen Dichtungen nicht erfahren.'

[44] ibid., 2, pp. 8, 14, 23.

[45] ibid., 1, pp. 13–14 on the tent of meeting: '. . . ist nicht unwahrscheinlich, dass Mose ein solches, obgleich in der beglaubigten Geschichte späterhin keins als mit diesem völlig identisch vorkommt, errichtet, und darin die einfache Lade mit den Gesetztafeln, welche ausser dieser nichts enthielt (vgl. 1 Reg. 8, 9) aufbewahrt haben.' On the Levites, see p. 170: 'Dass Mose seinen Stamm zur heiligen Kaste bestimmt, und, um durch ihn eine wohl organisirte Hierarchie zu begründen, ihr ohne eignen Landbesitz unter die übrigen Stämme vertheilt hatte, ist wahrscheinlich, doch die Gränzen des Einflusses, welchen er den Priestern bestimmte, nach den mythischen Darstellungen der nach ihm benannten Bücher gar nicht auszumachen.'

cult derived from Egyptian worship of Apis was part of the religion of the Mosaic period.[46]

The book of Joshua is regarded by Gramberg, following de Wette, as a very late composition, many of whose details can be shown to be based upon earlier books. In particular, Gramberg contrasts the claims of the book of Joshua that the land was subdued with the indications in Judges 1 that the Canaanites had not been driven out of many areas.[47] The book of Judges, on the other hand, is held to contain folk traditions that give some indication of the situation before the monarchy.[48]

The books of Samuel attest the religious freedom that obtained in the early days of the monarchy. The priesthood of Samuel indicates that priests did not have to be Aaronic or Levitical. The Davidic kings were also priests 'after the order of Melchizedek'.[49] Many sanctuaries were in use, and Yahweh was represented by a picture or image by way of the Ephod. There were also household gods.[50]

The bringing of the ark to Jerusalem represented the beginning of a desire to associate God with a particular place.[51] However, the Jerusalem cultus, culminating in the building of the Temple, remained a royal cultus, making little impact upon the ordinary people,[52] for whom the principal sacrifices were whole burnt offerings and sacrifices in which the worshippers shared in a sacred meal (zᵉbāhîm).[53] It is also clear that human sacrifice was not

---

[46] ibid., 1, p. 444.

[47] ibid., 2, pp. 190–207. For comparison between Joshua and Judges 1 see pp. 198–9. For Gramberg's general verdict on Joshua see p. 191; 'Der Zweck des Vf's ist durchaus ein unhistorischer, nämlich; (1) zu zeigen, dass Josua von Jehova nicht weniger begünstigt worden sey, als Mose, und nicht weniger grosse Wunder gethan habe, als dieser; (2) nachzuweisen, dass und wie Josua den grössten Theil des Landes Canaan erobert und vertheilt habe. Dass das erstere nur Mythen geben kann, liegt in der Natur der Sache; aber auch das Letztere wird vollkommen widerlegt durch die viel glaubwürdigeren Sagen des Buches der Richter und durch den Zustand, in welchem wir das Volk noch unter Saul und David vor den grossen Siegen des Letzteren finden. Übrigens ist die Theokratie hier, wie in den spätern Büchern überhaupt, ganz der Hierarchie dienstbar, und es geschieht z.B. selten etwas zur Verherrlichung Josua's, was nicht zugleich zur Verherrlichung des Cultus und der Priester gerichtet, wesshalb denn Vieles auch von diesem Standpuncte aus angesehn werden kann.'

[48] ibid., 2, p. 56.

[49] ibid., 1, pp. 183, 186, 218.

[50] ibid., 1, pp. 448–9. At the time of David, Gramberg envisages David saying to Abiathar (1 Sam. 23.9), 'bring the picture of Jehova here!' For household gods, see pp. 458–9.

[51] ibid., 1, p. 6.

[52] ibid., 1, p. 66.

[53] ibid., 1, p. 112: 'doch machen wir noch bemerklich, dass daselbst mehrere Male ein Brandopfer neben mehreren andern erwähnt wird: wahrscheinlich deswegen, weil es dem älteren, einfacheren Cultus natürlich war, nur ein Opferthier, welches dann gar nicht weiter benutzt werden konnte, der Gottheit ganz darzubringen und zu verbrennen, die andern aber zum Mahle zuzurichten und die Gottheit zu demselben nur einzuladen, oder ihr die Fettstücke davon, als Ehrengeschenke, auf den Altar zu legen.'

absent from Israelite religion at this time.[54] To serve at the royal sanctuary, priests of the family of Aaron were employed. Thus they were both priests and Levites; but this was true only of Levites who belonged to the family of Aaron.[55]

After the building of the Temple by Solomon, the worship of gods in addition to Yahweh seems to have been encouraged by the kings. Solomon is presented (1 Kings 11) as the founder of idolatry.[56] Prophetic opposition to the idolatry of the royal cult and the idolatry of the ordinary people who worshipped at local shrines led to the attempts of Hezekiah and Josiah to regulate worship. Josiah's reform saw the cleansing of the royal cult and the attempt to destroy the local shrines. This move inevitably led to a strengthening of the power of the priesthood, and to the elaboration of ritual.[57] This process is seen if Leviticus and Numbers are compared with Exodus.[58] Books compiled at the end of the Exile—Deuteronomy, 1 and 2 Kings and Joshua—begin to reinterpret history in terms of the centralization attempted by Josiah and made potentially possible by the Exile. The books of Kings, however, still preserve evidence of the diversity of practice at the time of the monarchy (for example, Elijah sacrifices on Mt Carmel), and have not yet reached the level of invention of the author of Chronicles.[59] Deuteronomy, however, perpetrates absurdities, such as equating priests with Levites against the evidence of Numbers that Levites were not necessarily priests.[60] The periods six and seven, from Ezra to the book of Chronicles, see merely a consolidation of the priestly power and religion at the expense of the theocracy. The theocracy is kept alive in the messianic hopes based upon the notion of the ideal king as God's representative.[61]

Because Gramberg did not live to write his further volumes that would

[54] ibid., 1, p. 115.

[55] On Levites see especially 1, pp. 187ff.

[56] ibid., 1, pp. 463, 502.

[57] ibid., p. 66: 'Das Volk sah den Jehovadienst im Tempel nur als einen Hofcultus an, und machte ihn freiwillig nie mit, ja die Könige selbst wussten ihm keine Herrschaft zu verschaffen, oder vernachlässigten und entweihten ihn gar: Hiskia ist der erste, welcher rechten Eifer für denselben und gegen die auswärtigen Heiligthümer zeigt; diese werden aber von Manasseh sogleich wieder hergestellt, und erst nach Auffindung des Gesetzbuches von Josia mit Erfolg zerstört, ohne dass jedoch des Volkes Wille sichtbar mit dem seinigen übereinstimmt.'

[58] ibid., 1, pp. 119, 132.

[59] ibid., 1, pp. 146–53.

[60] ibid., 1, p. 229; 'weit entfernt, die Priester sehr über die Leviten zu erheben, wie Leviticus, Numeri und noch mehr Ezechiel thun, stellt er die letztern ihnen schon in Ausdruck ganzgleich, indem er meistens, wie in einer erklärenden Apposition, die Priester [das heisst] die Leviten . . . zusammenfasst, wovon nur einige genauere Wiederhohlungen alter Gesetze eine Ausnahme machen, wesshalb wir denn, nach seinem Beyspiele, von Priestern und Leviten zugleich werden reden müssen.'

[61] see ibid., 2, pp. 564–665.

have dealt with dogmatics and ethics of the Old Testament,[62] it is only possible to guess at the assumptions upon which his treatment of Old Testament history is based. Although he acknowledged in many places his debt to de Wette, it is clear that he rejected de Wette's adherence to 'a new school of philosophy'.[63] He seems to have accepted that there was a 'natural development of the idea of sacrifice' such that elaborations in the cult would indicate a later period.[64] Gesenius, in a preface to the *Critical History*, claimed that Gramberg's work was entirely objective, and that the picture of the history of Israelite religion followed from the dating of the literature.[65] Gesenius's only complaint (perhaps an important clue to his own position) was that he missed any attempt to correlate the development of Israelite religion with the development of non-Israelite religions, and Gesenius supplied a few parallels from classical sources.[66]

(c) J. F. L. George

One of the most significant effects of Gramberg's *Critical History* was that it enabled J. F. L. George in 1835 to bring the de Wettian approach to its logical conclusion, for all that de Wette himself was critical of George's work.[67]

Johann Friedrich Ludwig George was born in Berlin in 1811.[68] He studied in Berlin, and at the time of writing his book *The Older Jewish Festivals* (1835), he was a devoted follower of Schleiermacher. In 1837, in response to Strauss's *Life of Jesus*, he published *Myth and saga: an attempt at a*

[62] Preface to vol. 1, p. xxviii.
[63] Preface to vol. 2, p. iv: 'Wenn de Wette aber ferner die Grundsätze einer bekannten neuen Philosophienschule seiner biblischen Dogmatik unterlegt, so entgeht er auch bey Darstellung der Theokratie dem Fehler nicht, in die Bibel hineinzutragen, was nicht in ihr liegt ... Weit entfernt, mir eine solche Ausgleichung zur Aufgabe zu machen, glaube ich nur dann völlig unparteyisch zu verfahren ...'
[64] ibid., 1, p. 95.
[65] Gesenius, Introduction to vol. 1, pp. ix–xiii.
[66] ibid., 1, pp. xiiiff.
[67] J. F. L. George, *Die älteren Jüdischen Feste mit einer Kritik der Gesetzgebung des Pentateuch*, Berlin 1835. For de Wette's review see *TSK*, 1836 pp. 935–81. His key criticism of George is: 'Unsere Kritiker [de Wette also includes Vatke and P. von Bohlen] bauen Vieles, wo nichts Alles, auf den Grundsatz, dass das Vollendete, consequent Durchgeführte der späteren Zeit angehöre und die Frucht einer geschichtlichen Entwickelung sey. Aber dieser Grundsatz, so einleuchtend er an sich seyn mag, wird in der Anwendung auf die israelitische Gesetzgebung keine allgemeine Anwendung finden.' For Ewald's estimate of George's book see *GGA* 1836 pp. 678–80. His view is that, 'die Weise der geschichtlichen Forschung, welche diess Buch zeigt, [ist] ziemlich unfruchtbar'.
[68] See the entry in *ADB*, 8, 1878, repr. 1968, pp. 710–2. See also Max Lenz, *Geschichte der Königlichen Friedrich-Wilhelms-Universität zu Berlin*, 2, 1, p. 484. The dedication of *Die älteren Jüdischen Feste* contains fulsome praise for the lately deceased Schleiermacher.

scientific development of these terms and its relation to Christian belief.[69]
However, George appears to have lost his Christian faith, and to have
deserted the theology of Schleiermacher for the philosophy of Hegel. After
occupying numerous teaching posts, he became professor of philosophy at
Greifswald in 1856, and remained there until his death in 1873. In view of
the fact that he developed the de Wettian approach to the point where it
anticipated Wellhausen in so many details, it is interesting to note that
George and Wellhausen overlapped briefly at Greifswald. Wellhausen took
up residence in Greifswald in October 1872;[70] George died at Greifswald in
May 1873. Whether there was any contact between the two men which
might have affected Wellhausen's work on the history of Israel is something
that it would be valuable to determine, if the means for so doing were
available.

George's *Festivals* is a brilliant book, especially in contrast with Gramberg's
tedious and laborious method of re-presenting the biblical material. It not
only contains shrewd insights into the dating of Old Testament material; in
its account of the history of the festivals, it provides suggestions about how
the festivals developed. The fact that so many of these suggestions are, from
a later standpoint, probably wrong, does not alter the fact that compared
with the work of Gramberg, and even de Wette, George's work has a
thoroughness and completeness which makes it very satisfying to read.

In the Introduction to *Festivals*, George acknowledged his indebtedness
to Vater, de Wette and Gramberg, and he also noted that Gesenius confirmed
by means of philology what de Wette had urged on other grounds about
the date of Deuteronomy.[71] George's fundamental point, against both de
Wette and Gramberg, was that Leviticus and Numbers and parts of Exodus
were *later* than Deuteronomy.[72] Thus, without actually identifying or
specifying the existence of a Priestly document, George put forward the
view, later to be fundamental to Wellhausen, that so far as the books of the
Pentateuch were concerned, Deuteronomy was not the *end* of a development,
but that it was rather part of the *beginning* of a development that was to end
in the formalized priestly religion represented in those parts of Exodus,
Leviticus and Numbers where priestly and ritual matters were to the fore.

George's dating of Leviticus, Numbers and parts of Exodus (by means of
a fragmentary hypothesis) as later than Deuteronomy dealt with the main
weakness of the de Wettian standpoint. The religious rituals and observances
in Leviticus and Numbers are undoubtedly more 'developed' (if 'complex'

---

[69] For an account of this book see my *Myth in Old Testament Interpretation*, Berlin 1974, pp.
    24–7.
[70] See R. Smend, 'Wellhausen in Greifswald', *ZThK* 78 (1981), pp. 141–76, esp. p. 144.
[71] George, *Die älteren Jüdischen Feste*, pp. 6–9.
[72] ibid., pp. 10ff. George's dating of Leviticus and Numbers as later than Deuteronomy was a
    stumbling block to de Wette. See the review referred to in n67 above.

equals 'developed') than they are in Deuteronomy, and much more representative of 'Judaism' (as opposed to 'Israelite religion') than is Deuteronomy. Yet both de Wette and Gramberg had tried to maintain that Deuteronomy was the latest of the Pentateuchal books, while at the same time arguing for a history of Old Testament religion that saw a post-exilic decline into legalism, priestly domination and formalism. Gramberg, as we have seen, partly tried to ease this difficulty by arguing that Josiah's law book was Exodus, or parts of it.[73] This at least enabled him to date Leviticus and Numbers to the beginning of the Exile. De Wette's half-hearted identification of Josiah's law book with Deuteronomy or parts of it left him with Leviticus and Numbers dated uncomfortably early. Further, in his treatment of the Levites, Gramberg had been obliged, on the view that Deuteronomy was later than Leviticus and Numbers, to regard the deuteronomic equation of priests and Levites as absurd.[74] George's new arrangement of the material solved this, and connected problems, elegantly.

George reasserted the de Wettian position, backed by Gesenius's philology, that Deuteronomy was Josiah's law book, and that it was later than the *historical* material in Genesis and Exodus. The *legal and cultic* material in Exodus, however, together with Leviticus and many fragments in Numbers were *later* than Deuteronomy. Old Testament history could be divided into three main periods;[75] first, an *epic* period or period of the early Theocracy. To this period belonged the historical material of the Pentateuch. The second period, the *lyrical* period, was that of the Theocracy in its prime, and to this period belonged some of the legal material of the Pentateuch, especially that in Deuteronomy. Here, George noted (following Gesenius) the rhetorical style of Deuteronomy,[76] and the fact that its laws appeal rather to the heart than to the head. This explains his assigning of Deuteronomy to the *lyrical* period. The third period was dominated by conscious rational thought (*Verstand*). It was the period of the Hierarchy[77] (domination by priests); its laws, as in parts of Exodus, Leviticus and Numbers, were directed to the head not the heart, and religious ritual was carefully prescribed.

The general picture of the history of Israelite religion that emerged was not dissimilar from that found in de Wette and Gramberg. A religion of essential freedom, with no central sanctuary or dominating priesthood was attacked by the prophets because of its idolatry. Where the prophetic denunciations failed, a law book attributed to Moses, and made the basis for Josiah's reform succeeded, at any rate in the changed circumstances of the post-exilic period. The religion of the post-exilic period was based upon

[73] See above, p. 59.
[74] See above, p. 62.
[75] George, op. cit., pp. 11–12.
[76] ibid., pp. 18–19.
[77] Note that Gramberg had seen a hierarchy taking over from the theocracy. See above p. 60.

worship in fixed ways at a central sanctuary under the control of the priests. This is George's general picture; but it will now be necessary to look in detail at some individual aspects of his position.

(i) *Centralization of worship*[78]

The Deuteronomic programme for centralization was a prophetic-inspired attempt to purify the cult from idolatry by getting rid of the high places. The stress in Deuteronomy upon worship at a single sanctuary is in marked contrast to Leviticus and Numbers, where worship at various places is envisaged, and this latter fact, on the face of it, favours an earlier date for Leviticus and Numbers. George argued, however, that since Leviticus and Numbers were written at a time (after the Exile) when the high places no longer existed, there was no need for these books to demand centralization; it was *tacitly assumed*.[79]

The fact that Deuteronomy was earlier than Leviticus and Numbers was supported by the absence from Deuteronomy of the tent of meeting. The tent of meeting in Exodus, Leviticus and Numbers was a back-projection of Solomon's temple into the time of the wilderness. It was a pure fiction not known at the time of the writing of Deuteronomy.

(ii) *The Priesthood*[80]

George took seriously the equation of priests and Levites in Deuteronomy and maintained that Levites had always had the *right* but not the *duty* to be priests. The situation in Deuteronomy corresponds to that in Genesis 49.7: the Levites were scattered throughout Israel, but according to Deuteronomy 18.5ff had the right, if they so wished, to minister at the central sanctuary. In Leviticus and Numbers, the Levites were *required* to be engaged in the service of God, and this increase in the number of ministers led to the situation in which Aaronic priests gained a superiority over the rest of the Levites. They became second-class ministers after the Exile, with Ezekiel 44.9ff constituting a bridge between the Deuteronomic and post-Deuteronomic situations. The high priesthood was probably not established until after the Exile, in spite of the reference to Hilkiah in 2 Kings 22.4, 8. Since the books of Kings were written after Deuteronomy, they could not always be relied upon to be accurate about the monarchic period.[81]

---

[78] George, op. cit., pp. 38–44.
[79] ibid., p. 41, 'die Einheit des Heligthums . . . stillschweigend *vorausgesetzt* wird' [George's emphasis].
[80] George, pp. 45–75.
[81] ibid., pp. 153–4.

(iii) *The passover*[82]

The passover festival was originally a festival of the barley harvest. It was then associated with the festival at which first-born sheep and cattle were offered to God. Since, like all sacrifices, such offerings ended in a meal, a festival in which unleavened barley bread and sacrificial animals were eaten came into being. This festival was then 'historicized' by being projected back into the time of Moses. The offering of first-born animals was 'mythicized' into the killing of the first-born of Egypt in the tenth plague. Prior to Deuteronomy, passover was a local festival, celebrated throughout the land. But it became a national festival, and thus was linked to the central sanctuary. The legislation in Deuteronomy reflects this development. After the Exile, the passover alone of the major festivals retained the element of the communal meal after the sacrifice. The accounts of the passover in Exodus 12—13 are largely post-exilic, although fragments such as Exodus 12.14–20 could reflect the pre-Deuteronomic situation.

(iv) *The Day of Atonement*[83]

The Day of Atonement, as described in Leviticus 16 was a post-exilic festival. It may originally have been a fast day, on which individuals brought offerings for their own sins. However, atonement on a national scale was necessary only in the face of a disaster such as the loss of the capital, and exile in a foreign land. In the post-exilic situation, the high priest offered sacrifices to atone for the whole nation. Azazel, to whom a goat was offered, was a demon; but since growth in belief in angels and demons was a late phenomenon in the Old Testament, the mention of Azazel was a further indication of the lateness of the festival and of the part of the Pentateuch in which it appeared.[84]

Conclusion

With George's *Festivals*, the de Wettian position reached the view of the history of Israelite religion that was to dominate critical Old Testament scholarship from 1878 onwards. Only in one or two respects were there differences from the position formulated by Wellhausen. First, George's position was not accompanied by a documentary hypothesis in which different documents corresponded to different stages of the development of Israelite religion: but he came very close to this. The narrative sections of Genesis and Exodus that George associated with the first or epic period of religion in Israel are not dissimilar from what the later Documentary

[82] ibid., pp. 85ff, 222–58.
[83] ibid., pp. 291ff.
[84] ibid., pp. 133–4.

Hypothesis called J and E. The parts of Exodus, Leviticus and Numbers dealing with ritual, and associated by George with the post-exilic period are not dissimilar from what was later called P. And it was common ground that Deuteronomy was the fixed point indicating the innovative centralization of the seventh century.

Second, George's view of the relationship in time between the legal parts of Exodus and Deuteronomy differed from what came to be later critical orthodoxy. George accepted that the laws of Exodus 21—3 were roughly contemporary with, or perhaps slightly later than those in Deuteronomy. Later critical orthodoxy was to decide for the greater age of the laws in Exodus, with the laws in Deuteronomy regarded as a re-formulation of the Exodus laws in terms of centralization. George's insistence that the Deuteronomy laws were the older was partly based on what might be called a remnant of the de Wettian view that literature can be dated by its 'spirit'. Deuteronomy was rhetorical, not precise in its use of law, and must therefore be older than Exodus. George did, however, appeal to the biblical material in support of his argument, and he saw a gradual development in the regulations about the release of slaves, culminating in the regulations about the Sabbath and Jubilee years. The textual progression, beginning from Deuteronomy 15 went through Exodus 21 to Exodus 23.11 to Leviticus 25.[85]

Granted that with George so much of the position to be advocated by Wellhausen had been formulated, why did it take over forty-nine years for the step from George to Wellhausen to be taken? The following chapters will attempt to present the various competing approaches to the history of Old Testament religion that eclipsed the results of those who continued what de Wette had begun.

[85] George also used the argument, hardly supported by the biblical evidence, that Deuteronomy possessed a more comprehensive coverage of law than the other books, and therefore must be earlier. See p. 28: 'Deuteronomium giebt nicht wie die übrigen Bücher nur über einige Gegenstände Bestimmingen, sondern es erstreckt sich über alle Zweige des Lebens, und umfasst alles, worüber man Gesetze erwarten kann.' For the argument about the release of slaves and the sabbath year, see pp. 28ff.

4

Vatke's 'Biblical Theology'

It was unfortunate for George that his *Jewish Festivals* was published in the same year as Vatke's *Biblical Theology* and Strauss's *Life of Jesus*. The antagonism caused by Strauss's book worked also against Vatke, who was regarded as 'an Old Testament Strauss'. Further, since George's *Festivals* was reviewed alongside Vatke's *Biblical Theology*, it could not help being tarnished by this association. Although it is idle to speculate about what might have been, it is worth wondering how the works by George and Vatke would have been received had Strauss's *Life of Jesus* been published several years later.

The author of the *Biblical Theology*, Johann Karl Wilhelm Vatke, was born in 1806 in the village of Behndorf, near Helmstedt. He studied under Gesenius in Halle and Ewald in Göttingen, before moving to Berlin, where he heard Neander, Schleiermacher and Hegel. In 1830, he became a *Privatdozent* in Berlin, and in 1831 began a collaborative friendship with D. F. Strauss, the friendship part of which lasted until Strauss's death in 1874.[1]

The *Biblical Theology* was published in 1835; its aim was to secure for Vatke a full professorship. However, a year before the book's appearance, Schleiermacher died, heralding the beginning of the dominant influence of the conservative Hengstenberg in the Berlin theological faculty. Hengstenberg was able to see to it that Vatke was never offered a full professorship, while warnings from the Minister of State responsible for universities, von Altenstein, saw to it that the *Biblical Theology* was never completed. Vatke's marriage to the daughter of a wealthy Berlin merchant solved his financial problems, and after 1850 he seems to have produced nothing. He died in 1882, aged 77.[2]

Vatke's *Biblical Theology* is never mentioned or described without being

---

[1] The standard biography of Vatke is by H. Benecke, *Wilhelm Vatke in seinem Leben und seinen Schriften*, Bonn 1883. For important discussions of Vatke see L. Perlitt, *Vatke und Wellhausen*, BZAW 94, Berlin 1965; Michael Brömse, *Studien zur 'Biblischen Theologie' Wilhelm Vatkes*, Diss. Kiel 1973. See also R. J. Thompson, *Moses and the Law in a Century of Criticism since Graf*, SVT 19, Leiden 1970, pp. 22–4, and *passim*. A section on the contemporary reviews of Vatke's *Biblical Theology* can be found in Brömse pp. 30ff.

[2] Brömse, op cit. pp. 18–25.

classified as Hegelian.[3] This is fair enough. Vatke became increasingly interested in Hegel's philosophy from 1828 onwards, and in the *Biblical Theology* he made no secret of his own Hegelian position. The opening 170 pages or so, and the concluding 120 pages or so he devoted to discussions of the nature of religion in general and of Old Testament religion in particular, and he cast these discussions in unmistakably Hegelian terms. However, the main part of the book, pages 177–590, is a critical account of the history of Old Testament religion; although organized around certain key Hegelian ideas, they constitute a profound and detailed analysis of many problems undoubtedly raised by the content of the Old Testament, and it is quite possible to read this section independently of the long opening and closing theoretical sections. Indeed, although it may be permissible to disregard the parts of the *Biblical Theology* that are blatantly statements about religion in Hegelian terms, the same cannot be done to Vatke's detailed treatment of the Old Testament text. Furthermore, it appears that later scholarship took seriously the historical-critical parts of the *Biblical Theology* while ignoring the theoretical parts.[4]

In what follows, a full exposition of the historical-critical section of the *Biblical Theology* will be attempted. Before this is done, however, some introductory comments will be in order. First, the treatment of the Old Testament in the *Biblical Theology* does not correspond closely to Hegel's discussion of 'Judaism' in his *Lectures on the Philosophy of Religion*.[5] In these lectures, the religion of the Old Testament is treated by Hegel under the heading of the 'religion of sublimity', a type of 'religion of spiritual individuality' midway between the religion of nature at the lower end of the scale, and absolute religion (Christianity) at the higher end of the scale. Hegel does not appear to use the Old Testament historically in order to describe religious conflict, with higher stages of religious consciousness emerging from lower stages as Israel's religion develops through history. His appears rather to be a reading of the Old Testament as a whole, in which he finds an entity called 'Judaism' which articulates in various ways the 'religion of sublimity'. Hegel mentions Job as a book which recognizes with submission that God is the unity that reconciles in himself the contradictions of injustice. Hegel expounds the 'Fall' narrative of Genesis 3, recognizing that it finds little echo elsewhere in the Old Testament, and he discusses the

---

[3] Wilhelm Vatke, *Die biblische Theologie wissenschaftlich dargestellt.* 1, *Die Religion des Alten Testamentes*, Berlin 1835 (there was no vol. 2). The Hegelian background is outlined by Kraus, *Geschichte der historisch-kritischen Erforschung*, pp. 194–9.

[4] cf. Brömse, op. cit., p. 54.

[5] G. W. F. Hegel, *Vorlesungen über die Philosophie der Religion, Sämmtliche Werke Jubiläumsaufgabe*, vols. 15–16, repr. Stuttgart 1965; ET, E. B. Spiers and J. B. Sanderson, 3 vols., London 1895. The Old Testament is dealt with in vol. 2 (16 of the *Sämmtliche Werke*), pp. 66ff; English, pp. 193ff.

dialectic of the *particular* claim of Jewish religion to possess the absolute God of all the nations. This latter section, indeed, is the only passage of Hegel referred to explicitly in the entire historical-critical part of the *Biblical Theology*.[6] What this amounts to, if my analysis is correct, is the fact that Vatke did not find in Hegel a ready-made interpretation of Old Testament religion that he simply expanded with the help of the critical method. Vatke's *Biblical Theology* represents a profoundly original interpretation of the Old Testament informed by certain Hegelian principles. What these principles were it is now time to state.

Most fundamental is the idea of development. Religion continually moves from the lower to the higher, and for Vatke, this has the far-reaching consequence that he rejects the de Wettian idea that post-exilic Judaism is a falling-away from the high points of Mosaic and prophetic religion. In this respect, Vatke stands close to the liberal British Old Testament scholars of the 1830s onwards who saw the religion of the Old Testament in terms of gradual and steady development. A second feature shared by Vatke with Hegel, but possibly influenced as much by Gesenius as by Hegel, is an interest in comparative religion.[7] The use of comparative religion was certainly a prominent part of Hegel's lectures on religion in general, and the *Biblical Theology* also makes considerable use of data about the religion of Israel's neighbours in its exposition of the phases of Old Testament religion. A third prominent feature used by Vatke is the dialectic between the 'religion of nature' and 'religion of spiritual individuality', in which there is a gradual movement towards ideas of divine transcendence and away from cruder ideas of the divine immanent in nature. This topic emphasizes how important it is to give Vatke a fair hearing; for however one wishes to explain it, there is no doubt that much space is devoted in the Old Testament to the struggle between faith in the transcendent Yahweh of Israel, and the fertility cults of Canaanites, closely associated with the cycle of the agricultural year.

If Hegel, in a general sense, was the starting point for Vatke's view of religion, his main guides in the critical method seem to have been de Wette and Gesenius. De Wette is referred to more than any other scholar, and he is described as the representative of the principles and results of the newer

---

[6] Vatke, *Biblische Theologie*, p. 443, 2n.

[7] cf. the comment on Hegel, in Charles Taylor, *Hegel*, Cambridge 1975, p. 496: 'Hegel's philosophy of religion is like all his work extraordinarily well researched, and full of interesting detail. As a work in comparative religion it would not stand up today in most of its passages, but it was remarkable considering what was available at the time.' Gesenius's interest in comparative religion is indicated by his preface to Gramberg's *Critical History* (see above p. 63).

criticism.[8] Gesenius is referred to principally with regard to parts of his Isaiah commentary that touch upon matters of comparative religion, while there are also several references to Gramberg's *Critical History*. On the whole, Vatke can be said to have provided a more profound treatment of matters discussed also by de Wette and Gramberg. He had clearly learned from them well, but was not afraid to criticize them where necessary. Thus he rightly points out the shortcomings of Gramberg's method of ascribing particular books of the Old Testament to particular periods, followed by an exposition of the books concerned as information about the religious ideas of that period.[9] This does not allow for the complexity of redaction, whereby books may contain information derived from several periods, a problem of which Gramberg was aware, but which he did not seem able to solve satisfactorily in his presentation.

Like Gramberg's *Critical History*, the *Biblical Theology* divides the history of the Old Testament religion into a number of periods, in this case eight. They are the Mosaic period, the period of the Judges, the age of David and Solomon, the tenth-ninth centuries, the Assyrian period, the Babylonian period, the Persian period, and the Macedonian and Maccabean period.

In Vatke's opinion, reliable sources for Old Testament religious history were available only from the period of the Judges and the time of David, with full certainty available from the eighth century.[10] Thus, in dealing with the Mosaic period, Vatke depended as much upon his theories about the development of religion in general as upon the Old Testament. The sojourn in Egypt and the departure from Canaan were accepted, from which the conclusion was drawn that the Hebrews of the Mosaic period were nomads, that their religion was the 'religion of nature' as in Egypt and the ancient Near East, and that it took the particular form of star worship.[11] This latter assertion was to be supported from Amos 5.15–16, which was taken to mean that the Israelites in the wilderness wanderings worshipped Saturn.[12] Vatke surmised that Saturn, portrayed as a bull, was carried in a

---

[8] *Biblische Theologie*, p. 179. Brömse's remark, op. cit. p. 90 that Vatke makes minimal use of de Wette is puzzling. Vatke refers to other scholars only rarely, and his references to de Wette outnumber references to other individual scholars.

[9] Vatke, p. 178.

[10] Among books whose historical value is limited to the time of composition, or the time of origin of their oral or written sources are the Pentateuch and Joshua.

[11] Vatke, p. 184: 'sowohl in Aegypten als während des Zuges durch die Wüste war die Mehrzahl des Volkes dem Naturcultus, und zwar dem durch ganz Vorderasien und Aegypten verbreiteten Gestirndienst ergeben.' Hegel's treatment of Egyptian religion under the division 'religion of nature' can be found in *Sämmtliche Werke*, vol. 15, pp. 451ff; English, vol. 2, pp. 101ff.

[12] Vatke, pp. 190ff.

tent. Other elements of Israelite worship of the time involved the symbolism of the serpent.[13]

Compared with de Wette, Vatke's view of the work of Moses was on the negative side.[14] Wedded to the view that religion could only develop and not degenerate, Vatke saw in Moses at best an initiator of what was later to become the full-blown theocracy. There was no institutional machinery of the type that would be necessary to sustain even a simple theocracy; Moses combined in his own person all the powers of authority over the people. Moses did not found a cult or establish a priesthood, and the simple laws that he promulgated could not have been the laws dealing with an agricultural and settled life that are attributed to him even in the Decalogue. On the other hand, he may have promulgated a simple Decalogue appropriate to the circumstances of the people.[15]

The positive work of Moses consisted of introducing the worship of Yahweh, and of being a mediator of a covenant between Yahweh and the people. Moses believed that Yahweh was the only God, and thought of his as a holy power. Moses banished from the worship of Yahweh all traces of nature worship, although he cannot have promulgated the commandment forbidding representations of Yahweh in the form that it is in the Decalogue.[16] The new religious element introduced by Moses was in conflict with the astral nature religion of the people; but the conflict thus introduced did not result in progress from the religion of nature to definite religion. This was not to happen for a very long time, until the capacity of the people had reached the point where the new revelation could take over entirely.[17] Thus the result of the work of Moses was that the people of Israel had two national gods, Saturn and Yahweh.[18]

---

[13] ibid., pp. 199–201.

[14] ibid., pp. 201 ff.

[15] ibid., p. 211: 'Aus dem Bisherigen ergiebt sich nun von selbst, dass Mose eine solche angebliche Staatsverfassung nicht könne gegründet haben, also auch nicht die Theokratie im strengeren Sinne des Wortes, da sie eine allgemeine Anschauung ist, die sich erst aus wirklich bestehenden Verhältnissen abstrahiren liess.'

[16] ibid., p. 299: 'Was die Sphäre des Göttlichen betrifft, so dürfen wir es als unzweifelhafte Thatsache annehmen, dass Mose den Glauben an Jehova, als den Einen Gott gehabt und sein Volk zu demselben verpflichtet habe, denn schon der Name: Jehova führt uns wenigstens in das Mosaische Zeitalter hinauf, wenngleich die etymologische Deutung desselben später sein mag.'

[17] ibid., p. 231: 'Die ganze Geschichte der Alttestamentliche Religion ist insofern ein beständiger Kampf und Sieg des Gedankens über das Natürliche, und wenngleich zwischen beiden Begriffen kein fliessender Uebergang stattfinden kann, so ist dennoch die Abreibung beider Seiten an einander als fliessend zu denken, bis der Begriff der Idealität d.i. die Idealität in der Totalität ihrer Momente und als selbständige, ausschliessende und über alles Andere übergreifende Einheit daraus als Resultat hervorging. Speculative Thätigkeit im engeren Sinne des Wortes zeigt der hebräische Geist erst in späteren Zeiten . . .'

[18] For a summary of the Mosaic period, see p. 251.

For the period of the Judges, Vatke disregarded the cycle of apostasy—
subjugation—deliverance—rule by a Judge—apostasy that forms the
framework of the book of Judges.[19] On developmental grounds, it was
impossible that the people as a whole should revert to a lower religious state
having achieved a higher one under the leadership of a Judge. The period in
fact saw the transition from nomadic life to settled life with its more
developed legal and ethical implications, yet there was no development of a
political state in this period. The nomadic stock of the Hebrews from Egypt
was enlarged by elements joining them in Canaan, and contact with the
local population brought its dangers.

Religiously, the period saw a struggle between the religion of Yahweh
and that of Baal and Astarte. Yahweh was worshipped in many places, the
cult was simple and there were few priests. Only a minority of people held
to the higher principles implicit in Yahwism. The period also saw the
beginnings of the prophetic groups and Nazirites. However, these prophets
were soothsayers rather than the prophets who would later preach the
transcendence of Yahweh.

Politically and ethically speaking, the life of the people was dominated
by the 'right of the strongest' familiar in societies in a 'state of nature'. This
can be seen from the warring, and the use of the *herem*, or total destruction
of the enemy. There were human sacrifices in this period, of which the
herem was also an example.

In reconstructing the period of David and Solomon, Vatke rejected the
widespread view that Samuel was the second founder of the theocracy after
Moses.[20] From the historical point of view, Saul was most likely made king
as a result of his victory over the Ammonites described in 1 Samuel 11.
Samuel, as a prophet, confirmed Saul as king, but almost certainly did not
anoint David during Saul's lifetime. Further, it is unlikely that Saul
attempted to reform Yahwism as implied in 1 Samuel 28.3. The earliest
Israelite kings were closer to Judges than Kings.

A major event was the building of the Temple, for which Solomon
employed a Phoenician architect. This introduced a new factor into the
religion of Israel, since the Temple incorporated Asiatic mythological
symbols.[21] These symbols belonged primarily to the sun god, whereas the
symbols of the worship of Baal were excluded from the Temple. Although

---

[19] For the whole period, see pp. 251–88.

[20] For this period see pp. 288–391. Presumably Samuel was held to be the second founder of
the theocracy because he initiated the kingship.

[21] Vatke, p. 323: 'Der salomonische Templebau übte auf den Cultus und allmälig auch auf
die religiöse Vorstellung selbst grossen Einfluss aus. Der Bau wurde von phönizischen
Künstlern und in phönizischer Kunstform ausgeführt, daher gewiss nach einem in
Phönizien schon vorhandenen Typus, was in Beziehung auf Construction des Ganzen und
einzelne dabei angebrachte Symbole höchst wichtig ist.'

the Temple was not a central sanctuary, it would later become the means of helping Israelite religion to move to a higher stage.

The Temple as originally constructed had no holy of holies separated from the rest of the sanctuary by a veil. The ark had no tent and no cherubim, and probably contained a sacred stone. The main effect of the Temple upon the cult was that it imparted to the latter a little more splendour; it did not, at this stage, increase individual self-awareness and feelings of transcendence. Regarding the priesthood, the emergence of Zadok into prominence indicated that the Jerusalem priests were *not* the descendants of Aaron, since Zadok was not thus descended.[22] The Levites were an order of ministers inferior to priests, although the word 'Levite' probably had more than one designation. There was certainly never a tribe of Levi as one of the twelve tribes.[23]

The ethics of the period were rudimentary. Here, Vatke made great play of the less reputable aspects of the lives of the families of Saul, David and Solomon. The section on this period ends with a complicated discussion of the relation between the sun god and the worship of Baal and Astarte.

Vatke seems to have been concerned to oppose a widespread view that Baal and Astarte represented the sun and the moon. He argued that although Baal and Astarte might originally have derived from sun and moon worship, they had come to represent the masculine and feminine principles of the power of nature.[24] The worship of the sun represented a higher form of religion than the worship of Baal and Astarte, and thus the Jerusalem temple with its introduction of the cult of the sun god brought Yahweh into contact with a higher form of religion. In an interesting discussion of the Samson sagas, Vatke argued that Samson was to be connected with the sun, and that the whole cycle reflected a movement from the worship of Baal to that of the sun god.[25]

The books of Kings in their present form were not reliable guides to the period of the divided monarchy.[26] The unfavourable treatment of Jeroboam's revolt overlooked the fact that Jeroboam was no worse than Solomon.

---

[22] Zadok's lack of connection with Eli and Aaron is discussed at length on p. 344, n2.

[23] ibid., pp. 346–7: 'Sehen wir hierbei von den verdächtigen Berichten der Chronik ab, und halten uns an die Bücher Samuelis und der Könige so wie an einige Stellen bei Jeremia und Ezechiel, so lässt sich jene Frage bestimmt verneinen, woraus dann weiter folgt, dass die Leviten in älteren Zeiten gar nicht für einen Stamm angesehen wurden und dass David's angebliche Verdienste um den Cultus als spätere unhistorische Sage zu betrachten sind.' See also p. 221.

[24] Vatke also had to meet the criticism that both the worship of the sun and that of Baal was represented by pillars or obelisks; cf. pp. 358ff.

[25] Vatke, p. 370: 'Wahrscheinlich hat sich die Sage von Samson früher ausgebildet, als der ältere Baalsdienst in den späteren Sonnendienst überging, und zeugt daher für das höhere Alter jener Vorstellung.'

[26] For this period see pp. 391–460.

Indeed, Jeroboam was more faithful than Solomon to the older religion of
Israel. Elijah and Elisha did not criticize Jeroboam's rebellion and religion,
but concentrated upon the ethical abuses of the kings of Israel. The assertion
of 1 Kings 12.31 that Jeroboam had instituted an illegitimate, that is, non-
Levitical, priesthood had to be rejected.

On the other hand, the Northern Kingdom was plagued with political
instability, while its religion lacked the inner dynamic to enable it to
progress. Judah, by way of contrast, enjoyed the stability of the Davidic
dynasty, as well as the new elements introduced by the Temple. The
prophets developed from being members of bands to becoming great
individuals. Transcendence began to be emphasized by stress upon Yahweh's
love for his people, and by the notion of his holiness.

Two discussions of biblical material relating to this period show Vatke's
method at work at its clearest. The first concerns Micaiah ben Imlah's vision
of the heavenly court of Yahweh in 1 Kings 22.[27] Vatke argues that this
narrative must originate from a period later than the ninth century, since
the heavenly hosts (as distinct from angels) developed from the worship of
astral bodies. This development would not have taken place as early as
presupposed by the Micaiah narrative. Angels, according to Vatke, are not
'personal', but are abstract manifestations of the power of Yahweh. The
second discussion concerns the patriarchal narratives. Vatke holds that in
the tenth–ninth centuries contacts with foreign nations began to help Israel
to encounter and absorb the elements that were later to be formed into the
patriarchal narratives and the primeval history of Genesis 1–11. In their
final form, these traditions evince a developed form of religion that indicates
that they cannot possibly belong to the period in which they are set.[28]

Dealing with the Assyrian period, Vatke sees in the preservation of Judah
in the face of the Assyrian threat an indication of divine providence.[29] This
period sees a spread of the worship of the sun god; but it also sees the
development of Israelite laws, and an increase in prophetic activity. The
transcendence of Yahweh is articulated in terms of the day of Yahweh, and
the notion of an 'end' of world history. The theocracy also develops
significantly, with Yahweh seen as lawgiver, lord, and protector of the
people. Also, the prophetic calls to repentance introduce an abstract element
which helps to increase the self-awareness of the ordinary people, and to
wean them away from the religion of nature.

Josiah's reform, in the Babylonian period, is a prophetic reform, backed
by the use of laws to regulate the common life. Vatke doubts whether the

[27] ibid., pp. 444ff.
[28] ibid., p. 455: 'Denn selbst in der scheinbar particularistischen Sage von den Patriarchen hat
das religiöse und volksthümliche Element auf der einen Seite so universelle Beziehung, auf
der anderen Seite einen so abstracten, prophetischen Charakter, dass seine Gestaltung nur
aus dem concret-historischen Hintergrunde der nach-davidischen Zeit begriffen werden
kann.'
[29] See p. 460–500.

law book was really found in the Temple, and he makes the unassailable point that in view of the dire consequences that its discovery had for the idolatrous servants of the Temple, its concealment in the Temple would have been a risky business.[30] His view of the law book is that it contained chapters 13, 19—24 and 32—4 of Exodus. One of the effects of Josiah's suppression of the high places where Yahweh had been legitimately worshipped was to increase the number of Levites wishing to assist at the Jerusalem Temple. Discussing the passover which Josiah ordered to be observed, Vatke posits astral origins for the passover ceremony, the lamb being associated with the astronomical Aries. The passover also expresses the holiness of first-born humans and animals. Its connection with unleavened bread and the departure from Egypt are developments long after the time of the exodus.

The fall of Jerusalem had the result that either the people continued a religion based upon Canaanite idolatry, or they took over the worship of the Babylonian gods. There was also the development of a new religious awareness, especially in Jeremiah. The chapters of Isaiah dealing with the servant of Yahweh called upon the Israelite people to be the bearer of the true religion and to spread this to all the nations of the earth.

In the post-exilic period, there is a greater stress than ever upon holiness, and the emergence of a developed symbolism of the theocracy. The laws and the cult are ascribed to Moses, and contact with Babylon and Persia brings knowledge of Satan, and belief in resurrection, as well as familiarity with traditions such as the Flood and the Tower of Babel. The ceremony of the Day of Atonement must date from this period because Azazel is a demon, and there is no Israelite belief in demons before this period.

The Persian period sees the arrival of the high point of Old Testament religion.[31] Idolatry disappears, religious and civil life is ordered by cultic

---

[30] See the continuation of p. 504, n2, on to p. 506: 'Die Erzählung von dem Auffinden des Gesetzbuches ist so unvollständig und ungenügend, dass man über den Ursprung und das Alter des Buches, so wie über das Zufällige oder Beabsichtigte seiner Bekanntmachung keinen rechten Aufschluss erhält.'

[31] Cf. the following important statements, first, about the end of the Babylonian period: 'Alle diese Einflüsse, welche grösstentheils auf den Parsismus zurückgehen, vermittelten sich allmälig mit der älteren Jehovareligion, und das Zeitalter des Exils bietet nur erst die Keime dar von dem grossen Assimilationsprocesse, wodurch mit der Zeit die Hauptmomente persischer Religion und Weisheit in's Judenthum und durch dessen Vermittelung ins Christenthum aufgenommen wurden. Da das Allmälige des Ueberganges selbst in der vorexilischen Zeit nachgewiesen ist, so lässt sich keine strenge Scheidung des eigentlichen Hebraismus und des durch jene Einflüsse bedingten Judenthums vornehmen' (p. 551). Second, this statement about the Persian period: 'Wir müssen nach dem Bisherigen eine doppelte Richtung des jüdischen Geistes im persischen Zeitalter unterscheiden, welche dem Princip nach zwar älter sind, in dieser Form aber erst jetzt in's Leben treten können: die streng-gestzliche auf der einen Seite, und die frei-reflektivende auf der anderen. . . . Die versöhnende Mitte jenes Gegensatzes bildete . . . die religiöse Lyrik, welche in diesem Zeitalter die höchste Blüthe erreichte, namentlich in Ansehung der tiefen Innigkeit und des klaren Selbstbewusstseins. Fasst man dann das letztere als den Einheitspunkt auf, in

ritual and by law, and there is a development of prayer. Only from the second century onwards is there the fatal transition to Judaism that results in the emergence of the Pharisaic and Sadducaic parties.

It is to be hoped that this lengthy account of Vatke's *Biblical Theology* will have enabled the reader to get a good idea of the flavour of the work. On the one hand, it will be obvious that Vatke's views about the development of religion led him to interpret the Old Testament material according to his preconceived notions. On the other hand, it has to be allowed that many of the questions to which he addressed himself need to be answered, if not necessarily in Vatke's terms. The type of social organization which bound the Israelites together in the time of Moses has to be considered, and it has to be asked whether that social organization can have borne the laws and rituals ascribed to Moses. It has to be asked why, if Moses instituted laws and rituals, the ordinary Israelites persisted in being idolaters for much of Old Testament history. It cannot be denied that the Temple was designed by a non-Israelite, constituted an innovation in Israelite religion, contained symbolism that was not germane to Yahwism, and became a focus for aspects of heathen religion during the reigns of many kings. Vatke did not invent the many problems that he discussed, and it cannot be denied that by addressing them in the way that he did, he issued a challenge to those who would disagree with him to produce a more coherent set of solutions to the problems.

As mentioned earlier, a noteworthy feature of the *Biblical Theology* was its refusal to see Josiah's reform as the beginning of a fatal degeneration in Judaism. For Vatke, ritual and law did not appear to be the monstrous things from which other Lutheran consciences recoiled. The cult and the law were positive things, freeing the Old Testament religion from idolatry and the religion of nature, and articulating a degree of self-awareness that made the worshippers aware of the gulf between themselves and a transcendent deity. Thus for Vatke, the Persian period saw the highpoint of Old Testament religion. To the extent that he could attribute no historical authenticity to the Patriarchal narratives, that he maintained that the work of Moses was minimal compared with what the Bible credits to him, and that the Pentateuch can, on his reckoning, have reached its final form only after the Exile, Vatke's position was in line with that of his critical predecessors from de Wette onwards. He brought to his work, however, a refinement of argument and an attention to detail that at the technical level advanced the critical method to a new standard.

---

welchen zuletzt alle Seiten des religiösen Lebens zusammengehen, so fällt überhaupt die Blüthe der Alttestamentlichen Religion als solcher, in dieses Zeitalter. Vergleichen wir jene beiden Hauptrichtungen mit den früheren Entwickelungen des hebräischen Geistes, so würden wir der levitisch-gesetzlichen Form Unrecht thun, wenn wir sie mit dem äusserlichen Formalismus in Sachen des Cultus, der levitischen Reinheit und der Sittlichkeit, den die älteren Propheten bekämpften, schlechthin identificiren wollten' (p. 566).

5

Confessional Opposition to the Critical Method

The two significant books of critical Old Testament scholarship of 1835, George's *Jewish Festivals* and Vatke's *Biblical Theology*, received a setback from the unfavourable reviews published by the established leaders of the 'new critical method'.[1] They also received severe criticism from the emerging Confessional orthodox groups of Old Testament scholars, led by E. W. Hengstenberg.[2] The influence of this group became a major factor in German Old Testament scholarship during the 1830s, and it lasted for nearly forty years. It affected not only German Old Testament scholarship, but British Old Testament scholarship also, as English translations of works by Hengstenberg, Tholuck, Keil, Hävernick, to name some representatives of this 'school', were published by T. & T. Clark in Edinburgh from the 1830s.[3]

Just as the representatives of the 'new criticism' were not straight-forwardly descended from the rationalists and neologists, so the Confessional orthodox scholars were not straightforwardly descended from the supranaturalists. Two movements were responsible for their presence as a force to be reckoned with: the movement towards unity between the Lutheran and the Reformed churches dating from the three-hundredth anniversary of the Reformation in 1817, and the so-called revival movement (*Erweckungsbewegung*) that began to affect churches in many parts of Germany from the first decade of the nineteenth century.[4]

These two movements were unrelated, yet both had their roots in the Enlightenment. One of the effects of rationalism and Neologism in the eighteenth century had been to take a critical stance in relation to the traditional confessions of faith such as the creeds and the Augsburg

---

[1] See Brömse, *Studien zur 'Biblischen Theologie' Wilhelm Vatkes*, p. 41, where he points out that the unfavourable reviews of Nitzsche, de Wette and Stähelin functioned as crown witnesses for the orthodox verdict on Vatke's *Biblical Theology*.

[2] See Brömse, p. 31 for Hengstenberg's reaction in *Ev.K-Z* for 16-1-1836.

[3] See the list on p. 176.

[4] See J. Cochlovius, *Bekenntnis und Einheit der Kirche im deutschen Protestantismus*, Die Lutherische Kirche, Geschichte und Gestalten, 3, Gütersloh 1980; E. Beyreuther, *Die Erweckungsbewegung*, Die Kirche in ihrer Geschichte, 4. 1, Göttingen 1977[2].

Confession. 'Enlightened' thought of the period could no longer feel strongly about theological issues that had divided Lutherans and Calvinists. With the need for national renewal following the defeat of Napoleon, and the approach of the three-hundredth anniversary of Luther's nailing his ninety-five theses to the door of the Schlosskirche in Wittenberg, Frederick Wilhelm III of Prussia proposed a union of Lutheran and Reformed Churches in his kingdom.[5] However, the movement towards unity was not restricted to Prussia; Hessen-Nassau, Rheinbayern, Rheinhessen and Baden were other principalities where union was initiated.[6] A practical outcome of such union schemes was that new attention was focused upon the church formularies, especially the Augsburg Confession.

The revival movement had its roots in the Enlightenment, in that it was a reaction to the secularization of that period, and to the impoverishment of Christian life that had resulted.[7] In the first instance, 'awakened' German Christians were untroubled by denominational differences. Increasingly, however, they began to find that the Augsburg Confession expressed for them theologically what their Christian experience had come to mean.[8] This was to have a profound effect upon the whole issue of church unity. No sooner had the union of Lutheran and Reformed Churches been achieved in Prussia in 1830, than doubts about it began to be entertained among those who had come to accord high authority to the Augsburg Confession. A union that had been initiated because 'Enlightened' thought had minimized doctrinal differences between churches, now became threatened by 'awakened' Christians who took a firm Confessional stand. In the 1840s, strenuous attempts were made in the United Church to safeguard Lutheran interests. Involved in these efforts were Old Testament scholars such as Hengstenberg, Delitzsch and von Hofmann. Thus matters of Confessional orthodoxy received particular attention in the middle of the nineteenth century in Germany, with important results for Old Testament scholarship.

At the centre of Christian experience for those affected by the revival movement was justification by faith in the atoning work of Christ. In turn, the atonement and the divinity of Christ became the starting point for interpreting the Bible, Old Testament as well as New Testament. The Bible was seen to be a unity, with the Old Testament pointing towards and being fulfilled in the New Testament.

[5] See Cochlovius, op. cit., p. 19.
[6] See K. F. A. Kahnis, *Der innere Gang des deutschen Protestantismus seit Mitte des vorigen Jahrhunderts*, Leipzig 1854, pp. 211ff. Union was achieved in 1817 in Nassau, 1818 in Rheinbayern, 1821 in Baden and 1822 in Rheinhessen.
[7] Cochlovius, op. cit., pp. 21–2.
[8] Cochlovius dates widespread interest in Confessionalism from the 1840s, although the interest of Steffens and Hengstenberg (see below) dates from the 1820s.

It would be wrong to understand the orthodoxy that resulted as simply a revival of Protestant scholastic belief in biblical inerrancy. It appears to have been based upon a renewal of spiritual life, expressed in terms of the Augsburg Confession. The Augsburg Confession itself contains no article of faith either about the authority or inspiration of the Bible. However, it was held to be an expression of biblical faith as understood by the principles of the Reformation. The Confessional orthodox Old Testament scholars of the late 1820s onwards could not reconcile the 'new criticism' with their Christian experience and doctrinal standpoint.

Before looking more closely at the historical development of Confessional Orthodoxy in Old Testament scholarship, it will be useful to illustrate more clearly what was at issue between the 'new criticism' and Confessional Orthodoxy. A good example is Hengstenberg's attitude to a treatise on the atonement by his predecessor in the Berlin chair, de Wette.

De Wette's *Commentatio de morte Jesu Christi expiatoria* was first published in 1813.[9] It had several aims, the chief of which was to argue that the interpretation of the death of Jesus as an atoning sacrifice did not derive from Jesus himself, nor from the Old Testament nor from Jewish messianic expectations of the first century AD, but from the disciples of Jesus after his death. Not unnaturally, de Wette contributed a careful study of the Servant passages in Isaiah 40—55, in order to show that they did not prophesy a suffering Messiah.[10] He also quoted extensively from rabbinic sources in order to show the lack of such a belief among first-century Jewry. His view of the death of Christ was that it was an expression of the love of God. Jesus, alike in word and deed showed that God was a God of love, and that it was not his will that any should perish. Jesus's death was a pledge and seal of the divine love, making unnecessary both the religion of good works and the need to approach God through animal sacrifices.[11]

De Wette's treatise received detailed treatment in one of the chapters of Hengstenberg's major work, his *Christology of the Old Testament*.[12] The chapter, entitled 'The Suffering and Atoning Christ in the Old Testament' characterized de Wette's work thus:

[9] Reference has been made to the reprinted version in *Opuscula Theologica*, Berlin 1930, pp. 1–148.

[10] Gesenius makes constant reference to de Wette's treatise in his *Commentary* on Isaiah. See Zweyter Theil, pp. 4ff, 12, 160.

[11] W. M. L. de Wette, *Ueber die Religion*, p. 441: 'In dem Blute, das er vergoss, strömte die unendliche Fülle der Liebe hin, die er für das Menschengeschlecht im Herzen trug; dieser Tod war das Siegel, das er seinem der Liebe geweiheten Leben aufdrückte; ja, er war das Pfand und Siegel der göttlichen Liebe selber, indem ihn Gott gesandt und dahin gegeben hatte, dass er die Menschen durch seinen Tod vom Verderben rettete.'

[12] E. W. Hengstenberg, *Christology of the Old Testament*, 4, Edinburgh 1858, pp. 332–364; German: *Christologie des Alten Testaments und Commentar über die Messianischen Weissagungen der Propheten*, Berlin, 1, 1829, pp. 252–92.

The question whether there is any reference in the prophecies of the Old Testament to a suffering and dying Messiah in general, or to his vicarious suffering and death in particular, has received from rationalism a most decided and negative reply.[13]

Hengstenberg's approach was based upon great learning and ability, but it eschewed entirely the historical-critical method as it had been developed up to his day. It can be summarized by saying that Hengstenberg used all his considerable abilities to defend a Confessional viewpoint, which viewpoint would be undermined if historical criticism were to be admitted as valid. The difference between the 'Rationalists' and their orthodox opponents was neatly summed up by Gustav Friedrich Oehler in 1840 in his *Prolegomena to the Theology of the Old Testament*:

> ... there are those who accept the religion of the Old Testament as a fact and who assume, indeed acknowledge and are convinced, that what was believed must also have happened; and there are those who see the content of the Old Testament belief as a product of religious expression whose historical basis must be discovered by means of the critical method, which itself depends upon the assumptions of modern consciousness.[14]

This, then, was the difference between the two sides: the Confessionalists accepted the witness to faith in the Old Testament (as seen through Protestant eyes), assumed the authenticity of the historical narratives in which the witness was expressed, and used scholarship to defend the authenticity of Old Testament writings and history. Those who embraced the critical method approached the Old Testament with a variety of

[13] ibid., p. 332. German p. 252. The first German edition (1829) has instead of 'Rationalism', 'die meisten neueren Theologen'. This is altered to 'Rationalismus' in the second edition (1856[7]). In this edition, the chapter is Appendix 4 to vol. 3, 2, pp. 86–92.

[14] G. F. Oehler, *Prolegomena zur Theologie des Alten Testaments*, Stuttgart 1845, p. 12. He distinguished between: 'dasjenige, was die alttestamentliche Religion als Thatsache annimmt und voraussetzt, auch als solche erkennen, somit überzeugt sind, dass das Geglaubte auch ein Geschehenes war; und zwischen denjenigen, welche in dem Inhalt des alttestamentlichen Glaubens zunächst nur ein Product der religiösen Vorstellung sehen, dessen geschichtliche Grundlage erst durch einen auf den Voraussetzungen des modernen Bewusstseyns beruhenden kritischen Process enthüllt werden könne.' Oehler's book is a valuable commentary on the various 'schools' of the mid-nineteenth century. Of Hengstenberg Oehler says: 'bei Hengstenberg hat in Bezug auf die Lehre die Einheit des A. und N. T. den Sinn, dass der neutestamentliche Lehrinhalt im A.T. bereits als fertige, abgeschlossene Verkündigung ist, nur vielleicht mehr 'zurücktretend', während der wahre Sinn vielmehr ist, dass das N.T. im A.T. wird, und desshalb nur so in ihm ist, wie bei jeden Organismus die höhere Entwicklungsstufe dem Keime und Vorbilde nach bereits in der früheren enthalten ist' (p. 68). Oehler describes Hengstenberg's *Theology of the Pentateuch* as 'ausgezeichnet' (outstanding).

assumptions: Friesian,[15] Hegelian,[16] developmental,[17] and the view that the Old Testament should be read 'neutrally',[18] but they were agreed that the historical-critical method was the basis upon which the 'true' course of Old Testament religion was to be discovered.

The most famous representative of Confessional orthodoxy was E. W. Hengstenberg, but preceding his influence in point of time was the influence of August Tholuck.[19] Tholuck was not primarily an Old Testament scholar, but he published in this field, and undoubtedly left his mark upon students attracted by the Confessional standpoint. Tholuck was born in 1799, studied oriental languages in Berlin, and seemed destined for an academic career. However, contact with the revival movement led him to dedicate his life to Christian scholarship, and to upholding the central Christian doctrines. He taught at Berlin[20] before being appointed to a chair at Halle in 1826 in succession to J. S. Vater. He died in Halle in 1877.

Tholuck's presence in Halle alongside Gesenius brought problems. Even before his appointment, Tholuck was in trouble through an address that he gave to the Continental Society in London in 1825.[21] The address was published in the *Missionary Register* for June 1825 and reprinted in the *Allgemeine Kirchenzeitung* for 16 October 1825. In the address, Tholuck described his religious instruction at school, in which Christ had been described as a good man, but a little fanatical.[22] He characterized the University of Halle as a 'seat of unbelief',[23] and implied that 'awakened' pastors and their congregations were being persecuted in parts of Germany. Two months later in the *AKZ*, Tholuck tried to extricate himself from the implications of the slur that he had cast upon the university to which he had been called, by claiming that the report of the address had been prepared

[15] So de Wette.

[16] So Vatke.

[17] So George.

[18] So Ewald, except that he also embraced 'developmentalist' ideas, as did some Confessionalists, e.g., Delitzsch and von Hofmann.

[19] On Tholuck see W. Schrader, *Geschichte der Friedrichs-Universität zu Halle*, 2, pp. 144–65, where the verdict is offered that Tholuck was too preoccupied with current dogmatic issues for his biblical scholarship to constitute a lasting contribution. The standard biography is L. Witte, *Das Leben Tholucks*, 2 vols, Bielefeld and Leipzig, 1884. See also *ADB* 38, pp. 55–8.

[20] In Berlin he was an *ausserordentlicher* Professor. See Walter Elliger, *150 Jahre Theologische Fakultät Berlin. Eine Darstellung ihrer Geschichte von 1810 bis 1960 als Beitrag zu ihrem Jubiläum*, Berlin 1960, pp. 39–41.

[21] See Lenz, *Geschichte der Königlichen Friedrich-Wilhelms-Universität zu Berlin* 2. 1, pp. 338–9.

[22] *AKZ* 1825, Nr 138, 16-10-1825, 'Ihnen nach war Christus ein guter Mensch, nur etwas schwärmerisch'.

[23] ibid., 'Jene preussische Universität, welche der grösste Theil der Theologie Studirenden bezieht, Halle . . . ist nun der Sitz des Unglaubens.'

from notes taken by a listener, and that it misrepresented him.[24] He acknowledged that rationalism could be combined with piety, and that although Professor Wegscheider in Halle was well-known as a rationalist, he always delivered his lectures in a thoroughly scientific manner. Tholuck made no reference to Gesenius. Unfortunately for Tholuck, in January 1826, the *AKZ* claimed to have irrefutable proof that the report of Tholuck's speech had been printed from the text used by Tholuck himself, an allegation that Tholuck did not answer.[25] This incident shows that little love was to be lost between the Confessional and the critical scholars, and the bitterness reached a new level when, in 1830, Hengstenberg publicly accused Gesenius and Wegscheider of teaching views that were contrary to the Confessional basis of the Halle theological faculty.[26]

Two early works by Tholuck indicate the shape of things to come. The first, published when he was only 22, and a *Privatdozent* at Berlin, was entitled *Several apologetic hints for the study of the Old Testament*.[27] It makes little reference to critical scholarship, except for commending Gesenius on philological matters. It stresses the importance of reading the Old Testament as an oriental book, and warns that misunderstandings can arise if this is not done. However, its main concern is to point out the close relationship between the Old and the New Testament. First, the morality of the New Testament rests upon the religious ideas of the Old Testament; second, the dogmatics of the New Testament are an explicit statement of the religious teaching of the Old Testament; third, Christ is the centre of all Old Testament prophecies, and the prophecies of the Old Testament receive their confirmation in the New Testament.

Two years later, in 1823, Tholuck published a book which was intended to be a reply to de Wette's novel *Theodore, or the Doubter's Ordination*. It was entitled *The Doctrine of Sin and the Redeemer, or the True Ordination of the Doubter*, and it was written in the space of three weeks.[28] In fact, it can bear no comparison with de Wette's novel, and is merely a series of letters between two students, Julius and Guido.[29] Its significance lies in its content

---

[24] *AKZ* 1825, Nr 172, 15-12-1825.

[25] *AKZ* 1826, Nr 15, 26-1-1826.

[26] See above, p. 51.

[27] August Tholuck, *Einige apologetische Winke für das Studium des Alten Testamentes*, Berlin 1821, ET, *Hints on the Importance of the Study of the Old Testament* (Biblical Cabinet, 2), Edinburgh 1833.

[28] A. Tholuck, *Die Lehre von der Sünde und vom Versöhner, oder Die wahre Weihe des Zweiflers*, Hamburg 1823; ET (of part of the book), *Guido and Julius: the Doctrine of Sin and the Propitiator*, London 1836.

[29] Nevertheless, in spite of its patent artificiality, Tholuck's 'reply' to de Wette achieved astonishing success. Elliger, *150 Jahre Theologische Fakultät Berlin* (p. 40) speaks of 'ein enormer publizistischer Erfolg', mainly because of the intensity with which it describes Tholuck's own religious convictions.

not its form. De Wette's hero, Theodore, decides to enter the ministry after
gaining a type of faith in which rationalism and positive religion are
reconciled in Friesian terms. In Tholuck's book, Julius experiences
conversion, as a result of which he decides to study theology, and tries to
win to faith his friend who started with theology but turned to philosophy.
The contrast between the vows of the two 'doubters' is clear. De Wette's
'doubter' attains to a faith which reconciles philosophy and theology;
Tholuck's 'doubter' experiences justification and new birth.[30] As one of a
number of appendixes, Genesis 3 is expounded, and it is asserted that Genesis
3 was written by Moses on the basis of oral tradition. The narrative reflects
a period when mankind was at a stage of childlikeness, perceiving reality in
a picture-like manner. However, Genesis 3 is not a philosophical myth. It
records the fact that mankind wished to become autonomous, and no longer
desired to recognize God's decrees as the highest law.[31] Genesis 3 and
Romans 7 are the two pillars on which the building, which is living
Christianity, rest.[32]

Ernst Wilhelm Hengstenberg was born in 1802, and went in 1819 to
Bonn where his principal teacher was the Arabist Freytag.[33] As a student, he
worked carefully through E. F. K. Rosenmüller's commentaries, from which
he will have seen the encyclopaedic, mildly rationalist approach. He bought
the second volume of de Wette's *Contributions*, and engaged in a study of
Kant and Fries.[34] His graduation as a doctor was based upon a critical edition
and translation of an Arabic text, but included among the theses of his Bonn
submission was the statement, 'the theological interpretation of the Old
Testament is without value'.[35]

In 1823, Hengstenberg went to Basel to be personal tutor to J. J. Stähelin.
He visited de Wette in Basel, and he taught Arabic at the Basel Mission in
addition to his duties as tutor. His year in Basel brought about a new
direction in his life, with far-reaching consequences for Old Testament
scholarship.[36]

Among the influences that played an important part were his contacts

[30] Tholuck's book is as concentrated upon one topic as de Wette's is expansive, containing
treatments of aesthetics as well as philosophy and theology. De Wette's is also a moving
love story of Theodore's relationship first with Therese, and second with Hildegard, who
converts from Roman Catholicism to become Theodore's wife.
[31] Tholuck, *Die Lehre von der Sünde*, pp. 232–38 (not included in the English translation).
[32] ibid., p. 38: das dritte Capitel der Genesis und das siebente des Römerbriefes, das sind die
Zween Pfeiler, auf denen des lebendigen Christenthums Gebaüde ruht . . .'.
[33] The standard biography is Johannes Bachmann *Ernst Wilhelm Hengstenberg. Sein Leben
und Wirken*. Gütersloh 1–2, 1876–80; 3, completed by T. Schmalenbach, 1892. See also
Lenz, vol. 2, 1, pp. 387ff and Elliger, *passim*.
[34] Bachmann, 1, pp. 77–8.
[35] ibid., p. 97; 'theologica Veteris Testamenti interpretatio nihili est.'
[36] For the Basel period, see Bachmann, pp. 124–72.

with the Basel mission, his study of the Augsburg Confession and of the writings of Luther, and another book written in opposition to de Wette's novel *Theodore*. This latter was Henrich Steffens's *Concerning False Theology and True Belief* (1823).[37] Steffens was not a theologian, but he was a prominent layman, who became professor of Natural Philosophy, Anthropology and Religious Philosophy in Berlin in 1832. He was later a prominent member of the continuing Lutheran Church that did not join the Union in 1820.[38] Steffens, in the book studied by Hengstenberg, wrote profoundly about the mystery of human sinfulness, and presented the case for the Bible as a revelation of the cause and remedy of sinfulness, a revelation inaccessible to human reason. Steffens argued that Luther would never have been party to the use of the notion of freedom in scholarship to the point where Christian faith itself could come under attack.[39] He saw the role of the scholar as a dedication to use all resources of scholarship for the purpose of confirming the Christian faith.[40] Hengstenberg read Steffens's book immediately after reading de Wette's *Theodore*, and commented that more notice needed to be taken of Steffens's point that the Bible should be read in the light of the confessions of the Church, so long as the spirit of inquiry was not thereby stifled.[41] Hengstenberg returned to Berlin in 1825 with his mind made up about his future use of scholarship. He visited Neander and Tholuck in Berlin, and as one of the theses in defence of his licentiate examination in 1825 declared: 'the Messianic idea in the Old Testament is no human invention, but truly from God. This idea is one and the same in all prophets and all times, although occasionally obscured by human weakness.[42] In an address to the Prussian Bible Society in October 1825 he lectured, with copious references to Luther, on Luther's view of the necessity of the written word to control the inner experience and reason of Christians. He outlined Luther's view of the blindness of human understanding of the things of God even among Christians, and he criticized those who had taught that nothing in the divine revelation should be contrary to human reason. With Luther, Hengstenberg asserted that reason must be subservient to the obedience of faith.[43] In 1826, Hengstenberg became an *ausserordentlicher* Professor, and in 1828 he succeeded to de

[37] Henrich Steffens, *Von der falschen Theologie und dem wahren Glauben. Eine Stimme aus der Gemeinde*, Breslau 1823.
[38] See Cochlovius, *Bekenntnis und Einheit der Kirche*, pp. 43, 46.
[39] Steffens, op. cit., p. 233: 'Es wäre thöricht, wenn wir glaubten, dieses Dilemma sei unserm Luther entgangen. Er sah sehr deutlich ein, welche Gefahr dem Glauben durch die Freiheit der Untersuchung drohte . . .'
[40] ibid., p. 234; 'Ein Lehrer der Kirche ist derjenige, der die Leitung aller Forschung zur Bestätigung des Glaubens erkannt hat; dadurch ist er geweiht.
[41] Bachmann, p. 160.
[42] ibid., pp. 228ff. See also Lenz, 2. 1, p. 333.
[43] The address is reprinted in Bachmann, 1, pp. 334–54.

Wette's chair, which had remained unfilled since 1819. He died in Berlin in 1869.

The aim of this chapter so far has been to indicate the exact nature of the Confessional opposition to critical scholarship. This opposition was based upon deeply-held convictions about human sinfulness and the doctrine of Justification. It regarded the Augsburg Confession as the statement of faith that enabled the Bible to be interpreted in a Christian manner. It placed limitations upon the unrestricted use of scholarship for the reason that human understanding was blind to the things of God, and that scholarship could not be allowed to undermine traditional Christian belief. That those convictions of Confessional orthodoxy did not necessarily entail Hengstenberg's interpretation of the Bible and no other, will be appreciated when Delitzsch and von Hofmann are discussed in a later chapter. Hengstenberg and his closest followers maintained traditional views of the authorship and authenticity of Old Testament writings. Moses was the author of the Pentateuch, and Isaiah of all 66 chapters of his book. Chronicles was historically authentic in its portrayal of Levitical religion, Zechariah was a unity. All these positions were defended with great learning.

Although his followers considered Hengstenberg's *Christology of the Old Testament* to be his masterpiece, he is perhaps to be seen at his most effective in his *Contributions to Introduction to the Old Testament* (1831–9).[44] The similarity of the title of this three-volume work to the title of de Wette's masterpiece was not accidental, and indeed, de Wette is often placed in the front line of Hengstenberg's attack upon critical views of the Pentateuch.

In the second and third volumes of his *Dissertations on the Genuineness of the Pentateuch*, Hengstenberg showed what a formidable advocate he could be. He did not eschew polemical statements such as the pronouncement:

> Such a work as the Pentateuch can be maintained as genuine, only as long as it is expounded as a sacred book. An inability to penetrate its depths—the exposition of it as a profane author—the diluting of its meaning, contain (in the germ) the denial of its genuineness.[45]

But having made his Confessional point, Hengstenberg moved squarely onto historical and literary ground. His first task was to consider the central question of the Samaritan Pentateuch, which figured in all discussions of the date of the Pentateuch.[46] Hengstenberg argued that the Samaritans had nothing to do with the ten tribes of the northern Kingdom. They were a heathen group transported to the area of the northern Kingdom in the

---

[44] E. W. Hengstenberg, *Beiträge zur Einleitung ins Alte Testament*, 3 vols. Berlin 1831–9. ET of vols. 2–3 by J. E. Ryland, *Dissertations on the Genuineness of the Pentateuch*, 2 vols, Edinburgh 1847.

[45] *Dissertations*, 1, p. 2; German, 2 (1836), p. ii.

[46] ibid., pp. 69–106; German, pp. 1–48.

eighth century. Consequently, the existence of the Samaritan Pentateuch in the Samaritan community did not entitle scholars to reason back to the possession of the Pentateuch by the ten tribes prior to their eighth century exile. The differences between the communities ruled out the possibility that the Samaritans had inherited the Pentateuch from the northern tribes. But this surprising conclusion prepared the way for a new line of attack upon critical views of the Pentateuch.

Vater, and to a greater extent, de Wette and Vatke, had employed the argument from silence, according to which there was little evidence in the books outside the Pentateuch of the existence of the books of Moses before the divided monarchy. Hengstenberg, on the other hand, regarded the argument from the Samaritan Pentateuch as of little moment because he believed that he could prove conclusively from Hosea, Amos, Kings and Judges the existence of the Pentateuch from before the monarchy.[47] Of course, his arguments assumed that Kings and Judges were reliable witnesses to the periods which they described; granted this assumption, Hengstenberg had no difficulty in adducing many allusions to the Pentateuch from the time of Hosea and Amos backwards in time. His treatment of Jeroboam's revolt, for example, argued that Jeroboam had deliberately modelled himself upon the revolt of Aaron against Moses as known from Exodus 32.[48]

The *Contributions* also contained a lengthy treatment of the divine names Yahweh and Elohim, whose aim was to show that Yahweh was as ancient a name as Elohim. The famous passage in Exodus 6.2, according to which the Patriarchs did not know the deity under the name Yahweh, in fact has nothing to do with the names used for God. 'Yahweh' denoted a profound aspect of the character of God, and it was this 'character' that was unknown to the Patriarchs.[49] Hengstenberg thus invoked theological meanings of the names Yahweh and Elohim in order to argue that those names could not be used in source division.

In dealing with many alleged contradictions and anachronisms in the Pentateuch, Hengstenberg argued in ways that seem from a modern standpoint to be much more like special pleading. The famous contradictions between the passover regulations in Exodus 12 and Deuteronomy 16, where

---

[47] ibid., p. 166: 'in every chapter of the prophets there are references to the Pentateuch which . . . critics have entirely overlooked; and they are so significant, so strongly affect the essential meaning, that he who does not perceive them, can never fully comprehend *that*'; German, pp. 122–3.

[48] ibid., p. 212: 'The expedients which Jeroboam employed in order to bring his innovations into agreement with the Pentateuch, and to set aside the prerogatives of Judah, were so violent, that the choice of these desperate measures is only conceivable by admitting that the conviction was general among the people, that the Pentateuch, as a complete whole, had Moses for its author, and was the common property of the whole nation'; German, pp. 179–80.

[49] ibid., pp. 278ff; German, pp. 248ff.

the Exodus passage implies that the passover lamb is to be sacrificed wherever one is, while Deuteronomy requires that it is to be sacrificed at the single sanctuary, was dealt with by means of the assertion that Deuteronomy was not speaking of the passover lamb at all, but of other sacrifices to be offered at passover time.[50] The mention of the town of Dan in Genesis 14.14 and Deuteronomy 34.1 before the capture of Laish and its renaming as Dan in the period of the Judges (Judges 18.29) was explained from 2 Samuel 24.6. Here, there is a reference to Dan-jaan—evidence for Hengstenberg that there was another town of Dan before and after the Danites captured and renamed Laish.[51] The most powerful part of Hengstenberg's position was that which argued for knowledge of the Pentateuch in books such as Hosea, Amos, Kings and Judges. However, even this advocacy could not show that it was to the Pentateuch *in its extant form* that allusion was made.

The influence of Hengstenberg can be divided into three phases. The first began in 1830, when Hengstenberg became editor of the *Evangelische Kirchenzeitung*, a journal dedicated to fighting Rationalism in all its forms. Hengstenberg was a tireless contributor and reviewer, as well as editor. In 1842, his influence was such that Delitzsch was in correspondence with him about the possibility of an academic post, and on the death of Gesenius in the same year, the minister responsible for appointing a successor sought from Hengstenberg an expert opinion on Hupfeld, the eventually successful candidate.[52] With the appointment of Karl Otto von Raumer as Prussian Minister of Culture in 1850, Hengstenberg's influence in the appointment to theological chairs reached its highest point.[53] Among scholars who either fully shared Hengstenberg's convictions, or who were sympathetic to them, the following can be named: C. F. Keil (Dorpat 1833–58, Leipzig 1859–88), H. A. C. Hävernick (Königsberg 1841–5), Michael Baumgarten (Rostock 1850–8), Franz Delitzsch (Rostock 1846–50, Erlangen 1850–67, Leipzig 1867–90), J. C. K. von Hofmann (Rostock 1842–5, Erlangen 1845–77), G. F. Oehler (Breslau 1845–52, Tübingen 1852–72), F. W. Schulz (Breslau 1864–88), A. F. Kleinert (Dorpat 1829–34), J. Bachmann (Rostock 1858–88). This list could be extended by reference to 'Hengstenberg scholars', who were not Old Testament specialists; further, scholars such as Delitzsch and von Hofmann produced their own students, some of whom were sympathetic to the Confessional approach.

If the Confessional orthodox scholars worked positively, from their point

---

[50] ibid., 2, pp. 309–310; German, vol. 3 (1839), pp. 377–8.
[51] ibid., pp. 157–8; German, pp. 192–4.
[52] See Siegfried Wagner, *Franz Delitzsch, Leben und Werk*, Beiträge zur evangelischen Theologie 80, Munich 1978, pp. 66ff. Wagner mentions that Tholuck opposed the appointment of Delitzsch to succeed Gesenius.
[53] See Lenz, 2. 2, pp. 279–80.

of view, in that they advanced conservative critical positions through their teaching and publications, they also worked negatively by hindering the advancement of critical scholars. Hengstenberg succeeded in preventing Vatke from ever becoming a full professor in Berlin, and we have seen that George made no progress in university life until he switched finally to Philosophy. Lenz bitingly summarized the Hengstenberg era as follows:

> ... it was the time in which Hengstenberg and his disciples sought for scientific honour by treating as historical facts the story of Balaam's ass, and Joshua's command to the sun to stand still over Gibeon; the time in which the courage to prove the authenticity of the Pentateuch or of the fourth Gospel opened firm expectations of a chair, which thing was permanently denied to Vatke.[54]

That this is far too harsh a judgement will be indicated when Delitzsch and von Hofmann are discussed; for these were Confessional orthodox theologians who were much more open to the spirit of their age than was Hengstenberg. Perhaps a more powerful criticism of the Hengstenberg era is that by being so overtly theologically dogmatic, it ensured by way of reaction that the critical method became increasingly secular, concerned not with Old Testament religion as a factor in contemporary faith, but concerned with it more as a monument of past history. Some of the things said, unfairly, about the 'Rationalists' by the Confessional orthodox came true, after the day of Confessional orthodoxy was over.

[54] ibid., p. 379.

6

Heinrich Ewald

The scholarly path marked out by de Wette and furthered by George and Vatke was opposed not only by the Confessional orthodoxy of Hengstenberg and his sympathizers; it was opposed by one of the greatest critical Old Testament scholars of all time, Heinrich Ewald.[1] In a memoir of Ewald, his pupil Wellhausen described him as the principal brake upon the progress made along the scholarly road by de Wette and Vatke.[2] Ewald's authority and influence prevented what Wellhausen regarded as the correct insight into the development of Israelite history from receiving much earlier recognition. No doubt from Wellhausen's standpoint, this was true. Whether this judgement was fair to Ewald is another matter.

The character sketch of his former teacher given by Wellhausen contains no surprises to those familiar with Ewald's prodigious scholarly output. Without Wellhausen's testimony it would still be easy to guess that in his lectures, Ewald blurred the line between what was plausible and what was certain, that he scarcely referred to the opinions of other scholars, that he tended to present only the results of his own research, and that he found it difficult to regard those who held opposing scholarly views as anything other than personal enemies.[3] Ewald was clearly an opinionated man, as

[1] The only book devoted solely to Ewald is by T. Witton Davies, *Heinrich Ewald, Orientalist and Theologian*, 1903. However, it is anecdotal rather than a serious study. The same is true of the treatment in Cheyne, *Founders of Old Testament Criticism*, pp. 66–118. For Diestel's treatment of Ewald see his index; it consists mostly of brief references; see especially p. 589. Kraus devotes two chapters to Ewald, pp. 199–208, but does not expound his system in any detail. For a treatment of Ewald's understanding of saga and myth see my *Myth in Old Testament Interpretation*, pp. 27–31.

[2] J. Wellhausen, 'Heinrich Ewald' reprinted in *Grundrisse zum Alten Testament*, ed. R. Smend, Munich 1965, pp. 120–38. See pp. 131–2: '... ich kann doch nicht anerkennen, dass Ewald auch auf diesem Gebiete [the reconstruction of the religion of Israel] die Bahn gebrochen und den Weg gewiesen habe. Das haben vielmehr de Wette und Vatke getan; er ist im Gegenteil der grosse Aufhalter gewesen, der durch seinen autoritativen Einfluss bewirkt hat, dass die bereits vor ihm gewonnene richtige Einsicht in den Gang der israelitischen Geschichte lange Zeit nicht hat durchdringen können.'

[3] Wellhausen, op cit., p. 120: 'In die wissenschaftliche Arbeit führte er den Hörer nicht ein; er liess ihn nicht mit suchen und finden, sondern offenbarte seine Resultate ohne weitere Begründung. In der biblischen Einleitung verlor er über die Vorarbeit seiner kritischen Analyse keine Worte, sondern setzte sie einfach als gelungen und sicher voraus'; p. 138: 'Wenn er nicht liebenswürdig und nicht leicht zu behandeln war, weil er Person und Sache gar zu leicht identifizierte, so war er doch ein Mann aus Einem Guss und von ungewöhnlicher Art.'

well as being an outstanding linguist and historian, and a man of principle prepared to suffer for his political convictions. Yet Ewald's eccentricities should not obscure the fact that he was very much a man of his times, and that his contribution to Old Testament criticism was not obscurantist. Ewald may not have been the direct forerunner of Wellhausen; on the other hand, he could be described as a clear anticipator of the work of the twentieth-century German scholars, Albrecht Alt and Martin Noth.

Ewald was born in 1803 in Göttingen, studied there, and apart from an exile of some eleven years spent in Tübingen, taught there for most of his working life. When Göttingen became Prussian in 1867, Ewald refused to take a new oath of loyalty, and he was removed from the university in 1867–8. He died in 1875. The exile from Göttingen to Tübingen was occasioned by Ewald's resistance, as a member of the famous 'Göttingen Seven', to the action of Ernst August in suspending the constitution of Hanover in 1837.[4] His principal teacher in Göttingen was Eichhorn, and in fact Ewald was cast somewhat in Eichhorn's mould. Eichhorn had been a critical scholar who nonetheless defended some traditional positions, such as the Mosaic authorship of the Pentateuch.[5] The results of Ewald's scholarship, though radical in comparison with Eichhorn's results, were nevertheless very much closer to the traditional reading of Old Testament history than were the reconstructions of de Wette, Gramberg, George and Vatke. As we shall see, Ewald was able to find pieces of authentic history in the patriarchal narratives, and was more positive about the Mosaic period and its aftermath than de Wette and the others could be.

In this more positive approach to the handling of the Old Testament material, Ewald was not only following his teachers. He was in tune with ancient history as it was developing at that time in Germany. In 1811–12, B. G. Niebuhr's History of Rome was published, in which it was demonstrated how classical legends and other literature could furnish a solid basis of history.[6] Further, a Göttingen colleague of Ewald's, Karl Otfried Müller published in 1825 his Prolegomena to a Scientific Mythology, in which the Greek myths were treated as containing information about earliest Greek history.[7] It was not, therefore, Ewald's individualism or eccentricity that led him to turn his back upon the scholarship of de Wette and the others. He

[4] See Gotz von Selle, Die Georg-August-Universität zu Göttingen 1737–1937, Göttingen 1937, pp. 273ff. Von Selle refers to Hans Kück, Die 'Göttinger Sieben', ihre Protestation und ihre Entlassung im Jahre 1837, Diss. Göttingen 1935.
[5] This viewpoint Eichhorn modified in the 4th edition of his Einleitung (1823–4).
[6] B. G. Niebuhr, Römische Geschichte, 1–2, Berlin 1811–12.
[7] K. O. Müller, Prolegomena zu einer wissenschaftlichen Mythologie, Göttingen 1825, repr. Darmstadt 1970. On this work see Rudolf Pfeiffer, History of Classical Scholarship 1300–1850, Oxford 1976, pp. 186–7. Ewald, Geschichte des Volkes Israel, 1, 'Göttingen 1843, pp. ix–x refers to Niebuhr, and 'an meinen unvergesslichen Göttinger Collegen K. O. Müller'.

firmly believed that he was using an objective historical method, and in the case of de Wette and Vatke, he could justifiably argue that these scholars allowed their philosophical theories of the nature of religion to dictate what *must* have been the course of Old Testament history. Not that Ewald was without his own, perhaps unconscious, assumptions about history and religion. He clearly believed, like Niebuhr, that history objectively reconstructed would show evidence of divine direction and oversight, and would confirm belief in God.[8]

The present chapter will be primarily concerned with Ewald's *History of Israel* which began to appear in 1843, and which was the first great critical work of this type to be written. However, it should be pointed out that Ewald did much preparatory research prior to beginning the monumental *History*. He published large works on the prophets and on the poets of the Old Testament.[9] He published in the fields of Hebrew and Arabic grammar, and he made a study of Arabic historical traditions and of Sanskrit literature, to which frequent reference was made in the *History*.[10] His work was characterized by exhaustive knowledge of every conceivable scrap of information that might illumine the point that concerned him at any given moment, and in the light of this great erudition he stated forthrightly the facts as they appeared to him, and as he believed them actually to have been.

This tremendous self-confidence is seen nowhere better than in the introduction to the first volume of the *History*, where he described the history of the literature of the Old Testament, as the necessary prelude to the reconstruction of the events. Ewald presented a complicated theory of literary composition, which envisaged a whole series of rewritings of large complexes of material until they reached their extant form. This theory will now be presented in some detail.

Ewald divided the historical traditions (the traditions that he used for the basis of his reconstruction) into three great works, each succeeding work later than its immediate predecessors. The earliest was the 'Great Book of

---

[8] Cf. Ewald, *History of Israel*, 1, London 1876, p. 5, German, 1, p. 9: 'The history of this ancient people is in reality the history of the growth of true religion, rising through all stages to perfection ... finally revealing itself in full glory and power, in order to spread irresistably from this centre, never again to be lost, but to become the eternal possession and blessing of all nations.' p. 7 (German, pp. 11–12): '... little cause has it to dread the strictest investigation of all its parts; since the profoundest examination ... will enable us to discern with greater and greater distinctness and certainty its actual course from beginning to end.'

[9] *Die Dichter des Alten Bundes*, Göttingen 1835–9, 1866–72; 2 *Die Propheten des Alten Bundes*, Göttingen 1840–1, 1867–8. ET, J. Frederick Smith, *The Prophets of the Old Testament*, London 1875–81.

[10] On these works, see Wellhausen, op. cit., pp. 122–3. See also the important essay by Ewald on ancient Hebrew festivals, 'De feriarum hebraeorum origine ac ratione' in *Zeitschrift für die Kunde des Morgenlandes*, 1839, pp. 410ff, and the discussion on this in the *GGA*, 1835, pp. 2025–37.

origins' comprising the Pentateuch and Joshua, then came the 'Great Book of Kings' comprising Judges, Ruth, Samuel and Kings, and finally there was the 'Great Book of universal history to Greek times' comprising Chronicles, Ezra and Nehemiah.

According to Ewald, the following was the course of the emergence of the extant Pentateuch and book of Joshua.[11] First, many ancient fragments were to be identified, such as Joshua 17.14–18, which was Joshua's speech to the tribes of Ephraim and Manasseh, whose stammering prose and hard, rough style indicated that it was written down soon after Joshua's death. Second, the 'Book of the Wars of Yahweh' (for the name see Num. 21.14) was a collection of fragments such as Numbers 21.14, 20, Exodus 15.1–18 (the 'Song of Moses'), probably also including Joshua 17.14–18 and a list of desert stations visited by the Israelites during their wilderness wanderings. Third, there was a biography of Moses, of which only Exodus 4.18 and Exodus 18 could be identified with confidence. Fourthly, there was a Book of Covenants containing Genesis 21.22–32; 26.28–31; 31.44–54 (covenants between Jacob and Laban, Isaac and Abimelech, Abraham and Abimelech), Genesis 49 (the 'Blessing of Jacob') and Exodus 24 (the covenant between Israel and God). The author, Ewald's 'First Narrator', wrote in the second part of the period of the Judges, and was responsible for uniting the patriarchal traditions known to him with the Mosaic biography. He also inserted into his work the Decalogue of Exodus 20.1–17 and made use of some of the other fragments mentioned earlier. Fifth, there was the 'Book of the Upright' (see Josh. 10.13; 2 Sam. 1.18) written in the time of Solomon.

Ewald next described the composition of a book which clearly had much in common with what later scholarship designated as the Priestly Code. It was entitled the 'Book of Origins' because of the recurrent phrase 'these are the generations . . .'. Its author was probably a Levite, and the book had a special concern for priestly legislation. It was written in the first third of Solomon's reign by Ewald's 'Second Narrator'.

It began with the creation story of Genesis 1.1—2.4 (a 'clear specimen' of its distinctive style), passing to the Flood, the expansion of the peoples and their scattering at the destruction of the Tower of Babel (Gen. 10–11) and then on to traditions about Abraham and the other Patriarchs, and Moses. Its description of the desert Tabernacle in Exodus 35—40 indicated that the Sanctuary of Solomon's Temple had been modelled on the Tabernacle. Legislation about priests and offerings found in Leviticus 1; 20; 23; 25.1—26.2, 46 and in parts of Numbers were also included. The author also made use of an earlier law-book, now found in Exodus 20.23—23.19.

A writer designated by Ewald as the 'Third Narrator' collected and wove

---

[11] *History of Israel*, 1, pp. 63–132; *Geschichte des Volkes Israel*, 1, pp. 73–164.

together traditions such as Genesis 10.25; 20.29–31, much of the Joseph narratives (Gen. 37, 39–47), Exodus 1.15—2.22; Numbers 11; 12.6–8 and Genesis 14 (a fragment possibly Canaanitish in origin). The 'Third Narrator' also made much use of the compilation of the earliest fragments of the 'First Narrator'. He was an inhabitant of the Northern Kingdom of Israel in the tenth or ninth centuries, and was especially interested in the workings of divine providence (as evident in the Joseph narratives), and in the prophetic movements. His work was to Israel what the 'Book of Origins' was to Judah.

The 'Fourth Narrator' wrote at the time of the great prophets of the ninth and eighth centuries. In his day, a messianic expectation had developed, and the writer was conscious of the graciousness of Yahweh and of the sinfulness of mankind. Thus he was responsible for the account of the origin of evil (Gen. 3), as well as the story of Israelite apostasy in the wilderness (Exod. 32–4), and the story of Sodom and Gomorrah (Gen. 18.1—19.28). He also had a sense of the promises to the Patriarchs being extended to all the nations, as in Genesis 12.1–3. He was not frightened to transfer ideas from his own age back to the earliest times, and thus it is to him that the worship of Yahweh by the Patriarchs must be ascribed.

The 'Fifth Narrator' worked up the first four books of the Pentateuch and Joshua to something like their present form, although he was not the last editor. He based his work upon the 'Book of Origins' and upon its chronological framework, and he was responsible for transposing some fragments of the material relating to sacrifices and ritual from their original position in the 'Book of Origins' to their positions as we now have them in Leviticus. He added the name 'Elohim' (God) to the name Yahweh in Genesis 2—3 and in his presentation of the Patriarchal and Mosaic history, he delayed the introduction of the name Yahweh until what is now Exodus 3.15. His specific contributions concern the relation of Israel and Judah to surrounding peoples, such as the Canaanites, Syria, Moab and Ammon, and thus he contributed Genesis 9.18–27; 15; 19.31–8; 27; Numbers 22—4. In handling his sources, he apparently omitted some of the material available to him.

The next contributor to the 'Great Book of Origins' was the writer of Deuteronomy, who probably was active in the second half of the reign of Manasseh in the seventh century, and who probably wrote in *Egypt*. The Deuteronomist sought to commend the old law in a manner to suit his times. He treated the material that already existed with a freedom that is not in evidence in earlier times, and sought to present to the people a new covenant declared by Moses (Deut. 27–30) in accordance with which Joshua acted. Joshua, indeed is his second hero, and many passages in Joshua were put in their extant form by the Deuteronomist. The book, deeply influenced by the prophetic activity which preceded the seventh century, was the basis of Josiah's reformation, and it was to the Old Testament what the Fourth Gospel was to the New Testament.

Deuteronomy existed in the first instances as an independent unit. Its combination with the literary work produced by the 'Fifth Narrator' was the work of the last editor or compiler of the Pentateuch and Joshua. This editor worked before the end of the seventh century, or at the latest before the Fall of Jerusalem (586 BC, according to Ewald). That he added material is shown by the insertion of the 'Blessing of Moses' (Deut. 33) into Deuteronomy. However, before the Fall of Jerusalem, according to the highly complex theory presented by Ewald, the Pentateuch and Joshua had reached their present form.

To describe Ewald's reconstruction of the literary history of the 'Great Book of Kings' and the 'Great Universal History' in the same detail as the literary history of the 'Great Book of Origins' has been presented would overburden the present text with technicalities. Thus, only salient points will be made in dealing with these other historical compilations.[12]

The raw ingredients of the 'Great Book of Kings' were, first, annals or State archives, which were kept from the time of David, and utilized in the books of Chronicles as well as in Samuel and Kings; second, a book of wars, including Judges 17—18; 19—21 as well as accounts of the exploits of Saul (1 Sam. 13—14) and David; third, a prophetic history (probably by a Levite) which covered roughly the extant books of Samuel and the beginning of 1 Kings; fourth, a book covering the same period as the third work, but preceded by an account of the period of the Judges. In the process of the gathering of these elements into the whole which is now Judges, Samuel and Kings, Ewald envisaged that some of the works had suffered the omission of material. For example, much had been omitted from between 1 Samuel 23—30, while chapters such as 24 and 26 had been inserted. Again, in the second part of 1 Samuel, a compiler had used only the salient parts of the story of relations between Saul, David and Jonathan, with a resultant unevenness.

The 'Great Book of Kings' reached its final form as a result of two Deuteronomic redactions, one soon after the reformation of Josiah and the other after the exiled Jehoiachin had been taken into favour in the Babylonian Court by Nebuchadnezzar's successors (2 Kings 25.27–30). The first Deuteronomic editor made great use of the prophetic history of the Kings, covering roughly 1 Samuel 1 to 1 Kings 2. He contributed his own material, with its distinctive Hebrew style, and his retention or omission of material was determined by his aim to present the period from the beginning of the time of the Judges to the time of Josiah in a way which expressed the

---

[12] For the 'Great Book of the Kings', see *History*, 1, pp. 133–68; German, 1, pp. 164–215. For the 'Great Book of Universal History' see *History*, 1, pp. 169–203; German, pp. 215–56.

Deuteronomistic ideas. The main work of the second Deuteronomic editor consisted of working the histories of the period of the Judges into their present form, of adding 2 Sam. 21—4, and of contributing the chapters 1 Kings 3 to 2 Kings 25 in their present form.

The 'Great Universal History'—Chronicles, Ezra and Nehemiah—was compiled about 323 BC by a Levite. So far as Chronicles is concerned, he utilized the canonical books of Samuel and Kings, the state annals, and a larger and later work on the period of the Kings which was not admitted to the canon. His aim was to write a universal history focused upon Jerusalem, tracing the Jerusalem of the post-exilic age back to the ancient Jerusalem, and setting the whole within a cosmic perspective stretching back to Adam. The Samaritan presence in the north constituted a people, 'of whose affinity with themselves the lords in Jerusalem would know nothing', and of whose existence the Chronicler recognized nothing. Whereas in the 'Great Book of Kings' the history of Israel was treated from a prophetic point of view, mentioning little about priesthood and worship, Chronicles treated the history from a priestly point of view, and could be described as a 'History of Priesthood'. With this remark, the brief presentation of Ewald's view of the origin and growth of the Old Testament historical traditions can end.

As one reviews Ewald's position, it is impossible not to admire the boldness of his scheme, and its attention to the smallest details. If its piling of hypothesis upon hypothesis, its multiplication of entities, its unverifiable assumptions of transpositions and losses of material, work upon us to the point that it comes as little surprise that few, if any, of Ewald's students wished to take his method any further, we must also acknowledge that it is only a little more complex than what we find, say, in Niebuhr's *History of Rome*. Judged in the light of the critical views of de Wette and his followers, Ewald's critical results yielded a more traditional view of the history of Israelite religion. Moses and his times were far more substantial in Ewald's reconstruction than in the reconstructions of the earlier critics. Large parts of the Pentateuch were, according to Ewald, in existence early in the monarchy, including parts of Leviticus. The books of Chronicles were not used as a foil to the books of Samuel and Kings so that anything that displayed developed priestly religion could be assigned a late date. Although Ewald dated Chronicles in the late fourth century, and acknowledged that the canonical books of Samuel and Kings had been used as a source, he did not reject as post-exilic fantasy the descriptions of Israel's religion in the early monarchy in priestly and Levitical terms. His account of the history of priesthood and sacrifice will be described shortly, as will be his interpretation of the Patriarchal narratives.

Judged in the light of modern critical views, Ewald's work seems to have lasted better than seemed likely at the time of Wellhausen. If it is fair to say that Martin Noth's view of the Deuteronomist as compiler is, with certain modifications, still the prevailing modern view, it is not very far removed from Ewald's treatment of the two Deuteronomists as compilers. Further, over-complex as was his work on the Pentateuch, he nevertheless observed many factors of which subsequent scholarship took cognizance, such as the Deuteronomic character of much of Joshua. Even after the new documentary hypotheses of the second part of the nineteenth century had triumphed over rival theories, it was still necessary for scholarship to begin to search for the fragments of which the sources were composed, and to theorize about their tradition history, even if no one was prepared to adopt the highly sophisticated composition criticism advanced by Ewald. In some respects, then, Ewald was far ahead of his day, for all that his achievements do not necessarily look so idiosyncratic in the light of what was going on in the classical scholarship of his time.

As a companion to the opening volumes of his *History of Israel*, Ewald published a volume entitled *The Antiquities of Israel* in 1848. This contained his account of the history of priesthood and sacrifice, together with other practices and ceremonies.[13]

There was no doubt in Ewald's mind that, in their extant form, the narratives about Abraham, Isaac and Jacob presented these heroes as 'types', expressing and embodying ancient Hebrew hopes and ideals.[14] Abraham, Isaac and Jacob could be compared with Agamemnon, Achilles and Ulysses, as well as with other classical and Indian heroes. Abraham was the type of the founding father, Sarah the type of the wife and Hagar the type of the concubine. Isaac was the type of the child, while his betrothal and marriage to Rebekkah were types of those institutions. There were also 'counter-types' in the characters of Lot (counter to Abraham), Ishmael (counter to Isaac) and Esau (counter to Jacob). These traditions of the ancient Hebrews, with home and domestic circles as their setting in life, had become fixed in the last few centuries before Moses.

By use of historical research, it was possible to reconstruct the following historical outline from these narratives which, in themselves, had little to say about the Patriarchs that was really historical. It was clear that the Hebrews had migrated to Canaan from the north-east.[15] The migration of Abraham was probably part of a larger migration which included the future peoples of Ammon and Moab, represented by Abraham's nephew Lot. Abraham himself probably dwelt in the south of Canaan, as indicated by the tradition linking him with Hebron.[16] In Genesis 14, Abraham emerged momentarily into the light of history, as the warrior fighting the kings of

---

[13] *Die Alterthümer des Volkes Israel*, Göttingen 1848; ET, H. S. Solly, *The Antiquities of Israel*, London 1876.
[14] See *History*, 1, pp. 290ff; German, pp. 341ff.
[15] ibid., pp. 277ff; German, pp. 327ff.
[16] ibid., pp. 305–6; German, pp. 360ff.

the cities of the plain (now covered by the waters of the Dead Sea south of the tongue—*el-lisān*).[17]

The figure of Isaac was a good deal fainter than that of Abraham; indeed the events of his life seemed to be copies of what had happened to Abraham.[18] On the other hand, it was likely that the threefold occurrence of the story of danger to a Patriarch's wife (twice in the case of Abraham, once in the case of Isaac) should be traced back to an incident in the life of Isaac.[19] Isaac seems to have inhabited the extreme south of Canaan.[20]

The religion of the Hebrews at this period was probably already monotheistic, the plural word Elohim (gods) having already lost its polytheistic implications. The Patriarchs erected simple altars and worshipped God under the name of El Shaddai.[21]

The Jacob narratives indicated the arrival from the north-east of a new wave of Hebrew migrants. These became fused with the Hebrew elements already in Canaan, thus giving rise to the description of Jacob as the son of Isaac and the brother of Esau. The later Edomite people, represented by Esau, was already present before the arrival of the Jacob elements. In order to present a picture of the essential unity of the Hebrews, Hebrew tradition described Jacob as being born in Canaan, as departing to the north-east to escape from Esau's anger, and as returning to Canaan from the north-east. The historical fact was that Jacob migrated from the north-east to Canaan, settling in the centre of the country. After the fusion between the Jacob-led Hebrews and the older Hebrew elements in Canaan, the new name Israel was used to designate the people.[22]

The new community was divided into twelve branches, and incorporated Canaanite as well as Hebrew peoples.[23] Its religion was still predominantly monotheistic, although there was an admixture of less pure elements brought from the north-east. In course of time, probably because of the rivalry and jealousy of the other branches of the community, the Joseph family (the later Ephraim and Manasseh) went to Egypt. Here, under the Hyksos, Joseph rose to prominence, and was later followed by the rest of the Hebrew community.[24]

The hostility that developed in due course between the Egyptians and the Hebrews was predictable, and it was the prophet Moses who led the Hebrews from Egypt towards the land Canaan. That Moses should have

[17] ibid., p. 301; German, p. 353.
[18] ibid., p. 340; German, pp. 386–8.
[19] ibid., p. 327, 1n; German, pp. 374, 388. In the first edition, Ewald holds that Gen. 26.1–33 is taken from *Abraham's* life story.
[20] ibid., p. 305; German, p. 359.
[21] ibid., p. 320; German, pp. 370ff.
[22] ibid., pp. 341–9; German, pp. 388–95.
[23] ibid., p. 381; German, pp. 421ff.
[24] ibid., pp. 404ff; German, pp. 444ff.

been brought up in the Egyptian court, that he fled to Midian after involvement in a killing, and that in Midian he became allied by marriage to the Kenite–Midianite nation were all likely facts of history.[25] However, Moses did not necessarily gain much from his Egyptian education. The memory of the Patriarchs and of their religion was still fresh in the time of Moses, and their religion was simple and sublime compared with the superstitions of Egypt. Moreover, during the absence of Moses in Midian, Aaron was working actively among the Hebrews in Egypt.[26]

On his return to Egypt, Moses sought permission to take his people from the country. The refusal of Pharaoh did not deter Moses, and the Israelites departed. The highly developed story of the plagues and the passover cannot have reached its extant form before the time of the great prophets.[27] After travelling initially to the north-east, Moses turned to the south in order to avoid hostile peoples. North of Suez, where the Red Sea gulf was narrow, and could be crossed at low tide, the Israelites negotiated the Red Sea. A pursuing Egyptian army was overwhelmed by a sudden inundation caused by an extraordinary flood tide.[28] The party now made for Sinai, where their numbers were swelled by loyal Kenites and Midianites. This explains how the whole company could muster 603, 550 fighting men.[29]

The religion which Moses mediated to his people in the wilderness was highly developed cultically, and was to be modified only slightly by later ages. Sacrifice had long been known to the Hebrews in all its varieties.[30] The religion of Moses led some forms to be rejected, and some forms to be modified. An ancient form of sacrifice from an altogether primitive age was retained in the form of the offering of the shewbread. Other ancient sacrifices retained were the cereal offering and the whole burnt offering.[31] The pre-Mosaic expiatory and guilt offerings developed in Yahwism to the point where expiatory offerings were usually public ceremonies, with the blood sprinkled or disposed of ostentatiously, while guilt offerings were private ceremonies preceded by appropriate reparation on the part of the worshipper.[32]

The religious calendar provided by Moses was an adaptation of the pre-Mosaic nature festivals, with their attention to the full moon on the

---

[25] *History*, 2, pp. 42–3; German, pp. 32a–b.

[26] ibid., pp. 36, 56; German, p. 27.

[27] ibid., p. 65; German, p. 50.

[28] ibid., p. 73. 1n; German p. 55, 1n.

[29] ibid., p. 46; German p. 32c. It is interesting to note Ewald's acceptance of a figure that had been such a feature of the criticism of Reimarus (see below p. 25). However, Ewald did not say that these men had taken part in the exodus.

[30] *Antiquities of Israel*, p. 25; German p. 24.

[31] ibid., pp. 27ff; German pp. 25ff.

[32] ibid., pp. 55–67; German pp. 58–72.

fourteenth and fifteenth days of the month.[33] The calendar envisaged that the year would begin at the spring festival of the full moon, and that this festival would be balanced six months later by the corresponding autumnal festival.[34] Each festival was preceded by an observance of penitence and expiation. For the spring, this was passover, originally observed on the 10th day of the month; for the autumn, it was the Day of Atonement. Each major festival ended with a celebration, but in the case of the spring festival, this was postponed until the feast of weeks to allow for bringing in the grain harvest.

The passover was a private and family observance of penitence; the Day of Atonement was a public ceremony. The name *Azazel* denoted a fiend or demon opposed to Yahweh. However, it was a mistake to equate Azazel with Satan.[35] As Israel later began to celebrate the great historical events of redemption, these celebrations were associated with the originally purely agricultural observances. Thus passover and the spring festival were associated with the Exodus and the autumn festival was associated with the wilderness wanderings. The most distinctive Mosaic bequest to the Israelites was the Sabbath, a sacrifice of time and work to Yahweh which was absolutely peculiar to Yahwism.

In order to carry out the sacrificial cult, Moses's own tribe of Levi assumed cultic functions, although only the descendants of Aaron and his brothers belonged to the higher priesthood.[36] There were, and continued to be, priests other than from the tribe of Levi; but the Levites gradually took over most of the priestly and cultic functions. The Levites not descended from Aaron or his brothers performed many tasks, and under David and Solomon provided the Temple choirs and musicians. The sacred objects of Mosaic religion included the ark of the covenant, the stone tables of the Decalogue, and the tabernacle of which the sanctuary of the Solomonic Temple would later be a copy.[37]

This, then, was the critical position that helped to stem the advance of the view of Israelite history initiated by de Wette, and developed by those who followed him. Its effectiveness lay in the fact that it was at one and the same time critical, traditional and theological. Ewald was able to dismiss the earlier critical view on critical grounds. At the same time, his account of the

[33] ibid., p. 349; German, pp. 354–5.

[34] ibid., pp. 354–64; German, pp. 360–73.

[35] ibid., p. 362; German p. 370. The prevailing critical view, based upon Gesenius, was that Azazel was to be equated with Satan and that since Satan was a late conception in Israelite religion, the Day of Atonement was introduced at a late stage. See above, p. 67.

[36] For the priesthood, see ibid., pp. 263ff; German, pp. 278ff.

[37] *History*, 2, p. 18; German, 2, pp.4–5. Again, Ewald's divergence from earlier (and later) scholarship is to be noted, according to which the descriptions of the tabernacle in the wilderness were back-projections of what the sanctuary of the Jerusalem temple was like. See above p. 66.

history of Israel in traditional terms, and his conviction that the history thus reconstructed disclosed the development of true religion, accorded with the Confessional approaches of Delitzsch and von Hofmann, as the next chapter will make clear. Further, for all those shocked by Strauss's *Life of Jesus* (1835), and to a lesser extent by Vatke's *Biblical Theology* of the same year, Ewald's outspoken criticism of the Hegelians put him close to, if not on the side of, the angels. As will be shown in a later chapter, the views championed by Ewald were successfully popularized in a less ultra-critical form by C. C. J. von Bunsen.

Yet for all his greatness, Ewald seems to have remained a lonely figure, and in his reviews of books, and in his articles in his *Jahrbücher der biblischen Wissenschaft* (1848–65), he constantly criticized the scholars of his day, young or old, dead or alive, critical or conservative.

His rivalry with Gesenius seems to have resulted from the fact that Ewald resented the accord given to Gesenius as the great Hebrew grammarian and lexicographer of the first half of the nineteenth century, for all that his own work was highly praised during his lifetime.[38] In Wellhausen's opinion, Ewald was unjust in his treatment of Gesenius.[39]

De Wette was similarly roughly handled by Ewald. True, on the occasion of his death, Ewald relented sufficiently to give de Wette credit for not following the exaggerations and falsehoods of the Hegelians;[40] but for long after his death, Ewald had many unkind things to say about de Wette. Typical are remarks such as, 'from my youth all I have learnt from him is how one should not proceed';[41] or 'De Wette possessed so little linguistic knowledge, and had so little idea how to handle the poetic and historical relations of the Psalms or how to recognize their true meaning and worth for religion, that it must have been a great joy to him to find in my work of 1835 such a great aid to a better all-round understanding of the Psalms.[42]

Other scholars to be treated harshly were Hupfeld, who had been unwise enough to write a highly critical review of Ewald's Hebrew grammar,[43]

---

[38] See Cheyne, pp. 82ff, and the generous account of Ewald's work in Diestel, pp. 567–9.

[39] Wellhausen, p. 126. In his own defence, perhaps acknowledging something of the force of the charges of unfairness, Ewald wrote, 'Niemand hat nachgewiesen oder wird nachweisen, dass ich Gesenius' oder de Wette'n ein Unrecht gethan . . .', *Jahrbücher der biblischen Wissenschaft* 7 (1854–5), p. 242. See also the *Vorrede* to *Geschichte des Volkes Israel*, 1, pp. xii ff. Gesenius had recently died when Ewald wrote the *Vorrede*, and Ewald devoted some space to a critical evaluation of Gesenius.

[40] *Jahrbücher* 2 (1849), p. 11 'Wirklich war ja de Wette keiner der gewöhnlichen Theologen: er hielt sich immer mit einem gewissen richtigen Gefühle fern von den Überspannungen und Faseleien der philosophischen Schulen . . .'

[41] *Jahrbücher* 4 (1851–2), p. 16.

[42] ibid. 8 (1856), p. 163.

[43] See Wellhausen, pp. 124–5. For a sharp attack on Hupfeld see *Jahrbücher* 7 (1854–5) pp. 245–8, in the course of which Hupfeld is described as 'ein kleinlicher bösartiger Kopf'.

Bleek, whose weaknesses were excused on the grounds that he had studied with Gesenius and de Wette in the days before biblical scholarship had developed,[44] and Hitzig, who was deemed to be no more scholarly than Hengstenberg.[45]

The conservatives, in both Germany and Britain received short shrift. Of Delitzsch's commentary on Genesis Ewald wrote, 'A more superficial, careless, empty and worthless writing on the first book of the Pentateuch than this could hardly be produced today by a doctor of theology and university teacher in Germany'.[46] Of a book by Hengstenberg he commented 'When one has read one of Hengstenberg's thick books, one has really read them all. Only two desires motivate him: the delusion that he honours Christ and the Bible better than most other contemporary scholars, and second, the obsession of crying out against "Rationalists"'.[47]

Such comments seem to have been the outbursts of a fundamentally insecure man, and it is no wonder that his later life was lonely. Yet, as expressed by Wellhausen, his pupils owed more to him than they realized:[48] and the same can be said of twentieth century Old Testament scholarship.

---

[44] *Jahrbücher* 11 (1860–1), pp. 148–9: 'muss man sich erinnern dass seine wissenschaftliche Ausbildung vor die Zeit fält in welcher Biblische Wissenschaft in unsern Tagen sich erst am freiesten und am höchsten entfaltete, und dass sie von Anfang an von de Wette und Gesenius zu abhängig war.'

[45] *Jahrbücher* 8 (1856), p. 169: 'die ganze Abhandlung zeigt am Ende bloss dass Hitzig nur nach einer andern Seite hin völlig ebenso unwissenschaftlich auswächst wie die Hengstenberge Delitzsch Hahne usw.'

[46] *Jahrbücher* 4 (1851–2), p. 36.

[47] ibid., 2 (1849).

[48] Wellhausen, p. 138.

7

Hofmann and Delitzsch:
Confessional Scholars with
a Difference

The varieties of standpoint within nineteenth-century German Old Testament scholarship are nowhere better demonstrated than in the cases of J. C. K. von Hofmann and Franz Delitzsch. The major work and influence of these scholars began in the 1840s and lasted to the 1880s. In the crucial period 1840–70, their work had the effect of providing further opposition to the progress of the critical method. Yet it would be wrong to suppose that they were simply followers of Hengstenberg and his school. Delitzsch probably stood a little closer to Hengstenberg than did Hofmann, whereas at a scholarly level Hengstenberg and Hofmann had little in common, and attacked each other in print.

Hofmann was by far the most adventurous thinker among the Confessional Lutherans of the mid-nineteenth century, and it may be for this reason that none of his writings were translated into English. Delitzsch, also, was an original and adventurous thinker, but he stayed much closer to Confessional orthodoxy than did Hofmann. In contrast to the latter, Delitzsch had the satisfaction of seeing many of his works translated into English, in which form they helped to consolidate conservative opposition to the critical method. The two men were colleagues in Erlangen from 1850 to 1867.

Johannes Christian Konrad von Hofmann was born in Nuremberg in 1810. He studied in Erlangen in 1827, and in Berlin from 1829 where he studied, among others, under the great historian Leopold von Ranke, and under Hegel, Schleiermacher and Hengstenberg.[1]

[1] The biography of Hofmann is by Paul Wapler, *Johannes v. Hofmann. Ein Beitrag zur Geschichte der theologischen Grundprobleme der kirchlichen und der politischen Bewegungen im 19. Jahrhundert*, Leipzig 1914. A valuable study, which places Hofmann in the context of theological thinking about the meaning of history is Gustav Weth, *Die Heilsgeschichte, Ihr universeller und ihr individueller Sinn in der offenbarungsgeschichtlichen Theologie des 19. Jahrhunderts*, FGLP 4, 2, Munich 1931. A useful exposition of Hofmann's system, despite its Barthian overtones, is by Eberhard Hübner, *Schrift und Theologie. Eine Untersuchung zur Theologie Joh. Chr. K. v. Hofmanns*, Munich 1956. Hofmann is also discussed, among other works, in F. Kattenbusch, *Die deutsche-evangelische Theologie seit Schleiermacher*, 1,

He was professor first at Rostock (1842–5), and then at Erlangen from 1845 until his death in 1877. Numerous attempts have been made to trace the influence of one or other of the great Berlin scholars upon Hofmann, not to mention the influence of Schelling and of Württemberg pietism.[2] However, Hofmann is probably easiest understood if one assumes no direct influences, but instead makes comparisons between his thought and that of those said to have influenced him. In such an exercise, already brilliantly executed by E.-W. Wendebourg in an article in 1955,[3] it becomes possible to see the many complex strands of Hofmann's position. Wendebourg compared Hofmann with Ranke, Hegel, Schelling and Schleiermacher. Initially, the present chapter will follow Wendebourg's exposition (omitting the comparison with Schleiermacher) with additional comments where necessary, before passing to a comparison of Hofmann with Hengstenberg, followed by a final summary. Delitzsch's relationship to Hofmann will be treated in the section on Delitzsch.

Hofmann's study of history under Ranke in Berlin made a sufficiently deep impression upon him to make him entertain thoughts about becoming a professional historian, and his earliest research and publication was in the historical field.[4] Wendebourg takes as a point of comparison between Ranke and Hofmann the four aspects of historical research and synthesis described by Ranke himself: (1) Exact knowledge of the individual events (Momente) of historical research; (2) the personal motives behind each; (3) the interaction of the events, the mechanism of the reciprocal influences of the leading personalities; (4) the universal context. These four aspects entailed an interrelationship between critical research based upon primary sources, and an attempt to understand events in a way that allowed not only for the contribution to historical events of individuals, but also for the necessities and inevitabilities that determined individual destinies and overruled individual desires, resulting in a texture of events in which 'progress' could

Giessen 1934[6], pp. 52ff; Christoph Senft, *Wahrhaftigkeit und Wahrheit. Die Theologie des 19. Jahrhunderts zwischen Orthodoxie und Aufklärung*, BHTh 22, Tübingen 1956, pp. 87–123; K. G. Steck, *Die Idee der Heilsgeschichte. Hofmann, Schlatter, Cullmann*, TS 56, 1959; H. Stephan and M. Schmidt, *Geschichte der deutschen evangelischen Theologie seit dem deutschen Idealismus*, Berlin 1960, pp. 183–8. On Hofmann's O.T. work see Diestel, *passim*, and Kraus, pp. 226–30.

[2] Senft, for example, tries to stress Hofmann's indebtedness to Hegel; thus: 'was Hofmann Inspiration nennt, der Hegelschen Selbstentfaltung der Idee im Grunde viel ähnlicher ist als dem, was die Orthodoxen darunter verstanden', op. cit., p. 96. Kattenbusch, op. cit., p. 53, sees indebtedness to Schelling; thus: 'Es ist die Idee Schellings von der Geschichte als einer Art von Dichtung Gottes zur Enthüllung selbst in einem Ablauf von sich steigernden Schöpfungen, die Hofmann auf den Inhalt und Charakter der Bibel anwendet.' Other examples could be given.

[3] Ernst-Wilhelm Wendebourg, 'Die heilsgeschichtliche Theologie J. Chr. K. von Hofmanns in ihrem Verhältnis zur romantischen Weltanschauung' in *ZThK* 52 (1955), pp. 64–104.

[4] For this section and its details, see Wendebourg, op. cit., pp. 66–75.

be seen, but not necessarily progress towards a particular goal. Ranke's approach was essentially empirical, and certainly not a Hegelian attempt to use history in order to demonstrate a philosophical thesis.

In Hofmann, we find a deep respect for empirical history, which in his biblical work, led him to favour the interpretation of prophetic books and prophecies in their historical setting. We also find the view that individuals are carried along by the tide of history, so that what they suppose to be their freedom is much curtailed. Above all, history is seen as something in which the part makes sense in terms of the whole.

In contrast to Ranke, Hofmann placed a limit upon what critical historical research could be allowed to do to the Bible. Such research was in order in the profane sphere, but not permissible when it came to the Bible. Philological and archaeological explanations were in order, but the historical facts presented in the Bible were unassailable, and needed to be expounded rather than examined. Thus Hofmann placed the Bible in a privileged position, while otherwise admitting the historical-critical method.[5] His other major difference from Ranke was that he believed that the purpose and centre of history was the coming of Christ. That was the great event to which not only biblical history moved; secular history surrounded and supported biblical history and derived its significance from the coming of Christ. In this viewpoint, Hofmann was further from Ranke's empirical approach to the 'meaning' of history and closer to Hegel's speculative approach.

The most striking similarity between Hegel and Hofmann (not necessarily the result of 'influence') was the conviction held by both that self-understanding on the part of the interpreter provided the clue to the meaning of history.[6] In Hegel's case, it was the Hegelian philosophy based

---

[5] Hofmann's main grounds for rejecting the historical-critical method were a priori. Christian self-consciousness mediated by new birth in Christ accorded fully with the history of salvation in the Bible. See Hofmann's *Weissagung und Erfüllung im alten und im neuen Testamente*, Nördlingen, 1, 1841, p. 51: 'Der Einklang zwischen unserm Heilsbedürfnisse und den berichteten Heilsthatsachen einerzeits und zwischen diesen und dem Ja der Bekräftigung derselben, das wir in uns vernehmen, andererseits, gewährt eine Gewissheit, welche durch keine Beweisführung gewirkt werden könnte. Unser Heilsbedürfniss weist zurück in einem Willen Gottes an den Menschen, dessen Verwirklichung auch an uns zu erwarten steht; die berichteten Heilsthatsachen sind dann Erfahrungen, ausser uns, das Zeugnis ihrer Bekräftigung eine Erfahrung in uns, deren Einstimmigkeit mit jenem Bedürfnisse keinen Zweifel an ihrer Göttlichkeit übrig lässt, wenn man nicht das Bedürfniss selbst verläugnet, mit welchem sie stimmen.' At the same time, he pointed to disagreements between critical scholars as evidence for the uncertainty of the historical-critical method. 'Wie vieles hat de Wette nur allein in der Kritik der Psalmen zurückgenommen!' (quoted in Wapler, op. cit., p. 77).

[6] On Hegel and Hofmann, see Wendebourg, pp. 75–84. For Hofmann's own account of his reaction to Hegel's thought see his letter to Delitzsch in Wilhelm Volck (ed.), *Theologische Briefe der Professoren Delitzsch und v. Hofmann*, Leipzig 1891, pp. 37–8. As a student in

upon the highest achievement of critical self-awareness that allowed the interpreter to see absolute spirit striving through history to achieve unity with individual spirit. In Hofmann's case, it was the experience of new birth in Christ that placed him in a position to understand the Christ event as the centre of history.[7] This entailed an essentially *subjective* standpoint. History itself was objective and real; but it could not be understood by those who studied it 'objectively' or 'externally'. Only those who were illuminated by the spirit of Christ could interpret history from within.

However, Hofmann's view of history as an organic and unfolding process differed from the Hegelian notion of progress through conflict and synthesis. History was the expression, in the world of mankind, of the love that pertained eternally to the persons of the divine Trinity, a love that not only created mankind but which strove to make mankind belong wholly to God.[8] In this particular case, Hofmann stood closer to the later philosophy of Schelling than to Hegel.

Hofmann's own view of his intellectual development was that he had read Schelling only comparatively late in life.[9] Thus, again, it may be wrong to look for the 'influence' of Schelling upon him, although we shall see in the section on Delitzsch that Schelling-type ideas could be propagated in various ways. A simple comparison between Schelling's later philosophy and Hofmann's teaching indicates that both had a more transcendent notion of God than did Hegel. For Hegel, 'god' and the world were so closely related as to be mutually necessary. Transcendence was mainly an awareness on the part of mankind that absolute spirit was not to be identified crudely with nature. For Schelling and Hofmann, God was independent of the world and the world was wholly dependent upon God.[10] However, according to Schelling the creation of the world was necessary for God, to enable his potentiality to become actuality. Only through the creation, and later through human history, do the 'distinct personalities' of the Trinity

---

Berlin, Hofmann heard Hegel on the proofs for God's existence, but was not inspired. When he later read Hegel's *Phenomenology of Mind* and *Philosophy of History*, he lost any taste for Hegel that he might have had.

[7] See the quotation in 5n above, and the following sentence from *Weissagung und Erfüllung*, p. 40: 'Die Selbstdarstellung Christi in der Welt ist der wesentliche Inhalt aller Geschichte.'

[8] See Hofmann's letter to Delitzsch in Volck, op. cit., p. 26: 'Das Innergöttliche erkannte ich als das Ewige, und das Geschichtliche als den Vollzug des Innergöttlichen.'

[9] See the letter quoted in Volck, pp. 37–8. It is interesting that Hofmann says here also that, 'Der einzige Philosoph, dessen Schriften ich vollständig und mit rechtem Bedacht gelesen habe, ist Spinoza'. But this was in connection with Hofmann's historical studies.

[10] On this point, see the study by Paul Collins Hayner, *Reason and Existence. Schelling's Philosophy of History*, Leiden 1967, pp. 68ff. For the comparison between Schelling and Hofmann, see Wendebourg, pp. 84–98.

become actual. History is part of the process by which God achieves complete self-expression.[11]

According to Schelling, human history began with the Fall. Created man (before the Fall and human history) was meant to live in harmony with the three potencies within God. This he did not do, and by distinguishing between good and evil created a disharmony within God. The first potency within God became the enemy of both God and man, sentencing man to death.[12] The second potency within God began the work of redemption within human history, finally overcoming the hostility of the first principle, and restoring the harmony of the Godhead. Human history was to be divided into (a) the time of the suffering of the Son (the second potency), the period of paganism and of the power of the first potency; (b) the time of the triumph of the Son, in which he has been elevated to Lord of Being. In all this, a distinction could be made between 'sacred' and 'profane' history in that in the Old Testament, knowledge of the true God was revealed to Abraham, and the history of the Hebrews was a history in a different category from that of other peoples.[13]

Hofmann's teaching fell far short of Schelling's gnostic-type speculations. The creation was an expression of the desire of the eternal Trinity to have fellowship with created mankind, a desire perfected and consummated by the incarnation of Christ, and his union with mankind. The Fall was not part of the ideal plan of God; but it did not radically frustrate the divine plan, and it was not the beginning of human history.[14] History came about because the eternal Trinity chose to become 'unequal' by expressing itself in temporal terms. Biblical history was *Heilsgeschichte* (salvation history) because it was from the outset an expression of the desire of God to create and to perfect mankind.

We can summarize the position reached so far: Hofmann believed that human history was dependent upon God the eternal Trinity, as the divine love was extended to mankind so that mankind might belong wholly to God. That this was so could not be deduced from history itself or even necessarily from the Bible read 'externally'. Knowledge of this meaning of history came only through appropriation of the new birth in Christ which the Church proclaimed, and which was confirmed by the study of the Bible. The Bible itself recorded the unassailable facts of the divine involvement in the history of God's people, the goal of which was the coming of Christ.

The next stage of this explanation of Hofmann's position will involve a

[11] For Schelling on creation and fall, see his *Philosophie der Offenbarung*, Lectures 13–17, in Manfred Schröter (ed.), *Schellings Werke*, 6. Ergänzungsband, Munich 1954, pp. 262ff.
[12] See Schelling in Schröter, op. cit., pp. 350ff; also Hayner, pp. 139ff.
[13] See *Philosophie der Offenbarung*, 39th lecture in Schröter, vol. 6, Munich 1928, pp. 511ff.
[14] See the presentation of Hofmann's views of creation and fall in Hübner, pp. 98ff. See also Hofmann's *Die Schriftbeweis*, 1, 1852, pp. 35ff.

comparison of his teaching with that of Hengstenberg, for here, the originality of Hofmann's position is seen most clearly. The comparison will start from the subject of prophecy.

For Hengstenberg, prophecies, in the sense of predictions about the future and their fulfilment, were both a fundamental part of divine revelation and a confirmation of the truth of the Bible.[15] Prophecies came essentially to chosen individuals, in visions or states of ecstasy, but without necessarily suspending their consciousness or their awareness of what was happening. Revelations thus received, even if they pertained to far-off events, were often articulated by prophets in such a way that it was possible for interpreters to think that events contemporary with the prophets were being spoken of. This, however, was a mistake. Further, prophecies did not necessarily predict everything that was to come to pass. The messianic work and reign of Christ, which was the centre of all prophecy, was foreseen only partially, and necessarily expressed in symbols and figures that needed to be interpreted. Prophecy understood in this way confirmed what was asserted in the fundamental formularies of the Church, that Christ was pre-existent, that his work was foretold in the Old Testament, and that his suffering and atoning death were the basis of redemption.

In Hofmann's view, this approach to prophecy had two weaknesses. First, it failed to do justice to prophets as men of their age, and second it reduced biblical history to a series of forecasts of what was to happen in the remote future.[16] This seemed to him to rob history of its reality as an organic process guided by God. Hofmann did not deny that prophetic forecasts could be found in the Old Testament; but he opposed Hengstenberg's attempt to find prophecies of Christ in the Old Testament from Genesis 3.15 onwards. For him, *History* was prophetic, not in the sense that forecasts about the future were made, but in the sense that there was an organic relationship between each segment of history, and what preceded and followed it.[17] History was guided and shaped by the self-same spirit of God who spoke through the prophets. In each particular age, prophets spoke to their own people; but under the divine guidance, each age was the necessary prelude to the next age, culminating in the coming of Christ. To the generations before Christ, that goal of history could not be apparent. In the fuller light of the coming of Christ, the whole spread of biblical history could be seen as the work of divine expression. Thus Hofmann's great work *Prophecy and Fulfilment*

---

[15] See Hengstenberg's account of the nature of prophecy in *Christology of the Old Testament*, 4, pp. 396–444; German, *Christologie des Alten Testamentes*, 1857², 3.2, pp. 158–217.

[16] See Hofmann in *Weissagung und Erfüllung*, pp. 3ff.

[17] Hofmann, op. cit., pp. 7–8: 'Israel in allen seinen Institutionen und in seiner Geschichte sey eine Weissagung auf die Zukunft, und wo die einzelnen Propheten weissagen, da habe der weissagende Geist, der in der Substanz des Volkes lebt, sich selbst zusammengefasst.' Hofmann is here quoting from Tholuck's *Das alte Testament im neuen Testament*, p. 17.

(1841–2) differed considerably from Hengstenberg's *Christology of the Old Testament*. The latter sought to defend the authenticity of the forecasts of the coming and suffering of the Messiah in the Old Testament. Hofmann's work sought to demonstrate the prophetic nature of Old Testament history *taken as a whole*, as an organic process directed by God.

Behind these differing approaches, doctrinal differences can be seen. Hengstenberg's view of revelation was what we would call today 'propositional'. What was communicated to prophets was essentially information, whose supernatural origin was demonstrated by the impossibility that humans could have such knowledge of the future. Not only the supernatural origin of the prophecies was demonstrated, but their content was authenticated, confirming the pre-existence of the Messiah and his atoning work. Hofmann's view of revelation was closer to what today we would call 'relational'. The truth of Christianity did not need to be demonstrated externally by the argument from prophecy. It was known by those who had been born anew in Christ. The purpose of biblical history was not to provide external proofs for the dogmas of the Church; it was to confirm the conviction of believers that the fellowship with Christ that they enjoyed was the goal to which all biblical history moved, as it was guided by the spirit of God. Thus the Bible supported and enriched that fellowship.

Hengstenberg's views of the Fall, and of redemption by the vicarious satisfaction of Christ, were in line with the orthodoxy of his day. Hofmann's views on these matters were by no means orthodox.[18] The Fall did not result from man deliberately and consciously turning away from God. Man was deceived by representatives of the world of the spirits who were in conflict with God. They misled him into an action which they promised would enhance his life. The promise turned out to be false, and there was a consequent frustration of the loving purposes of God towards mankind. However, this did not deflect God from the path that led to the incarnation, and history continued to be the unfolding of the process that led to supreme fellowship between God and man in Jesus Christ.

With a view of the Fall that minimized the place of sin, in the sense of rebellion against God, it is no surprise that Hofmann's view of Christ's redemption found little place for the sufferings of Christ as a satisfaction for sin.[19] Man's dilemma was not so much that he was alienated from God, but

[18] See Hübner, pp. 113ff.

[19] Hofmann's doctrine of redemption provoked a strong reaction on the part of a Hengstenberg follower, Friedrich Adolph Phillipi in 1856. For the events, see Wapler, pp. 239ff. Hengstenberg supported Phillipi against Hofmann, but was disappointed that Phillipi did not show that Hofmann's view of the atonement was an integral part of his whole system, and a concession to the spirit of the age. See Bachmann, *Hengstenberg*, 3, pp. 318ff.

that he was alienated within himself and to that extent not able to do as God wished. The work of redemption, prepared throughout biblical history, and culminating in Christ, was to enable man to overcome his self-alienation. Christ, as the second Adam, revealed the perfect manhood, and in fellowship with him, sinners knew the assurance of their fellowship with God, the defeat of Satan, and the possibility of life with Christ that was in full accord with God's will.

Thus we see in Hofmann a highly original theological position, uniting Pietistic convictions with a deep respect for the actuality of history, and a Schelling-like view of history as an expression of divine purpose. In the context of our discussion of the critical method in the nineteenth century, there is no need for the content of Hofmann's exegetical works on the Old Testament to be described. As has already been stated, Hofmann allowed no use of the critical method in the study of the Old Testament, save for grammatical and philological studies, and the use of historical studies to enable prophecies to be understood in their historical setting.[20] His work and influence opposed the progress of the critical method;[21] but he was a highly original and courageous thinker, and a remarkable witness to the very complex currents of thought in mid-nineteenth-century Germany.

Franz Delitzsch was born in Leipzig in 1813, and studied at the university of his birthplace.[22] After initial uncertainty as to whether to follow an

---

[20] Hengstenberg, *Christology*, 4, pp. 388–95; German *Christologie*, 3.2, Berlin 1856–7,[2] pp. 150–8, attacked Hofmann for being a rationalist in orthodox clothing, and for preferring a historical to a messianic interpretation of such passages as Genesis 3.15, 49.10, Ps. 45, 72, 110. Hengstenberg could see no essential difference between Hofmann and de Wette with regard to the origin of the Messianic hope: 'With both of them the Messianic idea is a patriotic hope, the natural product of certain circumstances connected with the nation. The prophecy is nothing more than a wish in disguise. It did not enter the minds of the people from above, but sprang from the soil of the nation itself, which looked forward to the future for the perfect satisfaction that the present denied' (*Christology*, 4, p. 393; German, 3.2, p. 155). Whether this is fair to Hofmann is arguable. There is some truth in Hermann Hupfeld's comment that for Hengstenberg, Rationalism was 'die tiefsinnige Kategorie in die Hengstenberg alles wirft was ihm entgegensteht'. See his article in *Deutsche Zeitschrift für Christliche Wissenschaft und Christliches Leben*, N F 4 (1861), pp. 269–92, at p. 282. The whole article provides a thorough critique of Hofmann from a critical standpoint.

[21] Hupfeld, op. cit., p. 276, numbered amongst Hofmann's followers Baumgarten (Professor in Rostock 1850–8 when he was dismissed), Kurtz (Church historian in Dorpat 1849–59, Professor of Old Testament, Dorpat 1859–70), Delitzsch and Nägelsbach (Classicist in Erlangen 1842–59) and *many* others. To what extent Delitzsch was a whole-hearted follower of Hofmann will be seen in what follows. However, his Genesis commentary of 1852 (see 25n below) was dedicated to Hofmann and Baumgarten.

[22] On Delitzsch in general, see the magisterial work by Siegfried Wagner, *Franz Delitzsch, Leben und Werk*, BEvTh 80, Munich 1978. This deals not only with Delitzsch, but is a mine of information about church and university affairs in Germany 1830–90. There is also a valuable chapter on Delitzsch's ecclesiology in Cochlovius, *Bekenntnis und Einheit der Kirche*, pp. 68–86. Cheyne, op. cit., pp. 155–71, is mostly concerned with Delitzsch's

academic career or a life dedicated to missions to Jews, he became a *Privatdozent* in Leipzig in 1842, and then in 1846 succeeded Hofmann in Rostock when the latter moved to Erlangen. From 1850 to 1867 Delitzsch occupied a chair in Erlangen, before returning to his native Leipzig, where he died in 1890.

In the present chapter, our concern will be with the Rostock and Erlangen periods of Delitzsch's life, for during the years 1842–67, he propagated conservative views about the authorship and interpretation of the Old Testament, and was thus another significant opponent of the historical-critical method. In his Leipzig years, and especially towards the end of his life, he became more accommodating to the critical method and its results; but he did not at that time contribute materially to the critical method.[23]

If the account is taken simply of Delitzsch's views on the authorship of biblical books, and on the interpretation of key works such as Genesis and Isaiah, he appears as a conservative scholar who was not entirely on the Hengstenberg wing, but who was much closer to the traditionalist position than to the advanced critics.[24]

In his Genesis commentary of 1852, Delitzsch argued that the Pentateuch was Mosaic rather than composed wholly by Moses; but his dating of the final redaction was very early.[25] Moses himself wrote the book of the law of Exodus 19—24, and the remainder of the laws were given orally by him during the wilderness wanderings. There also existed narrative works, one by a priestly Elohistic writer of the same generation as Moses, the other by

---

later phase, in which he was more sympathetic to the results of critical scholarship. Kraus, op. cit., pp. 230–41 presents a useful summary of Delitzsch's results as does Diestel, op. cit., *passim.* An intimate picture of the older Delitzsch is provided in his correspondence with Baudissin in Otto Eissfeldt and K. H. Rengstorff (ed.), *Briefwechsel zwischen Franz Delitzsch und Wolf Wilhelm, Graf Baudissin 1866–90,* Abhandlungen der Rheinisch-Westfälischen Akademie der Wissenschaften 43, Opladen 1973.

[23] For an account of how Delitzsch began to come to terms with the results of Pentateuchal criticism see Wagner, op. cit., pp. 233ff.

[24] Delitzsch, in the early editions of his Genesis commentary, accepted Hengstenberg's argument that there were clear traces of the Pentateuch in Hosea, Amos, etc. His main complaint against Hengstenberg was that the latter was too rigid, and had no sense of the organic and unfolding nature of history. See Delitzsch's highly perceptive book, *Die biblisch-prophetische Theologie, ihre Fortbildung durch Chr. A. Crusius und ihre neueste Entwicklung seit der Christologie Hengstenbergs,* Leipzig 1845.

[25] See *Die Genesis ausgelegt von Franz Delitzsch,* Leipzig 1852; also Wagner, op. cit., pp. 215ff. The 'early' German editions of the Genesis commentary (1853,[2] 1860,[3] 1872) were not, apparently, translated into English. The commentary on Genesis in C. F. Keil and F. Delitzsch, *Biblischer Commentar über das Alte Testament,* 1, Genesis und Exodus, Leipzig 1861, ET, Edinburgh 1864, is by Keil, and represents a more conservative position than is presented in Delitzsch's Genesis, editions 1–4. Delitzsch's more critical *Neuer Commentar über die Genesis,* Leipzig 1887, was translated into English under the title *New Commentary on Genesis,* Edinburgh 1888–9. By this time, of course, the critical method was well established in Britain.

a prophetic Yahwistic writer of a generation later, both of whom wrote in the spirit of Moses. The Pentateuch as a whole reached its present form in two stages. First, someone such as Eleazar the son of Aaron composed a work which utilized the materials existing at the time of Moses' death. Secondly, someone of the second generation such as Joshua expanded it, especially by adding Deuteronomy, a book that reached its present form in the land of Israel, and to which Joshua, or whoever the final redactor was, had contributed. However, Deuteronomy was essentially a free recapitulation of the older lawgiving composed by Moses himself.[26]

For scholars of the Hengstenberg school, this view of the origin of the Pentateuch conceded far too much to the critics.[27] At the same time, Delitzsch was firmly rejecting any view of the Pentateuch that could be used to support the reconstructions of de Wette or of Vatke, and he had a high view of the authority of the information contained in the Pentateuch.

In his commentary on Isaiah of 1866, Delitzsch defended the authorship of all sixty-six chapters, while providing a section on the history of the rationalists who had doubted the authenticity of parts of chapters 13, 14, 21, 23—7 and 34—5, and, of course, 40—55.[28] Hengstenberg himself could have written Delitzsch's condemnation of 'that school of criticism which will not rest till all miracles and prophecies, which cannot be set aside exegetically, have been eliminated critically',[29] and Hengstenberg would surely have endorsed Delitzsch's description of Ewald and Hitzig as 'hemmed in between the two foregone conclusions, "there is no true prophecy" and "there is no true miracle"'.[30]

If one looks at specific examples of Delitzsch's exegesis, one finds very traditional results. Thus, on the basis of Job 38.4–7, Delitzsch held that the angels were created before the creation of the material world, and that those angels who fell had already fallen prior to Genesis 1.2. The chaotic condition of the world as waste and void (*tohu va bohu*) in Gen. 1.2, before God commanded the chaos into order, was the work of the fallen angels. God

---

[26] For this whole paragraph see *Genesis* (1852) pp. 27–8.

[27] See the comment in the *Neuer Commentar über die Genesis*, p. 36: 'Die Hengstenbergische Richtung war mir nicht sympathisch, weil sie das Gewicht der gegnerischen Gründe zu wenig auf sich wirken lässt.'

[28] *Biblical Commentary on the Prophecies of Isaiah*, Edinburgh 1867, 1, pp. 56ff; German, *Biblischer Commentar über den Prophet Jesaia*, Leipzig 1966, pp. 20–45 (Pt 3.1 of C. K. Keil, F. Delitzsch, *Biblischer Commentar über das Alte Testament*).

[29] Ibid., p. 62; German p. 24.

[30] Ibid., p. 60; German, p. 23. See Delitzsch's continuation on p. 61; German p. 23: 'They call their criticism free; but when examined more closely, it is in a vice. In this vice it has two magical formularies, with which it fortifies itself against any impression from historical testimony. It either turns the prophecies into merely retrospective glances . . . as it does the account of miracles into sagas and myths; or it places the events predicted so close to the prophet's own time, that there was no need of inspiration, but only of combination, to make the foresight possible.'

was not responsible for this chaos; he *found* it, and transformed it into something good.[31]

Again, if we look at his exposition of Isaiah 53, we find Delitzsch interpreting the chapter in regard to the vicarious sufferings of Christ.[32] The Servant of God spoken of in Isaiah 53 does not become the object of divine punishment in his role as servant of God or as atoning saviour. In both cases he undertakes work that is pleasing to God. It is as he identifies himself with sinners that the servant subjects himself to that divine wrath 'which is the invariable correlative of human sin'.

However, for all his apparent support of conservative and traditional positions, Delitzsch, like Hofmann had embraced significant aspects of the German speculative and idealist philosophy of his day, and he sought to combine these insights with confessional theology and with biblical exegesis.

On Delitzsch's own admission, one of the most significant books in his development was Anton Günther's *Preparatory School for Speculative Theology of Positive Christianity* (1828–9).[33] In his *System of Biblical Psychology* Delitzsch wrote:

> For years the works of Anton Günther were my favourite study and a book by a friend of his, J. H. Pabst, who preceded him into eternity on 28 July 1838, entitled *Man and his History* (1830), which first called my attention to Günther, even attained the importance of a turning-point in my course of theological training.[34]

Anton Günther was a Roman Catholic priest who was born in Austria in 1793, and who studied philosophy at Prague and Vienna.[35] His attempted use of speculative philosophy in the service of theology led to his condemnation by the Roman Church in 1857, and to Günther's submission to Pius IX in the same year.[36] In the *Preparatory School*, he seems to have

---

[31] See Delitzsch's *System of Biblical Psychology*, Edinburgh 1875, pp. 75ff. German, *System der biblischen Psychologie*, Leipzig 1855, pp. 44–6. For Delitzsch's *very* complex account of the relationship between evil and the creation narrative of Genesis 1–3, see *Genesis,* pp. 116–17. The only English translation of this section known to me is in J. W. Colenso, *The Pentateuch and Joshua*, Pt 4, London 1864, pp. 137–9.

[32] Delitzsch's *Isaiah*, 2, pp. 317–18; German, pp. 514–15, 528.

[33] As far as I am aware, it is Wagner, op. cit., pp. 294ff, 439ff, who first stressed the importance of Günther for Delitzsch. Wagner supplies no detailed exposition of Günther; thus, a summary is attempted here. The book by Anton Günther is his *Vorschule zur speculativen Theologie des positiven Christenthums, In Briefen*, 1, *Die Creationstheorie* 2, *Die Incarnationstheorie*, Vienna 1828–9.

[34] *System of Biblical Psychology*, p. viii; German, p. iv.

[35] On Günther, see Peter Knoodt, *Anton Günther. Eine Biographie*, 2 vols. Vienna 1881. Vol. 1 is an autobiography by Günther up to the year 1828.

[36] See Knoodt, 2, p. 343. Some of Günther's followers mounted sustained opposition to the definition of papal infallibility, and became founding members of the Old Catholic Church.

attempted to use idealistic philosophy as an alternative to scholastic philosophy, as a foundation upon which to expound the Bible and theology.

The first volume of the *Preparatory School,* which consists of correspondence between an uncle and his nephew concentrates upon creation, stresses the eternity and self-sufficiency of God the Holy Trinity, and denies that God needed to create the world in order to 'become' the Trinity or to attain full self-awareness. The creation was an act of pure love, and there is no comparison between the being of God and the being of Man. However, the creation of man in the image of God does imply an analogy: God is unity in his being but trinity in his form. Man is trinity in his make-up—spirit, nature and humanity—but a unity in his form.[37]

The second volume, entitled *Theory of the Incarnation,* expresses a realist view of history, which sees history not so much as the self-expression of God, but as a dialectic between God's work of redemption and man's constant mis-use of his freedom.[38] However, God was able to choose and exalt Israel from among the nations, so as to work through a part of mankind for the salvation of all.

Important for Günther was the establishment of the Hebrew theocracy,[39] the law-giving and the proclamation of sin and forgiveness in the sacrificial cult and in the prophetic movement.[40] However, in the course of time, the cult became purely formal, and prophecy looked forward to the restoration of mankind. The Old Testament era did not produce the healing of the nation, and the incarnation of Christ expressed visibly what the prophets had merely intuited and spoken about.[41]

It is not clear when Delitzsch actually first read Günther. Siegfried Wagner indicates that Delitzsch referred to Günther in his commentary on the Song of Songs in 1851,[42] and there is also a reference to volume 2 of the

---

[37] Günther, *Vorschule,* 1, p. 102: 'kann die Creatur als solche das Wesen Gottes mit Gott nicht gemein haben, so hat sie doch die Form, den *modus existendi* mit Ihm gemein.'

[38] *Vorschule,* 2, p. 171: 'Gegründeten Anspruch aber auf den Primat in jenem metaphysischen Geschäfte hat der Begriff von der Willensfreiheit des Geistes und dem dynamischen Verkehre derselben mit der Gottheit, und jeder Versuch, die Geschichte speculativ zu behandeln ... muss sich an das Factum anschliessen, dass jener primitive Lebensverkehr durch den Missbrauch der Freiheit, wo nicht abgebrochen, doch in sich gebrochen ist.'

[39] *Vorschule,* 2, pp. 195ff.

[40] ibid., p. 197: 'Die innere Offenbarung musste zur äussern werden:—und Das geschah in der Gesetzgebung auf Sinai. Und Jetzt erst, nachdem dieser Moment der Uroffenbarung gerettet war, konnte das zweite Moment derselben sich in dem auserwählten Volke für die ganze Menschheit geltend machen und Gestalt annehmen. Diese Gestaltung aber im relativen Seyn war notwendig zugleich von den Formen der Zeit und des Raum's, diesen Grundformen des relativen Seyns, bedingt. In den Formen des Raums tritt der vorbildliche Opferdienst, in denen der Zeit die Prophezie auf.'

[41] ibid., pp. 200ff.

[42] Wagner, op. cit., p. 294.

Preparatory School in Delitzsch's *Biblical-Prophetic Theology* of 1845.[43] He could not have read Günther before 1830, since that year was the year of publication of Pabst's book from which Delitzsch learned about Günther. At any rate, in Günther, Delitzsch found an expression of Christian orthodoxy that was based upon a realistic view of biblical history which placed sin and redemption in the forefront, but which also enriched theology by means of the use of the speculative theology of the day. Günther's position provided Delitzsch with a standpoint from which he could both support and attack Hengstenberg and Hofmann, and on the basis of which he could work out an a priori view of revelation that excluded the radical results of biblical criticism.[44]

In his *Biblical Prophetic Theology*, Delitzsch subjected Hofmann's *Prophecy and Fulfilment* to a searching analysis. He criticized Hofmann's view of *Heilsgeschichte* for stressing too strongly the divine impulse in history, and for underestimating the importance of human freedom. It was not Ahasuerus but Solomon who was a type of Christ; God had chosen not the Persians but Israel. And this had its ground not in the divine plan of salvation, but in human freedom and response, which God was able to use.[45] There are strong echoes of Günther here.

While Delitzsch was grateful to Hofmann for his view of prophetic history, he believed that Hofmann had made at least two mistakes. First, Hofmann did not sufficiently allow that in the Old Testament, only a minority of the people actually chose the narrow road that led to salvation. The majority went their own way.[46] This was difficult to equate with Hofmann's idea that every segment of biblical history was a divinely intended preparation for the following segments. Human freedom was again being obliterated by stress upon divine causality. Second, Hofmann's position made it impossible for anyone in Old Testament times to have enjoyed salvation. According to Hofmann, the new birth involved being clothed with the new spiritual humanity declared in Christ, something impossible for the Old Testament period. Delitzsch stood with the traditional view that the faithful in the Old Testament had received salvation.[47] He

[43] *Die biblisch-prophetische Theologie*, p. 208.
[44] Delitzsch shared with Günther the conviction that biblical history was an expression of the divine movement towards redemption; therefore the facts of biblical history as presented in the Bible were unassailable.
[45] *Die biblisch-prophetische Theologie*, pp. 180–1.
[46] ibid., p. 234.
[47] ibid., pp. 248–50: 'In der Hauptsache hat die Kirche auch hier schon vor Alters die Wahrheit erkannt. Denn auf die Frage *an regeneratio etiam in V.T. obtinuit?* antworten unser Dogmatiker gegen die Socinianer bejahend: *fideles V.T. vere renati fuerunt*,' and 'Nach Hofm. kommt die Wiedergeburt einerseits zwar durch selbstbestimmende Hingabe an der Geist Gottes, anderseits aber durch die schon hienieden erfolgte . . . Ueberkleidung mit Christi gottesgeistiger verklärter Menschennatur zu Stande. Dieser physische, obgleich übernatürliche Process konnte nun freilich im A.T. noch nicht stattfinden.'

preferred to follow Baumgarten's view that the Old Testament gave the pre-history of the human nature in Christ.[48]

There is no doubt that Delitzsch's position was more realistic than that of Hofmann, and that it took Old Testament history even more seriously than Hofmann took it, quite apart from the fact that Delitzsch stayed much closer to orthodoxy than did Hofmann. However, Delitzsch was constantly described as a follower of Hofmann,[49] and there is no doubt that the resemblances between their positions were more than superficial. This can be seen most clearly in what is possibly Delitzsch's most characteristic work, his *System of Biblical Psychology* (1855).

The *System* brings together every aspect of Delitzsch's ability. It shows him as philologist, exegete, theologian and philosopher. The aim of the book is twofold. First, there is the intention to make explicit what is implicit throughout the Bible, the divine revelation about the nature of man in creation, fall and redemption:

> . . . under the name of biblical psychology I understand a scientific representation of the doctrine of Scripture on the psychological constitution of man as it was created, and the ways in which this constitution has been affected by sin and redemption.[50]

But second, such a system expounded would show the essential unity of the Bible, and would shed light upon its interpretation as a whole:

> And here at once is a system; to wit, a system of biblical psychology as it lies at the foundation of the system of the facts and the revelation of salvation; and such a system of biblical psychology is so necessary a basis for every biblical summary of doctrine, that it may be rightly said of the doctrinal summary which Hofmann's *Schriftbeweis* seeks to verify by Scripture, that from the beginning of the creation to the doctrine of the last things, a special psychologic system . . . supports it.[51]

In an opening discussion of the nature of God, Delitzsch argued, in Güntherian terms, for the absolute transcendence and self-sufficiency of the Triune God.[52] He opposed Hofmann's idea that the Bible knows only of an economic Trinity, a Trinity that expresses itself in creation and redemption.

[48] Michael Baumgarten (1812–89), who was *Privatdozent* in Kiel (1839–46) and professor in Rostock (1850–8) had studied under Hengstenberg as a post-doctoral student, and was attracted to Hofmann's position as well as to Schleiermacher. He was an individualistic and original Confessional thinker of a conservative kind, whose increasing concern with political affairs led to his dismissal from his chair in 1858. See the article and literature in *TRE* 5, 1980, pp. 351–2.

[49] See the references, e.g., in Wagner, op. cit., p. 223, 11n.

[50] *System of Biblical Psychology*, p. 16; German, p. 10.

[51] ibid., pp. 14–15. This is in the second German edition, 1861, p. 9.

[52] ibid., pp. 55–64; German, pp. 30ff.

On the contrary, without the Son and Spirit, the Father would not be God, and without a three-fold substance, God would not be the light, the love and the life. This eternal Trinity, Delitzsch held, was not philosophical speculation, but was the teaching of the Bible, which described the eternal majesty of God by means of the words *kāvōd* and *doxa*, glory. God was not only threefold in his self-revealing nature, he was seven-fold in his essential revelation, as shown by the passage in Revelation 1.4 which describes the seven spirits before the divine throne.

Before the creation, the world and mankind existed in the mind of God.[53] This was clear from passages of the Bible that spoke of those whose names had been written in the Lamb's book of life before the foundation of the world (Rev. 13.8), or which said of Jeremiah that before he was born God had known him and appointed him to be a prophet (Jer. 1.5). It was the case that God had fore-knowledge of how men would use their freedom, and determine their standing before God, so that the redeemed were loved from eternity and the condemned stood under his wrath. At the same time, this was not incompatible with the divine love for all mankind. To the objection that if human history exists in the mind of God in an ideal form, God cannot at one and the same time contemplate the ideal world and the actual world into which the ideal world is passing, Delitzsch replied that this problem was implicit in the Bible and was not of his making. At no point did the Bible suggest that the world and history were pantheistically parts of the proceeding of the Godhead itself.

In order to articulate the nature and constitution of man, Delitzsch attempted to reconcile the uses in the Old Testament of terms such as *ruah* (spirit), *nephesh* ('soul') and *neshāmāh* (breath), uses in which the first two terms were used sometimes interchangeably, sometimes in juxtaposition.[54] On the basis of Genesis 2.7, 'the Lord God ... breathed into his nostrils the breath of life; and man became a living soul', and the usage of the key terms noted above, Delitzsch concluded that the divine in-breathing not only gave life to man's material body, but also brought into being the soul (*nephesh*). The soul both reveals the presence in man of the spirit of God, and enables this spirit to be subjected to the corporeity of the person, and to combine its own vitality with the energies of the body. Delitzsch rejected the view expressed in Hofmann's *Prophecy and Fulfilment*, but later modified, that the spirit that ruled in man was the absolute spirit of God.

Delitzsch's account of the fall was cast in terms very similar to those we have encountered in Hofmann.[55] It was essentially a deceiving of mankind by false promises made by Satan: 'the primal sin of Satan was a direct, purely spiritual revolt against God; the primal sin of man was indirect revolt

[53] ibid., pp. 46–55; German, pp. 23ff.
[54] ibid., pp. 78–124; German, pp. 64ff.
[55] ibid., pp. 147ff; German, pp. 87–110.

corporeally effected against God—brought about by means of a masked power of deceit from without . . .'.[56] The effects of fall were also seen by Delitzsch in terms reminiscent of Hofmann and of Schelling, but firmly contained within Delitzsch's grasp of theological orthodoxy.[57] On the manward side, there was a disruption of the unity of man as body, soul and spirit. The spirit of man, which before the fall linked him in fellowship with God, and which guaranteed the harmonious unity of man, became severed from the service of God, and instead became a slave to mankind. 'The powers of the soul, at peace in God, fell into confusion, and kindled in passionate eagerness opposed to God'.[58] On the Godward side, man thus severed from God became the object of his wrath (*orgē*). There now began that most lengthy process of human restoration and redemption in the course of human history, a process so long because it was a work of free divine love that could not be otherwise executed. Closely involved in this history was the action of the divine Son, whose task it was to deliver mankind from divine wrath by the operation of love.

This latter idea is strikingly similar to Schelling's exposition of the second potency within God overcoming the first potency which had become wrath through the fall of mankind.[59] We have already seen, however, that Delitzsch would have rejected Schelling's idea that the fall and human history enabled God to become himself. How Delitzsch avoided Hofmann's dilemma which centred redemption upon the reconstitution of mankind but at the expense of a traditional understanding of the atonement is best illustrated by the quotation of a long and beautiful passage from Delitzsch.[60]

Man was now by nature a child of wrath (Ephesians 2.3)—one that had incurred wrath. He was no more a partaker of the divine nature (2 Peter 1.4); and if he were to become so again, not only was a change of disposition in God necessary, but an act of divine love, to lift him up out of the depth of wrath again to the altitude of the light. This act of divine love is the everlastingly decreed and temporally fulfilled redemption of men from wrath through the Son to love, who betook himself down into the depth of the Godhead's wrath, clothed the humanity, which had forfeited the divine likeness, took the wrath upon himself, and in himself annihilated it—and thus brought back the creature that had fallen from love, again to the principle into which it had been created.

The history of redemption, beginning in the Old Testament, was the historical expression of the eternal fact of reconciliation before God. Even in the first judicial sentences pronounced upon mankind, the promise of

[56] ibid., pp. 149–50; German, p. 91.
[57] ibid., pp. 151ff; German, pp. 92ff.
[58] ibid., p. 153; German, p. 94.
[59] See above, p. 108.
[60] *System of Biblical Psychology*, p. 172; German, p. 107.

salvation was present. The Protoevangelium of Genesis 3.15 contained the whole gospel, and pointed to Jesus the Son of God. So the Old Testament recorded the advance of Christ towards the purpose of his incarnation.[61]

In the remainder of the *System of Biblical Psychology*, Delitzsch did not expound Old Testament history, but rather examined the whole range of expressions in the Old and New Testaments for the human emotions and bodily appetites and functions. He also discussed death, resurrection and the future hope in the light of what he believed the Bible to teach about the constitution of man and God's economy of salvation.

Delitzsch and Hofmann indicate that in the middle decades of the nineteenth century, there existed a powerful Confessional orthodoxy that was not, however, rigidly conservative. It combined the piety and inner experience of the revival movement with an openness to contemporary philosophy. It was subjective in the sense that proof for the truth of the Bible was to be found in the mutual agreement of Christian experience and the biblical record of the saving history. The truth of the Bible was not to be demonstrated primarily externally, by showing the correspondence between the facts of the Bible and the dogmatic formularies of the Church. Delitzsch's *System of Biblical Psychology* is to be seen as a sophisticated attempt to expound the coherence of Christian belief with the assumptions of the whole Bible about human 'psychology'.

These confessionalists were also deeply concerned with matters of ecclesiology, especially as highlighted by the problems of church unity and its basis in the mid-nineteenth century. For them, the Bible, the Church and Faith stood in intimate relationship. Scholarship, as much of it as possible, was to be the servant of these, and not their master, hence the rejection of the results of the historical-critical method. Yet simply to see Delitzsch and Hofmann as hindrances to the critical method is not only unfair to them, it does not evaluate them as true representatives of the period in which they worked.

[61] ibid., p. 173; German, p. 108.

8

Christian Carl Josias von Bunsen: Diplomat and Scholar

It is not unusual for histories of Old Testament scholarship to devote little space to C. C. J. von Bunsen. Unless I have overlooked them, there are no references to Bunsen in Cheyne's *Founders of Old Testament Criticism* nor in Duff's *History of Old Testament Criticism*. Kraus provides five lines only,[1] while Diestel is the most forthcoming mentioning Bunsen's work on Egypt and his *Bibelwerk für die Gemeinde*.[2]

This comparative neglect of Bunsen contrasts remarkably with the fact that in *Essays and Reviews* of 1860, Bunsen was accorded the honour of an essay of some 40 pages, while other German critical scholars received no mention, or only the odd reference.[3] Thus, de Wette, Döderlein, Ewald, Paulus, Rosenmüller and Wegscheider are mentioned once each in *Essays and Reviews*, with a proper footnote reference only in the cases of Ewald and Wegscheider.[4] Any British reader of *Essays and Reviews* in the 1860s who was unfamiliar with German biblical criticism, might well have gained the impression that Bunsen was, in fact, the leading representative of the critical school, with Ewald a little way behind. In a note appended to the end of the fifth edition of the volume, Roland Williams indicated that since he had written his essay on Bunsen, more volumes of his *Bibelwerk* had been received, dealing with Isaiah and the Pentateuch, and he added:

> . . . even those who hesitate to follow the author in his details must be struck by the brilliant suggestiveness of his researches, which tend more and more, in proportion as they are developed, to justify the presentiment of their creating a new epoch in the science of Biblical criticism.[5]

[1] Kraus, op. cit., p. 170, refers only to Bunsen's *Bibelwerk für die Gemeinde*.
[2] Diestel, op. cit., pp. 575, 591, 614, 644, 749.
[3] Roland Williams, 'Bunsen's Biblical Researches' in *Essays and Reviews* London 1861[5], pp. 50–93.
[4] Williams, loc. cit., p. 74, refers to Ewald, pp. 438–53. Baden Powell, in 'On the study of the Evidences of Christianity', mentions Paulus and Rosenmüller (presumably E.F.K.) on p. 117 and Döderlein, de Wette and Wegscheider on p. 124. Specific reference to a work is made only in the case of Wegscheider. The latter, of course, was not strictly speaking a biblical scholar.
[5] *Essays and Reviews*, p. 434.

121

The concentration in *Essays and Reviews* upon Bunsen is perhaps more understandable when it is remembered that Bunsen had close links with Britain. Born in 1791 in Korbach (roughly 30 miles west of Kassel), he studied at Marburg and Göttingen, before eventually entering the diplomatic service.[6] From August 1838 to October 1839 he travelled extensively in Britain, while from 1842 to 1854 he was Prussian minister in London. As early as 1819, when he was residing in Rome, he had come to know Connop Thirlwall,[7] and he also established friendships with other liberal British churchmen such as Thomas Arnold (from May 1827)[8] and Julius Hare (from March 1833).[9] Because in the present book relationships between British and German Old Testament criticism are of fundamental concern, a chapter on Bunsen is included. To the question whether Bunsen deserves such inclusion in his own right, an affirmative answer can be found from no less a scholar than Ewald.

Perhaps no scholar in the history of Old Testament criticism has ever expressed his dislike of the work of other scholars in such harsh and uncompromising language as has Ewald. Typical examples have already

[6] For Bunsen's life see Frances Bunsen, *A Memoir of Baron Bunsen*, 2 vols. London 1868. The German edition, edited by Friedrich Nippold, *Christian Carl Josias Freiherr von Bunsen*, 3 vols., Leipzig 1868–71 contains additional material, and is the more valuable work. Sketches of Bunsen's life can be found in F. Max Müller, *Chips from a German Workshop*, 3, Essays on Literature, Biography and Antiquities, London 1880, pp. 358–405, with letters from Bunsen to Müller 1848–59, pp. 407ff. See also A. J. C. Hare, *The Life and Letters of Frances, Baroness Bunsen*, 2 vols., London 1879. Vol. 1, pp. 91–110, sketches Bunsen's life up to the time of his marriage to Frances Waddington. Two monographs deal with Bunsen's links with Prussia and Britain: Wilma Höcker, *Der Gesandte Bunsen als Vermittler zwischen Deutschland und England*, Göttinger Bausteine zur Geschichtswissenschaft 1, Göttingen 1951: Klaus D. Gross, *Die deutsch-englischen Beziehungen im Wirken Christian Carl Josias von Bunsens, 1791–1860*, Diss. Würzburg 1965. Bunsen's part in the founding of the Anglican-Lutheran joint Jerusalem bishopric is treated by Kurt Schmidt-Clausen, *Vorweggenommene Einheit. Die Gründung des Bistums Jerusalem im Jahre 1841.* AGTL 15, Berlin and Hamburg 1965. Schmidt-Clausen devotes much space to trying to demonstrate Bunsen's theological heterodoxy. A most valuable study of Bunsen's work as a theologian and biblical scholar is by Ortrud Maas, *Das Christentum in der Weltgeschichte. Theologische Vorstellungen bei Christian Karl Josias Bunsen*, Diss. Kiel 1968. See also the essays in Erich Geldbach (ed.), *Der gelehrte Diplomat. Zum Wirken C.C.J. v. Bunsen*, BZRGG, Leiden 1980.
[7] Frances Bunsen, *Bunsen*, 1, p. 149; German, 1, p. 345 gives the impression that Thirlwall met Bunsen in the spring of 1818. However, it is clear from J. J. Stewart Perowne and L. Stokes (eds.), *Letters Literary and Theological of Connop Thirlwall*, London 1881, p. 23, and A. J. C. Hare, *Life and Letters of Frances, Baroness Bunsen*, 1, pp. 138–41 that Thirlwall met Bunsen in Rome in March 1819. Thirlwall (1797–1875) was to become one of the translators of B. G. Niebuhr's *History of Rome*, translator of Schleiermacher's *Essay on St Luke*, an accomplished classical scholar and Anglican bishop.
[8] See Frances Bunsen, op. cit., 1, p. 315; German, p. 322. Gross, op. cit., p. 48, gives the impression that Arnold first met Bunsen in 1833.
[9] A. J. C. Hare, op. cit., 1, p. 397.

been given above. For Bunsen, on the other hand, Ewald seems to have had almost unreserved praise. Reviewing volumes 4–5 of Bunsen's *Egypt's Place in Universal History* (1856–7) Ewald wrote:

> These three volumes complete a work whose excellence and fame are familiar to all friends of better scholarship, and whose first three volumes appeared in 1845. In these days, it is seldom that a work such as this appears that can bring such honour to the name of German, both with regard to the content and the author.[10]

Reviewing Bunsen's *God in History*, vol. 1, Ewald wrote:

> One must thank him also for this work that he has begun. It could not have appeared at a more opportune time, and should very soon produce the beneficial results of which it is capable.[11]

Bunsen's regard for Ewald was, similarly, very great. He considered Ewald to have achieved a breakthrough in the study of Old Testament prophecy and poetry, and when Bunsen praised the superiority of German scholarship over that of England, France, Holland and Scotland, he undoubtedly thought of Ewald as one of the great representatives of German scholarship.[12]

On the other hand, Bunsen did not always agree with Ewald. He must have been one of the very few people who could disagree with Ewald without this being taken by Ewald as evidence for personal animosity. Thus Bunsen considered the book of Job to be a unity, wholly written by Jeremiah's secretary Baruch, whereas Ewald held that the Elihu speeches and the divine speeches (chs. 32—42) had been added later.[13] Bunsen dated the prophetic book of Joel to the reign of Rehoboam, who had begun to reign, according to Bunsen's chronology, in 975. Ewald placed the book of Joel in

---

[10] Ewald in *Jahrbücher der biblischen Wissenschaft*, 8, Göttingen 1856, p. 145.

[11] Ewald, ibid., p. 235.

[12] C. C. J. Bunsen, *Gott in der Geschichte oder der Fortschritt des Glaubens an eine sittliche Weltordnung*, 3 vols., Leipzig, 1857–8, ET, *God in History, or The Progress of Man's Faith in the Moral Order of the World*, 3 vols., London 1868–70. See 2, p. 148: 'Nachdem Herder zuerst den höhern dichterischen Gehalt der Propheten geltend gemacht, fügten die von ihm und der philosophischen Entwickelung Deutschlands angeregten Gelehrten, von Eichhorn bis Gesenius und Umbreit, der Herderschen Sinnigkeit und tiefen menschlichen Empfindung kritischen Scharfsinn und gründliche Forschung hinzu. Ewald endlich hat auch bei den Propheten in vielen Stücken eine neue Bahn gebrochen, nicht blos durch tiefere grammatische Forschung, sondern, auch durch Hervorhebung des alttestamentlichen sittlichen Ernstes.' See ibid., p. 384, where he gives as a reason for the non-acceptance of the Deutero-Isaiah theory outside Germany as, 'Die Vereinzelung der alttestamentlichen Philologie in Deutschland, ihr Aussterben nicht allein in Frankreich, sondern auch in England und Schottland, endlich der Verfall der grossen kritischen Schule Hollands . . .'.

[13] Bunsen, op. cit., 2, p. 477.

the reign of King Joash (Jehoash) of Judah, whose reign began in 877 according to Ewald.[14]

However they may have differed over details, Bunsen and Ewald were substantially in agreement that the critical study of the Bible would lead to a better understanding of that sequence of historical events in which God had been guiding the human race to a deeper understanding of the divine nature.[15] Like Ewald, Bunsen believed that it was necessary to work not from a philosophical presupposition, but from the realities of history. The main influences upon Bunsen were probably the historian Niebuhr, for whom Bunsen worked in Rome,[16] and Schelling, who was Bunsen's favourite philosopher.[17] Bunsen was, however, an original scholar, who combined the study of small details with the wish to construct large syntheses.

In a letter to his elder sister Christiana, dated 28 December 1817, Bunsen stated the aims to which he was to devote his scholarly research and writing. His desire for some time had been to trace 'the consciousness of God in the mind of man, and that which in and through that consciousness, He has accomplished, especially in language and religion'.[18] Reflection upon the subject brought him to the conclusion that 'God had caused the conception of himself to be developed in the mind of man in a twofold manner—the one through revelation to the Jewish people through their patriarchs, the other through reason in the heathen'.[19]

In pursuance of his desire to describe the development of the consciousness of God among mankind, Bunsen ascribed positive value to the early chapters of Genesis.[20] They hinted at the existence of an original human race that was created in about 20,000 BC. This human race lived in the region of China, but was driven from its 'paradise' by a natural catastrophe. Also, human

[14] ibid., p. 323ff.

[15] Cf. Bernhard Baehring, *Bunsens Bibelwerk nach seiner Bedeutung für die Gegenwart beleuchtet*, Leipzig 1861, p. 21: 'Bunsen gehört im allgemeinen zu denjenigen Philosophen, welche eine relative Erkennbarkeit Gottes durch wissenschaftliches Nachdenken für möglich und das Streben nach dieser Erkenntniss für die höchste Aufgabe aller denkenden Geister halten.'

[16] See Bunsen's letter to his sister of 13 October 1816 in Frances Bunsen, op. cit., 1, p. 104; German, p. 106: 'Niebuhr is more kind and affectionate to me, and as in Rome he will have leisure, I shall be able to learn from him, as a man and a scholar, more than from all other persons put together.'

[17] See Ortrud Maas, op. cit., p. 1. For similarities and differences between Bunsen and Schelling, see further pp. 26, 39ff, 49ff, 55, 74ff.

[18] Frances Bunsen, op. cit., 1, pp. 137–8; German, p. 138.

[19] ibid., p. 138; German, p. 139. Bunsen presumably had Hegel and Schelling in mind as philosophers who forced together the revelation through reason and the revelation to the Israelites.

[20] See *Gott in der Geschichte*, 2, pp. 138ff; Maas, pp. 40ff.

reason ceased to be directed to obedience to conscience and to avoid wrong-doing.

The original human race began to break up between 15,000 and 12,000 BC, the flood occurring between 11,000 and 10,000 BC. The original language spoken by the human race divided into two main groups—a Semitic-Hamitic group and a Turanian-Aryan group. Egypt became a bridge between the original human race and later ages, helping to preserve the sense of God in human reason.

The importance of Egypt for Bunsen is indicated by his book *Egypt's Place in Universal History*, the research for which was stimulated by Bunsen's friendship with the great German Egyptologist Karl Richard Lepsius.[21] Bunsen made a close study of Egyptian chronology, part of which had important implications for his view of Old Testament history. Bunsen placed the arrival of Jacob's family in Egypt not in the period of the Hyksos, as Ewald did, but earlier, in the reign of Sesostris II (or III), roughly 2650 BC. Abraham was thus dated in the twenty-ninth century BC, while Bunsen argued that the Exodus had taken place in 1320 BC. This meant the discarding of the figure 430 years for the period that the family of Jacob lived in Egypt (Exod. 12.40) and the figure 480 years as the period between the Exodus and the building of Solomon's temple (1 Kings 6.1).[22]

It was in his three-volume work *God in History* that Bunsen concentrated upon the divine revelation through the Israelite nation. Although he dated Abraham so early, Bunsen had no difficulty in asserting, on the basis of documents dating from the time of David and Solomon 1,800 years later than Abraham, that the latter was an historical person, to whom divine revelation was afforded.[23] But if Abraham was the first person to whom was revealed the unity of God and his providential government of the world, it was Moses who was the incomparable 'seer' of the divine revelation. Fundamental to Mosaic religion was the idea of an eternal and

---

[21] See Frances Bunsen, op. cit., 1, p. 344; German, pp. 349–50 for the beginnings of Bunsen's contact with Lepsius. Bunsen and Alexander von Humboldt persuaded Frederick William IV to send an expedition to Egypt in 1842, led by Lepsius. Lepsius's letters from Egypt were published in English translation, together with extracts from his work *Die Chronologie der Aegypter* in London in 1853, under the title *Letters from Egypt, Ethiopia, and the Peninsula of Sinai, with extracts from his Chronology of the Egyptians*. See below, p. 178.

[22] Bunsen, *Ägyptens Stelle in der Weltgeschichte*, 5 vols., Hamburg and Gotha, 1845–57; ET, *Egypt's Place in Universal History: an historical introduction in five books*, London 1848–67. See also the long discussion of Bunsen's chronology by Ewald in *Jahrbücher* 8, 1858, pp. 148ff. Ewald, *History*, 4, p. 302, German, 3.1, p. 476 put the descent of the Israelites at 1932 BC and assumed a fifteenth century date for the Exodus.

[23] Bunsen, *Gott in der Geschichte*, 2, pp. 163–4.

unbreakable covenant between God and mankind; between God who spoke through human conscience and mankind the bearer of the divine image.[24]

The task of the prophets was to proclaim, in practical circumstances, the fundamental principles of the unity of God, the unity of mankind, the fact that only with divine enlightenment could mankind understand the world, its history and its purpose, and that the will of God was to be expressed in ethical behaviour. The way of faith was the way of trust in the goodness of God and of his control over the world.

During the prophetic period, Bunsen saw the development of five prophetic ideas:[25] (1) The religion of the spirit is the religion of the future, and should become the possession of all mankind; (2) so that the religion of the spirit can become a reality, all outward forms of religion, which try to usurp its place, must disappear through the judgement of God; (3) the deliverance of Judah will come from a ruler, a scion of David, who will establish a kingdom of salvation and peace among mankind; (4) the conscious, pious, devotion of one's life to the nation and to humanity for the glory of the kingdom of God is the overcoming of the world and its kingdoms, and the reconciliation of mankind with God; (5) the Lord himself will come to judge the world, and will establish the kingdom of God through a human person; the kingdom will be carried on among mankind by the spirit of God.

It is to be noticed that in describing prophetic teaching under these headings Bunsen said nothing about sin and redemption, except for the reference to reconciliation in idea (4). His understanding of the nature of evil will be commented upon in a moment. In summing up the teaching of the Psalms under five headings, Bunsen came closer to the problem of sin and redemption. Thus, the third main idea of the Psalms is: 'Moral striving leads first to a recognition of sin as an estrangement from God which is healed by self-humility, and second leads to the joyful offering of oneself.'[26] The fourth idea is: 'Evil destroys itself as a result of the laws of the moral government of the world, which hold for individuals as for nations. What is good and true sustains itself and moves forwards.'[27] It can be seen from these quotations that Bunsen's was essentially an optimistic view of mankind,

[24] ibid., p. 179: 'Die weltgeschichtliche Grundidee des mosaischen Gottesdienstes ruht auf der Anschauung von dem ewigen, unzerstörbaren, unmittelbaren, ausschliesslichen Bunde Gottes mit den Menschen, dem Bunde des ewigen einigen Schöpfers, dessen endliches Ebenbild im Menschen wohnt, dessen Stimme in seinem Gewissen spricht.'
[25] For these 'ideas', see ibid., pp. 221, 238, 241, 249, 253.
[26] ibid., p. 261.
[27] ibid., p. 263.

although he acknowledged the reality of unbelief in ancient Israel.[28] Mankind had the capacity to overcome evil by responding to God's revelation about the unity of mankind, by trusting in his goodness and his providential governing of the world, by obedience to his laws, and by service of God and mankind. With such an optimistic view of things, Bunsen necessarily had to reinterpret what the Old Testament said about evil. Thus, Satan was described as an ancient Hebrew figure, who was a servant of God in the moral world order, as seen from the book of Job.[29] The name Azazel in Leviticus 16 did not refer to Satan. The name was originally *Hazazel* meaning 'the might of El, the strong God'. God was the avenger of sin, and the offering of the Day of Atonement was not a propitiation to an evil power.

Bunsen's general views on prophecy were not unlike those of Hofmann.[30] Prediction was the least important aspect of prophecy. What mattered more was the ability to see behind the outward course of events that divine government of the world that had the unity of mankind and the recognition of God as its goal. Messianic prophecies were, accordingly, treated historically. Isaiah 7.14 spoke of a child who would soon be born, and during whose childhood the land would be devastated so that he was obliged to eat milk and honey; but when his childhood was ended, the two kings threatening Judah would be humiliated.[31] Isaiah 9.1–7 referred to the birth of King Hezekiah,[32] while the Suffering Servant in Isaiah was none other than Jeremiah, who met his death by stoning in Egypt.[33]

Bunsen's general view of the history of the idea of God in the Israelite nation was supported by detailed exegetical work which is not without interest today. On the Pentateuch, Bunsen supported the 'supplementary hypothesis', according to which a writer of the eighth century had embellished the earlier narrative from Davidic-Solomonic times.[34] On the Psalms, Bunsen suggested three main periods of composition: a Davidic-Solomonic period (Psalms 1–72); a period from the divided kingdom to the Exile (Psalms 73–106); and a period of the second Temple (Psalms 107–

---

[28] ibid., p. 269 on Psalm 73: 'Diese Weltanschauung errang sich nach schweren innern Kämpfen der Sänger des LXXIII Psalms in einer Zeit, wo Viele in Israel den Glauben verloren, weil sie den Frevler so gedeihen und das Recht unterdrückt sahen. Nur wer reines Herzens ist, kann die richtige Weltansicht festhalten: aber der Gläubige findet sie auch bald bestätigt.'

[29] ibid., pp. 182–4.

[30] On prophecy generally, see ibid., pp. 148ff.

[31] ibid., p. 244.

[32] ibid., p. 245.

[33] ibid., pp. 204–6.

[34] ibid., p. 163.

50). However, the alphabetic psalms were later than the time of Jeremiah, since Lamentations was the model. There were no Maccabean psalms.[35]

Of greatest interest are Bunsen's views on the composition of Isaiah.[36] Bunsen ascribed four collections of oracles to the eighth-century prophet: chapters 1—12, 14.24—20; 21.11—23 and 28—33. The intervening material, 13.1—14.23; 21.1–10, 24—7; 34—5 Bunsen ascribed to Jeremiah's secretary Baruch, who was also the author of Isaiah 40—66 and Lamentations. Baruch's additions to the collections of Isaiah 1—33 were intended among other things, to enable each of Isaiah's four sections to end upon a positive note. Thus, 13.1—14.23, written by Baruch between 554 BC and 546 BC, announced the imminent fall of Babylon; 21.1–10, written between 559 and 555 foresaw Babylon's fall at the hands of the Medes; 24—7, written in 570 rejoiced over the fall of Moab and 34—5, written in 545 after Cyrus's victory over Croesus announced Edom's destruction and the blossoming of the hopes of Zion. Like Ewald, Bunsen believed that Isaiah 40—66 had been written in Egypt. Baruch had composed these chapters, according to Bunsen, at the same time that he wrote chapters 34—5. Bunsen's study of the composition of other books of the Old Testament was no less thorough.

Sufficient has now been written to indicate something of Bunsen's work, as it is related to the Old Testament, from his detailed discussions of the composition of individual books, to his genial account of Old Testament history, with its record of the development of what Bunsen believed to be the central features of the Israelite understanding of God.[37] Bunsen, like Ewald, propagated a thoroughly critical view of the Old Testament which was nonetheless in clear opposition to the views of de Wette, Gramberg, George and Vatke, when it came to the earliest history of Israel. Bunsen greatly admired Herder, and like that great figure of the previous century, had the confidence that it was possible to reconstruct world history, and to understand the divine impulse within it. In this latter regard, however, we should not overlook the similarities between Bunsen and Schelling, Bunsen's favourite philosopher. Bunsen was much more of an historian than Schelling was, but shared with Schelling a tendency to speculation about the earliest history of mankind which ensured that this aspect of Bunsen's work soon became outmoded.

[35] ibid., pp. 457–65.
[36] ibid., pp. 400–27.
[37] The present chapter has necessarily omitted reference to Bunsen's five-volume description of Rome (1830–42), and his hymn and prayer books for public and private devotion of 1833 and 1845. Another important publication, in which Bunsen expressed something of his general philosophy was *Hippolytus und seine Zeit*, 2 vols, Leipzig 1852–53, ET, *Hippolytus and his Age*, 2 vols, London 1852, a book to which the High Church party in England took exception.

The intention of Bunsen's *Bibelwerk für die Gemeinde (Bible for the People)* was to present the results of critical scholarship, as he saw them, to the ordinary congregation. How far this venture made any impression upon German congregations is a subject upon which I have seen no literature. Generally speaking, Bunsen's publications were as unfavourably received by the Hengstenberg party as they were unreservedly lauded by Ewald.[38] Whatever their effect may have been, they indicate once more the complexity of the critical positions to be found in Germany in the mid-nineteenth century.

The plan of the *Bibelwerk* is summed up in the introduction to the first volume: it is to provide three things:[39] (1) a translation of the Bible based upon the best text-critical work and the latest knowledge of Hebrew and Semitic languages; (2) an inquiry into the processes of composition, and to the source used by the biblical writers, with the aim of subjecting the texts to historical exegesis; (3) an attempt to see the history contained in the Bible as part of the history of the Kingdom of God. In fulfilment of this plan, the *Bibelwerk* is truly monumental, providing the reader with a history of biblical translation, a history of biblical interpretation, a translation of the text itself with textual and philological notes, and treatises on the modern knowledge of the world of the Bible. There is nothing to be found in the *Bibelwerk* that is not available elsewhere in Bunsen's writings. What excites admiration is Bunsen's confidence that the ordinary members of congregations would want and would use a work running to many volumes and several thousand pages, and that they would readily see the need for initiation themselves into the technicalities of textual and historical criticism. This confidence says something for Bunsen's ideal of the average member of a Lutheran congregation. To put things into perspective, British productions such as Horne's *Introduction*, which is discussed below, were substantial works by today's standards. It would, however, have been unthinkable in England at any stage of the nineteenth century, to have produced for congregations a work such as Bunsen's, executed in that supreme confidence that critical scholarship was there to emancipate, to enlighten, and to instruct readers into the ways of God's providence.

---

[38] See, for example, Hengstenberg's review of *Hippolytus und seine Zeit* in *Evangelische Kirchenzeitung* for October–November 1853. Bunsen's opinion of Hengstenberg was no more complimentary. See his comments on Hengstenberg's commentary on the Song of Songs in *Gott in der Geschichte*, 2, p. 475: 'Die Sache könnte nur lächerlich scheinen, wenn sie nicht eine Versündigung an dem Ernst der Forschung und der Heiligkeit der Bibel wäre, und wenn sie nicht einen Theil der neuen lutherischen Hof-, Staats- und Pastoraltheologie bildete, welche die Wissenschaft, und besonders die philologische Kritik der Heiligen Schrift "ad majorem Dei gloriam" zu unterdrücken suchte.'

[39] *Vollständiges Bibelwerk für die Gemeinde*, 1, Leipzig 1858, p. cii.

9

Various Critical Scholars:
Bleek, Hupfeld, Hitzig
and Umbreit

The previous chapters have attempted to describe the progress of German critical Old Testament scholarship from de Wette to George and Vatke, and the opposition to their positions that came not only from various types of Confessional scholarship, but from the critical scholarship of Ewald and Bunsen. In trying thus to highlight the major directions of scholarship, I have necessarily omitted reference to many scholars who contributed to Old Testament study both by their publications and their teaching. The present chapter seeks to remedy this defect in part. The scholars chosen all belonged to the front rank of scholarship, although, of their work, only that of Hupfeld was to make a substantial contribution to the progress of scholarship in the last third of the nineteenth century. They further represent the diversity of critical outlook in Germany in the mid-nineteenth century.

Friedrich Bleek was born in 1793 in Ahrensbök, roughly 15 km north of Lübeck, and began his studies at his home university of Kiel.[1] Two years later, in 1814, he moved to Berlin, where he studied under de Wette, the church historian Neander, and Schleiermacher. These scholars enabled him to find a positive theology that followed a middle path between rationalism and supernaturalism, and which fully accepted the critical method. From 1818 to 1821 he was a *Repetent* in Berlin, and would have been named as an *ausserordentlicher* Professor in 1821 had not the minister of state who had dismissed de Wette in 1819 baulked at appointing a de Wette student.[2] The title of *ausserordentlicher* Professor was bestowed in 1823, and Bleek remained in Berlin until 1829, when he moved to Bonn. Here, he spent the rest of his teaching life, until his death in 1859.

Bleek's literary output was comparatively small for a German professor,

---

[1] On Bleek see *ADB* 2, Leipzig 1875, pp. 701–2; Cheyne, pp. 142–148; Elliger, *150 Jahre Theologische Fakultät Berlin*, p. 38; O. Ritschl, *Die evangelisch-theologische Fakultät zu Bonn in dem ersten Jahrhundert ihrer Geschichte 1819–1919*, Bonn 1919, pp. 14ff; R. Smend, 'Friedrich Bleek 1793–1859' in *150 Jahre Rheinische Friedrich-Wilhelms-Universität zu Bonn 1818–1968*, Bonn 1968, pp. 31–41 (with further literature).

[2] Smend, loc. cit., p. 33.

and may have resulted partly from the undermanning of the theological faculty at Bonn, and the shortening of vacations by the Prussian government so as to restrict student political activity.[3] His principal Old Testament work, the *Introduction to the Old Testament*, appeared in 1860 after his death.[4] Otherwise, his Old Testament publications comprised a number of articles and several monographs.[5]

On the question of the origin of the Pentateuch, Bleek moved decisively away from de Wette's position, eventually arguing for the view that the priestly legislation in the Pentateuch was Mosaic.[6] In this, he may well have been reflecting the tendency in the Bonn faculty towards obtaining conservative results by means of the critical method. His position on questions of New Testament criticism was also marked by a growing conservatism.[7]

Hermann Hupfeld, although never one of de Wette's students, became one of his most faithful disciples, and claimed to be building upon de Wette in making a major contribution to the progress of the nineteenth-century Old Testament study.[8] Hupfeld was born in 1796 in Marburg, the son of a pastor who had embraced a Kantian theological rationalism.[9] His studies at his home university of Marburg introduced him to rationalizing biblical exegesis, which was, however, given an aesthetic dimension in the spirit of Herder and Eichhorn. He also studied under the supernaturalist Arnoldi. However, it was through private study that he reached the convictions that sustained his life's work.

In 1822, the medical need for recuperation gave him the chance to study Herder's *Spirit of Hebrew Poetry*, of which he said that in his opinion, it had done a greater service to Christianity than all dogmatic theologies together.[10]

---

[3] See Ritschl, op. cit., pp. 38–9.

[4] Friedrich Bleek, *Einleitung in das Alte Testament*, ed. Johannes Bleek and A. Kamphausen, Berlin 1860; ET, *An Introduction to the Old Testament* from the second edition (1865) by G. H. Venables, 2 vols., London 1869.

[5] See, for example, Bleek's 'Ueber Verfasser der in neuerer Zeit darüber geführten Untersuchungen' in *Theologische Zeitschrift*, 3 (1822) pp. 171–294; also, his 'Einige aphoristische Beiträge zu den Untersuchungen über den Pentateuch' in Rosenmüller's *Biblisch-Exegetisches Repertorium* 1 (1822) pp. 1–79; 'Beitragen zu den Forschungen über den Pentateuch' in *TSK* 1831, pp. 488–524.

[6] Diestel, p. 613; Smend, pp. 37–8. Bleek: arts. in Rosenmüller's *Repertorium* and *TSK* 1831.

[7] Smend, p. 40: 'Dass Bleek als Neutestamentler ein konservativer Kritiker gewesen ist, mag noch eine kurze Statistik seiner Urteile über die Echtheit der neutestamentlichen Briefe in den nachgelessenen Vorlesungen belegen ... Vergleicht man diese Liste mit derjenigen de Wettes, der in diesen Fragen auch schon weit rechts von den Tübingern stand, dann muss man Bleeks Position als einen Schritt zurück in Gang der kritischen Arbeit betrachten.'

[8] See below, n16.

[9] See Eduard Riehm, *D. Hermann Hupfeld. Lebens- und Charakterbild eines deutschen Professors*, Halle 1867; Cheyne, op. cit., pp. 149–55.

[10] Riehm, pp. 23–4.

He began to understand revelation as a process of historical development in which human freedom being compromised, the divine initiative led human understanding to even deeper perceptions of the truth. The Old Testament was an especial witness to this process.

So as to deepen his understanding of the Old Testament, Hupfeld went to Halle in 1824 in order to study under Gesenius. At this time, he also read the works of Fries, de Wette and Jacobi, and accepted their belief that at the basis of religion was 'feeling'.[11] His opinion of Wegscheider was that the latter misunderstood and caricatured the positions of Schleiermacher and de Wette.[12]

From 1825 to 1827, he was a *Privatdozent* in Marburg, being named as *ausserordentlicher* Professor in 1827, and then succeeding J. M. Hartmann as full professor on the latter's death in the same year. When Gesenius died in 1842, Hupfeld moved to Halle, where he worked from 1843 until his death in 1866.

In his scholarly work, Hupfeld held fast to a de Wettian theological position. He rejected the so-called positive criticism of Ewald and Hitzig, according to which it was possible to reconstruct Israel's earliest history with the help of research in ancient history. He preferred the so-called negative criticism of de Wette that was agnostic about many aspects of the early history of Israel, and content to deal with the literature and religion of Israel in general. Like de Wette, Hupfeld believed that in reason and in conscience, mankind possessed an intuition (*Gefühl*) of its divine origin and purpose. The Bible was a witness to the fact that God had established his Kingdom upon earth, and it endorsed, as a witness to the divine plan in Israel's history, the inner convictions afforded by reason and conscience.[13]

For the future progress of Old Testament studies, Hupfeld's most important book was his *The Sources of Genesis and the Manner of their Conflation* (1853).[14] Basically, Hupfeld distinguished within the source of the Pentateuch that primarily used the divine name Elohim (God), two

---

[11] Riehm, pp. 32–4. Riehm prints a letter in which Hupfeld says: 'Ich betrachte dieses als die mystische, unbegreifliche, blos in Gefühl vorhandene Grundlage der Religion, und die Nichtanerkennung einer solchen als das *proton pseudos* der kantischen Philosophie und des grossen Haufens der Rationalisten, sowie die Nachweisung und Begründung derselben als ein wahres Verdienst Jacobis, Fries und de Wettes.'

[12] Hupfeld, quoted in Riehm, p. 24: 'wie herrlich er sie missverstehe und travestire.'

[13] Riehm, p. 86: 'er mied die Wege der neuern historisierenden Kritik, bei deren Hauptvertreter Ewald und besonders Hitzig er, . . . das der Alterthumsforschung so nöthige Gefühl der Unsicherheit des Bodens und der Schwierigkeit der Aufgabe zu vermissen glaubte. Dagegen hielt er den von De Wette eingeschlagenen Weg der sogenannten negativen Kritik ein . . . .'

[14] H. Hupfeld, *Die Quellen der Genesis und die Art ihrer Zusammensetzung*, Berlin 1853. The book is based upon articles published in 1853 in the *Deutsche Zeitschrift für christliche Wissenschaft und christliches Leben*.

sources: an older priestly source and a younger narrative and civil legal source. Further, the priestly source was the basis, or groundwork, of the Pentateuch, to which had been added two further sources, the Yahwist source and the younger Elohist source. The effect of this theory was to re-create a documentary hypothesis of the origin of the Pentateuch, since Hupfeld believed that the first four books were the result of the combination of three originally separate sources. The rival supplementary hypothesis assumed that a Yahwist editor had interpolated material into the (undivided) Elohist *Grundschrift*.[15]

It is interesting that Hupfeld referred back to de Wette's *Contributions* in putting forward his documentary theory. To de Wette he accorded the honour of first having identified a *Grundschrift* for the Pentateuch, which was a Hebrew national epic composition, divided into four periods.[16] Hupfeld avowed that this aspect of de Wette's work had not received the attention that it deserved.[17] Hupfeld also maintained that de Wette had already noticed that there were two Elohists, although so far, I have not identified where de Wette did this.[18]

By distinguishing between an earlier and a later Elohist, Hupfeld had opened the way to a four-document hypothesis of the origin of the Pentateuch. His designation of the older (priestly) Elohist applied only to the *narrative* sections of Genesis and Exodus, to which it was possible to ascribe an early date, while holding that the cultic and sacrificial sections of Exodus, Leviticus and Numbers were later. As will be explained in Part 3, what yet remained was for the scope of the *Grundschrift* to be enlarged to

---

[15] For a useful survey of the developments at this period see Eduard Riehm, *Einleitung in das Alte Testament*, 1, Halle 1889, pp. 145–65.

[16] Hupfeld, *Die Quellen der Genesis*, pp. 2–3: 'De Wette zuerst eine zusammenhangende Urschrift unterschied, die die Geschichte der Gründung der Hebraeischen Theokratie als ein Hebraeisches Nationalepos und in epischer Weise—in vier . . . Perioden [darstellten].' See de Wette's *Beiträge*, 2, p. 31: 'Ich nenne das Ganze, das wir herzustellen versuchen, ein Epos . . . Es ist ein ächt hebräisches Nationalinteresse, ganz im Geiste des Hebraismus; es *ist das Epos der hebräischen Theokratie*' [emphasis de Wette's]. De Wette did not claim to be able to identify the epic narrative in its entirety. Hupfeld's aim was to identify it more exactly than hitherto, by exclusion of the younger (as he supposed) Elohistic elements. In general, de Wette preferred a supplementary and fragmentary approach, not a documentary one.

[17] According to Hupfeld, Tuch and Ewald had followed de Wette to some extent—a comment that prompted Ewald to the statement, 'die Grille de Wette's Ansichten von 1807 welche geradewegs zu Bohlen Strauss und allen übrigen höchst schädlichen Theologen dieser Art hinführten, in Bausch and Bogen als hohe Weisheit zu loben ist wahrlich zu stark'. See *Jahrbücher* 5, 1852–3, p. 240.

[18] De Wette, op. cit., pp. 142ff, followed Ilgen in regarding the Joseph story (Gen. 37; 39—43) as made up of two sources, Vater having defended the unity of the narrative. However, this does not necessarily prove Hupfeld's contention.

include the legal and cultic sections, and for the resultant whole to be declared to be post-Exilic.[19]

Ferdinand Hitzig reveals yet another side to the types of critical scholar to be found in mid-nineteenth-century Germany.[20] Throughout his life, he represented what can be called the purely philological, historical and archaeological side of critical scholarship. He was born in 1807 in Hauingen near Lörrach, in the northern part of the grand-duchy of Baden. He attended school in Karlsruhe, and then attended the grand-duchy's university in Heidelberg from 1824–5, where he was taught by the veteran rationalist Paulus. In 1825 he moved to Halle to study under Gesenius and then from 1828 to 1829 studied in Göttingen, where he had contact with Ewald. After a precarious spell as *Privatdozent* in Heidelberg from 1829 to 1833, he was appointed to a chair in Zürich from 1833 to 1861, returning in 1861 to Heidelberg as the successor to Umbreit, who had died the previous year.[21] Hitzig died in Heidelberg in 1875.

Hitzig was an admirer of the positive criticism, as opposed to de Wette's so-called negative criticism, but his confidence in being able to solve critical problems led to some very radical conclusions. He is perhaps best known as an arch-advocate of the Maccabean dating of the Psalms, ascribing Psalms 1–2 and 73–150 to the Maccabean period.[22] His commentary on Isaiah (1833) continued the exegesis of the prophet along the lines laid down in Gesenius's great Isaiah commentary,[23] and there followed commentaries on the twelve minor prophets (1838), Jeremiah (1841), Ezekiel (1847), Daniel (1850), Ecclesiastes (1847) and the Song of Songs (1855).

In his work on the prophetic books, Hitzig's strongly historical approach led him to reject the traditional interpretation of messianic prophecies advocated by Hengstenberg. For example, the servant of God in Isaiah 52.13—53.12 was interpreted collectively as Israel, with the death of the

---

[19] Hupfeld's other important works included a commentary on the Psalms (1855–62), and a perceptive book about Old Testament Introduction: *Ueber Begriff und Methode der sogenannten biblischen Einleitung, nebst einer Uebersicht ihrer Geschichte und Literatur*, Marburg 1844. Reference has also been made in the section on Hofmann to Hupfeld's penetrating, 'Die heutige theosophische oder mythologische Theologie und Schrifterklärung' in *DZCW* NF 4 (1861), pp. 269–92.

[20] On Hitzig, see 'Zur Erinnerung an Ferdinand Hitzig. Eine Lebens- und Charakter-Skizze' in J. J. Kneucker (ed.), *Dr Ferdinand Hitzigs Vorlesungen ueber Biblische Theologie und Messianische Weissagungen des Alten Testaments*, Karlsruhe 1880.

[21] Cheyne, op. cit., p. 120, wrongly gives the date of Umbreit's death as 1861.

[22] J. Olshausen, *Die Psalmen erklärt*, in *KEH*, Leipzig, 1853, was even more radical than Hitzig in Maccabean datings.

[23] See the remarks by Umbreit in *TSK* 1834, p. 957, that Hitzig's Isaiah commentary did not achieve an advance in Old Testament exegesis, but was rather a reworking, especially of Gesenius's work.

servant being the Exile in Babylon.[24] Hitzig's view of the history of Israelite religion strongly reflected an interest in comparative religion.

According to Hitzig, the great achievement of the Israelites was to have developed a religion of transcendence which avoided all forms of pantheism. This had come about because the Patriarchs and prophets had been concerned with truth rather than beauty, and had thus been saved from the snare of confusing the human with the divine, and of venerating what was beautiful in the natural world.[25]

The religion of the Patriarchs, the worship of El Shaddai, had been influenced by Persian religion, and El Shaddai was probably a translation of the Persian *Auromazda* (the good principle).[26] Although there was no trace of ontological dualism in Israelite religion, its sharply developed sense of distinction between good and evil derived from ancient Persia, and was reflected in Genesis 3. It was also clear from the Old Testament that pre-Mosaic religion involved worship of the stars. The twelve tribes had an astral origin, and Amos 5.26 was evidence for ancient star worship. Hitzig rejected the view that *Kaiwan* in Amos 5.26 was to be identified with Saturn, identifying it instead with Sirius.[27] From their position in the desert, the pre-Mosaic Israelites developed their star worship into the notion of a God who controlled the whole system of stars, and thus of the whole cosmos.[28]

When they went down into Egypt, the pre-Mosaic Israelites already possessed a religion that was in sharp contrast to the polytheistic and deified animal religion that derived from the worship of nature. Israelite religion was thus not indebted to Egypt. The name Yahweh, which dated from the time of Moses, was probably a translation of the Armenian *astuads* or *astvat*, which meant 'the existing one' (*der Seiende*).[29]

In describing the process of the development of Israelite religion, Hitzig did not suppose that this was purely a matter of human discovery. There was divine initiative involved; thus the spirit of Moses was 'prepared' to the point that when he discovered the name *astuad*, it expressed for him the truth about God of which he had become profoundly convinced.[30]

Hitzig's positive criticisms, then, led him to wide-ranging and far-reaching comparisons, which meant that his reconstructions were open to challenge at many points. It can be safely said that it was precisely because

---

[24] See Hitzig's *Jesaja-Commentar*, p. 564ff.; also 'Messianische Weissagungen' in Kneucker, op. cit., pp. 174–89.
[25] *Biblische Theologie* in Kneucker, op. cit., p. 14.
[26] ibid., pp. 29–30.
[27] ibid., pp. 30–3.
[28] ibid., p. 35.
[29] ibid., p. 38.
[30] ibid., p. 38.

his reconstructions were so precarious, as was the exegesis of the Old Testament which went hand-in-hand with the reconstructions, that his permanent contribution to Old Testament study was less significant than that of his contemporaries. On the other hand, he represented a tradition of use of comparative religion in Old Testament study that became a significant factor, and which is worth a study in its own right.[31] In the latter part of the nineteenth century the *Religionsgeschichtliche* 'school' in both Old and New Testament studies would continue the tradition.

Friedrich Wilhelm Karl Umbreit represented a tradition of critical scholarship totally different from that of Hitzig, and distinct also from the other scholars discussed in this chapter.[32] He was born in Sonneborn, near Gotha, in 1795, and studied under Eichhorn in Göttingen from 1814 to 1819. From here he went to Vienna in order to study under the orientalist von Hammer. In 1820 he became a *Privatdozent* in Heidelberg, in 1823 a professor in the philosophical faculty, and from 1829 a professor in the theological faculty until his death in 1860. As mentioned above, he was succeeded in 1861 by Hitzig. For many years, he edited, with C. Ullmann, the important *Theologische Studien und Kritiken*, a journal that represented moderate critical scholarship, and to which scholars such as de Wette and Lücke contributed regularly.

Umbreit's own account of his student days in Göttingen indicates how isolated from each other the German theological faculties could be, at any rate at the level of teaching. In Göttingen, Umbreit fully accepted the philological and mildly rationalist position of Eichhorn. Little indication was apparently given of what was going on elsewhere in theology.

> Of the new life, which held sway in Berlin, we learned and knew nothing. Schleiermacher's name I heard only in a lecture by Schulze, who taught Philosophy with Bouterweck, and who spoke about the *Speeches on Religion* in such a curious way that I soon repaired to the library so that I might at least once cast eyes on this so mysteriously designated book; but it was not available. I did at least hear about de Wette in the lectures on Old Testament introduction given by the young Planck, but I only discovered anything about Neander later, from his father who was living in Göttingen.[33]

It was the reading of Schleiermacher's *Dogmatics* after he had begun to teach in Heidelberg that freed Umbreit from the old rationalism and which

---

[31] See Gustav Mensching, *Geschichte der Religionswissenschaft*, Bonn 1948, and the literature given in J. Waardenburg, *Classical Approaches to the Study of Religion*, 2, The Hague and Paris 1974, pp. 4–11.

[32] On Umbreit see *ADB* 30 (1875), pp. 273–7 and arts. by C. Ullmann in *TSK* 1862, pp. 435–79 and by E. Riehm, in *TSK* 1862, pp. 479–511.

[33] Quoted in Ullmann, loc. cit., pp. 441–2.

helped him to accept the centrality of the person of Christ.[34] He began to find in the Old Testament not merely a most remarkable account of human development, but a fundamental part of divine revelation of a salvation that could not be attained by human efforts, and which was mediated via a chosen people towards all mankind.

Umbreit combined the philological approach of Eichhorn with the spirit of Herder, together with what he had learned in Vienna from von Hammer. His main published work dealt with the prophetic and poetic parts of the Old Testament, on Ecclesiastes (1818), Song of Songs (1820), Job (1824), and on the Prophets (1841–6). Umbreit interpreted prophecies in an historical manner, but so as to allow for a deeper significance beyond the particular historical circumstances.[35] His views on the historicity of Moses were closer to the traditional view.[36] At his death, Delitzsch wrote that the Church and Old Testament scholarship had lost a man who had completed the work begun by Herder; a man who had helped his readers to appreciate fully the human side of the Old Testament without overlooking its divine side.[37]

---

[34] ibid., pp. 452–3.

[35] See his articles in *TSK* 1830, pp. 1–24 and 1840, pp. 597–708. In the first, Umbreit opposed Hengstenberg's 'roh-occidentalischer Materialismus' in the matter of interpreting prophecies, but opposed the views of de Wette and Schleiermacher that prophecies were 'bloss unbestimmte Ahnungen'. In the later article, on Ps. 22 and Isa. 53, he again criticizes Hengstenberg and de Wette. He sees the psalmist as a contemporary of the figure portrayed in Isa. 53. The sufferer displays something of the 'reine Urbild des leidenden und sterbenden Erlösers'.

[36] See his review of K. F. C. W. Bähr, *Symbolik des mosaischen Kultus*, 1, Heidelberg, 1837, in *TSK* 1843 pp. 144–92, esp. p. 145: 'Gesetzt auch, die das Oberste zu unterst kehrende Kritik hätte Recht, was wir aber einzuräumen weit entfernt sind, und Moses wäre nur ein Nachbild der Propheten . . .'

[37] Ullmann, loc. cit., p. 471.

10

Conclusions to Part One

For the bulk of the sixty years to 1860 there were seventeen Protestant faculties of theology in the German states, in which Old Testament scholarship was seriously pursued. In addition, there were German-speaking faculties in Basel, Zürich and Dorpat (now Tartu in the Soviet Union), and a French faculty in Strasbourg which stood under German influence. The first thing that must be noted is the scale of the operation. In the twenty-one faculties presented on the chart on p. 142, there were often two Old Testament teachers per faculty, not to mention chairs of oriental languages in the philosophical faculties, and the aspiring scholars who were *Privatdozenten* or *ausserordentliche* professors. Most of these university teachers were productive scholars, a process reinforced by the fact that in order to gain a teaching post, a doctoral thesis and, in some cases, an additional licentiate thesis needed to have been presented and published.

During the same period in England, there were, until 1828, only two universities (Oxford and Cambridge) at neither of which was theology taught in any serious fashion, although both had long-established chairs of Hebrew. The establishment of the university of Durham and of King's College, London, in 1832 and 1828 respectively, greatly improved the English situation, but within the period 1800–60 the only other foundation was that of Owens College, Manchester (1851), which did not have a department of theology. Nonconformists, who were unable to take degrees at Oxford and Cambridge because of the necessity of subscribing to the thirty-nine Articles of the Church of England, maintained some excellent academies; in Scotland, there were four ancient universities with excellent reputations, while in Ireland, there was Trinity College, Dublin.

Granted, then, that the scale of Old Testament scholarship in Germany was enormous when compared with England, it is no surprise that Germany should have pioneered critical scholarship, and should have made strides, in comparison with which English achievements seemed elementary.

At the beginning of the nineteenth century in the German universities, the value of source-critical studies was admitted, even in cases where the older 'Neologists' were defending traditional views of biblical authorship, as in the case of Eichhorn defending Mosaic authorship of the Pentateuch until the fourth edition of his Introduction, or E. F. K. Rosenmüller retracting his earlier views on the composite authorship of Isaiah. Students

138

who went at this time to the main centres of theology such as Halle, Jena and Göttingen received a critical, mildly rationalizing training, while those who went to Leipzig heard the mildly critical, encyclopaedic teaching of the Rosenmüllers. The founding of the university of Berlin in 1810, and the presence there until 1819 of de Wette undoubtedly furthered that scholar's influence, and it is no accident that towards the end of the 1820s we find young scholars such as Gramberg elaborating the de Wettian approach. However, from the end of the 1820s we find the beginnings of the polarization brought about by the renewal movement (*Erweckungsbewegung*), as well as the divisions among critical scholars and, later, among Confessionalists.

From roughly 1830 to 1860, students would have found a distinct 'tendency' in the Old Testament teaching at any particular university, although this would have to be qualified by various local factors. For example, at Halle, students could choose between Gesenius and his successor Hupfeld on the one hand, and Tholuck on the other. Again, the Tübingen faculty in the 1830s housed the notorious 'Tübingen school' of New Testament and early church history along with the critically traditional Ewald, to whom the work of the Hegelians was an abomination. Making due allowance for such factors one can *generally* describe the situation as follows.

Faculties where the conservative Hengstenberg was able to exert influence came more and more to be Confessionally orientated, and to have Old Testament teachers who defended traditional viewpoints. This can be seen at Dorpat from 1833, at Königsberg from 1841, at Rostock from 1842, at Erlangen from 1845 (where the influence of Harless was also a significant Confessional factor), and of course, in Berlin itself. Tübingen remained conservative in Old Testament matters under Oehler (1852–72). Universities at which there was an acceptance of the critical method, but within the context of more conservative results, were Bonn (with Bleek 1829–59), Heidelberg (with Umbreit 1823–60) and Leipzig (with Tuch 1843–67). At Göttingen, Ewald represented the so-called positive, historical criticism, as did Hitzig at Zürich. The so-called negative criticism could be found at Basel (under de Wette, 1822–49), Halle (under Gesenius, 1810–42 and Hupfeld, 1843–66) and Marburg (at least during Hupfeld's tenure, 1825–43).

Underlying these various 'schools' of criticism was a variety of philosophical and theological standpoints. The main division was between the Confessionalists and the non-Confessionalists. The former placed a limit upon what critical scholarship could be allowed to attempt. At its most rigid, Confessionalism saw the role of scholarship as simply that of defending orthodox Lutheran positions as they were perceived in the nineteenth century (thus Hengstenberg and his closest allies). However, as the chapter on Delitzsch and Hofmann makes clear, there were also Confessionalists who, while not admitting the radical results of critical scholarship, were prepared to make important concessions to historical criticism and to idealist philosophy. In the work of Hofmann we can see an attempt to reconcile the insights of the historical study of prophecy with a philosophical view of history as an organic process, the necessary starting-point for the reconciliation being the church's proclamation of the new birth in Christ.

The non-Confessionalists did not place a Confessional limit on what criticism could be allowed to do; but their starting-points varied considerably, and fundamentally affected how criticism was employed. The exponents of positive criticism, such as Ewald, Bunsen and Hitzig, had a view of history as an organic process under the guidance of God. For them, criticism did not undermine faith but confirmed it by uncovering the actual historical process in which God dealt with mankind. There was something of the spirit of Herder in this approach, and we can probably add to the list Umbreit, as well as Vatke who held to the same basic tenets on Hegelian grounds, even if his results were negative and repugnant to the likes of Ewald.

The so-called negative critics worked within a philosophical framework which was more strictly Kantian, whereas the positive critics were more overtly idealists. Thus de Wette and his closest followers regarded religion as a matter of experience, feeling and *Ahndung*, and they looked to the Old Testament to provide examples of religion in these terms. Their so-called negative attitude was based upon their inability to see history as an organic process guided towards an ultimate purpose. One of their biggest differences from the positive critics lay in their hostile attitude to the post-exilic period of Old Testament religion and the Judaism that they believed it to evince.

The complexity of the critical approaches to the Old Testament in the period 1800–60 in Germany was undoubtedly a reflection of the complexities of intellectual life in Germany at this time. In a period which saw the continuing literary activity of Goethe and Schiller, the spread of the philosophies of Fichte, Hegel and Schelling (not to mention Fries), the rise of the modern historical method at the hands of such men as Niebuhr and Ranke, quite apart from the tensions brought about by the renewal movement and unity in the churches on the one hand, and the strivings for greater political democracy on the other, it is hardly surprising that Old Testament scholarship reflected and was affected by these tendencies. Although during this period Old Testament criticism achieved results that were irreversible and concrete, the many and differing bases from which scholars worked must not be overlooked, if the critical method at this time is to be properly evaluated.

Appendix:
Table of
Old Testament Professors
in Protestant Faculties
in Germany 1800–1900

The following table does not claim to be complete, or entirely free from errors, although every attempt has been made to ensure accuracy. In some cases, my sources disagreed among themselves, e.g., some giving the date of appointment, others giving date of commencement of duties, others differing without making it clear why.

Although the attempt is here made to list the Old Testament professors, this is impossible, especially in the earlier parts of the century, when faculties had a fixed number of chairs, with the occupants taking on more than one subject. Thus, de Wette, who is treated in the present book as an Old Testament scholar, also taught New Testament and Christian Morals.

The attempt has been made in the later part of the century to indicate professors of Semitic or Oriental languages by the sign ϕ, and *ausserordentlicher* professors by an asterisk. *Privatdozenten* have not been listed, although one or two may appear by accident. It is hoped that the plan will give an indication of the scale of German Protestant Old Testament scholarship in the nineteenth century.

DORPAT
- Hezel 1802-20
- Henzi 1820-9
- Kleinert 1829-34
- Keil 1833-58
- Kurtz 1859-70
- Volck 1863-98 ø

KÖNIGSBERG
- Hasse 1788-1806
- Vater 1809-20
- Olshausen 1821-34
- von Bohlen 1828-40
- Hävernick 1841-5
- Dorner 1843-7
- J. Olshausen 1853-8
- Sommer 1850-1900
- Cornill 1888-ø8

GREIFSWALD
- Kosegarten 1823-60
- Hahn 1851-61*
- Diestel 1862-7
- Vilmar 1867-72
- Wellhausen 1872-82
- Baethgen 1889-95

BERLIN
- de Wette 1810-19
- Bleek 1824-9*
- Hengstenberg 1828-69
- Vatke 1827-82*
- Dorner 1862-84
- Schrader 1875-89
- Dillmann 1869-94
- Baethgen 1895-1901

BRESLAU
- D. Schulz 1811-54
- Augusti 1812-19ø
- Schirmer 1819-27
- Middeldorpf 1815-58
- Oehler 1845-52
- Schulz 1864-88
- Kittel 1888-98
- Cornill 1898-1910

BONN
- Augusti 1819-41
- Bleek 1829-59
- Dorner 1847-53
- Schottmann 1859-66
- Gildemeister 1859-89ø
- Kamphausen 1868-1901
- Budde 1879-89*
- Koenig 1900-21

KIEL
- Eckermann 1782-1837
- Kleuker 1798-1827
- Hartmann 1811-38
- Dorner 1839-43
- J. Olshausen 1823-52
- Hofmann 1842-5
- Delitzsch 1846-50
- Baumgarten 1850-8
- Dillmann 1860-4ø
- Nöldeke 1864-72ø
- Klostermann 1868-1913

ROSTOCK
- Martini 1791-1804
- Ziegler 1791-1809
- Dahl 1804-10
- Hävernick 1834-41*
- Bachmann 1858-88
- Baethgen 1884-8
- König 1888-1900

Timeline axis: 1790, 1800, 1810, 1820, 1830, 1840, 1850, 1860, 1870, 1880, 1890, 1900, 1910, 1920

HALLE

Vater 1799-1809
Vater 1820-6
Gesenius 1810-42
Tuch 1838-41
Tholuck 1826-77
Hupfeld 1843-66
Riehm 1866-88
Schottmann 1866-87
Wellhausen 1882-5*
Kautzsch 1888-1910

JENA

Paulus 1793-1804
Ilgen 1800-2
Gabler 1804-26
Baumgarten-Crusius 1812-34
Hoffmann 1826-64
Köhler 1864-6
Diestel 1867-72
Schrader 1873-5
Siegfried 1875-1901

LEIPZIG

J.G Rosenmüller 1786-1815
Keil 1793-1818
E.F.K. Rosenmüller 1796-1835
Cramer 1819-24
Winer 1832-58
Tuch 1843-67
C.F. Keil 1859-88
Delitzsch 1867-90
Buhl 1890-8
Kittel 1898-1929

GÖTTINGEN

Eichhorn 1788-1827
Staeudlin 1790-1826
Ewald 1831-7
Ewald 1848-67ø
Dorner 1853-62
Bertheau 1843-87
Lagarde 1869-91ø
Duhm 1877-89*
Schultz 1876-1903
Smend 1889-1913
Wellhausen 1892-1913ø

MARBURG

Arnoldi 1789-1835
Hartmann 1793-1827
Hupfeld 1825-43
Gildemeister 1843-59
Dietrich 1859-88
Baudissin 1881-1900
Wellhausen 1885-92ø
Budde 1900-21
Jensen 1892-1928ø

GIESSEN

Hezel 1786-1801
J.E.C. Schmidt 1798-1831
Kühnöl 1809-40
Knobel 1838-62
Dillmann 1864-9
Hesse 1844-78
Baur 1849-60
Schrader Merx 1869-73 1873-5
Stade 1875-1906

HEIDELBERG

de Wette 1807-10
Paulus 1811-51
Umbreit 1823-60
Hitzig 1861-75
Merx 1875-1909

TÜBINGEN

Steudel 1817-37 | Dorner 1838-9 | Elwert 1839-41 | Oehler 1852-72 | Diestel 1872-9 | Kautzsch 1880-8 | Grill 1888-1913

ERLANGEN

Vogel 1808-34 | Ewald 1838-48 | Dreschler 1833-48o | Merx 1869-73 | Delitzsch 1850-67 | Koehler 1867-97

Berthold 1803-23 | Winer 1823-32 | H. Olshausen 1834-9 | Hofmann 1845-77

Kaiser 1816-48

WÜRZBURG

Paulus 1804-11

BASLE

Buxtorf 1813-29 | de Wette 1822-49 | J.J. Stähelin 1829-75 | Schultz 1864-72 | Kautzsch 1872-80 | Smend 1881-9 | Duhm 1889-1928

Orelli 1885-1912

STRASBOURG

Reuss 1834-88 | Schultz Baudissin 1872-6, 1876-81 | Budde 1889-1900 | Nowack 1881-1919

Nöldeke 1873-1910o

GENEVA

Hävernick 1832-4 | Elwert 1836-7

Schulthess 1796-1836 | Schlottmann 1855-9 | Ryssel 1885-9

ZÜRICH

Hitzig 1833-61 | Schrader 1863-70

Part Two
England 1800–80

11

English Critical
Old Testament Scholarship
prior to 1800

In the nineteenth century, Germany led the way in the development of critical scholarship. England lagged far behind, and only late in the nineteenth century was there anything like a widespread acceptance of the critical method in England, and then only with modifications occasioned by the developmentalist philosophy that came to prevail. It is well known that in the hundred years roughly from 1650 to 1750 the position was completely reversed. Germany, under the influence of Reformation orthodoxy and pietism, contributed to scholarship mainly at the level of philological studies. In England, however, the writings of the Deists contained a considerable onslaught against the Old Testament.

Specialists in the study of Deism have warned that Deism must not be thought of as a movement, or as an identifiable body of opinion.[1] Its representatives sometimes contradicted each other, and in any case, they tended to be individuals, and did not constitute a party or school. Recent research has stressed the importance of understanding the Deist writers in the context of the philosophical and political climate of the period.[2] English religious thought at this time was rejecting scholasticism, was inclined to nominalism, and was deeply involved with the spirit of humanism. The burning issues of the relation between Church and State had created in many thinkers a desire for tolerance, which in turn resulted in a search for a basic form of Christianity that could be accepted in private, without the tyranny of a State Church. There was also a Puritan element among certain liberal thinkers, which attacked the clericalism and ritual of the Church of England by attacking those parts of the Old Testament devoted to priesthood and ritual. The position of the Church of England in the immediate post-

---

[1] See C. Gestrich, 'Deismus', in *TRE* 8, Berlin 1981, p. 392: 'Das Phänomen *Deismus* ist schwerlich auf einen einheitlichen Begriff zu bringen. Soweit ein rationaler, aufs Moralische ausgerichteter monotheistischer Gottesglaube für ihn charakteristisch ist, lässt sich der Deismus nicht einmal einem bestimmte einzelnen Zeitabschnitt der europäischen Geschichte zuordnen'.

[2] See especially Reventlow, *Bibelautorität und Geist der Moderne, passim.*

Reformation period had often been justified by reference to the Old Testament, and by comparisons between the religious reforms initiated by Hezekiah and Josiah, and the reforms of Henry VIII, Edward VI and Elizabeth I.[3]

It is not part of the plan of the present book to give an account of the Deist controversy.[4] Instead, some indication will be given of the critical views that were advanced during the period 1650–1750.

The standard works on the history of Old Testament interpretation devote some space to the views expressed in Thomas Hobbes's *Leviathan* (1651), although, as Reventlow has remarked, the background to these views is usually passed over.[5] In *Leviathan*,[6] Hobbes was arguing for the authority of the State Church, ruled, under God, by a Christian king in its sovereign territory. No doubt he was motivated by a desire to deny the claims of the Church of Rome to authority in the matter of interpretation of Scripture; but he was equally opposed to private or individual religion without a corporate expression. His basic dilemma was to discover in what way the Bible was binding upon Christians. He accepted that if what the Bible taught accorded with the laws of nature, then it was clear that such laws were evident to all, and must be obeyed by all. But what of teachings or laws that did not fall into this class, such as the biblical teaching that there are such things as angels? In this and similar cases, there would be no obligation upon people to accept such teachings unless they were promulgated by the authority of the national church and the power of the sovereign. Thus Hobbes regarded as authoritative those books of the Bible declared to be canonical by the Church of England, and he looked for a form of rational Christianity in which the sovereign upheld the laws contained in Scripture.

Within the terms of his acceptance[7] of the authority of the Church in the

---

[3] For such comparisons see, e.g., Reventlow, pp. 155ff, on Bucer's *De regno Christi* (1550).

[4] In addition to Gestrich and Reventlow and the literature there cited, see the useful summary in A. Plummer, *The Church of England in the Eighteenth Century*, London 1910, pp. 92–101.

[5] For standard treatments of Hobbes in histories of Old Testament study see Liestel, pp. 357, 360, 493, 506, 520, 540, 551; Kraus, pp. 57ff. R. M. Grant, *A Short History of the Interpretation of the Bible*, rev. ed., London 1963, pp. 116ff. See also Cheyne's remarks on p. 11. Reventlow deals fully with Hobbes in pt. 2, ch. 3.

[6] *Leviathan or the Matter, Fame and Power of a Commonwealth Ecclesiastical and Civil*, ed. M. Oakeshott, Oxford 1946, has been used here.

[7] *Leviathan*, Pt 3, ch. 33 (Oakeshott, pp. 246ff. See pp. 246–7): 'But the question is not of obedience to God, but of *when* and *what* God hath said; which to subjects that have no supernatural revelation, cannot be known, but by that natural reason, which guideth them, for the obtaining of peace and justice, to obey the authority of their several commonwealths, that is to say, of their lawful sovereigns. According to this obligation, I can acknowledge no other books of the Old Testament to be Holy Scripture, but those which have been commanded to be acknowledged for such, by the authority of the Church of England.'

promulgation of Scripture, Hobbes entertained views about the authorship of biblical books, which were radical for the English scene at the time. The basis of these views was the simple one that internal evidence of the books themselves is our sole evidence for determining authorship.[8] On this view, Moses could not have written Deuteronomy 34.6, which states, of Moses's tomb, that no one knows its location 'to this day'. Other non-Mosaic passages were Genesis 12.6, 'the Canaanite was then in the land', and Numbers 21.14, where the writer cites 'The Book of the Wars of the Lord' as the source for accounts of the acts of Moses.[9]

Although Hobbes concluded that 'it is therefore sufficiently evident, that the five Books of Moses were written after his time, though how long after it be not so manifest',[10] he ascribed Deuteronomy 11—27 to Moses, and assumed that this is what had been discovered in the Temple by Hilkiah in the reign of Josiah.[11]

The book of Joshua was written 'long after the time of Joshua', because of its use of the phrase 'unto this day' (e.g., Joshua 4.9; 5.9; 7.26), signifying 'a time past, beyond the memory of man'. Similar considerations pointed to the conclusion that Judges, Ruth and the books of Samuel had been written long after the time of the events recorded in them, while in the case of the books of Kings and Chronicles, it was obvious from their content that they were post-exilic.[12] The book of Job, whose prose parts were added 'as a preface in the beginning, and an epilogue in the end',[13] was not a history but a work of philosophy. Jonah was not, strictly speaking, a prophetic book, but an account of Jonah's forwardness, and probably not by Jonah himself since he was the subject of the book.[14] Hobbes accepted a date for Daniel during the time of the Babylonian Exile, and held that it was not evident from Joel and Malachi when these prophets were active. In its extant form, the Old Testament was post-exilic.[15]

In *Leviathan*, Hobbes devoted considerable space to the enunciation of Christian doctrine on the basis of biblical teaching. On the whole, his

---

[8] ibid., p. 247: 'who were the original writers of the several Books of Holy Scripture, has not been evident by any sufficient testimony of other history . . . The light therefore that must guide us in this question, must be that which is held out unto us from the books themselves. . .'.

[9] ibid., p. 248.

[10] ibid., p. 248.

[11] ibid., pp. 248–9: 'the same (chs. 11—27) which having been lost, was long time after found again by Hilkiah, and sent to King Josias (2 Kings 22.8) 'who causing it to be read to the people (2 Kings 23) renewed the covenant between God and them.'

[12] ibid., p. 249.

[13] ibid., p. 250.

[14] ibid., p. 251.

[15] ibid., p. 251: 'But considering the inscriptions, or titles of their books, it is manifest enough, that the whole Scripture of the Old Testament, was set forth in the form we have it, after the return of the Jews from their captivity in Babylon . . .'

conclusions were traditional; but his discussions revealed sharp critical appreciation. He was quick to point out different senses in which the phrase 'word of God' could be used,[16] and he also provided a discriminating account of prophecy, in which prophets were prolocutors as well as foretellers.[17]

If Hobbes was an advocate of the authority of the National Church, John Locke stood for separation of Church and State, and saw religion as a private matter.[18] His contribution to biblical studies lay primarily in the field of the New Testament, where he concentrated upon the interpretation of the Pauline Epistles. Tholuck's verdict upon Locke's efforts in this sphere was that his paraphrases represented 'the most lamentable watering-down and trivializing' of Pauline theology.[19]

Locke's greatest importance for the present book is that he gave classical expression to the sort of philosophical outlook that, consciously or unconsciously, pervaded England in the eighteenth century, and for much of the nineteenth century. This outlook regarded revelation as something essentially external, approved by reason, accepted by faith (intellectual assent), and put into practice by moral conduct and by worship and prayer. The Bible was this source of revelation, and as such, was basically unassailable.[20] Even those who attacked the Old Testament did not doubt that it was revelation, with the notable exception of Thomas Morgan.[21] If parts of the Old Testament were attacked, it was on the (traditional) grounds that the coming of Jesus had rendered the ritual and civil laws of Moses inoperative;[22] or it was on the grounds that the Old Testament legislation was the Judaism that Paul had urged Christians to reject. Even radical attempts to demythologize the Old Testament did not cast doubt upon the information gained *after* demythologization. Another approach deemed the Old Testament legislation to be necessary revelation for the Hebrews because of their hardness of heart or the temptation of idolatry, with the implication that this legislation was not necessary for Christians. Thus, although some Deists went a long way towards undermining the practical authority of the Old Testament, in the course of which action they put forward radical critical ideas, nothing that they said tended towards the

---

[16] ibid., pp. 272–5.
[17] ibid., p. 275: 'The name of Prophet signifieth in Scripture, sometimes *prolocutor*; that is, he that speaketh from God to man, or from man to God: and sometimes *predictor*, or a foreteller of things to come . . .'
[18] Gestrich, loc. cit., p. 398. Reventlow's treatment of Locke is on pp. 401–69.
[19] The quotation is given by Gestrich, p. 399.
[20] See Reventlow, pp. 425ff.
[21] ibid., pp. 649ff.
[22] As stated in Art. 7 of the Thirty-nine Articles of Religion of the Church of England: Ceremonial Old Testament laws are not binding on Christians and civil laws are not necessarily binding.

breakthrough in Old Testament criticism achieved by de Wette and his followers.

In Locke's *Letter on Toleration*, we appear to find the view that none of the Mosaic law is binding upon Christians, whereas the *Reasonableness of Christianity* makes it clear that Locke accepted that the moral precepts of the Mosaic law were binding upon Christians.[23] The apparent contradiction may be resolved by assuming that, like Hobbes, Locke limited the application of Old Testament laws that were addressed to specific individuals in the Old Testament to those individuals, whereas moral precepts of the Mosaic law, if approved by reason, were binding upon all Christians.

In the writings of John Toland, we find one of the earliest English attempts to demythologize the Old Testament.[24] Toland is best known for his *Christianity not Mysterious* (1696), a work which took to its logical conclusion the view that nothing in revelation can be contrary to reason. Locke, indeed, had distinguished between 'certainty of knowledge' and 'assurance of faith' which latter depended upon divine revelation, although it is not clear how far Locke was prepared to go in radically subjecting assurance of faith to the test of reason. Toland had no inhibitions, and held that unless something could be understood, it could not be assented to. There could, therefore, be no 'mysteries' in religion, since it would be a contradiction to believe something that could not be understood; and anything that could be understood could not be a mystery.

In Toland's *Hodegus* of 1720, the author addressed himself to the account of the pillar of cloud and fire that accompanied the Israelites through the wilderness.[25] On the basis of comparative studies, he concluded that the cloud and fire were *one* manifestation of an actual fire which was carried in the Israelite camp in order to guide the vast multitude that made the journey. By day, the fire produced smoke, by night fire, and journeying at night was often necessitated by the climate, it being too hot to travel by day.[26]

In the account of the crossing of the Red Sea, the statement in Exodus

---

[23] J. Locke, *Epistola de Tolerantia* (1689), ed. R. Kibansky, Oxford 1968, pp. 115–16: 'True indeed, by the law of Moses, but that in no way obliges Christians. And surely you will not make everything laid down by law for the Jews into an example for all. Nor will it help you to cite the well-known, but in this case useless, distinction between the moral, judicial, and ceremonial law. For a positive law does not oblige anybody except those for whom it is laid down.' Cf. *The Reasonableness of Christianity as delivered in the Scriptures* (1695) in *The Works of John Locke*, 7, London 1823, p. 15: '... the moral part of Moses's law, or the moral law ... obliges Christians and all men, everywhere.' See also Reventlow, pp. 466–7.

[24] See Reventlow, pp. 480–503.

[25] J. Toland, *Tetradymus, containing Hodegus, Clidophorus, Hypatia and Mangonentes*, London 1720.

[26] *Tetradymus*, p. 6. Toland also makes the point that visible signals were needed for the camp, since 600,000 men would not all be able to hear the trumpet signals.

14.19 that the angel of God that preceded the Israelites moved to a position behind them was to be understood as follows: the angel was, in fact, the human bearer of the fire. The alteration of the position of the fire from front to rear was a ruse to fool the enemy about the exact position of the Israelites, a ruse that could be paralleled from other peoples.[27] The bearer of the fire was Hobab (the Hodegus, or pathfinder, of the title). He was the brother-in-law of Moses, a Kenite who knew the wilderness well.[28]

Toland's aim in *Hodegus*, according to his general preface to *Tetradymus*, was to demonstrate the authenticity of the Mosaic history as demythologized.

> The discoveries I made ... created in me a higher veneration for Moses, than even was instilled by my instructors, and on better grounds. ... Wherefore, my design in this publication, is to make Moses better understood, and consequently more easily believed: which is as well to defend him against those, who unreasonably believe him not at all, as also against those, who by their absurd belief render him incredible.[29]

Other examples of demythologizing in *Hodegus* include the explanation of the claim in Deuteronomy that during the wilderness period, the clothes and shoes of the Israelites did not wear out. The reason for this was that among the Israelites were the craftsmen who could provide new shoes and clothes. The apparent miracle derived from a misunderstanding of the hyperbolic mode of expression of the Old Testament.[30]

Historical and demythologizing exegesis of the Old Testament inevitably raised the question of the interpretation of prophecies, especially those relating to the coming of Christ. In the work of Antony Collins (1676–1729), the interpretation of prophecies in their strict historical sense was advocated, while Collins also maintained a Maccabean date for the book of Daniel.[31] Collins's views provoked much opposition, because the Old Testament prophecies of the coming of Christ constituted in the eighteenth, as in the nineteenth, century, part of the evidence for the divine revelation contained in the Bible. If the proclamation of Christ in Old Testament prophecy was denied, the way was open to severing the Old Testament from the New, since Deists on the whole found distasteful the miracles and legislation of the Old Testament. The logical step of discarding the Old Testament altogether was taken by Thomas Morgan in his *Physico-Theology* (1741), who also directed criticism against the immoral behaviour of Old

[27] ibid., pp. 28–9.
[28] ibid., pp. 51ff.
[29] ibid., p. ii.
[30] ibid., p. 30. On p. 24, Toland mentions the view 'undeniably prov'd', by 'men of immense learning, and most of 'em Divines by profession' that the Pentateuch is an abridgement of some larger history of the Israelites.
[31] Reventlow, pp. 596ff.

Testament figures such as David, in the spirit of Bayle's *Dictionnaire historique et critique*.[32]

Although Morgan's work marked the high-point of the Deist onslaught on the Old Testament, the Deist tendency was not to last long after the date of his works. The demise of Deism in England was not due to the ability of those who defended orthodoxy; it was rather that it struck no chord with non-intellectuals and was in any case unable to convince many people that natural religion *was* clear and manifest to reason.[33] The liberal thinking implicit in Deism was taken over, in the second half of the eighteenth century, into Unitarianism, where it found a home in an organized form of religious belief. As will be mentioned below,[34] Unitarians became, at the turn of the century, one of the most considerable factors in the knowledge and propagation of German criticism in England. English Deism was, from the 1740s, exported to Europe including Germany, where it deeply affected Reimarus, and played a part in the critical approaches developed by scholars such as Semler and Michaelis.[35] England reasserted traditional doctrines, with Butler's *Analogy of Religion* and Paley's *Evidences* becoming standard works lasting well into the nineteenth century.

However, the Deist controversy seems to have left its mark upon even orthodox English Old Testament scholars, and other theologians. The eighteenth century saw considerable interest in establishing the original text of the Old Testament, which was generally acknowledged to be corrupt in parts. The defects could be remedied by greater knowledge of the manuscript tradition of the Hebrew Bible, by use of the ancient versions, and by comparative philology. The Old Testament text was handled freely, and many emendations were proposed.

The celebrated new translation of Isaiah (1779) of Robert Lowth[36] shows how far an orthodox scholar was prepared to go in allowing reason to attempt conjectural emendation of the text which was thought to be corrupt. Lowth firmly rejected the idea that such use of reason undermined the divine revelation.

> If it be objected [he wrote] that a concession, so large as this, tends to invalidate the authority of Scripture; that it gives up in effect the certainty and authenticity of the doctrine contained in it . . . this . . . is a vain and groundless apprehension. Casual errors may blemish parts, but do not destroy, or much alter, the whole.[37]

[32] ibid., pp. 649ff.

[33] See the reasons for the collapse of Deism in Plummer, op. cit., p. 100.

[34] See p. 158.

[35] Reventlow, 'Das Arsenal der Bibelkritik des Reimarus' in *Hermann Samuel Reimarus*, pp. 44–65.

[36] Robert Lowth, *Isaiah: A New Translation, with a Preliminary Dissertation and Notes, Critical, Philological, and Explanatory*, 1799, n. ed., Glasgow 1822.

[37] ibid., pp. lxxviii–lxxix.

Lowth was prepared to allow the reason and judgement of readers to decide,

> whether the conjectural reading ... be more agreeable to the context, to the
> exigence of the place, to parallel and similar passages, to the rules and genius of
> the language, and to the laws of sound and temperate criticism.[38]

Lowth is most famous for his *Lectures on the Sacred Poetry of the Hebrews*,
delivered before the University of Oxford in 1753.[39] The main effect of
these lectures upon the future course of critical studies was to encourage the
use of criteria from secular poetry in evaluating the poetic mode of discourse
in the Old Testament. This was to stress the human side of the text, to treat
it 'like any other book'. Lowth accepted that the historical reference of
prophecies had to be taken seriously, although in the case of messianic
prophecies, he held firmly to the view that the coming of Christ was
predicted.[40]

By far the most remarkable results in critical scholarship in Britain, as the
eighteenth century drew to its close, were those of Alexander Geddes.[41] In
view of the fact that Geddes was a Scottish Roman Catholic, who trained
for the priesthood in France, it could well be argued that he has no place in
a book about English and German Old Testament criticism. However, his
critical work certainly played a part in shaping English orthodox attitudes
towards biblical criticism. He is therefore considered briefly.

Geddes was born in 1737 in Buckie, Banffshire, Scotland, and educated
at the Scottish seminary at Scalan, and at the Scots College in Paris, where
he studied from 1758 to 1764. From 1764 to 1780 he worked as a priest in
Scotland, resigning from his charge in May 1780 after friction with the
bishop, which was brought to a head when Geddes attended an Episcopalian
service. This latter incident shows Geddes's broad sympathies; he had regular
contact with Episcopalian and Presbyterian clergy during his period at
Auchin.

In 1781, Geddes went to London in order to fill a chaplaincy, but when
this post folded, he was asked by Lord Petre to undertake a revision of the
Douai–Challoner version of the English Bible, the version used by Roman

---

[38] ibid., pp. lxxxv–lxxxvi.

[39] *De sacra poesi hebraeorum*, Oxford 1753.

[40] See *Isaiah*, pp. 85–6, on Isaiah 7.14, where Lowth allows an 'obvious and literal meaning
of the prophecy', but goes on to assert, 'we may easily suppose, that, in minds prepared by
the general expectation of a great deliverer to spring from the house of David, they raised
hopes far beyond what the present occasion suggested ...'

[41] For what follows, I am greatly indebted to R. C. Fuller's *Dr Alexander Geddes. A Forerunner
of Biblical Criticism*, Diss. Cambridge 1968. I wish to thank Dr Fuller for permission to
refer to the dissertation, of which a revised edition is to be published by Almond Press,
Sheffield, in the series 'Historic Texts and Interpreters in Biblical Scholarship'. See also
Cheyne, pp. 4–12, and Kraus, pp. 1, 155f.

Catholics in Britain. However, because of the insistence of the Roman bishops that the Douai version was their responsibility, Geddes proposed to undertake a completely new version of the Bible. His project was announced in his *Prospectus of a New Translation of the Holy Bible* in 1786. In 1788 there appeared some *Proposals and Specimens*, to be followed by two volumes of his translation, in 1792 and 1797. In 1800 appeared his *Critical Remarks on the Hebrew Scriptures corresponding with a New Translation of the Bible.*

Geddes's work amounted to far more than a new translation.[42] In the first place, it was concerned to establish the original text of the Old Testament as accurately as possible, and it took full account of the work on the Hebrew manuscript tradition carried out by Kennicott and de Rossi. For his part, Geddes had a distrust of the massoretic tradition of the Hebrew text, and in dealing with the Pentateuch, he often preferred the readings of the Samaritan Pentateuch. He was also fully aware of the readiness of eighteenth-century scholars to emend the text where it was thought to be corrupt, and he was particularly familiar with the work in this field of Kennicott and Lowth.

The most significant part of his work, however, was in his prefaces to his translations, in which he offered opinions on the authorship of the biblical books, and on their interpretation. On the authorship of the Pentateuch,[43] Geddes rejected the view that it was written by Moses, and placed it somewhere between the time of David and Hezekiah. He rejected the documentary hypothesis of Astruc and Eichhorn. For example, he recognized the different character of Genesis 2—3 compared with Genesis 1, but did not accept that there had been two authors or sources. His approach to the composition was an early form of the 'Fragment Hypothesis', in the sense that Geddes identified passages that were 'interpolations', while not making it clear whether the interpolations were subsequent to the final main redaction.[44]

In addition to his remarks about authorship, Geddes addressed himself to the problem of the supernatural elements in the narratives, reaching a position close to that of Eichhorn, of whose work he knew and approved. Like Eichhorn and the Neologists Geddes wished to retain the historical basis of the narratives by removing the supernatural crudities. He was also worried about the moral crudities of the Old Testament, and said in no uncertain terms that directions such as those to slaughter the Canaanites totally, had wrongly been put into the mouth of God.[45]

Geddes's views on the supernatural and on the crude moral parts of the Old Testament inevitably led him to reject traditional views of biblical inspiration, although he does not seem to have offered an alternative view

[42] See Fuller, pp. 39ff.
[43] ibid., pp. 112ff.
[44] ibid., pp. 118–19.
[45] Ibid., pp. 141ff.

of inspiration. That the Old Testament contained revelation he did not doubt; but it was necessary to discover that revelation by the use of critical means. Geddes did not deny the possibility of the truth of the miracles recorded in the Bible, but denied that the matter of their historicity was settled by their being in an inspired book.[46]

When Geddes published his *Prospectus* in 1786, it was supported by Lowth and widely approved, not only because he sent complimentary copies to scholars and influential people at home and abroad. As his work proceeded, however, it drew more and more opposition. Geddes was officially censured by his bishop in June 1793, for failing to retract the comments in the preface to the first volume of his translation.[47] His association with Unitarians in the 1790s, and his intimacy with German scholars such as Paulus and Eichhorn were such as to increase suspicion in orthodox circles. Reviews and publications hostile to him began to appear. His importance for critical Old Testament scholarship in Britain seems to have rested on the role he played in helping to mediate German ideas through his Unitarian associates, on into the nineteenth century.

Whether he played a *substantial* role in the history of critical scholarship in general, is an open question. Reginald Fuller, in his excellent treatment of Geddes, tries to argue that a definite strand of critical influence can be traced from Geddes through Vater to de Wette and on to Ewald. He also believes that had Geddes lived to complete his work, he would have reached conclusions similar to those of de Wette.[48] Both claims are, I think, difficult to sustain. Geddes appears to have added little or nothing to Eichhorn's 'mythical' understanding of the Genesis narratives. The extent of his influence upon Vater is difficult to estimate, but even if we hold it to have been decisive, we have already seen that Vater's 'Fragmentary' approach did not lead him to the breakthrough achieved by de Wette.

It is unlikely that Geddes would have reproduced de Wette's early historical negativism independently. As Fuller himself shows, Geddes stood closer to the naturalism of Paulus than to the mythical historicism of Eichhorn, and Geddes stood in the tradition of the French enlightenment and English Deism. It is also unlikely that, as a Catholic by training, he would have entertained such negative views of ritual and priesthood as to place their Old Testament developed form in the despised period of 'Judaism'.

The writings of Geddes were carefully reviewed by German scholars, including Michaelis and Eichhorn.[49] They showed a dialogue between scholarship in Britain and Germany of a kind to suggest that such scholarship in Britain and Germany was a common possession of all thinking people,

[46] ibid., p. 124.
[47] ibid., pp. 187–8.
[48] ibid., p. 221, 225ff.
[49] ibid., pp. 177–8, 192–3, 203ff.

regardless of country. However, Geddes's death in 1802, and the Napoleonic Wars, which made links between Britain and the Continent of Europe difficult to maintain, ushered in a period of relative isolation of German from British Old Testament scholarship. It would be many years before such cordial links would not only exist, but assist the mutual advance of critical scholarship.

12

German
Old Testament Criticism
in England 1790–1859

The publication of *Essays and Reviews* in 1860, and of Bishop Colenso's writings on the Pentateuch in 1861 produced shock waves in English theology which will be referred to later in this book.[1] The object of the present chapter is to provide an outline of the knowledge of German Old Testament criticism that was available in England from about 1790. The fact that such knowledge was available does not entail that it was widely known. What was known and discussed in the study or the academic cloister did not necessarily penetrate to the average clergyman and his congregation in the first half of the nineteenth century. Our own recent theological history has witnessed the shock waves caused by a book such as *Honest to God*,[2] when the views presented in it were fairly commonplace in academic circles. On the other hand, it would be wrong to conclude from the outcry over *Essays and Reviews* and Colenso on the Pentateuch that the views contained in them had never before been aired in England. That this was not the case will be illustrated in the present chapter. No doubt they were revolutionary to people who had no opportunity to reflect on critical matters or who had been discouraged from doing so; and there were also not a few such people in the 1960s who reacted violently to *Honest to God*. But part of the reason for the hostile reaction to *Essays and Reviews* and Colenso came from the fact that a bishop, and other accredited ministers of the established Church had dared to put forward what had hitherto been known (if it was known at all) as the work of 'Rationalist' Germans.

Acquaintance with German Old Testament critical scholarship in England can be traced back to the 1790s, if not earlier. On the whole, this knowledge was at its deepest and keenest in the Unitarian circles which took over from Deism the spirit of radical dissent.[3] One such circle was to be found in

---

[1] See chs. 15 and 16.
[2] J. A. T. Robinson, *Honest to God*, London 1963.
[3] See Basil Willey, *The Eighteenth-Century Background*, Harmondsworth 1962, p. 175: 'Deism was professed by isolated freethinkers, while the Unitarian Congregation, having evolved by imperceptible stages from the older forms of dissent, retained a strong group-consciousness as a religious fellowship.'

Cambridge in the late 1780s, consisting of men such as William Frend, Robert Robinson, and George Dyer.[4] The Rationalist H. E. G. Paulus, who was visiting England in 1788, met the Cambridge Unitarians at a party in Jesus College on 8 October 1788, and maintained contact with several British theologians.[5] Other important Unitarians were Joseph Priestley, Theophilus Lindsey, Thomas Belsham and Thomas Beddoes.[6] Beddoes apparently possessed a large number of foreign periodicals, especially those published in Göttingen, and was fully aware of the work of Eichhorn and his followers. It was from Beddoes that Coleridge learnt about the work of the Göttingen scholars.[7]

Not only Unitarian circles were aware of German biblical criticism. The *Critical Review*, edited by an Anglican, contained between the years 1792 and 1799 reviews of such 'advanced' works as J. P. Gabler's edition of

---

[4] William Frend (1757–1841) was a fellow of Jesus College, Cambridge, until his expulsion on religious grounds. Robert Robinson (1735–90) was a Baptist minister in Cambridge, with strong radical views. George Dyer (1755–1841) moved in literary circles, including those of Coleridge and Charles Lamb. See Frida Knight, *University Rebel. The Life of William Frend (1757–1841)*, London 1971.

[5] See Knight, *University Rebel*, p. 67. Also, Thomas Sadler, *Diary, Reminiscences and Correspondence of Henry Crabb Robinson*, London 1872[3], 1, p. 83. Paulus corresponded with Geddes, and received letters 'from several of the bishops'. Robinson records that Paulus was not much pleased by English theologians.

[6] Joseph Priestley (1737–1804), a leading Unitarian and radical, who emigrated to America after a mob had burnt his house in Birmingham. Theophilus Lindsey (1723–1808), vicar of Catterick, who became a Unitarian and founded the Essex Street Chapel in London in 1774. Thomas Belsham (1750–1829), an Independent who resigned from his post at Daventry College and became tutor at the Hackney College (1786–96). Thomas Beddoes (1760–1808), medical doctor.

[7] On Beddoes and his influence on Coleridge, see Elinor S. Shaffer, *'Kubla Kahn' and the Fall of Jerusalem. The Mythological School in Biblical Criticism and Secular Literature 1770–1880*. It is difficult to know to what extent Coleridge was significant for the knowledge and influence of German Old Testament criticism in England. He visited Göttingen and heard lectures from Eichhorn in 1798, and he possessed a copy of Eichhorn's *Einleitung in das Alte Testament*, which he annotated, apparently in the first decade of the nineteenth century (see Shaffer p. 320, n31). Coleridge also read Gabler's edition of Eichhorn's *Urgeschichte* (Shaffer p. 321, n38). That Coleridge knew a lot about German criticism cannot be denied. How much of this knowledge he passed on, especially after he became theologically more orthodox, I do not know. His *Confessions of an Inquiring Spirit*, which contained some of his views of biblical interpretation was published posthumously in 1840, but had been read in manuscript by Thomas Arnold and others (Shaffer p. 320, n30). For other recent works on Coleridge and his relations with Germany and with Anglicans in the early nineteenth century, see Rosemary Ashton, *The German Idea. Four English Writers and the Reception of German Thought, 1800–60*, Cambridge 1980, and Stephen Prickett, *Romanticism and Religion. The Tradition of Coleridge and Wordsworth in the Victorian Church*, Cambridge 1976.

Eichhorn's *Urgeschichte*.[8] In actual fact, the review gave away little of the contents of the *Urgeschichte*, so that readers of the review could not have learned from it that Gabler accepted the two-source documentary hypothesis, that he demythologized the incident of the Fall, that he regarded Genesis 1 as a poetic composition expressing earliest man's understanding of how the world had originated, not to mention Gabler's theoretical discussion of types of myth and their relationship to the growth of ancient traditions. The reviewer blamed illness for his failure to outline the contents more fully, and contented himself with recording that 'the view taken of the second and third chapters of Genesis is highly deserving attention'. Gabler was praised for his observations on what many previous writers had said, as also for his acute defence of positions which, however, the reviewer could 'by no means accede to'. The reviewer was far more explicit about J. C. K. Nachtigall's *Gesänge Davids und seiner Zeitgenossen, nach Zeitfolge geordnet und bearbeitet*.[9] Full justice was done to this early attempt to place the Psalms in the context of an annual festival of Zion commemorating the bringing of the ark to Jerusalem by David. Not only did Nachtigall classify the Psalms according to their conjectured use at the festival—Psalm 24 at the gate of Zion; Psalm 132.8–9, 13–18 after the Ark had been deposited in its place—but he also expressed radical views about the state of preservation of the Psalms. In the words of the reviewer:

> Songs, in themselves distinct, have not been kept so; and others entire have been broken. Instances of the former remark occur in the 18th, 19th, 39th, 40th, 51st, 57th, and other psalms; and of the latter, in the 9th and 10th, which are three joined together, as are the 42nd and 43rd. Besides, many of these songs are but *membra disjecta*. Hence, rightly to understand these compositions, it will be requisite to arrange them according to their contents, and unite what would obviously make out the sense.[10]

Thus, readers of the critical review of 1798 were made aware of what we might call a fragmentary hypothesis of the Psalms. On the grounds of content, Psalms were dismembered into fragments and re-assembled, with the aim of reconstructing their liturgical use in the Temple. The reviewer noted that 'as few traces remain in the documentary history to guide an inquirer, many doubts with respect to the alleged hypothesis may arise'. Apart from this caveat, the reviewer commended Nachtigall's 'original and

---

[8] The editor was G. Gregory, translator of Lowth's *Praelectiones* on Hebrew poetry. I owe the information about the *Critical Review* to my Sheffield colleague in the Department of English Literature, Mr Derek Roper. For the review of the *Urgeschichte* (probably by Samuel Henley) see *Critical Review* (1795), pp. 549–50.

[9] *Critical Review* (1798) pp. 537–42.

[10] ibid., p. 539.

very interesting view'.[11] The pages of the *Critical Review* indicate a flow of critical works from Germany to England at the close of the eighteenth century.[12]

The turn of the century, however, witnessed a hardening against German critical work in 'establishment' circles. Changes among the contributors to the *Critical Review* meant that few, if any, works of German criticism were noticed.[13] Also, in 'establishment' circles it was easy to lump together radical dissent and critical views, and to see both as a threat not only to traditional Christian doctrines, but to the constitution of the land. There is the further point that at least during the Napoleonic wars, it was not easy to receive periodical literature and books from the Continent of Europe.[14] However, there were opportunities for links between Germany and England to be forged.

A remarkable link was forged by Henry Crabb Robinson, who studied in Jena from October 1802 to August 1805, and who initially lodged in the house owned by Jakob Friedrich Fries.[15] Not only did Robinson begin a friendship with Fries that lasted for many years;[16] he also joined the inner group of students whom Fries gathered around him. Robinson must surely have met de Wette during this period, although I have not found any documentary evidence of this. De Wette was a student in Jena at this time, and one of Fries's inner circle.[17] Robinson attended lectures given by Fries and by Paulus, and was acquainted with Griesbach.[18]

It is difficult to assess the significance of Robinson's German contacts for knowledge of German critical scholarship in England. Robinson became a barrister, and he moved in Unitarian and in literary circles, where he had met Coleridge as early as 1795.[19] On the other hand, he does not appear to

[11] ibid., p. 539.

[12] The following works, among others, were noticed between 1792 and 1799: J. C. Döderlein, *Salomons Prediger und Hoheslied*; E. F. C. Rosenmüller, *Scholia in Vetus Testamentum*; J. Simonis, *Lexicon manuale Hebraicum et Chaldaicum*, ed. J. G. Eichhorn.

[13] According to my colleague Mr Roper, Henley, the main reviewer of German theology, ceased to write for the *Critical Review* after 1799, and his successor was mostly interested in books dealing with comparative mythology.

[14] See below, note 23.

[15] See Hertha Marquardt, *Henry Crabb Robinson und seine deutschen Freunde. Brücke zwischen England und Deutschland im Zeitalter der Romantik*, 2 vols, Göttingen, 1964–7. Robinson's time in Jena is described in 1, ch. 3, 'Robinson als Student in Jena', pp. 125–208.

[16] See Marquardt op. cit., 2, p. 557 for a mention of Robinson's visit to Fries in Jena in 1829.

[17] A. Wiegand, *W. M. L. de Wette*, pp. 11–12.

[18] Robinson described Fries as the man who taught him the little that he ever clearly understood about Kant. Fries held English philosophy 'very cheaply' (Sadler, 1, p. 70). Paulus's lectures were always didactic and practical (Marquardt, 1, p. 129). See also Sadler, 1, pp. 82–3 for an account of a conversation between Robinson and Paulus. For Robinson's first visit to Griesbach, see Sadler, 1, p. 83.

[19] Sadler, 1, p. 17.

have met the liberal Anglicans until many years after his German student days, by which time the liberal Anglicans were already interested in matters German. Robinson met Julius Hare in 1825 in Cambridge, the first time that they had met since 1805, when Robinson visited the Hare Naylor family in Weimar.[20] Hare was then aged nine. Robinson did not meet Thomas Arnold until 1835, although he knew of Arnold's position.[21] We should probably conclude that the knowledge of German criticism possessed by Unitarian circles in England did not significantly influence non-Unitarians. As noticed above, the influence upon liberals such as Thirlwall and Arnold most likely came from contacts with Bunsen. Robinson did not meet Bunsen until 1829.

Before we consider the liberal Anglicans, it should be noticed that one of the very few works of German Old Testament criticism to be translated into English in the early part of the nineteenth century was J. D. Michaelis's *Mosaisches Recht*, published in 1814 under the title *Commentaries on the Laws of Moses*.[22] The preface to this book incidentally sheds some light upon aspects of communications between Britain and the Continent of Europe at this time. The translator apparently had the greatest difficulty in obtaining a copy of the German original, and when he finally obtained one, it was a copy in which a section from the *first* edition of *Mosaisches Recht* had been incorporated into the essentially *second* edition work. Considerable efforts to obtain a copy that was uniformly second edition failed, the work of translation was postponed 'for a considerable time' and then only begun after further efforts both at home and abroad to obtain a better copy had met with no success.[23]

In commending the work to the English audience, the translator spoke of *Mosaisches Recht* as Michaelis's acknowledged *magnum opus*, he noted its translation into other languages as well as earlier unrealized plans to render it into English, and quoted a glowing opinion from Eichhorn. On the other hand, the translator, identifying himself as a clergyman, stated that the book contained manifest mistakes, which he would have corrected in footnotes had it not been for the fact that the text as it stood ran to four volumes in the translation.[24]

Mosaisches Recht is indeed a fine work, presenting the Israelite legislation

---

[20] See Sadler, 1, p. 111, for the 1805 contacts with the Hare Naylors. See 2, p. 2 for the 1825 meeting with Julius in Cambridge.

[21] See Sadler, 2, p. 165 for the meeting with Arnold. In his reminiscences of the 1825 meeting with Hare (see n20) Robinson commented: 'The High Church party consider him a heretic on account of his intimacy with Bunsen and Arnold.'

[22] J. D. Michaelis, *Commentaries on the Laws of Moses*, tr. Alexander Smith, 4 vols., London 1814.

[23] ibid., pp. xxx–xxxi. The translator also remarks on 'the obstructed state of literary intercourse with the continent', p. xxii.

[24] ibid., p. xxii.

systematically, illuminated by studies from other disciplines. Michaelis never wavered in his support of Mosaic authorship of the legislation in the Pentateuch. On the other hand, Michaelis had a view of the relevance of the Mosaic legislation that can hardly have commended itself to 'establishment' readers in England in 1814. Michaelis asserted, following unspecified 'orthodox and sound divines', that the civil laws of Moses were not binding upon Christians, and he attacked the 'superstition' whereby attempts had been made to argue that the civil laws of Moses were not abrogated for Christians.[25] Michaelis presented the laws as a remarkable achievement of Moses: nonetheless, they were not the best possible laws; they were primarily suited to the very special conditions of Israelite life, and they were certainly not binding upon other nations living in quite different circumstances.[26] Positively, it could be said that what the Mosaic laws allowed (e.g., slavery, divorce for grounds other than adultery) was not a sin.[27] However, the legislation of the Old Testament was not to be applied unthinkingly to modern situations. Needless to say, in spite of his stress on the Mosaic origin of the laws, Michaelis's treatment stressed the human, relative and temporary nature of the ancient Israelite legislation.

In liberal 'establishment' circles, two of the most knowledgeable figures with regard to developments in Germany were Julius Hare and Connop Thirlwall. Hare, as has been mentioned, spent some time in Weimar with his family in 1804–5 at the age of nine. According to F. D. Maurice, Hare's eldest brother Francis, who initiated Julius into Greek, was an excellent German scholar, so that Julius 'could scarcely have avoided German studies even if he had desired to avoid them'.[28] The importance of German literature for Hare was such that he was to write in 1820 of his German books

> Above all, to them I owe my ability to believe in Christianity, with much more implicit and intelligent faith than I otherwise should have been able to have done, for without them I should only have saved myself from dreary suspicions, by a refusal to allow my heart to follow my head, and by a self-willed determination to believe, whether my reason approved of my belief or not.[29]

When Henry Crabb Robinson visited Hare's rooms in Cambridge in 1825,

---

[25] ibid., p. 5.

[26] See the heading to article 6, op. cit., 1, p. 17: '. . . the Mosaic Laws, though the best that the Israelites could bear, are not absolutely and universally the best, nor yet to be imitated by every people.'

[27] ibid., p. 6: 'It may . . . be politically inexpedient, but it is not sinful, in a sovereign, even in certain cases not specified by Christ, to permit married persons to separate, on account of their unyielding and irreconcilable tempers.'

[28] F. D. Maurice in the Introduction to J. C. Hare, *Charges to the Clergy of the Archdeaconry of Lewes, delivered at the Ordinary Visitations in the years 1843, 1845, 1846*, Cambridge 1856, p. xi.

[29] Hare to his mother in January 1820, quoted by Maurice, op. cit., p. xiii.

he was shown 'the best collection of modern German authors I have ever seen in England'.[30]

Hare was not an Old Testament scholar, and his contribution to Old Testament studies in England was indirect. His translation, with Thirlwall, of Niebuhr's *History of Rome* contributed to the development of the notion of progressive revelation in English thought; he defended the work of Bunsen against English opponents. Above all, he provided in Hurstmonceux a meeting point for Anglicans and others of a liberal disposition.[31]

Thirlwall was a school friend of Hare's, and a fellow undergraduate at Trinity College, Cambridge, in 1814.[32] His knowledge of German must have been gained early, for in 1819, when he visited the Bunsens in Rome, Frances Bunsen wrote to her mother:

> that he [Mr Thirlwall] had read Mr Niebuhr's Roman History proved him to possess no trifling knowledge of German, and as he expressed a wish to improve himself in the language, Charles ventured to invite him to come to us on a Tuesday evening . . . seeing that many Germans were in the habit of calling on that day . . . and Mr Thirlwall has never missed any Tuesday evening since. . . .[33]

Again, Thirlwall's effect upon Old Testament studies was indirect rather than direct, as the co-translator of Niebuhr. For his translation of Schleiermacher's *St Luke*, published in 1825, Thirlwall read works by Eichhorn, Paulus and Lücke.[34] We also find him in 1823 recommending to Hare, de Wette's novel *Theodore*: 'It is by Schleiermacher's colleague, de Wette, but without his name in the title page (two little volumes from which I have learnt more than from anything else I have read for a long time past)'.[35]

In orthodox dissenting circles, the controversy with Unitarianism produced an able work by John Pye Smith which showed acquaintance with German critical work. Smith's *Scripture Testimony to the Messiah*, first published in 1821, was occasioned chiefly by Thomas Belsham's *Calm*

[30] T. Sadler, *Diary*, 2, p. 2.
[31] See, for example, Frances Bunsen, *A Memoir of Baron Bunsen*, 2, p. 40; and the biography of Julius Hare by J. Merril Distad, *Guessing at Truth, The Life of Julius Charles Hare (1795–1855)*, Shepherdstown, 1979.
[32] J. J. Stewart Perowne and Louis Stokes, *Letters Literary and Theological of Connop Thirlwall*, London 1881, p. 22.
[33] A. J. C. Hare, *Life and Letters of Frances, Baroness Bunsen*, 1, p. 139.
[34] *Letters Literary and Theological*, pp. 71–80.
[35] ibid., p. 70. By 1823 de Wette was not, of course, Schleiermacher's colleague, having left Berlin in 1819. Whether Thirlwall's statement implies that he thought that de Wette was still in Berlin can only be a matter for speculation.

Inquiry into the Scripture Doctrine Concerning the Person of Christ.[36] In book 2, Smith examined the interpretation of the principal passages traditionally held to be prophecies of the coming of Christ, and in the process he had occasion to refer to de Wette, E. F. C. Rosenmüller, Michaelis, Gesenius, Döderlein, Ewald and Umbreit, to mention some. Smith's attitude to these German scholars was largely negative.[37] They were generally categorized as Anti-supranaturalists, scholars who denied revelation and the forecasting element in prophecy, and who hardly merited the designation 'Christian'.

Smith utilized Gesenius's commentary on Isaiah, and à propos of Gesenius's treatment of Isaiah 7.14 wrote, 'How true and melancholy is the reflection that, in this, our apostate and rebellious world, the misuse of learning is equally criminal and pernicious'.[38] Eichhorn is described as 'a man of splendid talents and prodigious acquirements, but awfully imbued with infidelity'. E. F. C. Rosenmüller, on the other hand, is praised for having altered his opinion in the 1821 edition of his *Scholia*, so that he is now prepared to refer some of the psalms to the future Messiah, and abandons some of his psalms interpretation in terms of actual events in David's or Solomon's reign. Even so, Rosenmüller is taken to task for saying that the author of Psalm 2 cannot have had 'our Saviour Jesus in his mind's contemplation'.[39] De Wette is described by Smith as the man who moves in the highest orbit of the class of Anti-supranaturalists: 'I might even say unrivalled among them as a scholar, a psychologist, a man of fine taste, and an acute logician'.[40]

Smith quotes a long passage from an article by de Wette in *Theologische Studien und Kritiken* for 1828 in which de Wette *appears* to adopt an attitude towards the notion of the Messiah that is so orthodox that Smith is led to exclaim 'after such admissions, we may well ask, Why should this great man object to the belief of direct revelation and inspiration?'[41] Almost certainly, Smith failed to understand the particular mediating theological position that de Wette represented, and in the light of which de Wette would not have cared to be labelled an Anti-supranaturalist.

We turn now to the knowledge of German criticism contained in the famous works of Hugh James Rose and Edward Bouverie Pusey of the close

---

[36] J. Pye Smith, *The Scripture Testimony to the Messiah*, 2 vols., London 1847⁴. The book went through several editions between 1821 and 1847, and my working copy was the fourth edition of 1847. It is acknowledged that reference to the 1847 version rather than the 1821 version spoils the attempted chronological treatment in this chapter; nevertheless, the picture of the state of knowledge of German criticism up to 1850 is not thereby distorted.

[37] Only Ewald appears to escape censure.

[38] Pye Smith, 1, p. 242, n122.

[39] ibid., p. 198.

[40] ibid., p. 130.

[41] ibid., p. 131.

of the 1820s. However, there will be no need to enter here into the controversy that arose between the two men about their views on German Rationalism, and the replies to each other that were occasioned.

Rose had been at Trinity College, Cambridge, with Julius Hare and Thirlwall, and in 1825 he published a series of sermons that he had preached before the University of Cambridge on 'the state of the Protestant Religion in Germany'.[42] Rose had visited Germany the previous year.[43] From Rose's sermons, and the very full notes that accompanied them in their published version, readers in the 1820s would have learned that in Germany there was a school of critics whose work could be compared with that of 'the most violent English Unitarians'.[44] The man chiefly responsible for this state of affairs was Semler, who having learned from his Pietist upbringing a view of the Church which ignored the necessity for teachers to defend the faith, had himself questioned the whole notion of canonicity, and had introduced a utilitarian criterion for judging the authority of a biblical work.[45] Further, he and others had presumed to investigate the character and disposition of the New Testament authors as a preliminary to interpreting their teaching, and he had insisted on the right of private judgement in biblical interpretation, something that the Church of England in its Articles certainly did not envisage.[46] A further complication was the influence of the philosophy of Kant in German theology, an influence which made theologians more concerned with sense than evidence, and which inevitably degenerated into mystical speculation.[47]

Regarding the content of German criticism, readers would have learned that the Mosaic authenticity of the Pentateuch had been attacked by Vater, de Wette, and Gesenius, and that de Wette and Gramberg had rejected the historicity of the books of Chronicles.[48] The mythical interpretation of Genesis as presented in the Gabler edition of Eichhorn's *Urgeschichte* was also outlined.[49] Of de Wette, Rose wrote, 'I never saw any writings more offensive than the early ones of de Wette, and was not aware of the change'—a change in de Wette's views had been claimed by Kaiser in his *Biblische Moral* (1821).[50]

---

[42] On Hugh James Rose (1795–1838) see J. W. Burgon, *Lives of Twelve Good Men*, London 1888, pp. 116–295. Rose's sermons were *The State of the Protestant Religion in Germany* in a series of discourses preached before the University of Cambridge, Cambridge 1825.

[43] See Burgon, op. cit., pp. 132–3.

[44] Rose, op. cit., p. 82.

[45] ibid., pp. 45–57.

[46] ibid., p. 103: 'The Church of England in her Articles, expressly assumes the exercise of an authority at variance with it' [the right of private judgement].

[47] ibid., p. 9.

[48] ibid., pp. 158–9.

[49] ibid., pp. 149ff.

[50] ibid., p. 136.

Rose adopted a very superior attitude towards the accomplishments of German theological scholarship. Paulus and his colleagues were learned, if by 'learned' was meant wide reading and the ability to distil information; but in Rose's view the German critics were not able to apply what they had collected, and accordingly could not be described as great scholars.[51]

Pusey's *Historical Enquiry into the Probable Causes of the Rationalist Character lately predominant in the Theology of Germany* (1828) was written, after his return from Germany, because of the distress that Rose's book had caused in Germany.[52] Much of it was devoted to the history of Protestant German theology since the Reformation, the lack of which in Rose's account was, in Pusey's view, a defect. In particular, there was a very long discussion of Spener, one of the founders of Pietism in Germany. Pusey traced the origins of the rationalizing tendency in German theology back to Pietism, its stress upon practical religion as a main criterion for authenticity, its possibility of being imitated by those who did not share its deepest convictions so that purely outward religion resulted, and its infiltration by philosophy, especially that of Wolff. The dissociation of the experiential religion from an outward and intellectual form of Christianity led, in the latter, to the school of Baumgarten and Semler, and their followers Michaelis and Eichhorn.[53]

For our purposes, we need notice Pusey's verdict on scholars such as Michaelis, Eichhorn and de Wette, names that would be most likely to be familiar to any English reader who had a vague inkling about German scholarship. In view of the fact that Michaelis's *Commentaries on the Law of Moses* had been made available to English readers in the previous decade, Pusey's verdict on the volumes was important: 'The commentaries on the Laws of Moses', he wrote '. . . are full of those perverted applications of mere civil, often of modern, principles, unfounded theories and low views . . .'.[54]

According to Pusey, Michaelis was 'destitute of that conviction, which

---

[51] ibid., pp. 144–5. In Rose's opinion, only Schleiermacher was a divine who was also a scholar. Even so, Schleiermacher's *Der Christliche Glaube* (1822) was 'difficult of comprehension' and Rose found that 'disagreeable feelings' were aroused in him by some of its expressions. Schleiermacher's *Reden* (1799) savoured strongly of pantheism (Rose, p. 136).

[52] See the letter of Pusey from Professor C. H. Sack of Bonn in Pt 1 of E. B. Pusey, *An Historical Enquiry into the Probable Causes of the Rationalist Character lately predominant in the Theology of Germany*, London 1828, pp. i–xv. The German reaction to Rose's book is also described by H. P. Liddon, *Life of Edward Bouverie Pusey*, 1, London 1894[4], pp. 146–52.

[53] Pusey, op. cit., Pt 1, pp. 128–32. Pusey also mentions (pp. 124ff) the part played by translations into German of English Deist writings. He notes that the translations of English apologists 'did but aggravate the evil and increase the rationalist tendency'. Part of the reason for this was that the apologists themselves were too exclusively intellectual in their approach.

[54] ibid., p. 135, n1.

can alone give a comparative insight into the real character of Revelation, and the harmonious relation of its several parts', and thus 'had no guide which might enable him to perceive what might be safely admitted, without detriment to the system itself'.[55]

As though Michaelis's views were not in themselves bad enough, they had influenced others, including Eichhorn, whose theories were 'constructed on the assumed human origin of every phenomenon in revealed religion'.[56] Of comments on de Wette, there are two in Part 1. He is described as one of the few remaining representatives of those who have converted doctrinal theology into contemporary philosophy, and that he is 'too much influenced' by Fries.[57] Elsewhere, it is noted that de Wette's 'really Christian faith' is 'obscured by his adherence to the Friesian philosophy'.[58]

Pusey deliberately avoided references to living scholars, and consequently, readers would have gained little idea from the *Historical Enquiry* about what the 'Rationalists' were actually proposing in Old Testament scholarship. The same is true of Part 2 of the *Historical Enquiry* published in 1830, and intended as a reply to the second edition of Rose's *Discourses*. In Part 2, Pusey softened his apparent attack upon the character of certain 'rationalists', while maintaining his opposition to their principles. He went as far as to say that he much preferred Semler, 'who doubted of the Apocalypse', to Eichhorn, 'who maintained its genuineness'.[59] There is also a footnote, which discloses what Pusey evidently accepted as the totally sincere struggles in the mind of de Wette, as he sought to reconcile his love for truth with the pain that he knew this would bring for those pious people who could not follow his free inquiry.[60]

Perhaps the most interesting section of Part 2 of the *Historical Enquiry* is that in which Pusey defends what he means by 'plenary inspiration' of the Bible, and in which he quotes numerous divines in support of his own apparent view at that time that belief in 'plenary inspiration' does not commit one to the view that the biblical writers were *entirely* free from error.[61] A distinction is made between what is necessary to be revealed (in which matters biblical writers are free from error) and matters relating to such things as dates or customs, in which they have no more accuracy than other writers writing about these things at the same time as the biblical

---

[55] ibid., p. 135.
[56] ibid., p. 137.
[57] ibid., p. 115.
[58] ibid., p. 177.
[59] Pusey, *Historical Enquiry*, Pt 2 (1830), p. 115.
[60] ibid., p. 114, note 2.
[61] ibid., pp. 66–87.

writers.[62] This indicates that orthodoxy of this period could contemplate errors in matters of fact in the Bible, without the admission in any way undermining belief in 'plenary inspiration'.

A book in the same genre as those by Rose and Pusey was E. H. Dewar's *German Protestantism and the Right of Private Judgement in the Interpretation of Holy Scripture*, published in 1844.[63] Dewar spent some time in Germany as a chaplain in Hamburg. He belonged to the Catholic party in the Church of England and expressed a pessimistic view of German theology and church life. The root problem of Protestant Germany was the belief that 'Christian doctrine admits of and requires to be constantly acted upon by the human intellect, to be ever searched into, developed, altered, improved'.[64] Like Pusey, Dewar blamed upon the infiltration of Wolffian philosophy into theology the exaltation of reason above revelation, and the subsequent subjection of the Bible to critical study. Semler's view that the biblical writings must be interpreted in the light of the circumstances of their composition, while true, was misapplied, because the method stood in judgement upon the Bible.[65] Among those who took up the viewpoint that led them to reject altogether any belief in the inspiration of Scripture were Michaelis and de Wette.[66]

Dewar's brief treatment of de Wette is interesting, because it shows how easy it was for de Wette's very sophisticated views to be misunderstood. Dewar stated that de Wette 'maintains that no reasonable ground can be adduced for the belief that Christianity is a special Divine revelation'.[67] He justified this by quoting a passage from de Wette's *Ueber Religion und Theologie*. However, it is clear from the quotation that he did not understand what de Wette meant by 'reasonable ground'. De Wette's point was not that Christianity was not a divine revelation, but that one could know that it

---

[62] ibid., p. 82: [Pusey quoting Powell's Boyle lectures] 'The great truths impressed upon their [the biblical writers'] minds neither obliterated their former knowledge, nor made it perfect. When they speak, for instance, of a Roman custom or a Jewish tradition, we are not to imagine that these things were revealed from above, nor to require greater accuracy in their accounts of them, than in other writers, who treat of the affairs of their own age, and their own country.'

[63] Edward H. Dewar, *German Protestantism and the Right of Private Judgement in the Interpretation of Holy Scripture*, Oxford 1844.

[64] Dewar, op. cit., p. 6. Dewar contrasted this with his own preferred view that 'Christian doctrine was from the commencement full and complete; that the duty of Christians, in respect to it, has never been more, and can never be more, than to hand it down to succeeding generations, pure, as it was delivered to the Saints'.

[65] ibid., p. 107.

[66] ibid., p. 112.

[67] ibid., p. 113.

was only by an act of faith (in the Friesian sense), and that the proposition could not be demonstrated by appeal to external arguments.[68]

Dewar's main reference to actual examples of biblical criticism was concentrated upon the New Testament, and upon the discussion of the relation of the Synoptic Gospels to each other. Here he showed quite detailed knowledge of many German writers on the subject. For Old Testament studies, his book would have led readers who knew little of German criticism to be suspicious of works by names whose New Testament efforts were condemned. De Wette, together with Schleiermacher and Lücke, was said to perpetuate in his theology the philosophy of Jacobi.[69]

The year before the publication of Dewar's *German Protestantism* saw the appearance of one of the most informative and fair-minded accounts of German criticism to be published in the first half of the nineteenth century in Britain. Its author, Samuel Davidson, was at the time resident in Belfast, and the book was published in Edinburgh; it could, therefore, be argued that it was not a representative of 'English' scholarship. However, Davidson was soon to move to England, where he would be dismissed from a chair in Manchester, and would spend the remainder of his long life in London. It will thus be mentioned in the present chapter.[70]

Davidson's *Sacred Hermeneutics* is a monumental work of over seven hundred pages, including a history of biblical interpretation from the time of the Apostolic Fathers of the Reformation.[71] Chapter 7 is a careful examination of modern German systems of interpretation, namely, the moral or Kantian system, the psychologico-historical system, the accommodation system, the mythic system, the rationalistic system and the pietistic system.

From the outset, it should be noticed with what care and insight Davidson differentiated between approaches which other writers constantly lumped together under the heading of 'rationalistic'; not that Davidson was a starry-eyed disciple of anything German. That he was not, is shown by his verdict on Kant's moral interpretation, that:

> It cannot be too much reprobated; and it is presumed, that very few in this country are careful to know, or solicitous to adopt it. The piety and practical character of our evangelism must ever repudiate it with deserved horror.[72]

---

[68] The quotation from de Wette given by Dewar reads: 'Dass das Christenthum göttliche Offenbarung sei, ist ein schlechthin gegebener Glaubensausspruch, d.h. ein ideales Urtheil, welches durch keine Verstandesgründe erwiesen werden kann.'

[69] ibid., p. 167. In ch. 14, there is a long discussion of Strauss's *Life of Jesus* and the influences upon it.

[70] Davidson will be considered further in ch. 14.

[71] Samuel Davidson, *Sacred Hermeneutics Developed and Applied, including a History of Biblical Interpretation from the Earliest of the Fathers to the Reformation*, Edinburgh 1843.

[72] ibid., p. 197.

However, such a verdict did not prevent Davidson from giving a fair account of Kant.[73] He saw that Kant's fundamental difficulty was the variance of moral parts of the Bible, and the moral imperatives supplied by practical reason, in which the Bible fell short of the imperatives of practical reason. But if the Bible proceeded from God with whom all things were perfect, how could it contain unworthy moral sentiments? Kant therefore devised a hermeneutic designed to make the Bible conform with the highest dictates of practical reason, in the process doing violence to the historical and literal sense of the text. Davidson was more successful in outlining Kant's position than in effectively opposing it, other than making the valid point that Kant compelled passages to teach what they were never intended to teach—a point conceded by Kant himself.[74]

By the psychologico-historical interpretation, Davidson meant the approach of Paulus and Eichhorn, who tried to defend the integrity of the biblical narratives by arguing that the psychology of the original writers/observers was such that they viewed the world very differently from ourselves:

> Whilst the inspired writers are viewed as honestly relating events according to their belief, truth and reality are carefully separated from their *impressions*. The sacred penmen are credulous simpletons, who exalted into supernatural events what more enlightened men would have explained in a rational way.[75]

Davidson recognized that the mythical approach was very similar to the psychologico-historical system, and conceded that in it, 'the historical is neither abandoned, nor lightly regarded'.[76] However, Davidson felt that the psychologico-historical approach was to be abhorred, for all that its 'infidelity' was better disguised than in some other systems.

A long and careful discussion of accommodation allowed that this principle had been used by the Church Fathers.[77] Jahn had maintained that the ancient view of accommodation extended it to include formal 'dissimulation, fraud and falsehood'. Davidson denied this. He allowed the existence of *formal* accommodation, that is, accommodation in the *form* of teaching, such as use of parables, proverbs and allegories. He also allowed that Christ had used *negative* accommodation, in the sense of not telling the disciples things that they could not have understood. What Davidson principally objected to was *positive* accommodation as used by Semler, according to which the biblical writers had so adapted their writings to the ignorances and prejudices of their age that it was necessary to take account

[73] ibid., pp. 193–7.
[74] ibid., p. 196.
[75] ibid., p. 198.
[76] ibid., p. 199.
[77] ibid., pp. 199–206.

of this factor in interpreting biblical texts. For example, belief in demons and angels was erroneous opinion, in which Christ and the apostles acquiesced. Davidson correctly linked this use of accommodation with the principle of the necessity of examining authors and their backgrounds critically before texts were interpreted. In Davidson's view, the historical interpreter who, with Semler, admitted positive accommodation, became 'a most dangerous expositor'. He further saw the danger that the historical grammatical method, which sought only to illumine the language and background of the text, would admit positive accommodation unobserved, to the detriment of exegesis. Davidson's refutation of this position turned on the impossibility of inspired writers deliberately conveying their truths by means of falsehoods. The view that they unwittingly employed falsehoods was not, of course, the accommodation view but the psychologico-historical view.

Davidson's account of the mythic interpretation showed his knowledge of German criticism at its most extensive.[78] Defining the mythic interpretation as one in which whatever appeared strange or miraculous was 'a peculiar dress suited to the rude notions of the times in which the writers lived', Davidson began by describing the theoretical basis of this position as found in Gabler's edition of Eichhorn's *Urgeschichte* and G. L. Bauer's *Hebräische Mythologie*.[79] He noted that the mythic approach had been worked out in relation to secular literature before being applied to the Bible, and he identified Eichhorn, Vater, de Wette, and 'rationalists in general' as users of the system. Davidson also rightly described J. F. L. George's *Mythus und Sage* as 'the most complete treatise on mythus and tradition which has perhaps appeared in Germany',[80] and he mentioned the commentaries on Genesis by von Bohlen and Tuch as providing examples of the violence done to the truth by the mythic approach.[81] Not unnaturally, most of Davidson's energy was devoted to an exposition and refutation of Strauss's *Life of Jesus*, and its philosophical determinants, and he considered that German scholars such as Neander and Tholuck had vindicated the credibility of the gospel history.

Davidson kept back his discussion of rationalistic interpretation until he had described the various other approaches. Strictly speaking, he argued, the other approaches could all be described as rationalistic, since the hallmark of rationalism was to take a system of philosophy, 'to which, as to a touchstone', they brought the doctrines of revelation. However, simply to

---

[78] ibid., pp. 206–17.
[79] ibid., pp. 207–8; and see my *Myth in Old Testament Interpretation*, ch. 1.
[80] See ibid., pp. 24–7.
[81] For P. von Bohlen, see below, p. 175. Tuch, the author of an important commentary on Genesis was professor at Halle (1838–41) and Leipzig (1843–67).

talk about rationalism would be to obscure important distinctions, as well as running the danger of objections from critical German scholars.

As an example of rationalistic interpretation, Davidson cited the exegesis of Isaiah 52—3 by scholars such as Paulus, Gabler, de Wette and Gesenius.[82] A passage obviously referring to the vicarious death and sufferings of the Messiah, and confirmed to be about this subject by the New Testament, was given an historical interpretation by the rationalists. Some referred it to the prophet Isaiah, others to the Jewish people, others to the prophetic group. Such was 'the respect paid to the sacred writers by Rationalism'.

Davidson concluded his chapter by referring to Pietism, and was scathing about the Pietist insistence on the priority of the internal light that guided faith and interpretation. That conversion was necessary if one was to understand God's word aright Davidson did not for a moment deny. But from its honoured beginnings, Pietism had given rise to totally undesirable directions in biblical interpretation.

A feature of Davidson's work in general was his provision of annotated bibliographies. In *Sacred Hermeneutics*, Davidson devoted fifty pages to an annotated bibliography of hermeneutical treatises from the Reformation to the nineteenth century—a bibliography that has retained its value.[83] Davidson includes full accounts of the content and principles of works by Baumgarten, Ernesti, Semler, Rambach, G. L. Bauer and Jahn. Of newer works he also noticed Schleiermacher's *Hermeneutik und Kritik*, and works by J. T. Beck and H. Olshausen. In spite of his many reservations about the theory and practice of the 'Rationalists' among those mentioned, Davidson never hesitated to commend what was good and valuable, exhibiting a degree of fairness to his opponents that was remarkable, and a knowledge of their work which was phenomenal.

Nine years before Davidson's *Sacred Hermeneutics*, in 1833, Henry John Rose, younger brother of Hugh James Rose, delivered the Hulsean Lectures in Cambridge on the subject of *The Law of Moses, viewed in connexion with the history and character of the Jews*.[84] The published version of these lectures contained an appendix in which was set out the 'times at which the Pentateuch and the Historical Books of the Old Testament are stated, by the Chief Continental authorities of recent celebrity, to have written or compiled'. The appendix was presented in tabular form so that the reader

[82] Davidson, op. cit., p. 220.
[83] ibid., pp. 677–725.
[84] Henry John Rose, *The Law of Moses, viewed in connexion with the History and Character of the Jews with a Defence of the Book of Joshua against Professor Leo of Berlin*, Hulsean Lectures for 1833, Cambridge 1834. On Rose see J. W. Burgon, *Lives of Twelve Good Men*, pp. 284–95. From 1837 to his death in 1873 he was Rector of Houghton Conquest in Bedfordshire, and Archdeacon of Bedford from 1866. In 1862 he contributed to *Replies to Essays and Reviews*.

could compare the date of composition of the Pentateuch and other books as advocated in the writings of Gesenius, de Wette, Gramberg, Bertholdt, Jahn, Eichorn [*sic*] and Rosenmüller.[85]

It is interesting to note that Rose was not able to use de Wette's *Contributions to Old Testament Introduction*, and that he was dependent upon Gramberg's references to de Wette's *Contributions* in his *Critical History of the Religious Ideas of the Old Testament*.[86] For de Wette, Rose relied otherwise upon the 1817 edition of the *Introduction to the Old Testament*, and for Gesenius he used the 1815 *History of the Hebrew Language and Script*.

In considering the views of the 'Neologists', as Rose called the scholars whose views he presented, Rose used the method of playing the scholars off against each other. If scholar A was correct, then scholar B was wrong, and vice versa. A hidden assumption seems to have been that the traditional views of the authorship of Old Testament books could be supported by showing that the alternative critical views were at variance among themselves. However, in the case of the books of Chronicles, Rose contributed a section in which he opposed the attempt of Gesenius to prove the lateness of these books on philological grounds.[87]

In this instance, it is a pity that Rose did not have access to de Wette's *Contributions*, since Gesenius's philological arguments were intended to back up the points made by de Wette on historical-critical grounds. Rose's arguments against Gesenius assumed that the *only* arguments that were convincing to Gesenius were philological arguments. Gesenius assumed that de Wette had proved his case, and made some philological observations designed to show how the author of Chronicles, in using Samuel and Kings, had misunderstood these source books. Rose seems to have assumed that the argument about the sources of Chronicles was primarily a philological argument, and he worked on the principle that if Gesenius's arguments could be modified or challenged, then the traditional view of the independence of Chronicles was safeguarded.

In the main body of his book, Rose provided one of the few expositions anywhere in English of Gramberg's *Critical History*, although he was hardly able to do justice, in a published version of public lectures, to Gramberg's 1,200 or so pages.[88] Rose seized particularly upon what he perceived to be the circular argumentation implicit in Gramberg's approach:

> . . . it is clear, that by the mode of proceeding any preconceived opinions may be found in the books of the Bible, and the whole may be forced into conformity with the results deduced from a part of them only.[89]

[85] *The Law of Moses*, pp. 202–8.
[86] ibid., p. 204 n1.
[87] ibid., pp. 220–7.
[88] ibid., pp. 70–2.
[89] ibid., p. 72.

However, Rose did not seem to appreciate that the same argument could also be brought against traditional views of composition and authorship. For example, the many unevennesses and indications of later passages in the Pentateuch were subjected to similar violence when they were forced into a scheme of unity of authorship which was deduced only from a part of the text.

The importance of Rose's book for our purposes lies in the fact that for English readers in the 1830s, it indicated that German criticism was not simply a matter of finding the sources Elohim or Jehovah in the Pentateuch. There was something much more fundamental at issue, and this was the relationship between the history of Israelite religion as presented by a surface reading of the Old Testament, and the German critical view that placed the developed Levitical religion of Israel in its later historical periods. Rose seems to have been one of the first scholars in England to address himself to this specific point.

Just over twenty years after the publication of Rose's Hulsean Lectures, English readers had the chance to see at first hand what a German critical work of the de Wette era of criticism was really like. The occasion was the publication of an English translation of von Bohlen's *Introduction to the Book of Genesis*.[90] This book, dedicated to Gesenius and de Wette, had been published in 1835, but like George's *Jewish Festivals* had been somewhat overshadowed by Vatke's *Biblical Theology* together with which it had in some cases been reviewed.[91] Whether this was the *first* de Wettian critical work to be made available to readers in England I do not know. Certainly, a translation of de Wette's 'Introduction' had been published in the United States in 1843.[92] How usual it was for American books to be obtained in England is a subject about which I know nothing.

The mention of translations from the German, however, brings us to a convenient point for noting that prior to the publication of the English version of von Bohlen's 'Genesis', there had been a steady stream of translations into English of *conservative* German works. Although many of these emanated from the Edinburgh firm of T. and T. Clark, there can be

---

[90] P. von Bohlen, *Introduction to the Book of Genesis, with a Commentary on the Opening Portion*, ed. James Heywood, 2 vols, London 1855. This was a translation and selection from *Die Genesis Historisch-Kritisch erläutert*, Königsberg 1835. The author was born in 1796 at Wüppel in the lordship of Jever, which is today a few miles to the north-east of Wilhelmshaven. He studied in Halle under Gesenius and at Bonn under the Arabist Freytag. From 1825 he taught in Königsberg, receiving in 1828 the chair of Oriental Languages. After a breakdown in his health in 1837, he spent some time in London and the Isle of Wight. He died in Halle in 1840.

[91] De Wette reviewed these three books in *TSK* 1837, pp. 953–1003, but said little about von Bohlen.

[92] W. M. L. de Wette, *A Critical and Historical Introduction to the Canonical Scriptures of the Old Testament*, tr. and enl. by T. Parker, 2 vols., Boston, Mass., 1843, 1850[2].

no doubt of their importance south of the border in disseminating conservative refutations of critical German positions, which positions were stated only partially, and were often presented as the work of impious men. Some of these early titles included:

E. W. Hengstenberg, *On the Interpretation of Isaiah lii.12–liii*, Biblical Cabinet, 9, Edinburgh 1832.

F. A. G. Tholuck, *Hints on the Importance of the Study of the Old Testament*, Biblical Cabinet, 2, Edinburgh 1833.[93]

F. A. G. Tholuck, *Guido and Julius: The Doctrine of Sin and the Propitiator ...* London 1836.[94]

E. W. Hengstenberg, *Egypt and the Books of Moses*, Biblical Cabinet, n.s., 3, Edinburgh 1844.

H. A. C. Hävernick, *A General Historico-Critical Introduction to the Old Testament*, Clark's Foreign Theological Library, 18, Edinburgh 1846.

E. W. Hengstenberg, *Dissertations on the Genuineness of the Pentateuch*, Edinburgh 1847.

Peter von Bohlen's *Introduction to Genesis*, which an English reader could have perused in 1855, consisted of a commentary on Genesis 1—11, with important additional material on the Flood added by the English editor. The introductory volume, preceding the commentary, argued against the Mosaic authorship of the Pentateuch and for the unhistorical nature of many of the historical narratives of the Pentateuch. Among the arguments used on this latter point was an exploitation of that old chestnut the 600,000 armed men that left Egypt at the time of the Exodus.[95] Here was a foretaste of what Colenso would develop so devastatingly six years later. The total company of Israelites, 2,500,000 would have been far too large to occupy the Sinai peninsula, and would have needed a level of fertility far higher than known in very favourable lands.

[93] For an account of the German of this book see above pp. 84–5.
[94] This translation of Tholuck's 'answer' to de Wette (see above p. 84) contained a preface by J. Pye Smith, from which it is evident that Pye Smith had not read de Wette's *Theodore*: 'The tendency of this book [*Theodore*] may not unreasonably be conjectured, when it is considered that the very clever and eloquent author deduces all religion from an innate propensity in the human mind, cherished and refined by reason and experience; that he excludes everything supernatural from the mission of Moses and the prophets, of Jesus and the apostles.' Pye Smith goes on to express his opinion of the 'hypocrisy for which we have no epithet of adequate abhorrence', that de Wette should make his doubter present himself for Lutheran ordination (preface to *Guido and Julius*, pp. xxviii–xxix). It is a pity that Pye Smith felt able to express himself so strongly about a book which he had apparently not read.
[95] *Introduction to Genesis*, 1, pp. 110ff.

On the composition of Genesis, von Bohlen adopted a position derived from the earlier writings of Ewald, and not unlike that advocated in the present century by Noth regarding the Deuteronomistic history. For von Bohlen, Genesis displayed a unity given to it by an eighth-century writer, who utilized many sources in the work of composition.[96] The idea that sources complete in themselves had been combined was rejected. Nonetheless, it was possible to detect a difference between the more primitive 'Elohim' passages, and the more sophisticated, national 'Jehovah' passages.

For the composition of the remainder of the Pentateuch, von Bohlen followed de Wette in finding no trace in the earlier historical books and the prophetic books of the developed levitical religion presupposed in parts of Exodus, Leviticus and Numbers. This type of religion he believed to have developed when there were weak kings on the throne permitting the development of priestly influence.[97] The book of Deuteronomy was the law book found in the Temple in Josiah's reign, and its 'discovery' was probably part of a well-conceived plan to revive the national consciousness in the face of Judah's enemies.[98] A comparison of its language with that of Jeremiah showed that it belonged to the seventh century. The levitical regulations were not made known to the people until after the reign of Josiah, and certainly not enforced until after the return from exile. The Pentateuch did not reach its final form until the period of the Exile.

Von Bohlen's 'Genesis' did not set out its results in a manner so as to make them transparently clear. His book displays some of the uncertainties of the 1830s. However, his view of the history of Israelite religion was clear. It exhibited progress from variety and laxity to greater regulation. The priesthood had become a powerful institution only towards the end of the monarchy and the elaborate levitical system was the end of a process, not an original revelation given to Moses. To trace the proper course of the development of Israelite religion was also to trace the history of the composition of the Pentateuch. English readers had in their hands in 1855 the germ of the position to be advocated some two decades later by Wellhausen.

Critical scholarship of the type of Ewald and Bunsen was made available to English readers, first, in the translation of Bunsen's *Egypt's Place in Universal History*, which began to appear from 1848, and second, in a

[96] ibid., pp. 304–11.
[97] ibid., p. 227: 'From the time of Samuel downwards, the religious system of the Israelites was only perfected by very slow degrees through the continued efforts of prophets, priests, and some individual princes . . . the levitical system arose contemporaneously and slowly under the government of weak kings . . . the festivals were not actually celebrated according to the levitical enactments until a very late period . . . the most important laws in the Pentateuch were never observed by the nation down to the time of the Babylonian Exile.'
[98] ibid., pp. 256ff.

translation of Richard Lepsius's *Letters from Egypt, Ethiopia, and the Peninsula of Sinai* in 1853.[99] Reference to Bunsen's findings on biblical chronology has already been made in a previous chapter.[100] In Lepsius's book, a long and detailed section on chronology reached the conclusion that for the early history of Israel, the actual figures given in the Bible, for example, the 430 years for the sojourn in Egypt at Exodus 12.40, were unreliable. On the other hand, the genealogical information in the Pentateuch agreed with the chronology of Egyptian events given by Manetho.[101] This led to the surprising conclusion that Abraham went down into Egypt only two hundred years before the Exodus.[102] The Exodus itself had occurred during the reign of Merneptah (Menephthes, as named by Lepsius) whose dates were 1328–1309 BC. Thus Abraham's descent would be placed in the latter part of the eighteenth dynasty, *after* the expulsion of the Hyksos.[103]

In justification of his handling of the biblical chronology, Lepsius referred to what Bunsen had written in the first volume of *Egypt's Place in Universal History*:

> The assumption that it entered into the scheme of Divine Providence either to preserve for us a chronology of the Jews and their forefathers by real tradition, or to provide the later commentators with magic powers, in respect to the most esoteric element of history, may seem indispensable to some, and absurd to others. Historical enquiry has nothing whatever to do with such idle, preposterous, and often fallacious assumptions. Its business is to see whether anything and if so, what—has been transmitted to us.[104]

To this account of knowledge of what was happening in German criticism there should be added a mention of the reviews of German works that appeared in a variety of journals and magazines. To describe them in detail will not add materially to the general position presented in this chapter. It may be helpful, however, to give some brief idea of the sort of books reviewed in the journals.

It would appear, on the basis of a literature search for reviews of German *critical* Old Testament scholarship in the first part of the nineteenth century, that reviewing in this field did not begin in earnest until the 1840s.[105] Bunsen's *Egypt's Place in Universal History* was reviewed in the *Edinburgh*

[99] R. Lepsius, *Letters from Egypt, Ethiopia, and the Peninsula of Sinai*, London 1853.

[100] See p. 125.

[101] *Letters from Egypt*, p. 490.

[102] ibid., p. 485.

[103] ibid., pp. 451, 470.

[104] ibid., p. 493.

[105] The search was undertaken by two students in the Postgraduate School of Librarianship, Sheffield, to whom I offer my thanks. However, I am to be held responsible for any inaccuracies in what follows.

Review for April 1846,[106] while the first number of the *Biblical Review* published in the same year considered Ewald's commentary on Job.[107] The August 1847 number of the *North British Review* noticed the American translation of de Wette's *Introduction*,[108] while the *British Quarterly Review* for 1851 discussed the second edition (1850) of the same work.[109] Kitto's *Journal of Sacred Literature*, which began publication in 1848, took considerable notice of German work in general, for example, Ewald on the prophets in vol. 10 (1853).[110] *The Eclectic Review*, vol. 103 (1856) reviewed Hupfeld's commentary on the Psalms,[111] while ahead of *Essays and Reviews*, the first volume of Bunsen's *Bibelwerk* was noticed in the *British Quarterly Review* no. 29 for 1859.[112] It goes without saying that many conservative German books, especially those of Hengstenberg, were reviewed between 1840 and 1859.

It should be clear from the comments of this chapter that the alarm caused by *Essays and Reviews* in 1860 and by Colenso on the Pentateuch in 1861–5 was not the result of a total ignorance in England up to 1859 of what was happening in German critical scholarship. It is, of course, difficult to know by whom, and how many of the books and articles mentioned in this chapter had been read. What is clear is that indications of the main methods and conclusions of German critical scholarship were available to English readers prior to 1860.

---

[106] Review by William Mure in *Edinburgh Review* 83 (April 1846), pp. 391–430.

[107] *Biblical Review* 1 (1846), pp. 23ff.

[108] *North British Review* 7 (August 1847), pp. 355–67.

[109] *British Quarterly Review* 15 (1851), pp. 453ff.

[110] *Journal of Sacred Literature* 10 (1853) pp. 329ff. See also the following articles in the same journal: 'German Rationalism in its early indications', by O. T. Dobbin, 1 (1848), pp. 126ff; idem, 'German Rationalism in Recent Developments', 1, pp. 257ff.

[111] *Eclectic Review* 103 (1856) pp. 612ff.

[112] *British Quarterly Review* 29 (1859) pp. 418ff.

13

English Critical Old Testament Scholarship 1800–57

The previous chapter has considered what could have been known about German critical scholarship in England in the first part of the nineteenth century. If the sample presented in that chapter is representative, it appears that German critical scholarship was more often than not mentioned in order to be refuted between 1800 and 1857. However, there was small but steady progress in England itself in the application of critical views to the Old Testament, and this progress will be sketched in the present chapter. One of the outcomes will be to show where critical thought stood on the eve of *Essays and Reviews* and Colenso's *Pentateuch*.

First of all, in what must necessarily be a sampling process rather than an exhaustive account of the subject, Adam Clarke's Genesis commentary of 1810 will be considered. The author was born in (Northern) Ireland in 1760 or 1762, and while spending his life in the service of the Methodist Church, he became a man of considerable scholarly attainments.[1] His knowledge of Hebrew he owed to a chance incident in 1783 in Bristol, when he acquired a Hebrew grammar purchased with a half sovereign that he found while gardening![2] *Genesis*, published in 1810, was the first part of his commentary on the whole Bible, which appeared from 1810 to 1825 in eight volumes.[3]

The commentary is written from a completely orthodox point of view; nevertheless, it is marked by an amazing openness. Clarke was not frightened to emend the text where necessary, and he did not shrink from bold hypotheses. The Mosaic authorship of Genesis and the rest of the Pentateuch

---

[1] See J. B. B. Clarke (ed.), *An Account of the Infancy, Religious and Literary Life of Adam Clarke*, LL.D., F.A.S., 3 vols., London 1833.

[2] ibid., 1, pp. 163–4. The grammar purchased by Clarke was by Cornelius Bayley, *An Easy Entrance into the Sacred Language, containing the necessary rules of Hebrew Grammar in English*, London 1782.

[3] Reference is here made to *The Holy Bible with a Commentary and Critical Notes* by Adam Clarke: the Old Testament, 1 (Genesis, Exodus, Leviticus, Numbers), London 1825. For the publication of Genesis in 1810, see *Life of Adam Clarke* (n1 above), 2, pp. 216ff.

was upheld, but allowance was made for the possibility that there had been interpolations into the text, most probably by Ezra. In Clarke's view, Ezra was acting under divine inspiration, and therefore the additions were 'of equal authority with the text'.[4]

In his exposition of Genesis 1, Clarke took great pains to reconcile the account with scientific theory of his day. Thus the light, created before the sun of the first day, was latent light, the light equivalent of latent heat. The sun, after Dr Herschel, was not a body but an atmosphere of 'various elastic fluids', which fluids had a phosphoric nature and gave out light. However, the sun did not itself provide heat for the earth. Rather, it acted upon the caloric or latent heat in substances and thus heat was produced.[5] Other scientific discoveries mentioned by Clarke included the skeleton of the mammoth, which was regarded as evidence for the mighty power of God's works.[6]

Clarke's treatment of Genesis 3 is an indication of how bold an orthodox writer could be in 1810. On the basis of comparative philology, with particular reference to Arabic, he maintained that the *nahash* of 3.1ff was not a serpent but a creature of an ape or orang-utang kind. The word *nahash* did not uniformly denote 'serpent' in the Old Testament, whereas what Clarke regarded as a similar Arabic root *hanasa* yielded the meanings 'seduced', 'ape' and 'devil'. The ape seemed to be a reasonable candidate for the seducer, since it would naturally have walked upright before it was cursed.[7] A most interesting point is Clarke's rejection of the fact that in the New Testament, the devil is described as a serpent. Clarke did not deny that the devil had been using the creature that seduced Eve. What he did deny was that appeal to the New Testament could settle an essentially Old Testament philological matter. The New Testament writers had taken 'serpent' from the LXX, and thus their views were not relevant to the discussion of the meaning of *nahash*. Clarke did not insist that all should follow him in his identification of the *nahash*. He wrote:

> I make it no article of faith, nor of Christian communion; I crave the same liberty to judge for myself, that I give to others, to which every man has an indisputable right, and I hope no man will call me a heretic, for departing in this respect from the common opinion, which appears to me to be so embarrassed as to be altogether unintelligible.[8]

[4] Preface to Genesis (page not numbered). Clarke also states, 'That there are a few things in the Pentateuch which seem to have been added by a later hand, there can be little doubt'.

[5] Clarke on Gen. 1.16ff.

[6] Clarke on Gen. 1.24.

[7] Clarke on Gen. 3.1.

[8] ibid. (the pages of the commentary are not numbered, although those of the General Preface are).

In his work on the remaining books of the Pentateuch, which followed closely upon Genesis, Clarke faced up squarely to many difficulties that would later be explained by the critical method. Thus, on Exodus 6.2–3, he explained the statement, contradicted in many parts of Genesis, that the Patriarchs did not know God as Jehovah, by presuming that the Patriarchs were aware of the name Jehovah, but not aware of its power and significance.

In its attention to small detail, Clarke's work was a rival, from the orthodox side, to the later calculations of Colenso. Thus, the size of Noah's ark and the amount of food for the animals it needed was carefully discussed. The figure of 600,000 armed men who left Egypt at the Exodus was calculated to imply a grand total of 3,263,000 persons, whose preservation in the wilderness was a mighty work of providence. At the crossing of the Red Sea, Clarke observed that if the wind that drove the sea back were sufficiently strong to have divided waters 28 yards deep, it would have had a devastating effect upon the Israelites and their cattle! Thus, Clarke supposed that the purpose of the wind was not to part the waters but to dry the sea bed once it was divided by a miracle.

In the biography of Clarke, it is recounted that someone remarked, in looking at Clarke's Genesis, 'Thank God, I never found these difficulties in the Sacred Record'.[9] These comments are a testimony to the degree of integrity that Clarke displayed as a commentator. No difficulty was passed over, and every branch of learning was appealed to in order to elucidate the biblical text. It is clear that in 1810, an orthodox commentator could be daring and original within the limits of traditional views on authorship and authority, and could even maintain that the New Testament use of the Old Testament was not necessarily decisive in a matter of philology.

The four-volume *Introduction to the Critical Study and Knowledge of the Holy Scriptures* by T. H. Horne, of which several editions appeared in the 1820s, was less daring than Clarke's commentary.[10] However, included in its mine of information about almost every aspect of the study of the Bible was a frank rehearsal of the difficulties inherent in a plain reading of the text. In facing these difficulties, Horne was ready to admit that the traditional text did not always exhibit the correct order, and he was prepared to correct the traditional text where necessary.

In the section of the book of Joshua, he pointed out that there was some 'accidental derangement of the order of the chapters in this book, occasioned

---

[9] *Life of Adam Clarke*, 2, p. 281. Clarke's biographer observes of the commentary: 'while he reasons strongly, and argues and insists earnestly on all matters of pure faith, and sound doctrine; it is everywhere clearly manifested, that in all those cases which may be classed as simple matters of criticism, or of curious investigation, his opinion is delivered with the candour of a liberal enquirer after truth' (pp. 281–4).

[10] Reference is here made to T. H. Horne's *Introduction to the Critical Study and Knowledge of the Holy Scriptures*, 4 vols., London 1825⁵.

probably by the antient [*sic*] mode of rolling up manuscripts'.[11] The true order of Joshua was 1.1–9; 2.1–24; 1.10–18; 3—11; 22; 12—21; 23—4. In 1 Samuel, where it was obvious that 1 Sam. 17 was prior to 1 Sam. 16, the true order should be 1 Sam. 16.1–13; 17; 18.1–9; 16.14–23; 18.10–30.

Where Horne did not advocate rearrangement, he allowed that in the text, some events were anticipated and that the natural order of others was reversed. Thus the creation of male and female at Gen. 1.27 anticipated the fuller accounts in Gen. 2.7 and 21–3. An example of inversion was Genesis 12.1 and 11.31, where the departure of Abraham from Haran (11.31) preceded the call to depart.[12] An example of the correction of the text was at 1 Chron. 20.3, where Horne read *wayāsem* instead of *wayāsar*, following the parallel passage in 2 Sam. 12.31 and seven MSS at 1 Chron. 20.3. The effect of the 'correction' was to remove the charge of cruelty against David. According to the traditional Hebrew text of 1 Chron. 20.3, David had *cut* the Ammonites with saws, etc. The 'corrected' text could mean no more than that he *put them to work* with saws, etc.[13] On the books of Chronicles generally, Horne allowed that their post-exilic author spoke and wrote a type of Hebrew that differed slightly from pre-exilic Hebrew. This explained some of the linguistic differences between parallel passages in Chronicles and in the books of Samuel and Kings. Also, the author of Chronicles had up-dated such things as place names.[14]

In a section entitled 'Apparent Contradictions between the Sacred Writers',[15] Horne mentioned many of the difficulties that critical scholarship explained by source criticism, and he defended the unity of the text. However, among the discrepancies noted were those between the two creation accounts of Genesis 1 and Genesis 2, the two pairs of all animals taken into the ark (Gen. 6.19–21), and the seven pairs of clean animals (Gen. 7.2), and the extermination of all the Egyptian cattle in Exodus 9.6 followed by the reference to Egyptian cattle as existing in Exodus 9.20.

In his *Introduction*, Horne was gathering together interpretations, some of which went back into the previous century. However, the work as a whole indicates that in the 1820s, many difficulties of a critical nature were recognized by orthodox scholars, and that in some cases, they were explained by assuming that the traditional text contained derangements of the order.

It is noteworthy that neither Clarke's commentary nor Horne's

---

[11] ibid., 2, p. 36.

[12] ibid., 1, pp. 545–6. The principle that there is no 'before' and 'after' in the Bible, i.e., that the events are not always related in the order in which they occurred, is, of course, an ancient principle of Jewish exegesis.

[13] ibid., 1, p. 572.

[14] ibid., 4, p. 58. Horne's argument is not unlike that offered by Gesenius on the language of Chronicles (see above, p. 52).

[15] ibid., 1, pp. 578ff.

Introduction seem to have been indebted in any way to literature in German. The annotated bibliography in Clarke mentioned only Latin works by German writers, while that in Horne mentioned only the German introductions to the Old and the New Testaments by Eichhorn. Of the English translation of Michaelis's *Commentaries on the Laws of Moses*, Horne wrote, 'It is much to be regretted that (these commentaries) are not free from that licentiousness of conjecture and of language, as well as tendency to scepticism, which are the too frequent characteristics of modern biblical criticism in Germany'.[16]

Granted that boldness among commentators upon the Old Testament from a traditional point of view was not unknown in England in the early 1800s, it comes as something of a surprise to read of the great outcry that arose in 1829 and 1830, when Henry Hart Milman's *The History of the Jews* was published by John Murray in the 'Family Library' series.[17] The outcry would be more easy for us to understand today if it were really the case, that, as A. P. Stanley wrote, *The History of the Jews* was, 'The first decisive inroad of German theology into England, the first palpable indication that the Bible could be studied like any other book',[18] or if it were really the case that 'he [Milman] was the first to introduce to public notice the Rationalistic School of Germany'.[19] It has already been shown in chapter 12 above how much was already available in England before 1829 on the subject of German critical scholarship, although perhaps this was not as conspicuous to the general public as would be any opinions appearing in the 'Family Library' series. However, what is really surprising to the modern reader of *The History of the Jews* is how *traditional* it is, and how *little* it displays any evidence of the influence of German scholarship. That it caused such a commotion at the time of its publication must serve as an indicator of how sensitive the Church and the general public were in 1829–30.[20]

[16] ibid., 2, p. 775.

[17] Reference is made here to H. H. Milman (1791–1868) *The History of the Jews*, Everyman edition, London 1909. This is a reprint of the 1863 edition, but differs from the edition of 1829–30 mainly in fuller notes. The main text is almost identical.

[18] A. P. Stanley, quoted in the Everyman edition of *The History of the Jews*, p. xii by Hartwell Jones. See his *Essays on Church and State*, p. 576.

[19] Hartwell Jones, ibid., p. xii.

[20] For further information on the reaction to the book see A. Milman, *Henry Hart Milman, D.D. Dean of St. Paul's. A Biographical Sketch*, London 1899, pp. 85ff: 'A wild storm of disapproval gathered, burst, and Sunday after Sunday Milman was denounced from University and other pulpits in most unmeasured language . . .'. See also S. Smiles, *A Publisher and his Friends. Memoir and Correspondence of the late John Murray*, 2, London 1891, pp. 298–301. In a letter in this volume from Milman to his publisher, John Murray, dated February 1830, Milman says, 'The often-repeated charge of following the Germans is rank nonsense. Except in one passage . . . *there is not one explanation of a miracle* borrowed from a German divine' (p. 300—the emphasis is Milman's). Milman, in the same letter, also argues that his exposition of miracles does not differ from that found in G. D'Oyley

The History of the Jews is based upon a straightforward 'surface' reading of the Old Testament, illumined with references to classical authors, to the accounts of travellers to the East, and to biblical scholars such as Richard Simon, John Spencer and J. D. Michaelis. Only rarely is the historical trustworthiness of the account questioned. There is no hint that it may be possible to detect sources in the Old Testament, nor that it may be possible to use these sources to provide a reconstruction of Israelite history at variance with the account presented in the Old Testament itself.

The history begins with Abram, a member of a pastoral family living at or near Ur, distinguished in his tribe as 'the worshipper of the one great Creator'.[21] His migration to Canaan is described, as is his sojourn in Egypt, where an outbreak of pestilence among the Egyptian royal family indicates to the Egyptian king that he has erred in taking Sarai into his harem.[22] Abram's rescue of Lot, who had been captured by the remnants of the retreating and defeated armies of Cherdolaomer is portrayed as accomplished by 318 of Abram's clan, plus members of neighbouring tribes, the success of such a small force being attributed to the lack of discipline of the soldiers of Lot's captors.[23] After the destruction of Sodom and Gomorrah and the birth of Isaac, Abraham receives the divine command to offer Isaac in sacrifice. Milman rejects the idea that this incident (Gen. 22) has anything to do with child sacrifice.

> . . . . the God of the Abrahamic family, uniformly beneficient, imposed no duties which entailed human suffering, demanded no offerings which were repugnant to the better feelings of our nature.[24]

Neither is it a rare example of a desperate propitiatory sacrifice.

> It was a simple act of unhesitating obedience to the divine command; the last proof of perfect reliance on the certain accomplishment of the divine promises. Isaac, so miraculously bestowed, could be as miraculously restored . . .[25].

With the second account (Gen. 20) of Abraham's needing to describe Sarah as his sister, and her removal to a harem and her subsequent restoration to Abraham, we meet the first comment by Milman that can be held to question the authenticity of the record. Milman remarks that the incident almost excites a suspicion that it is a variant tradition of the incident already

---

and R. Mant, *The Holy Bible with Notes explanatory* . . . Oxford and London 1817. Milman threatens to print his explanations and those of D'Oyley and Mant in parallel columns. Of the D'Oyley and Mant work, Horne, *Introduction* 2, p. 771 remarked, 'On the fundamental articles of Christian verity . . . this work may be pronounced to be a library of divinity'.
[21] *The History of the Jews*, 1, p. 32.
[22] ibid., p. 34.
[23] ibid., p. 36.
[24] ibid., p. 43.
[25] ibid., p. 45.

related in Genesis 12 and to be related in the story of Isaac (Gen. 26). At the same time, he points out that this critical observation is as old as Richard of St Victor (died 1173) and that 'the repetition is more simply accounted for if the book of Genesis was compiled from more ancient documents, a theory adopted by more learned men, and by some of the most rigid Scripturalists'.[26]

The story of Abraham, Isaac and Jacob follows the biblical account meticulously, as does the descent into Egypt, Joseph's governorship and the birth and preservation of Moses.[27] In his treatment of the plagues, Milman conspicuously avoids the temptation to treat them as natural occurrences exploited by Moses. On the redness of the Nile as a natural phenomenon, Milman makes the point well: 'that Moses should place any reliance on, or the Egyptians feel the least apprehension at, an ordinary occurrence, which took place every year, seems little less incredible than the miracle itself'.[28] While the 'corrupted waters' may have speeded up the births of the frogs who constituted the next plague, the most remarkable thing about the second plague was that it stopped immediately when Moses prayed that it should. In one day all frogs, except those in the Nile, were destroyed.[29] Again, in the plague of the thunder and hail, Milman sees only a miracle, which brings rain and hail at a time when such things were meteorologically inconceivable. However, if the plagues in Egypt were certainly miracles, the provision of the manna in the wilderness could be explained naturally, and had indeed been identified by travellers to Arabia as a product of the tamarisk.[30]

The period in the wilderness is accepted as the period when Moses promulgated the civil and religious law which was to be binding upon Israel for the rest of its historical existence. Milman writes:

> To what other period can the Hebrew constitution be assigned? To that of the Judges? A time of anarchy, warfare or servitude! To that of the Kings? When the republic had undergone a total change! To any time after Jerusalem became the metropolis? When the holy city, the pride and glory of the nation, is not even alluded to in the whole law![31]

Milman is certain that the legislation can only have been given in the

---

[26] ibid., p. 45, n1.
[27] ibid., p. 77: 'The daughter of the king, coming down to bathe in the river, perceived the ark, and, attracted by the beauty of the infant, took pity on it, and conjecturing that it belonged to one of the persecuted Hebrews, determined to preserve its life. By a simple and innocent stratagem, the mother was summoned, her own child committed to her charge, and, as it grew up, it became the adopted son of the princess who called it Moses, from Egyptian words signifying, drawn from the water.'
[28] ibid., p. 86.
[29] ibid., p. 87.
[30] ibid., p. 120.
[31] ibid., p. 122.

wilderness, and that the tabernacle and tent of meeting came into operation at this time.

The crossing of the river Jordan and the conquest of Jericho are described as miracles. The flow of the Jordan is arrested as the Israelites cross it, the walls of Jericho are falling flat at the blowing of the trumpets on the seventh day of circumambulation.[32] Milman does not make clear his position on the sun standing still at Gibeon at Joshua's request, although he observes that 'Many learned writers, whom to suspect of hostility to revealed religion would be the worst uncharitableness, have either doubted the reality or the extent of this miracle'.[33]

The period of the Judges is handled according to the letter of the biblical record, and attempts to explain away Jephthah's sacrifice of his daughter are opposed. Milman sees it as highly likely that 'a fierce Freebooter in a period of anarchy should mistake an act of cruel superstition for an act of religion'.[34] When we come to the story of David, however, the sort of rearrangement of chapters 16 and 17 of 1 Samuel, already to be found in the orthodox introduction of Horne, is assumed.[35] David, already anointed king by Samuel, defeats Goliath, and only several years later is introduced into the court of Saul as a musician and armour bearer.

For the rest, we can note simply that Milman records that according to some authorities, Elijah was fed by travelling merchants or Arabians, not ravens, while he withdrew to the brook Cherith,[36] that the son of the widow of Zarephath was not necessarily dead when Elijah restored him fully recovered to his mother,[37] and that there may be reasonable natural explanations for the defeat of Sennacherib's army at the siege of Jerusalem recorded in 2 Kings 18—19.[38]

Milman's *History of the Jews* not only presents a very traditional account of the history of ancient Israel, with occasional mild instances of rationalization; it contains a deep sense of the divine providence which sustained and directed the fortunes of the people of Israel, and which vouchsafed a unique revelation to mankind through them. Thus, writing of the patriarchal age, Milman can explain that:

Writers unfriendly to revealed religion, . . . have enlarged with malicious

[32] ibid., pp. 186–7.
[33] ibid., p. 187. V. F. Storr, *The Development of English Theology in the Nineteenth Century*, p. 113, is not accurate when he summarizes Milman as follows: 'The story in Joshua of the sun and the moon standing still was poetry, not fact.' Milman is much less explicit than this.
[34] *The History of the Jews*, 1, p. 213.
[35] ibid., pp. 229ff: 'The early history of David is involved in great, it should seem, insoluble difficulty. The events are here related in what appears the most easy and natural order.'
[36] ibid., p. 278. This suggestion can be traced back at least to medieval Jewish commentators.
[37] ibid., p. 278.
[38] ibid., pp. 305–6.

triumph on the delinquencies of the patriarchs and their descendants. . . . Had the avowed design of the intercourse of God with the patriarchs been their own unimpeachable perfection, had that of the Jewish polity been the establishment of a divine Utopia, advanced to premature civilization, an overleaping at once those centuries of slow improvement, through which the rest of mankind were to pass, then it might have been difficult to give a reasonable account of the manifest failure. . . . The one thing certain is, that Divine Providence designed the slow, gradual, and progressive development of the highest religious truth. The patriarchs . . . are not to be regarded as premature Christians. They and their descendants are the depositories of certain great religious truths, the unity, the omnipotence of God, not solely for their own use and advantages but as conservators for the future universal benefit of mankind.[39]

This profound sense of the divine providence guiding the Israelite people was to be a fundamental tenet of those liberal Anglicans whose work represented the next stage in the growth of English critical scholarship.

Their chief representatives were Thomas Arnold (1795–1842) and Frederick Denison Maurice (1805–72). Neither was an Old Testament scholar by training or by profession, but among their published works, sermons on the Bible were conspicuous. Both were deeply convinced of the importance of the Old Testament for the Church of their day, and both succeeded in making the Old Testament a text to be taken seriously, by freeing it from the orthodox methods of interpretation that prevailed in England at the time.[40]

A work which played an important part in shaping the thinking of the liberal Anglicans of the 1830s was B. G. Niebuhr's *History of Rome*, of which the first two parts appeared in 1811 and 1812.[41] It is well known that Arnold learned German in order to be able to read this work, and it was he who reviewed it in *The Quarterly Review* of 1825.[42] In 1825, the first part of an English translation appeared, prepared by two of the leading liberal Anglicans, J. C. Hare and Connop Thirlwall. It must also be remembered that Niebuhr had been the mentor of Bunsen, and that Bunsen had close links with Thirlwall, Arnold and other liberal Anglicans.[43] Niebuhr's history displayed a masterly use of the historical method in the interpretation of the legends and chronicles of Greek and Latin authors; but he also had the conviction that divine providence could be discerned in the events of Rome's history:

[39] ibid., p. 58.
[40] See my account of them in my A. S. Peake Memorial Lecture for 1981: 'Progressive Revelation: Its History and its Value as a key to Old Testament Interpretation', *Epworth Review*, 9 (1982), pp. 73–86.
[41] B. G. Niebuhr, *Römische Geschichte*, 1–2, Berlin 1811–12.
[42] See *The Quarterly Review* 32 (1825), pp. 62ff.
[43] See above p. 162.

Through the whole of their history we shall see how often all the virtues of the state and of the people would have been ineffectual, unless destiny had saved Rome in her perils, and paved the way for her triumphs. The nations and the men before whom Rome might have fallen appeared too late . . . these are events in which we cannot but recognize the finger of God.[44]

Three main themes can be isolated from the writings of Arnold and Maurice on the Old Testament: first, history in general and biblical history in particular have been, and are, under the direction of God. Second, this history constitutes the divine education of the human race. Third, at every stage of the unfolding historical process, choices of good and evil confront mankind, so that although there is, in human history, development of human moral and religious sensitivity, the issue of loyalty to the good and the challenge to suffer for what is right face each and every generation.

This third point is at the heart of the two sermons *On the Interpretation of Prophecy* published by Arnold together with a preface and notes in 1839.[45] In the first sermon, Arnold declares that prophecy is different from history, because it fixes our attention on principles,

on good and evil, on truth and falsehood, on God and on his enemy. . . . Prophecy . . . is God's voice, speaking to us respecting the issue in all time of that great struggle which is the real interest of human life, the struggle between good and evil.[46]

Of course, prophecies are often presented in the Old Testament in terms of particular persons and events, in which case they are to be interpreted in regard to those particulars.[47] But many prophecies, even if attached to specific circumstances, speak generally about the judgement of evil and the promise of salvation, and demand repentance of the hearers.

Thus, without any *artificial* appeal to a higher or spiritual sense of Scripture as opposed to the historical sense, but on the basis of the nature of the text itself, Arnold is able to plead for a new approach to prophecy. In the first instance, this does not require us to interpret prophecies as direct forecasts of the coming of Jesus. If he fulfils prophecies, it is because in him the principles at the heart of all prophecy—the struggle between good and

---

[44] Cited from B. G. Niebuhr, *The History of Rome*, tr. J. C. Hare and C. Thirlwall, 1, London 1847[4], p. xxviii.
[45] Thomas Arnold, *Sermons* 1, London 1844[4], pp. 367–449.
[46] ibid., pp. 376–7.
[47] ibid., p. 377.

evil and the demand for obedience—are perfectly exemplified.[48] This approach has the immediate advantage of making Old Testament prophecies speak more directly to the present-day reader. Understood as forecasts of the coming of Christ, they can become little more than static guarantees of the truth of the Bible or of Christian dogma. Seen as declaring God's voice in the matter of the struggle with evil, they can address the reader and question his own allegiance.

Arnold works out with great subtlety the implications of the fact that many prophecies are patently both historical and 'spiritual',[49] that those relating to the ideal Israel cannot be said to be fulfilled in the Church,[50] and that in the symbolism of prophecy, Babylon stands for the world as implacably opposed to God, while Egypt symbolizes the world in somewhat more neutral terms.[51]

In his preface to the two sermons, dated 1839, Arnold mentioned that although the views presented represented his own solution to the problem of prophecy, he had found similar views in Tholuck's first Appendix to his edition of the *Epistle to the Hebrews*, as well as in a notice of a German book on the Psalms in the *Theologische Studien und Kritiken*.[52] This latter work and its author are not named, but there can be little doubt that de Wette's small book *On the Edifying Interpretation of the Psalms* (1836) is meant.[53] It is interesting that Arnold mentioned by name Tholuck, who was considered to be orthodox by the traditionalists in Britain at the time, whereas he did not mention the name of de Wette, whom traditional circles branded as 'rationalist'. In fact, although de Wette's results may have resembled those of Arnold, they were based upon his Friesian view that prophecy is an expression of, and longing for, the ideal realm of values and harmonies, fulfilled on this earth most completely in Christ. Arnold's vision of the triumph of Christ's Kingdom owed much more to traditional orthodox ideas of the Christian hope. Nevertheless, his approach to prophecy opened

---

[48] ibid., p. 399: 'In this same manner it is that so many passages of the Old Testament are applied to Christ in the New Testament, which taken in their original place seem to refer to a subject much less exalted. And the reason of the application of them to Christ is this; that whereas all Prophecy is addressed to the hopes of the good and to the fears of the evil, so the perfect fulfilment of it, that is, the perfect satisfying of these hopes, and the perfect realizing those fears, is to be found only in the perfect triumph of good, and the perfect destruction of evil; of both which we have the pledge in the resurrection of Jesus Christ . . .'

[49] ibid., p. 406.

[50] ibid., pp. 409ff.

[51] ibid., pp. 415–27.

[52] ibid., p. 372.

[53] W. M. L. de Wette, *Ueber die erbauliche Erklärung der Psalmen. Eine Beilage zum Commentar über dieselben*, Heidelberg 1836. De Wette defends the view that Christ is essentially an innovator, and that his ministry would mean little if it had been fully anticipated in the Old Testament. De Wette thus defines various ways in which prophecy refers to Christ, without his uniqueness being compromised.

the way to a proper historical and critical study of prophecy, and one not
bogged down in the grammatical-historical level of exegesis.

The other two themes central to Arnold and Maurice, the divine
education of the Israelite nation and the divine control of that nation's
history, can be taken together, since the former is dependent upon the latter.
The idea of a progressive education allowed for an historical interpretation
of the Old Testament, in the sense that its moral crudities could be allowed
to be proper to their time, and thus not morally binding upon Christians;
yet Arnold and Maurice were not afraid to extract even from God's
commands to Joshua to destroy the Canaanites, spiritual truth for the
modern reader. In his essay *On the Right Interpretation and Understanding of
the Scriptures* (1832), Arnold stated firmly that 'the revelations of God to
man were gradual and adapted to his state at the several periods when they
were successively made', and he explained that there had been a training of
mankind by God, in the process of which God had given commands,
commands that would be subversive to later enlightened morality, but that
were no harm to mankind at a less enlightened stage.[54] Maurice, in a sermon
on the Flood, published in 1851, asked the question why God could not
force man to be perfect by divine fiat and replied:

> because . . . He had made man in his [*sic*] own image; because He had given him
> a Will; because He could only restore and regenerate him by restoring and
> regenerating his Will. Hence we have to read all the Bible through, of floods,
> famines, pestilences, earthquakes, anarchy, tyranny. It is throughout, the history
> of an actual government,—throughout, the history of an actual education; a
> government of voluntary creatures to teach them subjection;—an education of
> voluntary creatures to make them free.[55]

The two words 'government' and 'education' sum up the purpose of the Old
Testament witness to God.

The impression left upon the modern reader of Arnold and Maurice,
especially through their sermons, is that they were men who had really
discovered the power of the Old Testament for themselves and for their
hearers. They had been liberated by discarding the theory of verbal
inspiration, and had discovered how much the Old Testament said to their
own age. Indeed, in a sermon preached in May 1851, Maurice warned of
the dangers of supposing that one of the fundamental differences between
the Old Testament and the New was that the former only looked for

---

[54] Arnold, *Sermons*, 2, London 1831, 1844³, pp. 382ff.

[55] F. D. Maurice, *Patriarchs and Lawgivers of the Old Testament*, London 1851, 1855², p. 63.
See also Maurice's *The Kingdom of Christ*, London 1838, repr. London 1959, 2, pp. 139ff,
for his view of the history of Israel as that of the Jewish Commonwealth which paves the
way for the establishment of the Church.

material prosperity in this life, whereas the latter was concerned with a spiritual redemption beyond the grave:

> Is it possible that this is what the writers of the New Testament meant when they proclaimed that the Son of God had taken flesh and become man, and that thenceforth the Lord God would dwell with men and walk with them?... Do such words import, that the world in which God has placed us has lost some of the sacredness which it had before; that the visible has become hopelessly separated from the invisible; that earth and heaven are not as much united as they were when Jacob was travelling to the land of the people of the east; that now earth is merely a forlorn place, in which men are forced to stay a certain number of years, engaged in a number of occupations with which Heaven has nothing to do, while yet it is held that the preparation for Heaven is the great business of those who dwell here?[56]

Yet for all that Arnold and Maurice invited a liberal and inquiring attitude to the Old Testament, their position remained basically a traditional and conservative position. The picture of Old Testament history presented in the Bible was basically authentic. It might contain odd factual errors, but it was fundamentally true.[57] Arnold and Maurice did not seem to think that criticism could convincingly overturn the whole picture of Old Testament history, and Maurice was to be devastated when his protégé Colenso sought to demonstrate the 'unhistorical' nature of the Exodus and wilderness wanderings tradition.[58] This is not to condemn Arnold and Maurice for being men of their own times. It is a reminder that the best of critical thought in orthodox circles at this time was still very conservative when compared with the radicalism of de Wette and those who saw the history of Israel as he did.

Yet there was a book by an English writer published anonymously in 1847, and thus within the period of Maurice's activity mentioned above, which hinted at a radical view of Israelite history, and which treated parts of the Old Testament 'like any other book' in a way that makes Milman's *History of the Jews* seem ultra-orthodox in comparison. The writer was Francis W. Newman (1805–97), younger brother of John Henry Newman, and the book was entitled *A History of the Hebrew Monarchy from the Administration of Samuel to the Babylonish Captivity*.[59] Newman had been brought up in a strict Calvinist household, and had experienced 'conversion'

---

[56] Maurice, *Patriarchs and Lawgivers*, pp. 251–2.
[57] See Maurice, ibid., p. 152.
[58] See below, p. 234.
[59] On Newman, see G. Sieveking, *Memoir and Letters of Francis W. Newman*, London 1909. The book was published anonymously in London 1847. See J. E. Carpenter in *The Bible in the Nineteenth Century*, London 1903, pp. 125–6. Carpenter's comment that the book 'would now be considered deficient in critical grasp' is somewhat harsh.

at the age of fourteen. However, on gaining most brilliant honours at Oxford in classics and mathematics in 1826, he did not take his degree because he felt unable to make the necessary subscription to the Thirty-nine Articles.[60] Following a missionary journey to the East, in particular to the Turkish empire, he became progressively estranged from positive forms of religion. In 1840 he became Classical Professor at Manchester New College[61] (lately moved from York to Manchester), and in 1846 he was appointed to the chair of Latin at University College, London.[62]

In his preface to the *Hebrew Monarchy* he gave vent to some of his feelings about his own education, and about the necessity to subscribe to the Thirty-nine Articles in order to graduate:

> If the Hebrew history has hitherto been nearly a sealed book to us, it is because all the academical and clerical teachers of it are compelled to sign Thirty-nine Articles of Religion before assuming their office. It is *not* easy to conceive how little we might know of Greek history, if, from the revival of Greek studies, test-articles had been imposed with a view to perpetuate the idea of it current in the fifteenth century. . . . Moreover, so has the study of the Bible been crippled by the classical and mathematical system, that in this country little interest has been felt in our subject; and the biblical critic is perpetually driven to the learned Germans for aid.[63]

The Germans referred to in the course of the *Hebrew Monarchy* are Ewald and Hitzig, but that sparingly; the work displays deep historical insight and is beautifully written.

On the rise of Saul to the kingship, and the nature of Saul's reign, Newman is fully aware of the problems raised by the text, which made it difficult 'to extract a distinct and congruous narrative of these transactions'.[64] The description of the complete Philistine dominance of the Israelites (1 Sam. 13.19ff) was incongruous with the manner of Saul's appointment as king, and with his operation against the Ammonites, where his forces were well armed. Thus 1 Sam. 13.19ff was to be assigned to an earlier era, and described what was true only for a small portion of Israel. In fact, Saul was

[60] Sieveking, p. 12.
[61] ibid., p. 65.
[62] ibid., p. 106.
[63] *A History of the Hebrew Monarchy*, p. vi.
[64] ibid., p. 38. See also p. 42: 'In pursuing [Saul's] reign into its details, although our materials are multiplied, the difficulty of using them is great, owing to their fragmentary character. Some of the documents appear to be duplicates of others, representing events in substance the same, but with variations sufficiently notable; others involve incongruities which cannot always be removed by help of transposition. In short, we are by no means as yet in the region of contemporary and clear history.' See also the detailed discussion of the problems of the narrative of Saul's relationship with David on p. 56, n1.

probably forced upon Samuel as king by the elders of the tribe of Benjamin, on the basis of his remarkable strength and stature.[65]

Among the various difficulties presented by the narrative were: (a) Samuel's prerogative over Saul to offer sacrifice;[66] (b) the fact that Saul cannot both have been a 'young man', when he was elected and have had a son old enough to be a warrior;[67] (c) the impossibility that Saul could have achieved the victories ascribed to him in 1 Sam. 14.44ff. Of chapters 13— 14 Newman concluded, 'the more these two chapters are studied, the less historical value do they seem to have'.[68]

On the anointing of David by Samuel following the rejection of Saul, Newman argued it was doubtful whether such a 'useless ceremony' had actually been performed. The act was apparently known to no one, did not consciously affect David's conduct, and was never referred to later. If performed, it was 'a barren type'.[69] However, it was clear that a breach between Saul and Samuel occurred, and that subsequent to this, Saul looked with greater favour on the worshippers of foreign gods in an attempt to counterbalance the power of the prophets.

Two points of particular interest are first, that Newman consistently pillories the books of Chronicles for their inaccuracies and exaggerations. Typical is the comment, 'The details given us in 1 Chron. 27 concerning David's standing army cannot be received with any confidence, considering the prodigious credulity of that book in regard to figures'.[70] Secondly, he notes that from the time of Samuel onwards, names compounded with Jehovah or Jah become common, a point to be made much of by Colenso a decade and a half later.[71]

In dealing with the reign of Josiah, Newman discusses the law book discovered in his reign, and the related question of the composition of the Pentateuch. His argument is presented devastatingly. If the Pentateuch existed in a published form before the time of Josiah, how had things reached the condition to be found immediately before Josiah's reign? If

[65] ibid., pp. 42ff.

[66] ibid., pp. 43–4: 'To sacrifice was as much the right or duty of Saul as of Samuel, who affected not the priestly office; and to elevate a petty ceremonial affair of this sort into the basis of Samuel's feud with Saul indicates the misconception of a later time, when the priestly power had given far greater weight to such matters, when kings had ceased to officiate at the altar, and when it had become a cherished notion that Samuel was a Levite.'

[67] ibid., p. 44.

[68] ibid., p. 44. In Newman's view, the triumphs ascribed to Saul were borrowed from the reign of David.

[69] ibid., p. 51.

[70] ibid., p. 94, n3. See also p. 109, n1: 'David buys the floor of Araunah for fifty shekels of silver in 2 Sam. 24.24, but for six hundred shekels of gold in 1 Chron. 21.25. Such exaggerations are throughout characteristic of the Chronicles.'

[71] ibid., p. 95.

Josiah 'upheld the rites of Baal and Moloch, and left a graven image of Astarte in Jehovah's house, and, while acquainted with Leviticus, repented not; neither would he have repented when Deuteronomy rose from the dead'.[72]

But perhaps the book of the Law had been suppressed by Manasseh; however, this was most unlikely. If it had existed before Manasseh's time, numerous copies would have existed in the hands of the priests; and in any case, had Manasseh been guilty of such a grave offence as destroying the book of the Law of God, the Bible would surely have charged him with it.[73]

Newman's conclusion was that the first four books of the Pentateuch were to be regarded as a growth, not a compilation, and that from the time of Josiah's reform they began to receive both their final shape and public recognition. The book of the Law upon which Josiah's reform was based was not Deuteronomy only, for all that that book clearly stood apart from the rest by its style. However, it was clear that Deuteronomy was of recent (seventh century) origin, and it was a mistake to accuse Hilkiah and the priests of that time, of forgery:

> When we know what a Cyprian and a Chrysostom thought of 'pious frauds'; and how greedily a Justin Martyr could snatch at Sybilline forgeries which helped a Christian advocate, it would be vain to expect our own standard of simplicity in an Hilkiah, or any clear-sighted criticism in the Jewish people.[74]

Nothing as radical and far-reaching as this was to come from an English writer until the appearance of the later parts of Colenso's *The Pentateuch and Joshua* in 1871 and 1879. Meanwhile, Newman's views proved to be unacceptable even to a liberal such as F. D. Maurice. Preaching at Lincoln's Inn in November 1851, Maurice made a clear allusion to Newman's account of Saul's election when he referred to a way of presenting 'what is called the rationale of the Bible narratives, stripping them of their mystical and theological adjuncts, which I do not profess to follow'.[75] It is clear that for

[72] ibid., p. 335.
[73] ibid., p. 331.
[74] ibid., p. 318.
[75] Maurice, *The Prophets and Kings of the Old Testament*, London 1879[3], p. 19. Maurice continues: 'If I did, I should have to tell you that Saul was chosen by the people of Israel, because he was the tallest and strongest man among them; that while the novelty of royalty lasted, he retained his popularity; that he lost it partly through the influence of the prophet Samuel. I do not deny that such paraphrases may be an escape from the dryness and formality with which Scripture narratives are sometimes offered to us, as if they referred to beings of a different nature from our own; as if, because they speak of God, they have nothing to do with man. But I venture to doubt whether the phraseology of newspapers is after all the most real, the most human, the most historical . . .' We, today, are tempted to ask why Newman and Maurice cannot both have been right; why it is not

Maurice, Newman's kind of approach invited readers not to see the hand of
God at work in the ordering of Israel's affairs.

---

possible to reconstruct the history of Israel critically from the biblical material and to
preach on the basis of the particular witness which the narratives in their final form possess.
It seems that in the mid-nineteenth century, these alternatives were mutually exclusive,
even to some liberals.

14

Samuel Davidson and his Dismissal in 1857

We have already seen in Chapter 12 that an unrivalled knowledge of German critical Old Testament scholarship was possessed by Samuel Davidson. In 1856, Davidson published, as Volume 2 of the tenth edition of T. H. Horne's *An Introduction to the Critical Study and Knowledge of the Holy Scriptures*, a work of over a thousand pages entitled *The Text of the Old Testament*.[1] This book probably provided the most detailed information yet available in English about critical studies in Germany. It also cost the author his post of Professor of Biblical Criticism at the Lancashire Independent College, Manchester.

Davidson was born in 1806 at Kellswater, near Ballymena, in what is now Northern Ireland.[2] He was educated at the Belfast Academical Institution with a view to entering the ministry of the Presbyterian Church. In 1835, the College Examination Committee of the General Synod of Ulster nominated him to the post of Professor of Biblical Criticism at the Belfast Academical Institution.[3] In 1842 he resigned, having moved to a Congregational viewpoint.[4] In the autumn of 1842 he moved to England, on being invited to take up a professorship at the newly-founded Lancashire Independent College. Here, Davidson worked from the opening of the College in 1843 to his enforced resignation in 1857.

Early in 1854, Davidson received a request from the publishers of Horne's *Introduction* to revise the volumes on the Old and New Testaments.[5]

---

[1] Samuel Davidson, *The Text of the Old Testament Considered; with a Treatise on Sacred Interpretation; and a brief Introduction to the Old Testament Books and the Apocrypha*, London 1856, 1859². Vol. 2 of *An Introduction to the Critical Study and Knowledge of the Holy Scriptures* by Thomas Hartwell Horne, Samuel Davidson and Samuel Prideaux Tregelles, London 1856¹⁰. Only Davidson's volume of the 1856¹⁰ edition of the whole work was reissued in a new edition in 1859. In the present chapter, reference is made to the 1859 edition, which differs only marginally from the 1856 version.

[2] See *The Autobiography and Diary of Samuel Davidson*, ed. by his daughter, Edinburgh 1899, p. 7.

[3] ibid., p. 13, where it is not clear to which institution, if any, Davidson was attached. I am grateful to Prof. J. M. Barkley for the information given above.

[4] ibid., p. 15.

[5] ibid., p. 36. This part of the *Autobiography* is in fact written by J. Allanson Picton.

Davidson declined to undertake a revision on the grounds that progress in biblical criticism called for a complete rewriting. He was now requested to rewrite both volumes, and again declined, on the grounds that he had recently published an introduction to the New Testament. It was finally agreed that Davidson should rewrite the volume on the Old Testament.

On the face of it, the volume should not have caused any alarm in orthodox circles. In writing on the subjects of inspiration and infallibility, Davidson put himself firmly on the side of orthodox divines who maintained that the Bible was free from error regarding doctrine, reproof, correction and instruction in righteousness, but was not necessarily infallible in matters unconnected with religion.[6] Thus, where the Bible touched upon astronomy, geology, botany and physiology, etc., it did so in terms popularly held by the people to whom the biblical writings were originally addressed. Again, in small matters of historical detail, it was not to be supposed that the biblical writers were infallible; and if small discrepancies were found, this in no way affected the religious truths propounded by the inspired writers. If Davidson was heretical on inspiration and infallibility, then so were Pye Smith, Archbishop Whately, Thomas Scott, Bishop Heber and W. J. Conybeare. Moreover, Davidson pointed out that no less a person than Tholuck had shown that the view that the Bible was infallible in its *entire* contents as opposed to its *religious* contents had emerged only in seventeenth-century Protestant circles.[7] The early Church and the Reformers had distinguished between essential truths of religion and non-essential points.

Any fear that Davidson would misuse this mild and orthodox 'liberalism' would have been disabused by his brief comments on the content of the books of the Old Testament. On Genesis 2—3, he held that the 'natural and safe interpretation' was to regard the narrative as 'a literal account, in plain prose, of the origin of the human race and their fall'.[8] Davidson was prepared to consider sympathetically the mythic view of the chapters, so long as this interpretation was concerned with how the facts were presented, and did not question the facts themselves. In the account of creation, the biblical writer used the ideas current among his readers, lest what he wrote would be unintelligible. 'He was not a natural philosopher, but a religious teacher raised up and qualified by God for the purpose of conveying moral and spiritual ideas to the Jews and to the world at large'.[9]

Davidson noted that parts of Exodus had been subjected to the mythic interpretation, on account of the miraculous elements in the narratives. However, it was safer to understand the narratives in their plain, historical

---

[6] Davidson, *Text of the Old Testament*, pp. 375ff.

[7] ibid., p. 372. In the 1859 edition, following page 376 are pages (369) to (376) [*sic*]. The references to Whately, Scott, Heber and Conybeare are not in the 1856 edition.

[8] ibid., p. 576.

[9] ibid., p. 577.

sense, 'leaving miracles and wonders to remain as they are; since they are appropriate and worthy of the Deity in a scheme of human redemption essentially supernatural'.[10] Of the famous passage in Numbers 24.17, 19 traditionally interpreted as referring to Christ, Davidson affirmed that he did believe it to apply to Christ, though not exclusively. 'Probably its *springing* or *germinant* fulfilment belongs to David; its *final* fulfilment to Christ'.[11]

However, to any reader who associated the inspiration of the Bible with acceptance of traditional views of the authorship of the books, Davidson would have become suspect as soon as he began to deal with the authorship of the Pentateuch. Beginning with the statement that the generally-received view in Germany was that of the supplement-hypothesis, he examined in great detail the arguments for supposing that Genesis to Numbers was composed of two main sources, the older Elohim and the younger Jehovah documents.[12] In many cases, Davidson judged that the grounds for alleging the separated sources were not convincing; but there were sufficient cases where attempts of orthodox defenders of unity such as Keil and Hengstenberg had failed, that Davidson was inclined to admit the validity of the documentary theory. On the authorship of Deuteronomy, he was convinced that the style and language of the book showed it to be by a different author from the other four books.

A careful discussion of the meaning of 'unity' distinguished between original unity and the unity of the final version,[13] and argued that grounds put forward by Keil for an *original* unity of the Pentateuch did not show that the unity could not have been achieved by a later redactor assembling his sources. Davidson's view of the composition of the Pentateuch was that Moses had substantially written Deuteronomy as well as the laws that formed the basis of the Sinai covenant, and other pieces such as wilderness itineraries.[14] The remainder of the Pentateuch was derived from the two sources, the Elohim and Jehovah documents, which Davidson, following Hupfeld, believed had been written independently of each other. That these sources had been written after the time of Moses could be argued from internal evidence; and Davidson dated the Elohim document in the time of Joshua and the Jehovah document in the period of the Judges.[15] The whole

[10] ibid., p. 581.
[11] ibid., p. 585.
[12] ibid., pp. 593ff.
[13] ibid., p. 612.
[14] ibid., p. 616.
[15] ibid., p. 631.

had been redacted in the early period of the monarchy, at which point some of the features such as the 'post-Mosaica' had been inserted.[16]

Davidson insisted that the position adopted in no way undermined either the authority of the Pentateuch or biblical teaching about its origin. He allowed that Moses had written parts of it, something upheld by the authority of Christ and the apostles. But nowhere did the Bible require belief that Moses had written the *entire* Pentateuch, and if there was an ancient tradition to this effect, that tradition must be modified by the results of a careful examination of the text. What could be inferred about the authorship of biblical books from an examination of the text itself was to be preferred to what was said by tradition.[17] Further:

> Inspiration does not stand or fall with certain names; as some would lead us to suppose it does. . . . Joshua was inspired as well as Moses. So was Eleazar. So were many others whose names we may not know. . . . If divine authority be claimed for them because Moses wrote them, divine authority should also be claimed for them because they were written after him by unknown persons.[18]

So far, only an outline has been given of the conclusions that Davidson drew from his study of the material. It needs to be added that in the course of his discussion, Davidson provided much information about positions held by critical German scholars, positions that he often rejected. Thus readers would have been made aware that German scholars found in the Pentateuch contradictions, doublets, later modifications of law, and differences of style and language; that some critics dated Deuteronomy in the seventh or sixth centuries. Readers would also have been presented with the arguments of orthodox scholars such as Keil, Hävernick and Hengstenberg, many of which Davidson accepted, but which often received the damning verdict that they proved too much and resorted to obviously far-fetched lengths. Among the critical scholars, the names de Wette, Vater, Hupfeld, Tuch, Stähelin, von Bohlen, to name only some, are found.

On books outside the Pentateuch, Davidson adhered much more closely to traditional views. Although he accepted the chronological difficulties in the book of Judges, and was inclined to view some of the Judges as contemporaries and not as succeeding one another,[19] he strongly defended the unity of the book of Isaiah, and the unity and Danielic authorship of the

---

[16] Post-mosaica: passages referring to Moses in the third person, such as Num. 12.3; also, passages using the phrase 'to this day', implying a considerable interval of time between event and narrative.

[17] ibid., p. 632.

[18] ibid., pp. 632–3.

[19] ibid., p. 650: '. . . it is likely that some judges, usually reckoned successive, were contemporary, ruling over different districts.'

book of Daniel.[20] On the books of Chronicles, he rejected the view that Samuel and Kings had been used as sources, and preferred the idea that a common source had been used.[21] He firmly repudiated the historical conclusions drawn from those who maintained the dependence of Chronicles upon Samuel and Kings:

> From the sections common to the books of Samuel, Kings and Chronicles, conclusions have been deduced by the Rationalist party very prejudicial to the historical character of the last work. Misconception, ignorance, inaccuracies, exaggerations, a peculiar doctrinal and mythological way of thinking, a partiality for the Levitical worship and for the pious Kings who were addicted to the Mosaic law, and hatred to the kingdom of Israel, have been attributed to the writer; by virtue of which, it is alleged, he has violated historical truth, or distorted and falsified the history of earlier times.[22]

Gramberg and de Wette were especially named as supporting these 'weighty charges'. Davidson believed that most of de Wette's arguments had been answered by Movers, Hengstenberg and Keil; but he conceded that not all the sources used by Chronicles were 'all alike trustworthy and accurate'.[23] Vagueness and exaggeration sometimes resulted because the writer had followed tradition, and on the whole, Davidson believed that Chronicles was inferior to Samuel and Kings 'in regard to historical details'.[24] But this admission did not take away the inestimable value of Chronicles for Hebrew history.

Davidson's contribution to Horne's *Introduction* was published in October 1856. The following month, the College Committee was made aware of the fact that letters had been received expressing alarm at the religious opinions contained in Davidson's volume.[25] The letters had, apparently,

[20] For Isaiah, see ibid., pp. 835ff. In rejecting the deutero-Isaiah theory, Davidson wrote: 'it appears to us, that incorrect views of the nature of biblical prophecy lie at the basis of much that is here set forth' (p. 853). On 'the book of the prophet Daniel' [sic] see pp. 905ff, esp. p. 934: 'In whatever light we regard the prophetic book before us, the difficulties of accounting for its origin in the Maccabean period are infinitely greater than any which lie against the Daniel-authorship.' The observation of J. Allanson Picton in the Davidson autobiography, that 'as to such books as . . . Daniel, his views were substantially the same as those now generally held by intelligent orthodoxy: that in their existing form they all belong to later periods of Hebrew literature than those to which they were traditionally assigned' (pp. 43–4) is incorrect.
[21] ibid., p. 682.
[22] ibid., pp. 684–5.
[23] ibid., p. 685.
[24] ibid., p. 686.
[25] For what follows, see Picton's contribution to Davidson's autobiography, esp. pp. 41–67. See also Thomas Nicholas, *Dr Davidson's Removal from the Professorship of Biblical Literature in the Lancashire Independent College, Manchester, on account of alleged Error in Doctrine*, London and Edinburgh, 1860.

been partly occasioned by a letter written by Dr S. P. Tregelles, the third
co-author with Horne and Davidson, to the *Record* newspaper, in which it
was indirectly alleged that Davidson had not upheld the plenary inspiration
of the Bible. Accordingly, a committee was appointed to inquire into the
allegations that certain of the views expressed in Davidson's volume were
'unsound'. It duly reported in February 1857. Between February and June
1857, when Davidson resigned, he was required to explain and to re-express
those parts of his book which may have caused offence, or misunderstanding.
His response was to produce a small book entitled *Facts, Statements, and
Explanations*,[26] in which he argued for the essential orthodoxy of his
position. Among other points, he showed that Horne himself, whose
orthodoxy nobody suspected, had written in the first volume that the
biblical writers were not 'inspired in every fact which they related, or in
every precept they delivered'.[27] Davidson's *Facts, Statements, and Explanations*
was deemed to be not satisfactory by a majority of the Committee, and a
resolution was narrowly passed stating that the Committee's confidence in
him as a professor was 'greatly shaken'. Davidson requested that the grounds
against him should be explicitly stated, a request which was declined. His
resignation then followed.

Before proceeding any further, comment must be made upon a fringe
allegation against Davidson, namely that of plagiarism. In 1857 there
appeared an anonymous book entitled: *Dr Davidson: His Heresies,
Contradictions, and Plagiarisms*.[28] The authors alleged that in some parts of
his volume, Davidson was 'absolutely dependent' upon other authors
without this being acknowledged. Elsewhere, Davidson's work was alleged
to be 'a patchwork of materials taken from sources either altogether
unacknowledged, or acknowledged in such a way as to conceal the extent
of his obligation'.[29] The authors asserted that 'Vast portions of his book
ought to have been placed within inverted commas, and nothing less than
these will satisfy the demands of literary honour'.[30]

With these observations should be compared the following remarks from
German reviews of the 1856 volume and of Davidson's 1862–3 *Introduction
to the Old Testament*. Writing on the former, Bleek stated that in discussing
the Pentateuch;

[26] S. Davidson, *Facts, Statements and Explanations*, London 1857.
[27] T. H. Horne, *A Summary of the Evidence for the Genuineness, Authenticity, Uncorrupted
Preservation, and Inspiration of the Holy Scriptures*, London 1856, p. 528. (vol. 1 of Horne's
Introduction). The same passage is found in earlier editions, e.g., the fifth, London 1825, p.
521.
[28] Anon. [Two Graduates], *Dr Davidson: His Heresies, Contradictions, and Plagiarisms*, London
and Manchester 1857.
[29] ibid., p. 81.
[30] ibid., p. 91.

the author bases himself largely on Keil's presentation, so that he gives this presentation in its particular points and arguments, sometimes completely, sometimes in summary form, and then adds his own opinion. Sometimes he agrees with Keil, sometimes he disagrees, but often his verdict rests upon no particular grounds, and is given in too general a way without any detailed proof.[31]

Kamphausen, reviewing the later work pointed out Davidson's indebtedness to German fundamental research. The divisions of Exodus and Deuteronomy were taken by Davidson from Bunsen's *Bibelwerk*, his section on Chronicles was indebted to Keil, and that on Job to Hupfeld. Kamphausen concluded that 'the author reveals an acquaintance with our specialist literature that is truly astonishing'.[32]

In the light of these observations, it is instructive to compare parts of Davidson's 1856 volume with German literature. In what follows, the comparison is made only with Keil's *Introduction*. However, the results are striking. In the section on the 'authorship and date of the Pentateuch', Davidson followed Keil, not only in his general divisions, but in the particular cases that were discussed. Sometimes, his wording was almost identical to that of Keil, as will be seen from a comparison of Davidson's text with that of the English translation of Keil published in 1869.[33]

Alleged discrepancies in the Pentateuch

DAVIDSON	KEIL
Genesis 27.46—28.9, where Jacob is sent to Mesopotamia to procure for himself a wife; and Genesis 27.41–5, where he is obliged to flee thither to avoid Esau's wrath.[34]	Between Genesis 27.46—28.9, where Jacob is sent away to Mesopotamia to obtain a wife, and Genesis 27.41–5, according to which he is compelled to fly from Esau's wrath.[35]

[31] F. Bleek in *Theologische Studien und Kritiken*, 1858, p. 372: 'Der Verfasser legt meistens die Keilsche Darstellung zu Grunde, so dass er diese in den einzelnen Behauptungen und Argumenten, zum Theil vollständig, zum Theil zusammenziehend, ausführt und dann sein Urtheil hinzufügt, theils billigend, theils verwerfend, aber vielfach das Eine und das Andere ohne gehörige Begründung, in zu allgemeiner Haltung, ohne speciellen Beweis.'
[32] A. Kamphausen in *Theologische Studien und Kritiken* 1863, p. 798.
[33] The advantage of comparing Davidson with a *translation* of Keil is that the latter represents an independent, contemporary English rendering of the German edition on which Davidson was allegedly dependent.
[34] Davidson, *Text of the Old Testament*, p. 596.
[35] K. F. Keil, *Manual of Historico-Critical Introduction to the Canonical Scriptures of the Old Testament*, trs. G. C. M. Douglas, 1, Edinburgh, 1869.

DAVIDSON	KEIL
In Genesis 30.25–43, the narrative gives a different account of the manner in which Jacob obtained his riches from that contained in Genesis 31.4–48.[36]	The narrative of Jacob's manner of acquiring wealth, Genesis 30.25–43, differs from that in 31.4–48.[37]
According to Genesis 26.34, Esau took two wives, Judith the daughter of Beeri the Hittite, and Basemath the daughter of Elon the Hittite, to whom he added, according to 28.9, Mahalath the daughter of Ishmael, the sister of Nebajoth.[38]	According to Genesis 26.34, Esau took two wives: Judith the daughter of Beeri the Hittite, and Basemath the daughter of Elon the Hittite; to whom he added, according to 28.9, Mahalath the daughter of Ishmael and sister of Nebaioth.[39]

In this section entitled 'Discrepancies', there are no fewer than twenty instances with close agreement either in wording or substance, after the manner of the examples given above, between Davidson and Keil as the principal grounds for source division are considered. This pattern continues into section 2, a discussion of doublets and the following section, on *usus loquendi*. It is true that after the introduction of each example the Davidson text differs from the Keil text; after all, Keil was stating examples so that he could disprove them, while Davidson, in putting forward the same examples, was on the whole inclined to believe that they proved the existence of sources.

In a section discussing the supposed allusions to the Pentateuch in books of the Old Testament outside the Pentateuch, we find again that Davidson's text exhibits close agreement with Keil's. The following is an example showing verbal agreement at its closest in this section:

DAVIDSON	KEIL
Joel presupposes the existence of the Levitical worship, and presents obvious references to the Pentateuch, sometimes verbal ones, as in 2.3 to Genesis 13.10.[40]	Joel not only assumes the existence of the Levitical worship, but he also furnishes distinct references to the Pentateuch, sometimes in its very words. Such are . . . 2.3 to Genesis 13.10.[41]

[36] Davidson, ibid., p. 596.
[37] Keil, ibid., p. 106.
[38] Davidson, ibid., p. 597.
[39] Keil, ibid., p. 107.
[40] Davidson, ibid., p. 628.
[41] Keil, ibid., p. 172.

To be fair to Davidson, he acknowledges here that he is outlining the position of Hengstenberg and others, a position that he does not entirely accept. However, the similarity in detail between his text and that of Keil is striking.

If we turn from the Pentateuch to Chronicles, we find ample justification for Kamphausen's observation of Davidson's dependence upon Keil, observations made by Kamphausen not about the 1856 book but to Davidson's 1862–3 volumes. However, the observations are pertinent to the 1856 volume. The table of parallels between Chronicles, and Samuel and Kings is identical in the Davidson and Keil books.[42] There is also a closeness of content and language in the verbal description of the relationship between Chronicles, and Samuel and Kings, of which the following example is typical.

DAVIDSON	KEIL
Primary facts again, are added in the Chronicles which do not appear in the Kings, as the companies that are come to David at Ziklag, and the warriors that come to him at Hebron (1 Chron. 12); his preparations for building the temple (22); the number and distribution of the Levites and priests (23—6).[43]	The following matters are taken up, which are not mentioned in the books of Samuel and Kings: The list of mighty men who came to David at Ziklag, and that of the warriors who made him king at Hebron (1 Chron. 12). David's preparation for building the Temple (1 Chron. 22). The enumeration and arrangement of the Levites and priests (1 Chron. 23–6.)[44]

A most striking parallel is found in the comments of the two authors on the use made by the negative critics of their view of the dependence of Chronicles upon Samuel and Kings. Thus Davidson:

> Misconception, ignorance, inaccuracies, exaggerations, a peculiar doctrinal and mythological way of thinking, a partiality for the Levitical worship and for the pious kings who were addicted to the Mosaic law, and hatred to the kingdom of Israel, have been attributed to the writer.[45]

Keil exonerates the Chronicler from the charge of falsifying history,

[42] cf. Davidson, op. cit., p. 677 with Keil, 2, 1870, pp. 53–4. The pagination in the 1856 and 1859 editions is identical.

[43] Davidson, ibid., p. 678.

[44] Keil, ibid., p. 80.

[45] Davidson, ibid., p. 45.

whether this were to be charged upon him on account of misunderstanding or want of information, of inexactness or exaggerations, of a peculiar dogmatico-mythological way of thinking, of a predilection for the Levitical mode of worship or a partiality for pious kings who were devoted to that worship and to the law of Moses, or of hatred towards the Ten Tribes of Israel.[46]

The way in which the ideas expressed by Keil are reproduced in their exact order by Davidson, albeit in different words, can leave little doubt that Davidson was deeply indebted at this point to Keil, not to mention other points.

However, the object of the present operation is not to renew the charge of plagiarism against Davidson, but rather to place his achievements in their correct perspective. The fact that his arguments and examples, at any rate when discussing the Pentateuch and Chronicles, followed so closely those of Keil does not entail that Davidson had copied Keil without reflecting deeply upon what could or could not be proved from the arguments adduced. The number of examples that can be brought to support the view that there are contradictions or doublets in the Pentateuch is finite, and if one is going to follow these through in order of their appearance in the text, there is bound to be similarity of presentation when scholarly works are compared. Davidson did not agree with many of Keil's conclusions, and he enlarged his discussions of particular passages with reference to other German critical and conservative works. That he had read these works carefully there can be no doubt.

On the other hand, it is clear from the comparison of Davidson with Keil that it would be mistaken to suppose that Davidson's 1856 volume was the totally original fruit of independent study of the text and of German criticism. The last comparison given above shows that Davidson, in itemizing the charges brought against the historicity of Chronicles by 'rationalists', was not constructing a synthesis from his own reading of 'rationalist' treatments of Chronicles, but was largely following points made by Keil. Again, I have no desire to condemn Davidson for doing this. Scholarship must always be dependent to some extent upon the work of others. In writing his 1856 volume, Davidson evidently relied heavily upon the model provided by Keil's *Einleitung* in his sections on the Pentateuch and Chronicles, and perhaps he was similarly dependent elsewhere in the book. However, in following the model, Davidson exercised his own judgement, and incorporated his extensive reading of other German authorities. Those who charged him with plagiarism were not making totally groundless allegations. If, however, the 1856 volume is to be judged for its impact upon its readers and not in the light of its composition criticism, it must be acknowledged that Davidson presented Old Testament

[46] Keil, ibid., p. 80.

introduction as a serious matter based upon detailed consideration of the text. He outlined some of the positions maintained by critical German scholars, and while not agreeing with them, in some cases he provided those who wished to consider matters further with the resources to do so. In the area of the Pentateuch, he conducted his inquiries with an openness of mind for which he paid a heavy price. His work was remarkable and courageous, whatever the sources that he drew upon.

After his resignation from the Lancashire Independent College, Davidson moved to Hatherlow in Cheshire, where he worked as a private tutor.[47] During this period, he worked at the three-volume *Introduction to the Old Testament*, which was published in 1862–3.[48] In this work, Davidson took a more radical position on some matters compared with the 1856 volume. His acceptance of Hupfeld's distinction between the elder and the younger Elohist was now complete,[49] and the younger Elohist was seen to be much closer to the Jehovist than to the elder Elohist. . . . The date of composition of the latter was now brought down from the period of Joshua to that of Saul,[50] the younger Elohist was dated *c*.880 BC,[51] while the Jehovist source was dated to the reign of Uzziah, probably written in the north.[52] But Davidson's biggest shift of position was with regard to Deuteronomy, which was now dated to the seventh century;[53] and the book of Joshua was believed to have been a continuation of the combined Elohist and Jehovist sources, redacted before the composition of Deuteronomy.[54]

It is idle to speculate on whether these more radical ideas were present to Davidson's mind already in 1856, and whether at that period he felt constrained to practise his criticism within the terms of the doctrinal basis of the Independent College; or whether the bitterness of his enforced resignation subsequently led him to adopt a more radical stance. Certainly, in his pre-1856 period he had no qualms about maintaining friendships with so-called Arians, such as T. D. Hincks.[55]

In 1862, Davidson was elected to the post of Scripture Examiner in the University of London, and took up residence in London, where he numbered liberal thinkers, including Unitarians, among his friends.[56]

---

[47] Davidson, *Autobiography*, p. 80.
[48] S. Davidson, *An Introduction to the Old Testament*, London and Edinburgh, 1862–3.
[49] In the 1856 volume, Davidson mentions Hupfeld's theory of a younger Elohim document (p. 595), but does not appear to incorporate the theory into his own view of the composition of the Pentateuch.
[50] Davidson, *Introduction*, 1, p. 50.
[51] ibid., p. 51.
[52] ibid., p. 50.
[53] ibid., p. 383.
[54] ibid., p. 424.
[55] Davidson, *Autobiography*, p. 16.
[56] ibid., pp. 80, 85.

Around 1870, he began to worship with Unitarians, and occasionally, in the Church of England.[57] Although he lived on until 1898, dying at the age of 91, it would be fair to say that his latter years were ones in which he did not exert significant influence upon British scholarship, although he kept up his critical studies to the last.

During his lifetime, Davidson's contacts with Germany were extensive. In the pre-1856 period he had visited Neander, Hupfeld and Tholuck, and in 1848 had received the honorary degree of D. Theol. (which he usually represented as DD) from Halle.[58] He became on intimate terms with Hupfeld, Tholuck and Ewald (to mention Old Testament specialists) and corresponded with Bleek. He felt a particular sympathy for de Wette, perhaps because both he and de Wette had suffered dismissal.[59] It is entirely fitting that he is the only nineteenth-century British Old Testament scholar to have a chair at an English University named after him—that in Old Testament at King's College, London.

[57] ibid., p. 95.
[58] ibid., pp. 21–8.
[59] ibid., pp. 299–300.

15

'Essays and Reviews' 1860

The story of the writing of the seven essays that were collected together in 1860 in *Essays and Reviews* has been told many times, as has the account of the aftermath of the publications, the proceedings against two of the essayists, and the judgements of the Court of Arches and the Judicial Committee of the Privy Council. The facts will not be rehearsed here.[1] Rather, the present chapter will be concerned with what *Essays and Reviews* contained on the subject of Old Testament criticism.

In general, it can be said that *Essays and Reviews* does not mark any advance in the critical method. Its importance lies rather in the way in which it indicates a growing tide of opinion against traditional orthodox opinions; a readiness of liberals to come out into the open. Of the seven essayists, six were clergymen of the Church of England, of whom one[2] was vice-principal of a theological college. The essays that will be discussed are those by Frederick Temple on 'The Education of the World', Roland Williams on 'Bunsen's Biblical Researches', Charles Goodwin on the 'Mosaic Cosmogony' and Benjamin Jowett on 'The Interpretation of Scripture'.

It is tempting to compare Temple's essay, 'The Education of the World' with Lessing's celebrated 'The Education of the Human Race', and the comparison has often been made.[3] However, the essay seems to owe as much to the views of liberal Anglicans, such as Arnold or Maurice, as it does to Lessing. Its basis is the distinction between nature and culture, between the world investigated at the level of the natural and physical sciences, and the world viewed from the point of view of mankind as the bearer and

---

[1] See, for example, Cornish, *A History of the English Church in the 19th century*, 2, pp. 215–44; Chadwick, *The Victorian Church*, Part 2, pp. 75–90; R. T. Davidson and W. Benham, *Life of Archibald Campbell Tait, Archbishop of Canterbury*, 1, London 1891, pp. 275–325 (valuable for its record of correspondence between F. Temple and Tait); R. E. Prothero and G. G. Bradley, *The Life and Correspondence of Arthur Penrhyn Stanley, D.D.*, 2, London 1893, pp. 30–44; H. P. Liddon *et al.*, *Life of Edward Bouverie Pusey*, 4, London 1897, pp. 38–68; Maurice, *Life of F. D. Maurice*, 2, pp. 382ff.; E. G. Sandford, *Memoirs of Archbishop Temple*, 1, London 1906, pp. 219ff.

[2] Roland Williams.

[3] Thus, in *Replies to Essays and Reviews*, Oxford and London 1862, E. M. Goulburn reviewed Lessing's essay together with Temple's. Ewald, *GGA* 1861, pp. 1172–4 noted that Temple's essay was written without reference to Lessing, but was 'doch wie eine heutige Erneuerung derselben'—a judgement that is open to question.

developer of civilization. From this latter viewpoint, the history of the world is broadly a history of the progress of mankind, a progress which entails that what was once hardly conceivable to adults is now common knowledge to children.[4] Thus it is possible to talk about the education of the world, and to apply to mankind as a whole the analogy of growing up from childhood, through youth to adulthood of an individual person.

The stages of this process—a process under divine direction, since education requires an educator—are summarized as those of rules, examples and principles; or in theological terms, the law, the Son of Man, the gift of the Spirit.[5] In biblical terms this means that the Old Testament corresponds to the law or to rules, and the New Testament corresponds to the Son of Man, or to examples in the sense of the example of the life of Jesus Christ.

Even within the Old Testament itself, the essayist maintains, the process of education can be discerned. 'The earliest commands almost entirely refer to bodily appetites and animal passions',[6] including violence and sensuality. However, following the division of mankind into classes (presumably a reference to the story of the tower of Babel in Genesis 11), the education of the human race begins. It appears to be concentrated upon one particular class in the first instance—the Hebrew nation—since people belonging to the other classes, while making some progress, distorted and adulterated the divine element in the laws and natural religions that they possessed,[7] until they were called to play their part in a renewed education of all mankind following the establishment of the Church.[8]

In the Old Testament the Mosaic system, the beginning of the educative process, was a series of precise and peremptory commands on moral and social matters, which allowed no freedom of conduct or of opinion, and which were given no explanation or justification; however, with the emergence of the prophets, a new spirit can be seen. The burden of prophetic preaching is not the observance of precepts, but sensitivity to the wider laws of 'brotherly kindness, truth and justice'.[9] There is an appeal to individual conscience. Yet while 'the teacher pleads instead of dogmatizing', the child is not yet old enough to be left to his own devices!

He is not yet a man. He must still conform to the rules of his father's house,

---

[4] F. S. Temple, 'The Education of the World' in *Essays and Reviews*, London 1860. (References are here made to the 5th edition, 1861. See pp. 1–4).

[5] ibid., pp. 4–5.

[6] ibid., p. 6. Temple presumably has in mind the earliest commandments in Gen. 1—9: what food mankind can eat, that he must be fruitful and multiply, that he must avoid bloodshed.

[7] ibid., p. 15.

[8] In the later part of the essay, Temple describes the contributions of Greece, Rome and Asia to the progress of mankind, including Christendom.

[9] ibid., p. 9.

whether or not those rules suit his temper or approve themselves to his judgement.[10]

The Exile and its aftermath teach deeper lessons yet, but result in a paradox. On the one hand, Israelites received a check, in the development of some of the outwardness of post-exilic Judaism. On the other hand, during this same period there was a development in prayer and spirituality, in preaching and in the study of the Bible. Thus:

> The Jewish nation had lost very much when John the Baptist came to prepare the way for his Master; but time had not stood still, nor had that course of education whereby the Jew was to be fitted to give the last revelation to the world.[11]

This account of the growth of Old Testament religion did not overlook the constant backslidings of the chosen people. But the essayist preferred to see these backslidings in educational rather than in religious or moral terms. The disobediences were not so much 'wilful backslidings from an elementary truth within the reach of children'; they were rather, 'stumblings in learning a very difficult lesson—difficult even for cultivated men'.[12]

The remainder of the essay deals with the New Testament and the development of doctrine, and not directly with the Old Testament. However, the characterization of modern man as having reached the point of toleration and of openness to truth whatever the latter's source, provides a standpoint from which the Old Testament can be interpreted. Mankind no longer needs the precise dogmatic formulae of earlier ages, and it is providential that the Bible does not provide such things. The Bible is cast in historical form, it expresses its insights in terms of the times in which it was written, and although it may still arouse the conscience, it may not now overrule conscience.[13] The Bible has the power to speak differently to succeeding ages, and thus there is no one final and static way of interpreting it.

The Bible is to be interpreted fearlessly, in the confidence that faith has nothing to fear from any kind of investigation:

> If geology proves to us that we must not interpret the first chapters of Genesis literally, if historical investigations shall show us that inspiration, however it may protect the doctrine, yet was not empowered to protect the narrative of the inspired writers from occasional inaccuracy; if careful criticism shall prove that

---

[10] ibid., p. 9.
[11] ibid., p. 11.
[12] ibid., p. 12.
[13] ibid., p. 44: 'When conscience and the Bible appear to differ, the pious Christian immediately concludes that he has not really understood the Bible.'

there have been occasionally interpolations and forgeries in that Book, as in many others; the results should still be welcome.[14]

Dr Temple concluded by asserting that of all theological tasks, that of the study of the Bible was the most pressing for his day.

This summary will have served to show that Temple set his view of the Old Testament in the framework of a sort of theological humanism. As the author of the 'reply' to Temple in *Replies to Essays and Reviews* was quick to point out, Temple's essay contained no reference to the 'fall' or to the atonement. As we have noticed above, Temple's reference to Israel's constant disobedience and apostasy was seen in educational terms, as the painful grasping of truths that are not easily learnt, rather than as the expression of a deep insight into man's fallenness.

However, this concerns us less than the fact that when all is said and done, Temple's reading of the broad outline of the Old Testament is entirely traditional. The law precedes the prophets, and an historical progression is seen even in the nature of the prohibitions of the opening chapters of Genesis compared with what later follows. These opening chapters exhibit prohibitions against bodily appetites and animal passions. Whatever Temple may have thought about *when* the opening chapters of Genesis were written, he seems to see in them an expression to earliest mankind of the divine educator.

We also notice Temple's attempt to regard the post-exilic period as a period of advance, despite the 'loss' that is exhibited in the religion of the Sadducees and Pharisees. All liberal forms of English thought which embraced developmentalist ideas had to come to terms with a paradox which was solved in German radical circles by the distinction between Hebrew religion and Judaism. Thus, Temple's defence of free inquiry in biblical studies comes not from a scriptural principle or from the facts of the text itself, so much as from an optimistic theological humanism, which sees all truth as coming from one divine source, whether that is recognized or not.

The essay on Bunsen's biblical researches by Roland Williams is unsatisfactory in several respects.[15] In the first place, one wonders what anyone would have made of it who was unfamiliar with Bunsen's writings. The style of the essay is allusive, and seems to hint at a discussion with which the reader is supposed to be thoroughly at home. Secondly, it is strange, to a modern reader, that Bunsen should be the subject of a whole chapter. In the chapter on Bunsen above, some grounds were provided for justifying this concentration upon Bunsen: his close connection with England, with the liberal Anglicans, and his belief in the providential ordering of the history

---

[14] ibid., p. 47.
[15] Roland Williams, 'Bunsen's Biblical Researches', pp. 50ff.

of mankind.[16] However, even allowing for Bunsen's prestige in certain circles in England, the claim that 'no living author's work could furnish so pregnant a text for a discourse on biblical criticism'[17] seems excessive.

Williams's opponent in *Replies to Essays and Reviews*, Henry James Rose, made the complaint that the essayist had misrepresented German scholarship by not mentioning the work of conservative German scholars such as Hengstenberg and Hävernick.[18] A modern critical response is more likely to be that he misrepresented critical German scholarship by his almost exclusive concern with Bunsen.

The picture that emerges from the essay is the correct one, that Bunsen had largely vindicated the biblical history by setting it in the context of scholarship in the area of ancient history. Abraham and Moses are historically dated; the 'historical reality of the Exodus' is vindicated and 'a new interest is given it by its connexion with the rise and fall of great empires'.[19] But if Bunsen is a vindicator of the broad outline of Old Testament history, it is clear that he rejects traditional views of the composition of biblical books. The Pentateuch is Mosaic, but not by Moses. Some Old Testament books are 'expanded from simpler elements'. Books such as Isaiah, Zechariah and Daniel are not the works of one author, and Bunsen's interpretation of prophecies is historical, not messianic. The Immanuel child of Isaiah 7.14 is a child to be born in the reign of Ahaz, while the servant of Isaiah 53 is probably Jeremiah.[20]

As in Temple's opening essay, so here, it is the idea of the divine education that is the point of departure for biblical investigation, and which is the uniting principle of the results. God has been pleased to educate men and nations, and he has done this 'within the limits of humanity and its shortcomings'.[21] Bunsen's work 'vindicates the work of the Eternal Spirit'.

> If such a Spirit did not dwell in the Church the Bible would not be inspired, for the Bible is, before all things, the written voice of the congregation. Bold as such a theory of inspiration may sound, it was the earliest creed of the Church, and it is the only one to which the facts of Scripture answer.[22]

Any reader not familiar with the work of Bunsen or of Roland Williams may well have learned from this essay that biblical criticism freely investigated the composition of biblical books, and the historical meanings

[16] See above p. 122.
[17] Williams, p. 53.
[18] H. J. Rose, 'Bunsen, The Critical School, and Dr Williams' in *Replies to Essays and Reviews* p. 70.
[19] Williams, p. 58.
[20] ibid., pp. 68–9.
[21] ibid., p. 77.
[22] ibid., p. 78.

of prophecies; that it vindicated the general presentation of Old Testament history, and that it did its work confident in its faith in a divine educator of mankind whose workings were clearly discerned in the sacred pages.

By far the most interesting essay of the collection for the present writer is that by C. W. Goodwin, a Cambridge layman, on the Mosaic cosmogony.[23] This essay is an elaboration of the simple point that:

> ... the object of a revelation or divine unveiling of mysteries, must be to teach man things which he is unable and must ever remain unable to find out for himself; *but not physical truths, for the discovery of which he has faculties specially provided by his Creator.*[24]

In elaborating this point, the essayist discusses at some length the attempts to reconcile Genesis 1—3 with geological and similar discoveries in W. Buckland's *Geology and Religion* (1820) and other writings, T. Chalmers' *Power, Wisdom, Goodness of God* (1833), H. Miller's *Testimony of the Rocks* (1857), and J. Pratt's *Scripture and Science not at Variance* (1858). It is not necessary here to describe these various attempts to harmonize Genesis with science by means of assuming that the days of creation were geological ages, or that ages intervened between each day, or that much happened before the first day of creation.

Goodwin's contention is that Genesis records not poetry, but science— the science of the writer's day—and remarkably accurate science, granted the knowledge then available. He denies that there was revealed to the biblical writer a description of the origin of the universe, 'which has misled the world for centuries, and in which the truth can now only with difficulty be recognized'. He accuses two defenders of the science of Genesis thus:

> Both these theories divest the Mosaic narrative of real accordance with fact; both assume that appearances only, not facts, are described, and that in riddles, which would never have been suspected to be such, had we not arrived at the truth from other sources.[25]

He asks:

> How can it be otherwise when the task proposed is to evade the plain meaning of language, and introduce obscurity into one of the simplest stories ever told, for the sake of making it accord with the complex system of the universe which modern science has unfolded?[26]

The essayist's attempt to show that the defenders of the Mosaic cosmogony are guilty of the grossest form of eisegesis, is eminently successful. Yet it can

---

[23] C. W. Goodwin, 'Mosaic Cosmogony', *Essays and Reviews*, pp. 207ff.
[24] ibid., p. 208, italics mine.
[25] ibid., p. 249.
[26] ibid., pp. 249–50.

be argued that his own conclusion is a form of eisegesis also. Fastening, like the fellow-essayist that we have considered, on the idea of progressive education, he declares that the biblical writer has 'seized one great truth, in which, indeed, he anticipated the highest revelation of modern inquiry— namely, the unity of the design of the world, and its subordination to one sole Maker and Lawgiver'.[27] Yet even so, the Genesis account as a whole is not a divine utterance but a human utterance, 'which it has pleased Providence to use in a special way for the education of mankind'.[28]

Owen Chadwick has written of Goodwin's essay that it was of little importance, since many educated members of the clergy and laity accepted its thesis that Genesis could not be reconciled with science as to the origin of the world.[29] This seems an odd comment when it is considered that some of the attempts to reconcile Genesis and science dealt with by the essayist had been published not long before 1860. Further, Goodwin's essay provoked a trenchant reply in *Aids to Faith*, in the form of an essay by A. McCaul, the professor of Hebrew and Old Testament at King's College, London.[30] Some of McCaul's conclusions are:

> We are astonished to see how the Hebrew prophet, in his brief and rapid outline sketched 3000 years ago, has anticipated some of the most wonderful of recent discoveries, and can ascribe the accuracy of his statements and language to nothing but inspiration. . . . Moses describes the process of creation as gradual, and mentions the order in which living things appeared, plants, fishes, fowls, land-animals, man. By the study of nature geology has arrived independently at the same conclusion. . . . If he did not possess the knowledge, then his pen must have been guided by superhuman wisdom. Faith has therefore, nothing to fear from science.[31]

The writer of the essay, 'The Creative Week', in *Replies to Essays and Reviews* G. Rorison, was much more sympathetic to Goodwin, and as contemptuous of the harmonizers as Goodwin himself. 'Mr Goodwin', he wrote, 'cannot be blamed for chastising palpable subterfuges', and he continued, 'The worst *dis*-service to the cause of divine truth is that contributed by contorted science and sophisticated exegesis'.[32] Rorison's own view of Genesis 1 was that it was a psalm of creation, exhibiting an internal parallel structure when days 1–3 were set over against days 4–6. Of the *science* of Genesis 1, Rorison

---

[27] ibid., p. 253.

[28] ibid., p. 253.

[29] *The Victorian Church*, Part 2, p. 76.

[30] W. Thomson, *Aids to Faith. A Series of Theological Essays*, London 1861. McCaul's answer to Goodwin is entitled, 'The Mosaic Record of Creation'. It refers consistently to a German scholar Hüpfeldt—presumably Hupfeld—whose works McCaul can hardly have read at first hand, otherwise the misrepresentation of the name is very careless.

[31] McCaul, pp. 232–3.

[32] G. Rorison in *Replies to Essays and Reviews*, pp. 332.

required only that Moses should have been inspired to write an account that would suffer no harm by the advent of scientific knowledge. 'Insight into the geological past it is unnecessary to suppose that the inspired penman either needed or had given him'.[33] Where Goodwin was assailed, it was only in respect of his characterization of the writer of Genesis as a 'Hebrew Descartes or Newton'. All in all, Rorison was rightly pleading for an understanding of Genesis 1 which was first and foremost *theological*. Goodwin's essay, for all its excellence, failed to do this. When Colenso sought to insist on the opening chapter of Genesis as an essentially theological statement, however, he was to be accused of denying its truth and inspiration.

Benjamin Jowett's essay 'On the Interpretation of Scripture', added little to the other essays as regards the Old Testament. Its *Leitmotif* is progressive education and progressive revelation. 'The education of the human mind may be traced as clearly from the book of Genesis to the Epistles of St Paul, as from Homer to Plato and Aristotle'.[34] Criticism is a necessary part of the state of maturity which the human race has now attained, and the interpretation of the Bible ought to be open to modern discoveries instead of being a defensive and apologetic business.

The strength of Jowett's essay lies in his analyses of prevailing attitudes, and in his alternative proposals, such as the one that we should define inspiration as, 'That idea of Scripture which we gather from the knowledge of it.'[35] He teaches that the fundamental level of interpretation is the discovery of the meaning which it had to those who first wrote and those who first heard or read it, and he enlarges upon the necessary procedures for this discovery. However, he would not limit the meaning of the Bible to the intentional level alone, and he admitted an inexhaustible and infinite character of Scripture. Yet this was not an open invitation to any sort of uncontrolled or fanciful exegesis. Its message as a whole is to be gained by a careful interpretation of each writer with the continuity that makes up the whole of the Bible. That continuity is the progressive unfolding of the revelation of God, reaching its climax in Jesus.

We can assume that Jowett would not have wanted to go in for any radical criticism of Old Testament history or religion, and that like the liberal Anglicans and his fellow essayists, he was confident of the reliability of the broad picture of history presented in the Old Testament.

For his opponents, Jowett was altogether too open to non-theological factors. A careful and scholarly article in *Aids to Faith* by C. J. Ellicott, Dean of Exeter and Professor of Divinity at King's College, London, went much of the way with Jowett when it came to the advocacy of the grammatical,

[33] ibid., pp. 328.
[34] B. Jowett, in *Essays and Reviews*, p. 402.
[35] ibid., p. 347.

historical and contextual level of interpretation.[36] But Ellicott felt that Jowett did not go far enough, and that his weakness lay in his refusal to accord authority to the 'rule of faith' adumbrated in the early Christian centuries. For Ellicott, the doctrines contained in the Creeds were authoritative guides to interpreting Scripture because they were, 'the epitome of that from which it has been properly conceded that Scripture ought to be illustrated and expounded'.[37]

For him, to interpret Scripture by itself was to allow as authoritative that movement from the New Testament to the classical formulations of the early centuries of the significance of Jesus as Son of God and saviour, in the light of which alone the Bible could be understood as *Christian*.

The reply by Canon Christopher Wordsworth in *Replies to Essays and Reviews* was written in a very different spirit—polemical, sarcastic and at times unscrupulous—as he wheeled out accounts of the alleged depravity of German critics with the warning that this was where the theology implied in *Essays and Reviews* would lead.[38] He fastened upon Jowett's famous dictum that the Bible should be interpreted 'like any other book' and complained that this was impossible, since the Bible had God as its author, . . . a fact which had fundamental implications for its interpretation.

Wordsworth rightly took Jowett to task for some observations about the state of German scholarship that were either careless, or indicated that Jowett knew little about German biblical scholarship. Jowett had claimed that:

> among German commentators there is, for the first time in the history of the world, an approach to agreement and certainty. For example, the diversity among German writers on prophecy is far less than among English ones.[39]

How anyone familiar with Ewald, Bunsen, Hitzig and Hupfeld on the critical side, not to mention Hengstenberg, Delitzsch and von Hofmann on the conservative side, can have made such a statement it is impossible to say, and Wordsworth did not spare Jowett on this point. However, of the two main replies to Jowett, only that of Ellicott was such as to map out a path of responsible orthodox scholarship.

In Germany, the publication of *Essays and Reviews* and the hostile response that followed, was greeted with a certain amount of puzzlement in critical circles. An article in the *German Journal for Christian Scholarship and Life*

[36] C. J. Ellicott, 'Scripture, and its Interpretation' in *Aids to Faith*.
[37] ibid., p. 447.
[38] C. Wordsworth, 'On the Interpretation of Scripture' in *Replies to Essays and Reviews*. Wordsworth makes great play of the (admittedly) wayward life of F. Bahrdt, and holds Bahrdt's teacher, J. S. Semler to be responsible through his teachings, to which Wordsworth compares Jowett's.
[39] Jowett, p. 340.

stated that German readers would not find in the volume what one had a right to expect from Christian scholarship.[40] In particular, exception was taken to what was claimed to be the division of the meaning of the Bible into religious truths and moral truths, with the former being treated according to the analogy of the growth and development of an individual.[41] Our view of the relation between ethics and religion is quite different, stated the reviewer.

Ewald was little more complimentary in *GGA*.[42] After reflecting for half-a-dozen pages on the fatal influence of the High Church party in England, and the lack of any scholarship in England, he turned to the individual essays. That by Goodwin was praised in that it represented those English scholars who did not take Genesis 1 literally. On the other hand, Goodwin was censured for not indicating the results of German interpretation of Genesis 1. Jowett and Williams were both, justly, accused of being superficial in the treatment of their subject, while Temple's contribution did not meet the standard to be expected of a successor of Thomas Arnold as headmaster of Rugby School. Ewald took exception to Temple's characterization of Jesus as chiefly an example.[43] The hostile reaction that the essays had produced in England was an adverse reflection on the opponents of the essayists.

For the purposes of the present book, *Essays and Reviews* indicates several things. First, that there was a significant gap between critical Old Testament scholarship in England and Germany. The highest praise that an Ewald could find for the essayists was based on the fact that they were critical scholars in principle. However, the difference between the criticism is well summed up, on the one hand by Ewald's references to the superficiality of the essays, and on the other hand, by Roland Williams's remark on Bunsen that 'for those who seek results, there is something wearisome in the elaborate discussions of authorities'.[44] The desire for results without the supposed tedium of massive attention to detail and to argumentation seems to have been typical of even the critical British scholarship of the time.

Second, *Essays and Reviews* indicates how conservative and traditional critical scholars were when it came to the Old Testament. Third, we see

[40] *Deutsche Zeitschift für christliche Wissenschaft und christliches Leben*, NF 4 (1861), p. 95.
[41] Ibid., pp. 95–6: 'Wir halten es für keine angemessene Aufgabe, die heiligen Schriften in einen religiösen (resp. metaphysischen, speculativen) und einen moralischen Gestandtheil zu zerlegen, den ersten dann für einen solchen zu erklären, der auf vielfach kritisch—durchlöcherten Zeugnissen beruhend, in den Prozess der Vergeistigung durch das fortgeschrittene Individuum geworfen werden müsse, während der moralische als der allein wesentliche stehen bleibe . . .'
[42] *GGA* 1861, pp. 1161–80.
[43] Ewald, p. 1174: 'Ist aber Christus nicht unendlich mehr! und wo sollte denn das dritte und letzte Weltalter eigentlich beginnen?'
[44] Roland Williams, p. 53.

already well established the lines on which critical Old Testament scholarship was to run when the critical method was generally accepted in academic circles from the 1880s. Progressive revelation, progressive education: these were to provide the main clue to Old Testament interpretation. They entailed acceptance of the general reliability of the history and religion of Israel as presented in the Old Testament. The efforts of Colenso to demonstrate the historical *inaccuracy* of some of the most fundamental of the 'historical' traditions would prove unacceptable to many liberals.

16

John William Colenso

Close on the heels of *Essays and Reviews* and the controversy which its publication aroused, there appeared towards the end of 1862 the first part of J. W. Colenso's *The Pentateuch and the Book of Joshua critically examined*. Over the next three years, Part 1 was followed by four more parts, while parts 6 and 7 were published in 1871 and 1879 respectively.[1] Taking Parts 1–7 as a whole, it is not an exaggeration to say that Colenso's *Pentateuch* was one of the most original British contributions to biblical criticism in the nineteenth century. It was also not without importance for the history of biblical criticism as a whole.[2]

Colenso was born in 1814 in Cornwall, and entered St John's College, Cambridge to read mathematics in 1832, where, after a struggle against financial difficulties, he was placed second wrangler in the examinations of 1836.[3] In 1837 he was elected as a fellow of the college. After some years as a mathematics master at Harrow and a short spell as tutor at St John's College, Cambridge, Colenso became rector of the parish of Forncett in the diocese of Norwich in 1846. Meanwhile, he had come to know F. D. Maurice, and had been impressed by Maurice's universalism and by his book *The Kingdom of Christ*. Maurice officiated at Colenso's marriage in 1846. In 1853, Colenso was appointed Bishop of Natal, and arrived in the colony in January 1854.

It would appear that Colenso's theological training, such as it was, had not exposed him to anything like biblical criticism, and that it was as a result of the questioning from one of his native Zulu converts that Colenso began to be profoundly dissatisfied with the conservative views that he embraced.

Between 1861 and 1862, Colenso began to study the Pentateuch with the help of works by Hengstenberg, Kurtz and Ewald (the latter's *History* in

[1] J. W. Colenso, *The Pentateuch and Joshua critically examined*, London, 7 parts, 1862–79.
[2] This is not the opinion of the standard German books on the history of Old Testament criticism. Kraus makes no reference to Colenso at all, while Diestel, acknowledging that Colenso's work brought life and movement to the stagnation of British scholarship, denies that his work achieves any particular advance in scholarship. See Diestel, p. 649.
[3] The standard biography of Colenso is G. W. Cox, *The Life of John William Colenso, D.D., Bishop of Natal*, London, 2 vols, 1888. See also Peter Hinchliff, *John William Colenso*, London 1964.

German), and dissatisfied with all of these, he set about writing the first draft of Part 1 of the *Pentateuch*.[4] It so happened that the curator of the museum and library in Cape Town was W. Bleek, son of Friedrich Bleek, and through his offices Colenso was able to obtain the *Introductions* by de Wette and Bleek. Other books obtained by Colenso were Hävernick's *Introduction*, Hengstenberg's *Dissertations*, and the first volume of the *Historisch-Kritisch Onderzoek* published by Abraham Kuenen in Leyden in September 1861. In the middle of 1862, Colenso travelled to London in connection with charges brought against him by Bishop Gray of Capetown and others, resulting from his *Commentary on the Epistle to the Romans*. In England, Colenso continued his reading, his revision of earlier drafts, and his writing. Of Davidson's *Introduction* of 1862–3, Colenso described the first two volumes, which he saw after he arrived in England in 1862, as 'the most able work which has yet appeared in England on the subject of biblical criticism'.[5]

Part 1 of *The Pentateuch and Joshua* shows unmistakable signs of the impatience that had been aroused in Colenso by what he considered to be the totally unconvincing attempts of orthodox writers, especially Hengstenberg and Kurtz, to deal with the practical implications of the numbers of Israelites who were in the wilderness following the Exodus. His starting-point was the figure of 600,000 males aged 20 and upwards who journeyed, together with their wives, children and cattle from Rameses to Succoth, according to Exodus 12.37–8. But Colenso's argument did not rest upon this figure alone, as some of his critics supposed. He appealed also to the figure of 603,550 warriors of Numbers 1.46, which latter figure itself was the total obtained from a detailed census of the tribes (Num. 1.20–43), and to the 603,550 men who were numbered at Exodus 38.26 at the collection of the tax for the construction of the tabernacle. The charge that Colenso's position could be demolished by allowing that the 600,000 in Exodus 12.37 was a scribal error was unfounded.[6] There can be no doubt of the accuracy

---

[4] See Colenso's own account of his studies in *The Pentateuch and Joshua* Pt 1, esp. pp. xvff. Of Hengstenberg, Colenso wrote to F. D. Maurice on 11 September 1862: 'For Hengstenberg's works, certainly, I do feel something like contempt, for his arguments are often dishonest—I can use no milder term—and that with a prodigious affection of honesty and censure of others as suppressing the truth from interested motives.' See Cox, 1, p. 196. Of Ewald, Colenso wrote to Maurice on 5 September: 'Ewald, in fact, is far wilder in his hypothesis and far more rash in his conclusions than I should wish to be. It is not because he is too *conservative* that I cannot agree with him, but just for the very contrary' (Cox, 1, p. 191).

[5] *The Pentateuch* 1, p. xvi.

[6] The remark in O. Chadwick, *The Victorian Church*, Pt 2, London 1970, p. 92, 'Conservative critics cheerfully jettisoned the figure of 600,000 as a scribal slip and so ruined Colenso's book', may create the impression that Colenso's case rested solely on this figure. In fact, as Colenso insisted, and as his fairest critics accepted, the figure of 600,000 could not be regarded as a scribal slip, whatever else it was.

of Colenso's claim that the biblical writers *intended* to convey that there were over 600,000 men in the wilderness, and thus some two to two-and-a-half million people in all.

Colenso's attack on the historical accuracy of the Exodus and wilderness traditions followed lines to be found a century earlier, for example, in Reimarus.[7] Colenso, however, was far more detailed. He showed that it was impossible for the seventy people of Jacob's family who went down to Egypt to have increased to over two million in a matter of four or five generations. He estimated how long the column of Israelites would have been from Egypt to the Red Sea, and how large would have been the settlement in Egypt where the Israelites were living alongside Egyptians from whom they were ordered to ask for jewels, silver, gold, and clothing (Exod. 12.35). Using his familiarity with sheep husbandry, he estimated that the Israelites would have had two million sheep and oxen for the two million plus population, and that, assuming five sheep to one acre, an area of 25 square miles of grazing would have been needed for the sheep alone.[8] On the basis of Numbers 3.43, which records that among the Israelites there were 22,273 first-born males, Colenso noted, following Kurtz, that if there were 900,000 males in all (the 600,000 are only those aged 20 and upwards) the ratio of first-born males to the grand total of males implied that there must have been an average of 42 boys in each family. Even if there were certain concessions made, for example, an allowance for the mortality of first-born males who were not then included in the 22,273, this still produced the result that each married woman bore on average 15 sons and 15 daughters; and that only one man in ten could have had a wife or children![9]

Perhaps the most amusing parts of Colenso's first volume are those dealing with the sacrifices, and worship. He pointed out that there were apparently only *three* priests in the wilderness: Aaron and his two sons Eleazar and Ithamar. These three were required to perform the following tasks. First, on the assumption that two million people would produce 250 births each day, the two prescribed offerings (Lev. 12.6–8) would amount to 500 sacrifices, which on the assumption of five minutes for each would involve nearly 42 hours a day for the three priests. At the passover, following the Deuteronomic regulations, it would have been necessary for the blood of some 120,000 lambs (one to every 15 to 20 persons) to be sprinkled, probably in the space of two hours; that is, the lambs would have been killed at the rate of 1,000 a minute by the three priests. Most

---

[7] See above, p. 25.

[8] *The Pentateuch*, Pt 1, chs. 2, 9–12.

[9] ibid., ch. 14. The problem of the ratio of first-born males to the total number of males (22,273 to approx. 900,000 according to the biblical figures) was well known, and discussed, among others, by J. D. Michaelis and Hävernick.

burdensome of all for these three overworked officiants would be the fact that because the sanctuary was in the middle of the encampment of the two million Israelites, and because, for certain offerings, it was necessary for the priests to dispose of remains 'outside the camp', a journey of some six miles would be necessary from the sanctuary to 'outside the camp' on each occasion. Again, the Deuteronomic regulations (Deut. 23.12–14) about relieving the calls of nature, where this had to be done 'outside the camp' would have involved considerable travelling for those unlucky enough not to be on the outskirts of the camp.[10]

So far, Colenso had not made any real advance beyond what had already been done by the Deists and by Reimarus, as Ewald was to remark in a highly critical review, although he had done his work very thoroughly.[11] In Part 2, he began to show much greater maturity and originality as a biblical critic. The early sections of Part 2 rehearsed the well-known arguments in favour of the final redaction of the Pentateuch and Joshua being later than the time of Moses and Joshua. The arguments included the post-Mosaica, references to ancient sources such as the 'Book of Jashar', and the statements in the biblical text about names or institutions existing 'to this day'.[12] However, for the rest of Part 2, he began to argue that the writer of the Elohistic document, which formed the basic framework of the Pentateuch, was Samuel.

Colenso's main line of argument was that the divine name Elohim was the only such name in use until the time of Samuel, when the name Yahweh was introduced, probably by the prophet himself.[13] The Elohim document must have been written before the name Yahweh was widely used, but could scarcely have been written before the time of Samuel in view of the conditions prevailing in Israel.[14] Therefore, Samuel was the likely author of the document.

Colenso's demonstration of the introduction of the name Yahweh in the time of Samuel rested upon two main arguments. First, throughout the whole of the Pentateuch and Joshua, there are only two names compounded with Yahweh, that of Joshua himself, and that of Moses's mother Jochebed. Otherwise, all names were compounded with El. Second, Colenso argued from the Davidic psalms that a change from the use of Elohim to Yahweh in these psalms could be discerned. Before this last point is elaborated, it is

---

[10] ibid., chs. 6, 20–1. Colenso (p. 62) based his estimates of the birth-rate upon the statistics for a week for London given in *The Times* of 3 September 1862. The population of London was roughly the same size as the Israelite camp in the wilderness, granted the accuracy of the biblical figures.

[11] For Ewald's remarks see above n18 of the Introduction, p. 8.

[12] *The Pentateuch*, Pt 2, chs. 1–6.

[13] ibid., p. 262.

[14] Colenso has in mind the period of the Judges, culminating in Israel's struggles with the Philistines.

important to note that Colenso regarded the books of Chronicles as unreliable. In Chronicles, many names compounded with Yahweh are to be found from the family of Jacob onwards. Colenso's view was that Chronicles, if taken at its face value, by alleging that so many pre-Mosaic names were compounded with Yahweh contradicted the view of Exodus 3.14 and 6.2–3 that the name Yahweh was not known before the time of Moses.[15]

Probably, Colenso's argument from the use of divine names in the Davidic psalms is the part of his position that today would seem to be most untenable.[16] In the first book of Psalms (1—41) there are many psalms ascribed 'to David' and using the divine name 'Yahweh'; but very few have titles relating the psalms to events in David's life. In later psalms, especially in the so-called 'Elohistic Psalter', some Davidic psalms have some quite explicit titles connecting individual psalms with events in David's life. The scholarly view today is that the psalms of the 'Elohistic Psalter', especially Psalms 42—80, originally contained the divine name Yahweh, and that at some stage, for reasons as yet not satisfactorily explained, Yahweh was replaced editorially by Elohim. This is usually justified by comparing Psalms 14 and 53.[17]

Colenso argued in exactly the opposite direction. Starting from the historical notices attached to the titles of psalms such as 52, 54, 56, 57, 59 and 63, noting that they referred to the earlier part of David's life, and that the divine name used in them was predominantly Elohim, he concluded that David had used this divine name in the first part of his life.[18] The psalms in book 1 (1—40) were held to be later than those in book 2, and were thus evidence for David's use of Yahweh in *later* life. An examination of Psalm 68 also supported the view that David initially used Elohim as the usual divine name.[19]

At the end of part 2, Colenso had reached the following position:[20] he accepted the supplementary hypothesis of the authorship of the Pentateuch, holding that the basic Elohistic document was written by Samuel and that the Yahwistic work was an enlargement and an amplification. Authors in the latter days of David and the early part of Solomon's reign were responsible. The book of Deuteronomy was written 'about' the time of

[15] ibid., p. 237: 'It is scarcely possible to doubt that the Chronicler has simply *invented* these names' [names compounded with *-iah* from Jacob's great-grandchildren downwards, e.g., in 1 Chron. 2].
[16] See Pt 2, chs. 12–17.
[17] See J. W. Rogerson and J. W. McKay, *Psalms* (Cambridge Bible Commentary), 1, Cambridge 1977, pp. 4–5.
[18] *The Pentateuch*, Pt 2, pp. 269–70.
[19] ibid., chs. 15–16.
[20] The results are summarized in Pt 2, pp. 353–67.

Josiah and 'as some suppose by the hand of the prophet Jeremiah'.²¹ There
had been Deuteronomic interpolations into the books Genesis—Numbers
and Joshua. Colenso had noted Hupfeld's suggestion that there were two
Elohists, an elder and a younger Elohist, but contrary to Hupfeld, said that
if there were two, 'they were men of the same age, who wrote in the same
spirit'.²²

Part 3 of *The Pentateuch*, published in 1863, dealt almost entirely with
Deuteronomy, and is a section-by-section examination of that book, with
asterisks marking paragraphs in which there was especial evidence for the
composition of the book long after the time of Moses. There are also
detailed examinations of the Hebrew vocabulary of Deuteronomy which
show the difference of this vocabulary from that of the rest of the Pentateuch,
and its similarity to the prophets, especially to Jeremiah. Colenso regarded
as carrying considerable weight the references to the Kingdom in 17.14–
20, clearly a reference back to the time of Solomon, and the reference to the
independence of Edom, which implied a date at least around the time of
Ahaz. However, the lack of implicit reference to Deuteronomy in the reign
of Hezekiah, and the condemnation in Deuteronomy of the worship of the
sun and moon, something which had grown in the reign of Manasseh, put
the composition of Deuteronomy in the latter part of Manasseh's reign, or
the earlier part of Josiah's. Of these possibilities, Colenso preferred the
latter.²³

Part 4 of *The Pentateuch* deals with Genesis 1—11, and can be divided
into two main sections. The first seeks to demonstrate the composite nature
of these chapters, and to divide them into two sources, the Elohistic and the
Jehovistic. The division is based upon a detailed verbal and stylistic
examination of the text, with reference, when necessary, to the ancient
versions where they differ from the Hebrew text as to the divine name. The
distinctive and recurring phraseology of the Elohistic source is noticed, as is
the difference between the two sources as to the word for 'destroy'.²⁴ The
anthropomorphic character of the Jehovist source is commented on.

By pointing out the two sources separately,²⁵ following on from the
detailed analysis, Colenso enables us to see easily how close his results were
to the commonly accepted modern source-division of Genesis 1—11. The
main exceptions were his assigning of 7.6–9 to the Elohistic source (a
difficult passage to assign, in any case)²⁶ and his assigning of the whole of

²¹ Pt 2, p. 359.
²² ibid., p. 355.
²³ See the summary of the results in Pt 3, pp. 611–18.
²⁴ Pt 4, p. 31.
²⁵ ibid., ch. 7, 'The Elohistic Narrative of Gen. 1.1—11.26'; ch. 8. 'The Jehovistic Passages in
Gen. 1.1—11.26.'
²⁶ S. R. Driver, *Introduction to the Literature of the Old Testament*, 9th ed., p. 14 assigns 7.7–10
to J 'in the main'.

chapter 10 to the Jehovistic source.[27] How far, in this division, Colenso was dependent upon other scholars is difficult to say. He freely indicates that he had Hupfeld, Tuch, Ewald and Delitzsch before him, to mention the works of only some scholars, and he must have owed something to Hupfeld, at the very least. Colenso is certainly attracted by Hupfeld's view that the Jehovist is a coherent and complete source rather than a series of supplements. At the same time, Colenso seems to have been such an independent person, that it is unlikely that he did not weigh every consideration very carefully before reaching his conclusions.

The second half of Part 4 is a discussion, section by section, of Genesis 1—11, the main purpose of which is to demonstrate that it cannot be accepted literally, and to refute those who assert this. We are back to the Colenso of Part 1, and it has to be admitted that he does his work devastatingly.

He is at his most brilliantly destructive in discussing the flood.[28] He pictures how the ark was inhabited: with snails and insects as well as animals and birds. He estimates how many sheep there must have been to satisfy the carnivores for over a year, in addition to the sheep meant to be preserved. He imagines the drudgery of the daily routine of Noah and his family, feeding all these animals, birds and other creatures, renewing their litter, and disposing of their excrement. He wonders how some insects got on which do not normally live in pairs, the bees, for example. He ponders the difficulties of temperature. Not only would the ark contain animals from hot climates, but reindeer would be there too. And when the ark finally grounded upon Mt Ararat, 17,000 ft above sea level, it would have been very cold indeed in the ark.

The grounding on Mt Ararat raised the difficulty that Everest and other Himalayan mountains are higher than 17,000 ft; yet the account says (Gen. 7.19) that all the high mountains were covered. This raised, in turn, the question whether the flood was a universal deluge or only a partial one, and here, Colenso was able to expose the arguments of orthodox writers, who tried to retain a literalist view of the narrative by supposing only a partial inundation—unfortunately, against the plain sense of the text that the flood was universal. Arguments from geology also figured, with a consideration of claims such as that by Lyell, that there was no geological evidence for a universal flood.[29]

A delightful point made by Colenso concerns how the various animals, once released from the ark in the neighbourhood of Mt Ararat, got to the parts of the world in which they are now known. How did the wingless

---

[27] Driver, op. cit., p. 14, assigns only 10.8–19, 21, 24–30 to J.

[28] Pt 4, pp. 176–210.

[29] ibid., p. 198.

dodo reach the island of Mauritius, or the wingless apteryx New Zealand! Did the kangaroo jump all the way to Australia? And so on.[30]

In dealing with Genesis 1, Colenso was able to give examples of orthodox writers who maintained the literal integrity of the narrative only by taking liberties with the text.[31] Some assumed that the days of creation were long epochs, others, that long intervals supervened in between the days. There was the problem that if the sun and moon were not created until the fourth day, then the earth would have existed without its solar system. An orthodox answer to this, again, according to Colenso, ignoring the obvious and plain meaning of the text, was that on the fourth day God did not *create* the sun and moon, but simply caused them to become visible. Some orthodox supporters of this view even went so far as to claim that for a long period, the earth was not dependent upon the sun for its light and heat, and that scientific discoveries proved that at this time, the earth had enjoyed a uniform temperature over its entire surface.[32]

If Colenso demonstrated the absurdities of the attempts to defend the literal authenticity of Genesis 1, he also held the account to be inspired, in that it expressed the great principles that (1) God was the creator and preserver of all things; (2) man was made in God's image; (3) what God had made was very good.[33] The clothing in which these principles were expressed, as could be seen from comparisons with other nations' creation stories, was not to be taken as literal science.

In dealing with the fall in Genesis 3, Colenso drew attention to Delitzsch's theories, already noted in chapter 7, that in the course of creation, demonic powers entered the world and corrupted it, so that new creations of plants, beasts and birds became necessary, beginning on the third and sixth days. He also noted Delitzsch's view that the serpent, used by the Evil One to corrupt Eve, probably had a quite different form from that familiar after its cursing.[34] Colenso countered by saying that geology showed that the serpent had the same form as it had now, long before the advent of man. The same was true of the ground and its produce. Briars and thorns existed before the emergence of man, and could not have been the result of a cursing *after* the disobedience of mankind. Again, it was clear that death existed before mankind did, and had overtaken all kinds of living creatures in many ways.

Some sharp thrusts against a literal reading of Genesis were also made by

---

[30] See especially p. 178.

[31] ibid., ch. 10.

[32] ibid., p. 102. Colenso is here opposing A. McCaul in his essay, 'The Mosaic Record of Creation', in W. Thomson (ed.), *Aids to Faith. A Series of Theological Essays*, London 1861, pp. 189–238.

[33] Pt 4, pp. 111–12.

[34] ibid., pp. 137–41. Here, Colenso provides the only English translation of this material from Delitzsch's 1852 *Genesis* commentary known to me.

Colenso, arising from the table of the nations in chapter 10.[35] Here, Canaan, is described as a son of Ham, whereas Eber, the eponymous ancestor of the Hebrews, is a descendant of Shem. This fact prompted Colenso to reflect upon the linguistic data to be found in the Old Testament. Recently-discovered Phoenician inscriptions[36] indicated that Phoenician was substantially the same as Hebrew; and certainly, the Old Testament itself assumed that Hebrews had no difficulty in communicating with Canaanites, whereas the mother-tongue of Abraham must have been some form of Aramean. It followed that after the Patriarchs had settled in Canaan, they had immediately dropped their native Aramean, and had begun to use the Hebrew of the Canaanites. So quickly and perfectly did they attain this that when they went down into Egypt, beginning a sojourn there of at least 215 years, they retained a mastery of pure Hebrew uncontaminated by Egyptian. This contrasted with the fortunes of the Jews of the Babylonian exile, who soon introduced Aramaisms into their language. Moses, although brought up in the Egyptian court, and although sojourning among the Midianites for forty years, was yet able to write perfect Hebrew, assuming him to have been the author of the Pentateuch.

But, of course, there was another explanation of these odd linguistic facts, and this was that the records about Abraham and the Patriarchs, and about the Exodus and Moses had been written down *after* the Hebrews had finally settled among the Canaanites and had adopted their language.

By the time he had published Parts 1–4 of the Pentateuch, Colenso had written over 1,100 pages, not counting the lengthy prefaces to Parts 2–4, in which he defended himself against his opponents. Part 5, published in 1865, added a further 640 pages, although there was no significant advance on his general position, but rather certain refinements backed by a most exhaustive analysis of the biblical material. Part 5—and this is important—was almost exclusively concerned with the book of Genesis.

Colenso returned, in particular, to a matter that he had considered earlier, namely Hupfeld's theory that a younger Elohist could be distinguished from the main Elohist. Colenso concurred in this view, supporting his position by a detailed analysis of the distinctive language of the Elohist as over against the Jehovist and the second Elohist, with consequent reference to the factors, such as duplications, which then distinguished the second Elohist from the Jehovist. However, in two very interesting respects, Colenso differed from Hupfeld. First, he was not convinced that the second Elohist and the Jehovist

---

[35] ibid., ch. 23.

[36] ibid., p. 252. Phoenician inscriptions had been discovered in June 1845 in Marseilles and the Eshmunazar inscription had been discovered at Sidon in 1855. Colenso based his discussion upon the material in Bleek's *Introduction*. For a contemporary discussion of the texts see H. Ewald, *Erklärung der grossen phönikischen Inschrift von Sidon . . .*, Göttingen 1856.

were different authors. He could find no consistent linguistic criteria for maintaining that there were two distinct authors, and his conclusion was:

> It seems to me very probable that the Jehovist may be identical with the second Elohist, and the difference observed in the use of the Divine Name may be only due to some change of *plan*, or to some change of *circumstances*, in the writer himself.[37]

Second, Colenso was convinced that the Second Elohist and the Jehovist did not provide independent narratives, which had been incorporated into the whole. The material designated by these names were *supplements* to the main Elohistic document.

The dating of the work of the main Elohist and of the Second Elohist and the Jehovist is discussed in great detail, with the same general conclusions reached as in Colenso's discussion in Part 2. A slight, but significant modification of his position was that the main Elohist was no longer identified absolutely with Samuel. Colenso presented a scheme, which correlated his writers with certain prophets:

	BC	CONTEMP. PROPHET
Elohist	1100–1060	Samuel
Second Elohist = Jehovist	1060–1010	Nathan
Second Jehovist	1035	Gad
Deuteronomist	641–624	Jeremiah

But he contented himself with saying that 'some great and good men' such as the prophets named, must have written the material designated as Elohist, etc.[38]

The mention of the Second Jehovist makes it necessary to say that Colenso posited in all four Jehovists, by which he meant four stages of the work of the Jehovist, of which the first stage was that which was (a little confusingly) described as the Second Elohist. Colenso gave the dates and size of his Jehovist as follows:

J[1] (Second Elohist)	336 verses, latter part of Saul's reign.
J[2] (Jehovist)	462 verses, second decade of David's reign.
J[3]	269 verses, latter part of David's reign.
J[4]	297 verses, beginning of Solomon's reign.[39]

[37] *The Pentateuch*, Pt 5, p. 67.
[38] ibid., p. 180.
[39] ibid., p. 183.

The reasons for distinguishing between four stages of the Jehovist work were mainly internal historical reasons. For example, Genesis 10.1–7, 13–32 were assigned to J[4] on the grounds that the extended geographical knowledge indicated in these verses had to be later than Samuel's day, and probably reflected contact, in Solomon's reign, with the maritime people of Tyre and Sidon.[40] It can be seen that Colenso's work as a literary and historical critic grew in sensitivity and confidence the more he did it.

An important section in Part 5 deals with the Levites.[41] Here, Colenso compared the Chronicles material on the Levites with that in the historical books, especially 1 and 2 Samuel. His occasion for so doing was his discussion of the blessing of Levi in the Blessing of Jacob in Genesis 49. Colenso reiterated what had been argued originally by de Wette, that in what was said about Levites, the books of Chronicles were untrustworthy, and that the Levites were relatively insignificant in Israel, at least until the middle part of David's reign. The implications of this observation for a history of Israelite priesthood, were not, however, taken very far by Colenso.

Six years elapsed between the publication of Part 5 and that of Part 6 in 1871, and in this intervening period, Colenso significantly altered his opinion about the composition of the Pentateuch in one respect. It has been observed above that Part 5 dealt almost entirely with Genesis. Part 6 dealt with Exodus through to Joshua, and argued that the legislative and cultic passages in the Elohist document belonged to the latest parts of the Pentateuch to be written, probably during and after the Babylonian Exile. In his earlier volumes, he had assumed that the legislative and cultic parts of the Elohistic source, together with its narrative parts, were the oldest parts of the Pentateuch. Thus, a very significant shift of opinion had now taken place in Colenso's mind. Clearly, H. K. Graf's *Die geschichtlichen Bücher des Alten Testaments* (1866) and A. Kuenen's *De Godsdienst van Israel* (1870) had an influence upon Colenso, but as ever, he did not accept their views uncritically, and in presenting his own latest scholarly opinions he went into everything in the minutest detail. Part 6 of *The Pentateuch* runs to over 800 pages!

Colenso's starting-point for his change of opinion was the similarity between the book of Ezekiel and Leviticus 26.[42] This led to an examination of the vocabulary of Ezekiel and of Leviticus, and to the establishment of the position that Leviticus 18—27 must have been written during the Babylonian Exile, on the grounds that Leviticus 18—27 and Ezekiel share features of expression and of vocabulary not found elsewhere in the Old Testament.

---

[40] ibid., p. 94.
[41] ibid., ch. 15. 'The Levites in the time of David.'
[42] Pt 6, ch. 1. 'Ezekiel the writer of L.XXVI.'

Colenso turns next to Deuteronomy, and argues that the original form of the book, that which was found in the Temple in 621 BC, consisted of chs. 5—26, and 28. He then goes on to show first, that what he calls L.L. (Later, or Levitical Legislation) can be found in Exodus, Leviticus, Numbers, and Joshua, and second, having identified it and 'removed' it, he reconstructs what he calls O.S. (the Original Story) in Exodus, Numbers, Deuteronomy and Joshua. A discussion of the passover in Deuteronomy 16 brings the conclusion that the passover was originally a spring festival of the sun-god, adapted from the Canaanites by the Israelites, at which festival first-born sons were offered in sacrifice to Yahweh.[43] The O.S., for example, in Genesis 22 (the 'binding' of Isaac), shows no sign of surprise at the command of God to Abraham to offer his son as a sacrifice, and Colenso supposes that this practice endured long in Israel, and that it was the Deuteronomic law that first enjoined the substitution of an animal for the human first-born. It followed, of course, that the connection of the passover with the Exodus from Egypt was secondary.

By the end of Part 6, Colenso's view of the composition of the Pentateuch and the historical books was as follows:[44] by the time of the early years of the reign of Solomon, there existed the O.S., a narrative work running from Genesis 1.1 to the beginning of 1 Kings. It was made up of the narrative parts of the Elohist and of the various Jehovists, and it took the story of Israel from the Patriarchs through the Exodus, Conquest and Judges to the reigns of Saul and David. It remained in this form until the time of Jeremiah, perhaps deposited beside the ark in the Temple. Jeremiah added to the O.S. various 'Deuteronomic' touches, as well as Deuteronomy 5.26 and 28. Later, he added Deuteronomy 1—4, 29—30, and he also completed the history of the Hebrew monarchy on the basis of older, perhaps official, materials. During the Exile, Ezekiel wrote Leviticus 18—20, and 26 and he was followed by various priestly writers who were responsible for the L.L. passages. The Pentateuch was almost complete by the end of the period of Ezra.

Eight years were to pass before Colenso, four years before his death, produced in 1879 the seventh and final part of the *Pentateuch*, a volume of over 700 pages. The main purpose of Part 7 was to defend Colenso's opinion that the *narrative* parts of the Elohist source were the oldest, whereas the *legislative* parts were the youngest portions of the Pentateuch. On the one hand, as Colenso admitted, his acceptance of the lateness of the legislative parts of the Elohist called in question the arguments of his earlier volumes, in which he had identified the Elohist source as a whole, narrative and legislative parts, on the basis of similarity of vocabulary and expression. On

[43] ibid., pp. 428ff.
[44] ibid., pp. 616ff.

the other hand, there had joined the lists of those advocating the lateness of the whole of the Elohist (or Priestly document as critical orthodoxy came to call it) the young Julius Wellhausen.[45]

It is impossible to reproduce here the wealth of detail and argument with which Colenso still maintained that the narrative parts of the Elohist were the oldest part of the Pentateuch. He remained convinced that the Deuteronomic and the L.L. material had been interpolated into the O.S., of which the Elohistic narrative was a prime component, but he was forced to concede that the similarity of style between the (early) narrative parts of the Elohist and the (late) priestly work of the L.L. was due to a conscious imitation by the priestly writers of the style of the Elohist narrative.[46] At the same time, Colenso saw no vital principle at stake, and he declared himself to be open to the possibility of being convinced that he was wrong about the early composition of the Elohist narrative.[47]

In addition to discussing the Pentateuch, Colenso addressed himself in Part 7 to many other books of the Old Testament, reiterating his belief in the unhistorical nature of the version of Israelite history given in the books of Chronicles, and showing that the priestly and levitical religion of Israel was unknown in the original forms of the historical books and in the prophetic books.

Looking at all seven parts of *The Pentateuch*, a work of some 3,500 pages including the prefaces and appendices, it is difficult not to regard it as the most remarkable achievement by a British scholar in the field of Old Testament criticism in the nineteenth century. It took account of German criticism in a manner that had not been done before, and more than this, it subjected German scholarship to a scrutiny probably unrivalled in Britain until the work of S. R. Driver and W. R. Smith. Colenso was his own man, prepared to back his own position, yet at the same time open to persuasion. In reaching his critical views he showed an attention to detail and an expenditure of energy worthy of an Ewald; and withal, he was a remarkable missionary bishop, who not only mastered the Zulu language, but published a grammar and dictionary of the language as well as translations of the New Testament and parts of the Old Testament into Zulu. From 1861 until the end of his life, he was constantly engaged in disputes with his opponents in

---

[45] In his articles in *Jahrbücher für Deutsche Theologie* 21–2 (1876–7).

[46] Pt 7, Appendix 152, p. 137 (note that the pages of the Appendices are numbered 1–216, at the end of the main part of the book, numbered 1–528.

[47] ibid., Preface, p. xxxi. Colenso takes the opportunity of disagreeing with Ewald about the work of Moses. In the preface, p. xxxii, he asserts that scholarship would be greatly assisted if the notion of the 'creativity' of Moses were altogether abandoned.

South Africa and England who regarded him as a dangerous heretic, and he was also a critic of British colonial policy towards the Zulus.[48]

It would appear that Colenso's most immediate impact upon critical scholarship was via the Dutch scholar Kuenen. It was Colenso's *Pentateuch* Part 1, which convinced Kuenen of the lateness of the narrative parts of the Elohist source, and although Colenso did not judge his own work in this way, Kuenen's shift in opinion was to have profound consequences for Old Testament criticism.[49]

Colenso's impact upon British Old Testament criticism is harder to guess. Cheyne, in *Founders of Old Testament Criticism*, indulges in his usual tactic of criticizing anyone who does not reach his [Cheyne's] critical position in one leap. Colenso is thus scolded for missing the truth 'on that very important point . . . the unity of the laws and narratives of the *Grundschrift*'. This leads Cheyne to the assessment that Colenso 'is a genuine but not an eminent critic', and that 'he was not qualified to do thoroughly sound constructive work either in historical criticism or in theoretic theology'.[50] Rather patronizingly, Cheyne remarks, 'Let us be thankful for all that he did in breaking up the hard soil, and not quarrel with him for his limitations'.[51] This latter observation, about breaking up the hard soil, is, however, very significant.

It is not possible in the present work to consider the many attempted refutations of Colenso that appeared subsequent to the publication of Part 1 of *The Pentateuch*.[52] These 'refutations' can be said to be based upon four main lines of approach. First, there was the view that if Colenso could be shown to be incorrect on one point in his argumentation, then the whole

---

[48] See Cox, op. cit., 2, p. 319: 'From this time (1873) to the end of his life a marked change is seen in the direction of the Bishop's energy. Thus far he had been fighting for freedom of thought in the search for facts on behalf of his fellow-countrymen; henceforth he was to be a champion striving to secure bare justice, if not mercy and forebearance, for the native tribes within and without the borders of Natal.'

[49] See Kuenen's statement in the *Theologische Tijdschrift* (July 1870), translated in *The Pentateuch*, Pt 6, p. xxx: 'The critics of the Continent are busy in building up, but in so doing are making use of materials which are rejected by Colenso on very just grounds. As regards myself, I gladly admit that I have had my attention drawn by him to difficulties, which I had before not at all or not sufficiently considered. And as regards the view prevailing in Germany—when it appears that Ewald, Bunsen, Bleek, and Knobel, one by one, have been brought by the English Bishop to the necessity of revising their theories— there is no reason truly for calling this method antiquated or his reflections obsolete.' (I have not been able to discover the effect on Ewald and the others to which Kuenen refers, and I can only conclude that Colenso did not accurately translate the Dutch. In the Introduction to A. Kuenen, *The Hexateuch*, London 1886, p. xv, the passage is translated: '. . . inasmuch as Ewald, Bunsen, Bleek and Knobel were every one of them logically bound—if they could but have seen it!—to revise.')

[50] Cheyne, p. 203.

[51] ibid., p. 203.

[52] Some of the titles of the 'refutations' are given by Hinchcliff, op. cit., p. 109, n4.

position that he maintained fell to the ground. Thus, some of the defenders of orthodoxy fastened upon only one or two points in the argument, and were satisfied that they had won, even if they showed only that Colenso's use of evidence could be given an alternative explanation. Second, there were those who defended the text by not taking it literally (for example, by saying that the flood was not universal, when the text makes it clear that it was), by positing textual corruptions or by indulging in mild rationalism. Then, as now, it was acceptable for conservatives to rationalize the text, but heresy for known liberals to do so. Third, there were those who assumed that the difficulties pointed out by Colenso had been overcome by special miracles or examples of divine providence, so that Colenso's main crime was that of failing to accept the miraculous. Fourth, there were those who argued that in assuming the lateness of Chronicles, Colenso was stating his conclusions in his premises. Once the authenticity of what is presented in Chronicles is accepted, the argument ran, then all becomes clear. However, nobody was able to produce what *today* looks like an effective answer to Colenso, and indeed, the attempts at refutation look today like the last desperate defence of a paradigm that was soon to collapse.[53] Colenso's significance may well lie in the way in which he broke up the hard soil in Britain, exhausted the credibility of the older defences of orthodoxy, and showed to a younger generation of scholars facts in the Bible that orthodox schemes could no longer explain. To Colenso more than to anyone else, may be due the fact that in *scholarly* circles from the 1880s, the defenders of the old orthodoxy were hardly to be seen, and the field was dominated by a new critical, if critically conservative, school of scholarship.

In one liberal quarter, Colenso's efforts were not at all appreciated. It is a tragic part of his life that the appearance of *The Pentateuch* destroyed his friendship with F. D. Maurice.[54] It is hardly surprising that Maurice, whose 'liberal' position was very traditional when it came to Old Testament history, should have looked with such horror on Colenso's apparent undermining of his view of Israel's history as a providentially guided process

---

[53] Probably the most important attempt to dispose of the early parts of *The Pentateuch* was E. H. Browne's *The Pentateuch and the Elohistic Psalms in Reply to Bishop Colenso*, London & Cambridge, 1863. Hinchliff, pp. 110ff, outlines this book briefly, and believes that the reply 'is impressive even to the modern reader'. Although I cannot share that opinion, I thoroughly endorse Hinchliff's remarks on p. 112 about the dangers of misrepresenting and trivializing both Colenso's writings and those of his more able and fair-minded opponents. The summary in Chadwick, *The Victorian Church*, 2, p. 91, 'He [Colenso] had no sense of history, no idea how to criticise documents, no wide reading, and no profundity of mind', if correct, is also a devastating condemnation of Colenso's opponents and the many forms of special pleading which they employed to support their literalist interpretations of the Pentateuch.

[54] See Cox, 1, pp. 188ff, for Colenso's letters to Maurice, and Maurice *Life of F. D. Maurice*, 2, p. 510, for Maurice's reaction.

culminating in the Christian Church. The qualification 'apparent' is important, since Colenso does not seem to have seen his work as other than an obedient response to the God of truth; but not for the last time was there a clash of interests in British scholarship between those whose liberalism stopped short of criticizing the surface story of Old Testament history, and those whose source-critical work questioned the surface story radically. How this was resolved in British scholarship will be seen below in Part 3.

What was at issue between Colenso on the one hand, and his opponents including Maurice on the other hand, was not merely how the Old Testament was to be interpreted, but what was the basis for Christian hope and belief. Colenso's orthodox opponents saw the ultimate basis of their faith as a supernatural communication from God contained in the Bible. If the opponents were Low Churchmen, the Articles of the Church of England supported this view. If the opponents were High Churchmen, as was the case in South Africa, the teaching of the Catholic Church required the support of a Bible free from radical criticism. In the case of Maurice, the locus of revelation had probably shifted from the text of the Bible to the history which the text recorded. In his case, an attack on a traditional reading of biblical history by means of source and historical criticism was equally unwelcome.

Colenso possessed a remarkable trust in the universal love of God for all mankind, expressed supremely in Jesus Christ. This made him, at one and the same time, such a remarkable missionary and such a fearless critic. Not unlike some of the critics of the late eighteenth century in Germany, whose pietistic upbringing gave them a certainty from which standpoint they could investigate freely, Colenso was deeply rooted in a faith which criticism could only confirm and strengthen. There is, however, a connection between his later critical views and the battles which he fought in South Africa.

The main issue at stake in South Africa was whether bishops such as Colenso and his Metropolitan, Bishop Gray of Capetown, were bishops of the Church of England or bishops of the Church of South Africa.[55] Gray, backed by High Churchmen in Britain, wished to set up a self-governing High Anglican church, free from the English legislation which regulated the Church of England, and which had upheld the right of critical inquiry into the Bible.[56] Colenso was deposed from his bishopric by a so-called synod of the South African Church, although in England, the Judicial Committee of the Privy Council refused to recognize the deposition, and declared Colenso to be Bishop of Natal.

This controversy was reflected in Colenso's later critical work in that he

[55] See Cox, 2, ch. 3.
[56] In the judgements arising from *Essays and Reviews*.

was deeply antipathetic to Roman Catholicism, and to what he saw as the
romanizing tendencies of the High Church party, and Bishop Gray. That
the Levitical Legislation could be shown to be a late phenomenon in Israelite
religion, and the particular concern of the (for Colenso) discredited author
of the books of Chronicles, was a help and comfort for Colenso in his
opposition to the High Church party, and in his quest to make known to
the Zulus the universal love of God. He saw the discrediting of priestcraft as
one of the most important results of the modern criticism of the Pentateuch,
and he regarded the rise of biblical criticism as the providential gift of God
to the Church at a time when what he, Colenso, regarded as the evils of
priestcraft and ritualism were once more establishing themselves.[57]

It is difficult to know whether Colenso's later critical work accepted the
lateness of the levitical system because this reinforced his theological position
or whether he was led by purely critical considerations to a position that
was obviously theologically congenial to him. What is important to notice
is that in the controversy between Colenso and his opponents on the critical
questions, there were underlying theological issues which strongly affected
the debate.

Colenso was far more than a mathematician dabbling with biblical
figures and dimensions. By unremitting labour in the midst of an incredibly
demanding life as a missionary, he mastered, as probably no English scholar
had before him, the technicalities of Old Testament criticism. Many of his
observations are now commonplace in Old Testament scholarship, and
anyone who cares to read through all seven parts of *The Pentateuch* will be
confronted with problems which cannot be overlooked today, even if not
all of Colenso's answers remain valid. Colenso's view of the Bible was
summed up in these words in Part 6:

> There is no infallible Book for our guidance, as there is no infallible Church or
> infallible Man. The Father of spirits has not willed it thus, who knows best what
> is needed for the education of each individual soul, as well as that of the race. But
> He gives us light enough upon our path that we may do our work here faithfully
> and fear no evil. And the pure in heart will see God face to face in many a page

[57] See *The Pentateuch* Pt 6, p. 631: 'Perhaps, the most important result of the criticism of the
Pentateuch is this, that it strikes a death-blow at the whole system of priestcraft, which has
mainly been based upon the notion that the Levitical Laws in the books of Exodus,
Leviticus and Numbers, were really Mosaic, or rather of Divine, origin.' p. 635: 'Let it not
be said that these all, with the sprinkling of blood, point to the blood of Christ as "of a
lamb without blemish and without spot". With our present knowledge of the time and
manner in which the L.L. originated it is impossible to believe this.' p. 637: 'How, indeed,
could these narrow priestly notions set forth in any way the sacrifice of Christ? As if any
other sacrifice were pleasing to God than that living sacrifice of loving obedience, faithful
unto death, though it be the death of the cross ... which Christ offered in his life and
death.'

of the Sacred Book—will recognise the Divine Revelation of all that is good and true throughout it—will hear God's voice, and feel His Living Word come home to the heart, and that it must be obeyed.[58]

There can be no doubt that the writer of these words was prepared not only to follow the truth wherever it seemed to lead critically; he was also prepared to obey the voice of God as it came to him through the sacred book.

[58] *The Pentateuch*, Pt 6, p. 626.

17

English Critical Old Testament Scholarship 1864–80

While the upheavals caused by *Essays and Reviews* and by the publication of the successive parts of Colenso's *Pentateuch* were still having a profound effect in ecclesiastical circles, critical scholarship continued to make steady, if moderate, progress. The publication of A. P. Stanley's *Lectures on the History of the Jewish Church* in 1863 and 1865 (Part 3 dealing with the post-Exilic period did not appear until 1876) was a significant event.[1] Apart from Milman's *History of the Jews*, Stanley's lectures represented the first attempt by an English scholar to produce a 'History of Israel' on a scale approaching that of Ewald's celebrated *History*. Stanley had been asked to be one of the contributors to *Essays and Reviews* but had declined on the grounds that he did not consider the time right for such a venture.[2] This same caution can be detected throughout his *Jewish Church*; yet arguably, it was precisely because he proceeded so warily that he was able to produce a work that undoubtedly commended the critical method to fair-minded people.

Stanley's biographers described *The Jewish Church* as 'the work of a moralist who is writing historically'; they complained, not unfairly, that it was often very hard to discover what Stanley thought had taken place, and that in the critical sense of the word history, the work was 'unhistorical'.[3] Certainly, very little idea can be gained from the lectures themselves of what critical principles, if any, underlay them. Stanley did not begin the lectures with a discussion of the sources for our knowledge of Israel's history

---

[1] A. P. Stanley, *Lectures on the History of the Jewish Church*, London, First Series 1863, 1865³, Second series, 1865, Third series, 1876. It is an interesting reflection on the organization of theological studies in England at this time that Stanley gave the earlier series of lectures as Regius Professor of Ecclesiastical History at Oxford. Stanley (1815–81) was successively fellow of University College, Oxford (1838–51), canon of Canterbury (1851–6), professor of Ecclesiastical History (1856–63), dean of Westminster (1863–81). See R. E. Prothero and G. C. Bradley, *The Life and Correspondence of Arthur Penrhyn Stanley, D.D. Late Dean of Westminster*, 2 vols, London 1893.

[2] *Life of A. P. Stanley*, 2, p. 31.

[3] ibid., p. 249. See also pp. 110–15.

and a critical assessment of their value or otherwise. His critical remarks are to be found here and there in the course of the exposition.

On the composition of the Pentateuch there is a note which appears to acknowledge 'the probability that the laws did not assume their present shape till a much later period'.[4] Even so, this did not rule out the probability that the sacrificial system was 'in full force' during the period of the wilderness wanderings. The main difficulty that Stanley saw was that of the apparent conflict between the Pentateuch as expressing authentic history and the prophetic denials that Israel offered sacrifices to Yahweh in the wilderness (Amos 5.25; Jer. 7.22). Stanley's solution was that the wilderness sacrifices of the Israelites 'had a real existence, but stood on a much lower level than the rest of the Mosaic institutions'.[5]

Stanley was more forthcoming about his views on the Pentateuch in letters which he wrote to Colenso after the publication of Part 1 of *The Pentateuch and Joshua*: 'The apportionment of the Elohistic and Jehovistic portion (after the first four chapters of Genesis) has always seemed to me very precarious'.[6] He also felt that Colenso made too much of arguments from silence. He was offended most of all by Colenso's use of the word 'fictitious', since he held that 'from the time of Abraham downwards there is a distinct, though not exclusively historical, narrative'.[7]

On the books of Chronicles, Stanley's view was that although these were late compositions, probably post-Ezra, they represented the work of many generations, and that they supplied for the voids in the books of Kings material that could only have come from the levitical 'caste'.[8]

In the light of what has been written above, it should come as no surprise to discover that in his lectures, Stanley made no reference to critical scholars or theories of the radical or 'negative' type. So far as I am aware, there is no mention of de Wette or Vatke among the Germans, nor of von Bohlen or Francis Newman among writers of works written in or translated into English. On the other hand, Ewald held an honoured place in Stanley's esteem. In his preface to vol. 2, Stanley referred to Ewald's 'great work' on the history of Israel, and to his 'no less important' work on the prophets. Elsewhere, Stanley alluded to 'the German scholar, to whose investigations

---

[4] *Lectures on the Jewish Church*, 1, p. 169, n2. (Reference is to the 3rd edition, 1865.)

[5] ibid., p. 169, n2.

[6] ibid., p. 101. Against this remark has to be set Stanley's account of a conversation with J. H. Newman in 1864 (ibid., p. 341): 'I urged the evidently composite character of Genesis. This he at once acknowledged. "It struck me the moment I first read those chapters in Hebrew. There must be two documents. And I mentioned it to Pusey, who seemed to acknowledge it. Would he acknowledge it now?" A.P.S.: "I think not."' Of course, Stanley and Newman may have been discussing Gen. 1—3 rather than the whole of Genesis.

[7] ibid., p. 103.

[8] *Jewish Church*, 2, pp. 417–8.

we owe so much in the study of the Older Dispensation',[9] or to 'the great Hebrew critic of our age'.[10] Yet any reader of Stanley's lectures who had not read Ewald (the English translation of his *History* did not appear until 1876) would have gained no idea of the critical nature of that scholar's work. A reader would have noted Stanley's opinion that Ewald's critical analysis savoured of 'arbitrary dogmatism' to many English readers and that Ewald assigned 'special dates and authors to the manifold constituent parts of the several books of the Old Testament',[11] but that was all.

Stanley's lectures, then, were a straightforward account of Old Testament history, following closely the biblical story, and treating as fully historical figures all the great Israelites from Abraham onwards. The difficulties presented by the accounts of Saul's rise to the kingship, difficulties so shrewdly analysed by Francis Newman, were overcome by the simple device of harmonization.[12] Stanley accepted that Saul had been privately anointed by Samuel, publicly elected by the people, and renewed in his kingship following his defeat of the Ammonites at Jabesh Gilead. On the notorious figure of 600,000 armed Hebrews who left Egypt at the time of the Exodus, Stanley took comfort from the fact that 'the great German scholar defends the correctness of the original numbers'.[13] He noted that one commentator wished to reduce the figure to 600, and declining to enter into the critical arguments, preferred to concentrate on 'what remains true under either hypothesis'.[14] Not for Stanley Colenso's agonizing over these figures, nor Colenso's conviction that if 600,000 was the correct reading (which it undoubtedly is), then the narrative was unhistorical.

In dealing with the problem of Joshua 8.30–5, according to which Joshua built an altar on Mt Gerizim when the Israelites had conquered only Jericho and Ai, Stanley observed, incorrectly, that Joshua came to Shechem in the Hebrew text immediately after the capture of Jericho and in the LXX immediately after the capture of Ai, and thus he felt able to follow Josephus who placed this incident at the close of Joshua's life.[15] The sun standing still

[9] *Jewish Church*, 1, p. 286.
[10] ibid., p. 371. See also the conversation with Newman, *Life of A. P. Stanley*, 2, p. 341: 'I then gradually led to Ewald; and he regretted the ignorance of German . . . I spoke of the great merits of Ewald . . .' Stanley first met Ewald at a congress in Dresden in 1844. See *Life*, 1, pp. 329–30. In 1839, Stanley had visited Bonn, and had met Bleek, among others (ibid. p. 221).
[11] *Jewish Church*, 1, p. xiv. Other scholars referred to include F. D. Maurice (2, p. v), Pusey (e.g., 2, p. 425, n2) and J. D. Michaelis (numerous references to the English translation of *Mosaisches Recht*).
[12] *Jewish Church*, 2, pp. 7–13.
[13] ibid., 1, p. 124. Ewald is referred to in the footnote.
[14] ibid., p. 125.
[15] ibid., p. 279, n1. In fact, 8.30–5 follows 9.2 in the LXX, numbered by Rahlfs as 9.2a–f. Ewald, *History*, 2, p. 234, n2, rightly identified 8.30–5 as a Deuteronomistic interpolation.

over Gibeon was a piece of poetry, not to be taken literally;[16] the Red Sea
was parted at the Exodus by a hurricane, although it was best not to enquire
too far into the mystery of what had happened.[17]

Stanley was at his most 'critical' in handling the development of priesthood
and sacrifice.[18] He regarded both institutions as Israelite borrowings from
other nations, albeit imbued with the distinctive spirit of Israelite faith.
However, these aspects of the Mosaic system were inferior to the other
elements, as the prophetic witness indicated. The priests and Levites were
seen as a cross between soldiers, farmers and butchers, whose office demanded
technical rather than spiritual qualifications. The Temple resembled a
slaughter house rather than a cathedral or a church. The institutions of
priesthood and sacrifice preferred dogma, ceremony and antiquity to
morality and devotion, and the crime of Caiaphas was:

> the last culminating proof that the opposition of the Prophets to the growth of
> the Priestly and Sacrificial system was based on an eternal principle, which carries
> with it a rebuke to the office which bears the name of Priesthood throughout the
> world.[19]

The value of the priesthood and its system lay in its persistence. Where
monarchy ended and prophecy fell silent, priesthood and sacrifice endured.
Thus, even if priesthood was the 'mere skeleton of the Jewish Religion' it
was also its backbone. If it was the husk, it was also a hard shell.

A feature of the earlier lectures was the constant reference to 'Arabia', and
to 'Arabian' parallels. In 1852–3, Stanley had visited Egypt and Palestine,[20]
and had published in 1856 a book of 550 pages entitled *Sinai and Palestine*.[21]
It was on the basis of his travels and researches that Stanley was able to
make, in his *Jewish Church*, assertions such as:

> Every English pilgrim to the Holy Land . . . is delighted to trace and record the
> likeness of patriarchal manners and customs in the Arabian chiefs. To refuse to
> do so would be to decline the use of what we may almost call a singular gift of
> Providence. The unchanged habits of the East render it in this respect a kind of
> living Pompeii . . . in the case of Jewish history we know the outward appearances
> through the forms of actual men, living and moving before us, wearing almost
> the same garb, speaking in almost the same language, and certainly with the same
> general terms of speech and tone and manners.[22]

[16] *Jewish Church*, 1, pp. 247ff.
[17] ibid., p. 130.
[18] ibid., 2, pp. 406–26.
[19] ibid., p. 426. For F. D. Maurice's negative reaction to this part of Stanley's lectures see the
correspondence in *Life of A. P. Stanley*, 2, pp. 250–2.
[20] See *Life*, 1, pp. 444–64.
[21] *Sinai and Palestine in Connection with their History*, London 1856.
[22] *Jewish Church*, 1, p. 11.

Claims such as this, which sound so extravagant today, undoubtedly confirmed Stanley in his view that Old Testament history from the time of Abraham had happened substantially as recorded in the Bible, and could be the basis for the moral lessons which Stanley drew from it.

The importance of Stanley's lectures, for the progress of critical scholarship, lay in the way in which he was able to show that the abandoning of 'orthodox' views of inspiration and the acceptance of criticism did not inevitably lead to irreverence and unbelief. The lectures showed that treated like any other book, and set within the history and culture of its time of origin, the Old Testament could be both illuminated and illuminating. In Stanley's hands, the 'Jewish Church' became an assembly of real people, responding to the educative hand of God in real situations. The purpose of the Old Testament was not to provide data about geology and astronomy,[23] but to teach about the purposes of God for his people, which had led to the fullness of revelation in Jesus Christ. Probably, Stanley judged better than anyone else at the time on the liberal front how best the liberal cause could be advanced.[24]

Among the 'founders of Old Testament criticism' introduced by Cheyne is a scholar, M. M. Kalisch, who is not mentioned by Diestel, Kraus or Duff, yet who undoubtedly made an important contribution to the progress of Old Testament studies in England. He was, in fact, born in Germany in 1826, but came to Britain as a political refugee following the upheavals of 1848.[25] A Jew, his published works included a four-volume commentary on the books of Genesis, Exodus and Leviticus and a well-known Hebrew Grammar. Because his scholarly works were written in English they are considered here.

Kalisch, especially in his later work, can be described as a liberal Jew of great learning and discernment. He referred to traditional Jewish commentators, to early critical German scholarship, especially the works of de Wette, Gramberg, George and Vatke, to the work of conservative scholars, and to classical and modern writings having a bearing upon comparative religion. He was thoroughly independent in his judgements. For example, he referred to de Wette and the others more often to criticize

---

[23] See the long discussion apropos of Joshua's victory at the valley of Ajalon, *Jewish Church*, 1, pp. 249ff. In Stanley's view, the clash between Galileo and the Church of Rome had established the principle once for all that 'the Bible was not intended to teach scientific truth'. As Stanley well observed (p. 249, n1), 'The expression "the stars in their courses fought against Sisera" (Judges 5.20) has never been distorted from its true poetical character, and has, therefore, given rise to no alarms and no speculations'.

[24] See *Life of A. P. Stanley*, 2, pp. 115–16, where he expressed his opinion that the lectures would be 'condemned by the advanced liberals as not going far enough, while those who are reputed "orthodox" will try to suppress it'. An 'orthodox' reaction can be found in E. B. Pusey's *Daniel the Prophet*, Oxford and London 1864, pp. xxvi, 619–27.

[25] See Cheyne, *Founders of Old Testament Criticism*, pp. 204–8.

them than to agree with them; and his positions depended upon a minute and careful examination of the text.

Of Kalisch's earlier commentaries, on Exodus (1855) and Genesis (1858) little needs to be said.[26] They seem, on the face of it, to be reasonably traditional in critical matters, and where a liberal spirit is displayed, it is in the recognition that a literal reading of the text cannot be reconciled with modern scientific discoveries, and that the especial genius of the biblical writers had to do with the mediation of *religious* truths.[27] In the two parts of the commentary on Leviticus, however, which appeared in 1867 and 1872, Kalisch put forward his own reasons for regarding as post-exilic many parts of Leviticus, and similar material in the other middle books of the Pentateuch. He offered reconstructions of the history of Israelite priesthood and sacrifice which in broad outline, though not necessarily in details, agreed with what George had proposed in 1835, and what Wellhausen was to propose in 1878.

At one level, his conclusions were based upon considerations drawn from what was generally believed at the time about the development of religion. Thus, on expiatory offerings, Kalisch believed that these entailed a developed sense of religious awareness, and were thus 'late' sacrifices in ancient Israel.[28] But at the most fundamental level, his conclusions were based upon the biblical text, and the signs of development and adaptations which he detected there.

On priesthood and sacrifice, Kalisch's views coincided with earlier critical opinions. Thus, the earliest sacrifices were the whole burnt offerings and they did not need an established priesthood to offer them. This could be done by elders, heads of houses and others. The priestly and levitical power grew only gradually and did not become fully established until after the Babylonian Exile, when there was no monarchy to keep it in check.[29] There was no evidence in the historical books of the Old Testament that the Levitical system was known before the Exile, and the books of Chronicles did not present a reliable picture on this score.[30] Leviticus was later than

---

[26] M. M. Kalisch, *A Historical and Critical Commentary on the Old Testament with a New Translation*, London, 1855 (*Exodus*), 1858 (*Genesis*) 1867 (*Leviticus* pt 1) 1872 (*Leviticus* pt 2).

[27] See the discussions on 'religion and science', in *Genesis*, pp. 1–41, 137–46.

[28] See the sections in *Leviticus*, Pt 1, entitled, 'History of Sacrifices among the Hebrews', pp. 14–50, 'The Sin-Offering and the Trespass-Offering', pp. 249–82.

[29] See *Leviticus*, Pt 1, pp. 640–59, 'A Historical Sketch of the Origin and Growth of the Order of Priesthood among the Hebrews'.

[30] ibid., pp. 33–4: 'He [the author of Chronicles] shows neither the ability nor the desire for writing an impartial and faithful history. Recognising no higher, scarcely knowing another, interest than that of Levitical priesthood, he is betrayed into the most obvious and invidious prejudices against all other classes and intellectual pursuits. He, therefore, deserves no authority whatever as a source of history, at least on points connected with public worship . . .' For further details, readers are referred *inter alia* to de Wette and Gramberg.

Deuteronomy for various reasons. Not only did Deuteronomy not refer to any of the detailed levitical legislation, the theological outlook of Leviticus was more developed and refined than that of Deuteronomy, thus confirming its lateness.

On the other hand, it is possible to find a certain equivocation in Kalisch about the date and composition of Leviticus. In his view, it consisted of various 'codes', which had been brought together.[31] In some cases, it was possible to detect the work of later editors or revisers who interpolated material into the codes so as to regulate new practices. Thus Leviticus 6.1–11 and 12–16 (English 6.8–18, 19–23) were 'early' in origin, while 6.17—7.7 (English, 6.24—7.7) represented the attempt of a reviser to interpolate material about sin offerings into a section dealing with burnt offerings.[32] This explained the language, 'in the place where the burnt offering is killed shall the sin offering be killed . . .'. The regulations for the (later) sin-offering were incorporated into those for the (early) burnt offerings. Kalisch was thus operating with a 'crystallization' hypothesis for the origin of Leviticus, and this makes his work immensely interesting from the modern point of view. In the context of the nineteenth century, however, his importance lay in his championing of a viewpoint which anticipated Wellhausen's account of the history of Israelite priesthood and sacrifice.[33]

A very different sort of work on the Old Testament appeared in 1877 in the form of J. B. Mozley's *Ruling Ideas in Early Ages and their Relation to the Old Testament Faith*.[34] This series of lectures, delivered in Oxford in 1874–5 to a graduate class of whom many were later to occupy prominent academic and ecclesiastical positions,[35] advanced no new critical theories, and indeed did not mention any established critical theories. Its references to secondary literature was sparing, with Michaelis on the laws of Moses, Milman on the history of the Jews and Stanley on the Jewish Church

[31] ibid., pp. xxiv–xxxv.
[32] pp. 541–4.
[33] See the summary on ibid., pp. 33–4: (1) The Levitical ordinances were neither known nor carried out before the exile . . .; (2) The execution of those ordinances argues a degree of religious education utterly at variance with the multifarious forms of idolatry to which the Hebrews were addicted up to the sixth century; (3) The priests whom history proves to have long been powerless and needy, appear in the Levitical law as men of influence and wealth . . .; (4) The Deuteronomist is more lenient and less authoritative in some of the Levitical injunctions; (5) The Book of Leviticus . . . bespeaks a very matured stage in the internal history of the nation; (6) The minuteness of the sacrificial ritual laid down in Leviticus accords perfectly with the spirit of post-Babylonian times, and finds a faithful reflex in the thoroughly Levitical Books of Chronicles.
[34] J. B. Mozley, *Ruling Ideas in Early Ages and their Relation to Old Testament*, London 1877, n. ed. 1896 (to which reference is here made).
[35] See the list of those who attended the lectures in *Letters of the Rev. J. B. Mozley, D.D.*, ed. by his sister, London 1885, page 343. It includes H. S. Holland, M. Creighton, J. R. Illingworth and R. C. Moberly.

predominant. However, the lectures reveal clearly a tendency that was powerfully at work within quite respectable orthodox circles, and which was to open the way for a limited admission of critical scholarship in the last two decades of the century.

J. B. Mozley (1815–78) was one of the early young Tractarians, and a friend of J. H. Newman before and after the latter's conversion to Roman Catholicism.[36] Although he became a little distanced from the High Church party, he remained on cordial terms with Pusey.[37] He was not sympathetic to the Anglican liberals. His essay in response to Stanley's biography of Thomas Arnold was decidedly cool,[38] and his attitude to Stanley himself was that he liked the man more than his opinions.[39] He had little respect for *Essays and Reviews*[40] and contempt for Part 1 of Colenso's *Pentateuch*.[41] Yet in regard to *Essays and Reviews* we see a reaction that is quite significant for his published lectures on the Old Testament.

On 22 February 1861, R. W. Church wrote to Mozley on the subject of *Essays and Reviews* as follows:[42]

> There is a spirit and tendency about the book, as there was in Hampden and the Oxford Movement, which is undeniable, whatever may be said about garbled extracts. And I suppose that it is quite possible and likely that a heavy blow may be dealt to the opinions—a much heavier than the writers dreamt of provoking. But unless there is also a strong argumentative answer to them, it is such mere provisional work. *People will go on asking these same questions, and raising these same difficulties* . . . I am afraid that the row will prevent for the present any quiet and hopeful pursuing of these questions, and certainly I should like to see some of them more fully examined, and even the real limits of the danger precisely drawn.

Mozley replied on 11 March, 'I feel much the same with respect to *Essays and Reviews* that you do. It goes against the grain to join an assailing mass'.[43]

Mozley seems to be at one with R. W. Church in thinking that the

---

[36] See *Letters of the Rev. J. B. Mozley, passim.* Newman was Mozley's tutor at Oriel College, Oxford. Mozley himself was a fellow of Magdalen College, Oxford (1840–56), vicar of Old Shoreham (1856–71) and Regius Professor of Divinity at Oxford (1871–8).

[37] See Pusey's letter of 7 February 1871 on the occasion of Mozley's appointment to the Regius chair at Oxford, in *Letters of the Rev. J. B. Mozley*, p. 318. Mozley's reply is contained in Liddon's biography of Pusey, 4, p. 221.

[38] See J. B. Mozley, *Essays Historical and Theological*, 2, London 1878, pp. 1–67, esp. p. 67: 'Would that Arnold had stuck to his natural department and not left it for the open world,—for the public arena of theology!'

[39] See, for example, *Letters of Rev. J. B. Mozley*, p. 262.

[40] ibid., pp. 248–51.

[41] ibid., p. 253.

[42] ibid., pp. 248–9, italics mine.

[43] ibid., p. 249.

writers of *Essays and Reviews* face up to vital questions and have an element of truth, but go about their task in a way that will not provoke the right sort of reply. By the time that Mozley published his *Ruling Ideas*, he had accepted totally one of the *Leitmotifs* of *Essays and Reviews*, namely, progressive revelation or progressive education;[44] but the liberal work, to which Mozley's lectures bears closest resemblance, is Arnold's essay 'On the Right Interpretation and Understanding of the Scriptures'.

Arnold's essay and Mozley's lectures have as their central concern the moral problems raised by the Old Testament, in general in the divine commands to the Israelites to exterminate their enemies, and in particular in the command of God to Abraham to offer Isaac as a sacrifice. Both writers refer to Butler,[45] and both ask the question about what evidence or miracle would be necessary to convince a person that God was commanding him to kill a human being. Both reach the same answer. In Arnold's words, 'the revelations of God to man were gradual and adapted to his state at the several periods when they were successively made'.[46] Mozley's answer, basically the same, is worked out far more elaborately and in the context of an implicit theory, stated in the title of the lectures, about the general state of mankind in Old Testament times.

Mozley sees, as the fundamental difference between modern man and man in Old Testament times (also 'primitive' man, as found in the Bedouin), the lack of understanding of the rights of individual human beings on the part of ancient/'primitive' man. This point is illustrated comparatively from classical and Arab sources, and is applied to the Old Testament in various ways.[47] As applied to the sacrifice of Isaac it has the following implications:

> [the sacrifice] required the particular state of ideas in the world at that time, and the defective state of ideas respecting the right of the individual man, for this great act to be brought out. Without those ideas it could not have been the subject of Divine command, having evidence that it *was* a Divine command: a miracle would not be evidence to *us* that God bade a father kill an innocent son: if it was, as it was, evidence to Abraham, it was because that clear idea of the individual right, which involved the inviolability of life, did not exist in his age as it does in ours.[48]

[44] Not only do these, and similar, phrases occur again and again in *Ruling Ideas*; there is a chapter entitled, 'The End the Test of a Progressive Revelation'.

[45] *Ruling Ideas*, p. 31: 'On the Right Interpretation and Understanding of the Scriptures', in *Sermons*, 2, p. 393. Mozley refers to the latter part of Pt 2, ch. 3 of Butler's *Analogy*. It is not clear to me whether Arnold is paraphrasing the same passage, or referring to another part of *Analogy* that I have not identified.

[46] Arnold, *Sermons* 2, p. 382.

[47] For his 'Bedouin' information, Mozley relied upon Michaelis's *Commentaries on the Laws of Moses*; see, e.g., *Ruling Ideas*, pp. 287–9.

[48] *Ruling Ideas*, p. 57.

It was necessary, then, to judge the Old Testament not in terms of the parts, but in terms of the whole; not in terms of the beginning, but in terms of the end.[49] Scripture was progressive, and as God used each stage to lead to a higher level of understanding, the lower level became obsolete. Lower stages did not express God's ideal morality, but a morality *accommodated* to the 'action of the day', to use Mozley's phrase. The Old Testament was to be interpreted, then, making full allowance for the ruling ideas that governed and limited at each individual point of time the capacity for human reason to understand the divine command. In the course of the divine education, an important stage was reached when Ezekiel 'proclaimed a more perfect idea of the Divine justice, as checked by the inherent limits of human individuality and responsibility'.[50]

It is instructive to compare Mozley's lectures with Christopher Wordsworth's reply to Jowett in *Replies to Essays and Reviews*. There, Wordsworth fiercely attacked the notion of accommodation as applied to the New Testament;[51] but above all, he contended for a view of the Bible very different from that contained in Mozley's lectures. For Wordsworth, the Bible is an organic whole, with the interpretation of the Old Testament governed by Jesus' use of it recorded in the New Testament. Again, the messianic prophecies contained in the Old Testament constitute a series of anticipations of the coming of the one, who would expound in the Old Testament the things concerning himself. For Mozley, the Old Testament is an organic process, which leads to the Christ by divine education. There are no references in the lecture to Old Testament prophecies, and only one instance of a dominical reference to the Old Testament—one which in no way forecloses how the Old Testament should be approached.[52] Mozley's lectures imply that the Old Testament must be interpreted like any other book, with clues about the level of the moral understanding of people in Old Testament times supplied from comparative studies. The lectures show us that by 1874–5, at least one representative of the Oxford Movement had reached the position of liberal Anglicans of an earlier generation.[53] This is an indication of how the critical method was able to make such decisive inroads in England after 1880.

To conclude the chapter, two further factors affecting the spread of the critical method in England can be mentioned. The first is the translation

---

[49] ibid., p. 251.

[50] ibid., p. 125.

[51] *Replies to Essays and Reviews*, pp. 480ff.

[52] *Ruling Ideas*, p. 7. The New Testament passage is John 8.56: 'Your father Abraham rejoiced to see my day . . .' Mozley's account of prophecy (e.g., p. 16) would no doubt have led to him being labelled a 'Rationalist' by Hengstenberg, had the latter been alive to evaluate him.

[53] It is remarkable that Mozley should both have such an antipathy to Arnold and yet be so close to him on the moral interpretation of the Old Testament.

into English of liberal works from Germany. Whereas Clark's 'Foreign Theological Library' and 'Biblical Cabinet' had concentrated on conservative German works, the 'Theological Translation Fund Library' of Williams and Norgate began to make available works by Ewald and Kuenen.[54] At the same time, Ewald's *History of Israel* began to appear in English translation.

The other factor was the critical work of Scottish scholars, notably, A. B. Davidson and W. R. Smith. Although their contribution up to 1880 strictly falls outside the scope of the present book, the effect of their work must not be overlooked, and Robertson Smith's post-1880 importance will be considered below.[55]

[54] In this series were published Ewald's *Prophets of the Old Testament*, 5 vols., 1875–81; *Commentary on the Psalms*, 2 vols 1880–1 and *Commentary on Job*, 1882; Kuenen's *The Religion of Israel to the Fall of the Jewish State*, 3 vols., 1874–5. Ewald's *History of Israel* was published by Longman's, 5 vols., 1867ff. The same firm published his *Antiquities of Israel*, 1876.

[55] See below p. 275. On A. B. Davidson and W. R. Smith see Cheyne, pp. 212–28. W. B. Glover, *Evangelical Nonconformists and Higher Criticism in the 19th century*, London 1954, pp. 59–61.

18

Conclusions to Part Two

German Old Testament scholarship entered the nineteenth century with something like twenty Protestant faculties in which the subject was taught, allowing for the closures and reorganizations that occurred in the first two decades of the century. In the year 1800, there existed a tradition of critical scholarship in which the investigation of the authorship and sources of Old Testament books was taken for granted, and whose results were readily available in works such as Eichhorn's *Introduction*. As a calling for a young, aspiring theological student, Old Testament studies were a possibility for which he would prepare by undertaking original research and publication, thus adding to the Old Testament critical enterprise. From the theological point of view, an aspiring Old Testament scholar could, with respectability, be a Supranaturalist if he inclined to traditional orthodoxy, or a Neologist or Rationalist if he felt inclined to draw more radical conclusions from his critical biblical studies. As the century wore on, several types of Confessional orthodoxy took the place of supranaturalism, while more critical views could be expressed in Friesian-de Wettian, Hegelian or speculative-idealistic forms. There was also the growth of the modern historical method.

At the beginning of the nineteenth century in England, Old Testament scholarship in an institutional sense can hardly be said to have existed at all. This does not mean that there was no research or writing on matters affecting the Old Testament. On the contrary, the chairs of Hebrew and Arabic at Oxford and Cambridge provided opportunities for important work to be done in these areas; commentaries on the Old Testament were written, and particular interest was paid to how the customs and manners of the East could throw light on the Bible. This activity was carried out, however, by learned gentlemen, who came from various walks of life. Some would be fellows of Oxford and Cambridge colleges, others would be Anglican and dissenting clergymen, the former working mainly from their parsonages, the latter either from their manses or in the dissenting academies. Taken as a body, these people did not constitute the kind of institution of biblical scholarship that existed in Germany. The conditions did not exist in England, in which a young scholar might aspire to become a biblical specialist and would need to gain a doctorate and to publish an original work as necessary steps towards his aspiration.

The studies that held pride of place in the two English universities were

classics, philosophy, mathematics and natural sciences, and most men, who
intended to be ordained or who hoped to gain a college fellowship, studied
one of these subjects. The philosophy would most likely be classical, but
among modern philosophers, Berkeley, Hume and Butler would be read.

Whereas Germany began the nineteenth century with an established
tradition of critical Old Testament scholarship, England entered the same
period deeply affected by a conservatism which flowed from the Methodist
and Evangelical revivals of the second half of the previous century. In some
respects, this conservatism was open to limited applications of biblical
criticism. We have noticed that scholars were prepared to emend the text
or to use comparative philology in order to suggest new interpretations.
Belief in plenary, as opposed to verbal, inspiration, did not require that
every single detail in the Bible should be accurate. However, none of this
freedom within the conservatism of the time began to approach anything
like the results of German biblical criticism of 1800. There was no soil
prepared in England into which the critical method could be planted and in
which it could flourish.

Similarly, there seems to have been little variety of theological outlook
as compared with Germany. Naturally, one could choose between being an
Anglican, a Methodist, an Independent and a Baptist; but a traditional
orthodoxy reigned supreme in these Churches, once the doctrinal-
ecclesiastical differences were set aside. If a person wished to entertain even
mildly radical views, judged from today's standpoint, and remain within
some sort of religious association, Unitarianism offered the only real
possibility. This can be seen, for example, in the case of Mary Ann Evans
(George Eliot), who, having broken with a once deeply-held Anglican
Evangelicalism, took refuge eventually in the company of Unitarians.[1] Had
she been born in Germany, her hesitations about certain aspects of orthodoxy
as represented at the time would easily have been accommodated into one
or other of the strands of liberal Protestant thought.

As the century continued, it was not the case in England that attack on
the critical method was mounted from various types of confessional
orthodoxy. The first concern of English scholarship, from the late 1820s,
was to ensure that German critical scholarship was kept out of England, and
biblical criticism was firmly identified with unbelief and with the
undermining of Christianity. Any theologian with sympathy for German
achievements could be sure of hostility directed from all sides of an
overwhelmingly orthodox establishment. As the reaction to Milman's
History of the Jews shows, simply to try to present biblical history as though
it were like secular history, was deemed to be an attack on pious belief. At

[1] Mary Ann(e) Lewes (née Evans) (1819–90) was the translator into English of D. F. Strauss's
Life of Jesus. She is better known as the novelist George Eliot. See Gordon S. Haight, *George
Eliot: a biography*, Oxford 1968.

the same time, the Pusey of the late 1820s was prepared to make suggestions about a revision of the English Old Testament, basing most of the suggestions upon the lexicon of Gesenius.[2]

From the mid-1840s, following Newman's conversion to Roman Catholicism, the burning ecclesiastical question in England was the future of the Church of England in relation to Roman Catholicism. There were undoubtedly great fears among orthodox Anglicans that if Liberalism were to gain any substantial footing in England, this would increase the numbers of those embracing Roman Catholicism. A hardening of orthodox attitudes can thus be detected in England in the middle of the century, but for quite different reasons from the growth of Confessional orthodoxy in Germany in the same period. The fact that Confessional orthodoxy existed in Germany at this time, however, was significant for England in that it became possible for English churchmen to believe that German criticism had been disproved by a reassertion of orthodoxy. Thus, any attempt or desire to further German criticism in England could be regarded as a retrogressive step from the point of view of scholarship, as well as something intrinsically abominable. In 1856, a reviewer in the *Journal of Sacred Literature and Biblical Record* could exclaim, of the appearance of von Bohlen's *Genesis* in English:

> It is rather too bad to have all von Bohlen's monstrous sceptical fictions thrust upon the English public, without a word to intimate that they have long ago been blown into the air by competent scholars.[3]

The *Journal of Sacred Literature*, which appeared in four series between 1848 and 1865, is an excellent index of what was happening in biblical scholarship in England during these years. When it was refounded in 1855 as the *Journal of Sacred Literature and Biblical Record*, an editorial under the title, 'The Study of the Bible, in what Spirit it should be pursued' set out the *Journal's* position:

> This Journal is conducted on the principle that good men, by the use of the gifts which God has conferred upon them, may throw light on the sacred pages, even while they arrive at different conclusions ... we would admit nothing which we believe to be of sceptical source or tendency, but we cannot call anything sceptical, or neological, or heterodox, because it does not harmonize with *our* sentiments.[4]

Within these limits, many contributions were offered from the kinds of persons engaging in academic pursuits described above. German publications

[2] I owe this information to the Rev. A. G. Livesley, who has spent several years investigating the sources of the marginal notes which Pusey made in an English Bible in 1827–8.
[3] *Journal of Sacred Literature and Biblical Record*, 2 (1856), p. 469.
[4] ibid., p. 14.

were noticed, some were reviewed, and in general, a hostile attitude to 'Rationalism' and 'Neologism' was maintained. At some points, distinctively liberal intentions can be discerned. Thus, in a review of Kalisch's commentary on *Genesis*, we find qualified approval of Kalisch's view that the Bible teaches us religious lessons rather than providing scientific information. The reviewer wrote:

> It may be thought that this verges on the mythic theory, and, as far as it admits that the statements of Genesis on natural phenomena do not always correspond to objective truth, it does so. But can this be avoided?

The reviewer, after considering the matter further, concluded that it was best to:

> ... maintain the truth of the religious teaching, but at the same time to admit the human element, so far as is requisite to produce harmony between the respective lessons of the monumental and documentary revelations; no danger can arise from this, if the study is pursued in a reverent spirit ....[5]

This last observation of the reviewer touches on a fundamental point. As the 1850s came to an end, biblical criticism was still identified in England with infidelity and unbelief. Unfortunately, the events of 1857 and later only served to reinforce this prejudice.

When Samuel Davidson was forced to resign his chair in 1857, a correspondent wrote to the *Journal of Sacred Literature*:

> If Dr Davidson can be proved not to have rejected the truths of revelation ... then the storm raised against him resolves itself into a mere veto upon biblical science, and freedom of enquiry into the meaning and condition of Holy Writ ... substantially, we believe this to be the true account of the matter.[6]

Had Davidson not adopted more radical views, both critically and theologically subsequent to his resignation, he would have constituted a powerful argument for the freedom of the investigation of the Bible within the limits of orthodoxy. As things turned out, his subsequent opinions only reinforced the 'critical scholarship equals infidelity' prejudice. The same can be said of Colenso, whose critical Old Testament work followed charges of theological heterodoxy against him, arising from his *Epistle to the Romans*, and of some of the contributors to *Essays and Reviews*, who were considered to be unsound on the atonement (Jowett) or tarnished by their association with Bunsen. This, then, was the situation in England as the position advocated by Wellhausen began to gain the predominance in Germany.

A word must be said about the lack of discussion in this book of the

[5] ibid., 7 (1858), p. 258.
[6] ibid., 6, p. 388.

impact of Darwin's *Origin of Species*, published in 1859. There is no discussion for two reasons. First, if recent writers are correct, the impact of *The Origin of Species* as initiating a battle between science and religion has been exaggerated.[7] Second, in the discussions about Old Testament scholarship of the period, there is surprisingly little reference to Darwin. From *Essays and Reviews*, the various parts of Colenso's *Pentateuch* and Stanley's *Jewish Church*, one gets no indication of an almighty conflict occasioned by Darwin. In some liberal circles, Darwin was held to have given a new dimension to the argument from design.

Well before 1859, orthodox defenders of the Mosaic cosmogony had been exercised by the findings of astronomers, physicists and geologists, and this fact occasioned the essay by Goodwin in *Essays and Reviews*. So far as the study of the Old Testament was concerned, *The Origin of Species* does not seem to have arrived like a bombshell. It does not seem to have raised, for orthodox writers on the Mosaic cosmogony, any questions, with which they were not already trying to deal in the wake of geological discoveries earlier in the nineteenth century.

[7] See J. Moore, *The Post-Darwinian Controversies*, Cambridge 1979; S. Gilley and Ann L. Loades, 'Thomas Henry Huxley: the War between Science and Religion' in *The Journal of Religion*, 61 (1981), pp. 285–308.

Part Three

England from 1880 and Germany from 1860: The Streams Converge

19

Germany from 1860: the Path to Wellhausen

Around 1860, the following measure of general agreement among critical scholars had been reached. Regarding the Pentateuch and Joshua, it was accepted that Deuteronomy had been composed in the seventh century BC, and that Deuteronomistic editorial work in the seventh or sixth centuries had brought the Pentateuch and Joshua to the form in which we now have them, barring some minor post-exilic additions. The books Genesis to Numbers and the pre-Deuteronomic Joshua were the work of the Yahwist. He had used an even earlier book, the so-called *Grundschrift* or Book of Origins, which was a priestly composition containing the basic narrative of the Pentateuch from Genesis 1, and including the levitical legislation in parts of Exodus, in Leviticus and in parts of Numbers. The Yahwist had supplemented, or added his own matter to, the already-existing *Grundschrift*.

This general position allowed for some variations of detail. For example, it was a matter of debate how much of the levitical legislation went back to the time of Moses, and how much of it represented traditions known largely only to priestly circles but definitely originating after the building of the Temple. Again, it was a matter for debate whether the *Grundschrift* could be divided into an older and a younger Elohist, and whether the younger Elohist and the Yahwist were narrative sources complete in themselves or simply collections of additional material. The important points of agreement seem to have been that the Yahwist had added to the earlier *Grundschrift*, and that Deuteronomy and Deuteronomistic material had been added to the Yahwistic work. The *disagreements*, especially about how much material was Mosaic, enabled differing reconstructions of Israel's history before the monarchy to be made.

In regard to the remainder of the books of the Bible, opinion was divided as to the historical value of Chronicles. The prophetic books were everywhere in critical circles interpreted historically, with the unity of authorship of books such as Isaiah and Zechariah denied. The poetic books (including what we now call the 'Wisdom Literature') were treated, in the spirit of Herder, as essentially poetic compositions. They will not figure in the present discussion.

By the time of the appearance of Wellhausen's *History of Israel* in 1878, the view presented above of the origin of the Pentateuch and Joshua had suffered radical alteration, with the result that Wellhausen was able to reconstruct Israelite religious history in a way that resembled the reconstructions of George and Vatke. The story of the development of Pentateuchal scholarship from Graf to Wellhausen has often been told, and it is not intended to reproduce it in detail here. Probably the best account that exists in English is that in the introduction to the English translation of the second edition of A. Kuenen's *An Historico-Critical Inquiry into the Origin and Composition of the Pentateuch* (1866).[1]

Karl Heinrich Graf's *The Historical Books of the Old Testament* appeared, according to Kuenen, in 1865, although dated 1866.[2] As Wellhausen observed,[3] it was similar to de Wette's *Contributions* in that it consisted of two parts, the second (pp. 114–257) dealing with the books of Chronicles, the first dealing with Genesis to the end of 2 Kings. Like de Wette, Graf argued for the untrustworthiness of Chronicles in order to remove the support of that book for the view of Israelite religion that saw priestly-levitical institutions as dating at least from Solomon. Graf's two main contributions were first, that he denied the unity of the so-called *Grundschrift*, and argued that its legislation was *later* than that of the book of Deuteronomy. Second, he argued that the work of the Deuteronomist had consisted of combining the *narrative* parts of the *Grundschrift* and the whole of the Yahwist with Deuteronomy and Deuteronomic material. The *priestly* material, composed in imitation of the style of the narrative parts of the *Grundschrift*, was added *after* the Exile.

The next major development is usually held to be T. Nöldeke's essay, 'The so-called *Grundschrift* of the Pentateuch', in his book *Investigations in the Criticism of the Old Testament* (1869).[4] Nöldeke's main aim was to re-establish the unity of the *Grundschrift* which Graf had disputed, and Nöldeke attempted this by a painstaking analysis of the Pentateuch. He also argued that the *Grundschrift* as a whole was pre-exilic, appealing to what he took to

---

[1] For useful accounts, including that of Kuenen, see R. Kittel, *Geschichte der Hebräer*, 1, Gotha 1888, pp. 33–9 (history of criticism up to Graf), 39–43 (criticism since Graf) (ET, *History of the Hebrews*, London 1895 (vol. 1), pp. 36–43, 43–8); E. Riehm, *Einleitung in das Alte Testament*, 1, Halle, 1889, pp. 145–65; A Kuenen, *An Historico-Critical Inquiry into the Origin and Composition of the Hexateuch*, London 1886, pp. xi–xl.

[2] K. H. Graf (1815–69) studied in Strasbourg under Reuss (see n8 below). He did not gain a university post, and spent his life as a schoolmaster. His *Die geschichtlichen Bücher des Alten Testaments. Zwei historisch-kritische Untersuchungen*, Leipzig 1866, is generally regarded as providing a new impetus in Old Testament criticism. For Kuenen's comment about the date of appearance of the book, see *An Historico-Critical Inquiry*, p. xix.

[3] J. Wellhausen, *Geschichte Israels*, 1, Berlin 1878, p. 4, n1. This observation is lacking in the second edition, *Prolegomena zur Geschichte Israels*, Berlin 1883.

[4] Theodor Nöldeke, *Untersuchung zur Kritik des Alten Testaments*, Kiel 1869; pp. 1–144 are the essay, 'Die s.g. Grundschrift des Pentateuchs'. Nöldeke (1836–1930) was professor of Oriental Languages at Kiel (1864–72) and Strasbourg (1873–1906).

be references to the *Grundschrift* in Amos and Hosea.[5] His view of the *order* of the redaction of the sources was roughly the standard critical view: (1) *Grundschrift*; (2) Yahwist (incorporating the second Elohist); (3) a redactor who combined (1) and (2); (4) the Deuteronomist who added his material to (3). On the *dating* of the sources, as opposed to the *order* of their redaction, Nöldeke allowed that it could not be proved that the *Grundschrift* was the oldest.[6]

By 1869, the following choices *vis-à-vis* the *Grundschrift* existed: *either* it was a unity, in which case it was either early (say, tenth–ninth centuries) or post-exilic; *or* it was not a unity, in which case its *narratives* were early and its *laws* were post-exilic. So far, the only possibility that had not received serious support was that it was a unity and was post-exilic. This possibility now came to be championed.

In Germany, the first person to do so was August Kayser, in his *The Pre-Exilic Book of Israel's Earliest History and its Expansions* (1874) in which it was maintained that 'the Elohistic document, the so-called *Grundschrift*, was composed in its entirety (historical and legislative portions alike) after the return from the captivity'.[7] Kayser, like Graf, had been a student of the eminent scholar from Alsace, Edouard Reuss,[8] who had entertained and taught the possibility that the priestly law was post-exilic, as early as 1834.

[5] Nöldeke, pp. 138 ff. With Hos. 1.3, he compared Lev. 19.29.

[6] ibid., p. 141. 'Auf keinen Fall darf man die Forderung aufstellen, dass die Grundschrift von allen ausführlichen Quellen des Pentateuchs gerade die älteste sein sollte. Recht wohl möglich ist das immerhin, aber erwiesen ist es noch nicht.'

[7] August Kayser, *Das vorexilische Buch der Urgeschichte Israels und seine Erweiterungen*, Strasbourg 1874. The mention of Germany in the text is a reminder that the scope of the present book precludes detailed references to scholars such as Kuenen and Reuss. The contribution of A. Kuenen (1828–91) is described fully by S. J. de Vries, *Bible and Theology in the Netherlands*, Cahiers bij het Nederlands Theologisch Tijdschrift 3, Wageningen 1968, pp. 65 ff. (For Kuenen as a whole, see pp. 56–76). It was Kuenen who, convinced by Colenso's *Pentateuch*, Pt 1, and Graf's *Die geschichtlichen Bücher*, proposed privately to Graf that the *whole* of the *Grundschrift* was post-exilic. Graf proceeded to advocate this view in *Archiv für die wissenschaftliche Erforschung des Alten Testaments* 1 (1869), pp. 466–77, without acknowledging his indebtedness to Kuenen.

[8] Edouard Reuss (1804–91) was born in Strasbourg, but studied *inter alia* in Göttingen (under Eichhorn) and Halle (under Gesenius and Tholuck). In 1834 he became the equivalent of an *ausserordentlicher* Professor at the Protestant Theological Faculty in Strasbourg. As early as 1834, he advocated the view that the law was later than the prophets, but did not publish his findings, because of the outcry over Vatke's *Biblical Theology*. His twelve theses are set out in Wellhausen's *Prolegomena*, p. 4, n1, of which two give the essence of his position: (6) Les prophètes du 8e et du 7e siècle ne savent rien du code mosaïque; (10) Ezéchiel est antérieur à la rédaction du code rituel et des lois qui ont définitivement organisé la hiérarchie. According to Kittel, *Geschichte der Hebräer*, 1, p. 39, Reuss had expressed his opinions in 1850 in his article, 'Judentum' in Ersch and Gruber's *Allgemeine Encyclopädie* sect. 2, vol. 27. On Reuss, see further Ch. Th. Gérold, *La Faculté de Théologie et le Seminaire protestant de Strasbourg 1803–72*, Strasbourg and Paris 1923, pp. 140 ff.

Kuenen, in his valuable survey, mentions the importance of Bernhard Duhm's *The Theology of the Prophets as the Basis for the inner History of the Development of Israelite Religion* (1875) in the discussion as a whole.[9] Duhm's basic view was that for the religion of Israel to develop, there were needed individuals who were sensitive to the divine leading. These were the prophets, and they were to be studied not as though they were dependent upon the Mosaic theocracy, but as prior to the theocracy in its developed form. Deuteronomy was an embodiment of the prophetic teaching of Hosea and Isaiah, not a reworking of earlier priestly legislation; from which it followed that the priestly legislation was *post*-exilic.

It was left to Julius Wellhausen to give expression to what Kayser and Duhm were saying in Germany, and to what others were saying elsewhere, and to give it such forceful and brilliant expression that a 'paradigm shift' began to be established.[10]

It is usual, in descriptions of this period, to make passing reference to Wellhausen's articles, published in 1876–7 in the *Yearbooks for German Theology* on the composition of the Hexateuch, and to concentrate instead upon his *History of Israel* of 1878.[11] Yet it is arguable that the articles are as important as the *History*, if not more important, and brief examination of them here will not only show how Wellhausen argued on critical grounds for the relative dating of the sources; it will indicate the degree of flexibility that he allowed, and which was further refined by subsequent scholarship.

Wellhausen began his investigation by considering Genesis 1—11,[12] and by isolating the *Grundschrift*, which he here called 'Q'—an abbreviation of the Latin *quatuor* (four) because he held the source to contain four covenants

---

[9] Kuenen, op. cit., p. xxxv, B. Duhm, *Die Theologie der Propheten als Grundlage für die innere Entwicklungsgeschichte der Israelitischen Religion*, Bonn 1875. Duhm (1847–1928) studied in Göttingen and was an *ausserordentlicher* Professor in Göttingen 1877–89, when he succeeded R. Smend in Basel, remaining there until his death.

[10] On Wellhausen, see, in addition to the standard works, R. Smend, 'Julius Wellhausen (1844–1918)' in *Theologen des Protestantismus im 19. und 20. Jahrhundert*, Stuttgart 1978, pp. 166–80. See also Smend's articles, 'Wellhausen in Greifswald', *ZThK* 78 (1981) pp. 141–76; 'Wellhausen und das Judentum', *ZThK* 79 (1982) pp. 249–82; also the article in Issue 24 of *Semeia*, which number is wholly devoted to 'Julius Wellhausen and his "Prolegomena to the History of Israel"'. Wellhausen (1844–1918) was professor at Greifswald (1872–82), Privatdozent and *ausserordentlicher* Professor at Halle (1882–5), professor of Semitic Languages at Marburg (1885–92) and professor of Oriental Languages at Göttingen (1892–1918).

[11] J. Wellhausen, articles (1876–7) in *Jahrbuch für Deutsche Theologie*, 21 (pp. 392–450; 531–602); 22 (pp. 407–79); reprinted in *Die Composition des Hexateuchs und der historischen Bücher des Alten Testaments*, 1889. Reference is here made to the 4th edition, Berlin 1963. Wellhausen had completed the material contained in the articles, probably in 1875.

[12] Wellhausen, *Composition*, pp. 2–14.

(*Vierbundesbuch*).[13] The isolation of the *Grundschrift* in Gen. 1—11 was generally agreed by critical scholars. Turning to what remained, the material of the Jehovist,[14] Wellhausen argued that this material was not a unity. Its basic core was Genesis 2.4b—3.24; 4.16–24; 11.1–9. To this had been added the Jehovist account of the Flood in Genesis 6—10, as well as 4.25 ff.; 5.29; 4.1–15; 10.16–18a. Even then, the Jehovist material was not in its final form. The Flood story, for example, had suffered from later additions. Wellhausen thus advocated a *supplementary* view of the growth of the Jehovist material in Genesis 1—11. The Jehovist in these chapters did not arise out of the combination of sources, but out of additions on two or more occasions of supplementary material to the core: Genesis 2.4b—3.24; 4.16–24; 11.1–9. A vital conclusion from this argument was that it was not the case that the Jehovist had supplemented the *Grundschrift*. The Jehovist material had had its own complex literary history, and when that had been completed, a redactor had combined the Jehovist with the *Grundschrift* of Gen. 1—11.

In chapters 12—16 of Genesis,[15] Wellhausen found evidence of the existence of Hupfeld's younger Elohist, an originally complete and independent work which ran parallel with the Yahwist. This source (E) was particularly distinct in Genesis 20—2. It had been combined with the Yahwist source by the Jehovist,[16] but not before the Yahwist source itself had suffered various interpolations. A conspicuous example of an interpolation in the Yahwist source before it was combined with E was Gen. 12.10—20. Thus for these chapters (12–26) Wellhausen advocated a Yahwistic core which had been *supplemented*, before it was combined with E. The redactor of J and E, the Jehovist, was to be distinguished from the redactor who combined this material with the *Grundschrift*.

In the analysis of chs. 27—36,[17] Wellhausen went a step further. In chs. 25.19—28.22, excluding 26.1–33, the Yahwist and Elohist accounts had been woven together so closely *that it was often impossible to disentangle them*. This could only be achieved with confidence when the divine name was present. This led to the important conclusion that the manner of the redaction together of the Yahwist and Elohist strands was different from

---

[13] Wellhausen does not himself use the term *Grundschrift*. I have used it so as to try to make it clear how Wellhausen's discussion related to the findings of scholarship prior to Wellhausen. As will become clear, Wellhausen did not regard the *Grundschrift* as the work of one author. Its core, 'Q', underwent various expansions before it was combined with other material to form the *Grundschrift*, or Priestly Code (P), as it is now usually called.

[14] Wellhausen distinguishes between the Yahwist (J), a mainly narrative source, which uses the name Yahweh for God, the Elohist (E) a source similar to J, which uses the name Elohim for God, and the Jehovist (JE), who combined J and E into a single work.

[15] ibid., pp. 15–29.

[16] See n14 above.

[17] ibid., pp. 29–50.

the manner of their combination with the *Grundschrift*, and this confirmed the point that J and E were combined together *before* a redactor combined them with the *Grundschrift*.[18]

For the remainder of his discussion of the *narrative* sections of the Pentateuch and Joshua,[19] Wellhausen continued to argue that the originally separate Yahwist and Elohist strands had been combined into a single work before their combination with the *Grundschrift*. A new point was the stress on the freedom with which the combination of J and E had been carried out.[20] In the section dealing with the law-giving at Sinai, Wellhausen described the redactor of J and E as an *author* (*Verfasser*) rather than a mere combiner.[21]

Wellhausen's view of the origin of the so-called *Grundschrift* was very sophisticated. He distinguished between Q—the book of the four covenants (*Vierbundesbuch*)—and the Priestly Code, which latter was the *Grundschrift* in its final form. Q was a narrative source, found especially in Genesis; but it also contained legal material, for example, in Exodus 25—9, and Leviticus 9.[22] It had been subject to enlargements, before it was incorporated with earlier and later material to form the Priestly Code (i.e., the *Grundschrift*). How Wellhausen envisaged the composition-history of the Priestly Code will now be sketched briefly, and of necessity inadequately, granted the intricate detail of Wellhausen's investigation.

Wellhausen did not go into great detail about how Q had been enlarged and re-edited in its *narrative* and non-legal sections, but he gave as an example of how Q was enlarged before it became part of the Priestly Code, a discussion of Genesis 1.1—2.4a.[23] He held that the original form of Q had described the creation of mankind in *seven* not six days, in the following order: *day (1)*, light and darkness; *day (2)*, division of waters; *day (3)*, creation of plants; *day (4)*, creation of the stars; *day (5)*, creation of fishes and birds; *day (6)*, creation of mammals; *day (7)*, creation of man. The account as a whole probably began, 'And the earth was waste and void . . .'.

Wellhausen's main concern was with the legal and cultic parts of Q, which these he began to investigate closely beginning at Exodus 25. The section Exodus 25 to Leviticus 9, had as its basic core Exodus 25—9 and

---

[18] See the important summary, p. 50.

[19] ibid., pp. 58–134.

[20] ibid., p. 72: 'Man sieht: so wenig sich in JE Ex. 1—11 die Scheidung ins Einzelne hinein durchführen lässt, so ist doch die Tatsache evident, dass dies Geschichtswerk auch hier wie in der Genesis aus J und E zusammengesetzt ist, durch die Hand eine Bearbeiters, der viel freier mit seiner Vorlage verfuhr und sie dadurch viel mehr zu einem Ganzen verschmolz, als es der letzte Redaktor mit Q und JE getan hat.'

[21] ibid., p. 94: 'Der Jehovist ist hier mehr als Redaktor, er kann als der eigentliche Verfasser des Abschnittes von der Gesetzgebung auf Sinai gelten.'

[22] ibid., pp. 134–49.

[23] ibid., pp. 184–6.

Leviticus 9, containing the instructions to build the Tent of Meeting and to institute its rites. Exodus 35—9 were a later reproduction of chs 25—9, with the tabernacle as the chief object of concern. Chs. 30—1 were a later addition to chs. 25—9, but they were earlier than chs. 35—9. From Leviticus 9, the original core of Q continued with 10.1–5, 12—15, and ch. 16. Wellhausen was uncertain whether the author of 10.1–5, 12—15 had himself included the independent chs 11—15, or whether these chapters had been added by another hand.

The discussion of Leviticus 17—26 was very important.[24] Wellhausen maintained that these chapters were older than Q and thus independent of them, but that they had been added to the Priestly Code *after* Q had been incorporated in the Code. As arguments for Leviticus 17—26 being older than Q, Wellhausen adduced, among other arguments, the fact that Leviticus 17.1–9 stood closer to Deuteronomy in its attitude to the centralization of the cult than to Q. Also, Leviticus 17.1–9 differed from Q in the matter of so-called secular slaughtering. Again, Leviticus 26, which was by the author of the collection Leviticus 19—25 had close affinities with Ezekiel and with Deuteronomy 28. That Leviticus 19—26 had been added to the Priestly Code, after Q had been incorporated into the Code, was proved by Leviticus 24.1–9, where there were remains of Q. It was clear that in this part of the Priestly Code, Q material had been excised in favour of Leviticus 17—26, although traces of Q remained at this point.

These complicated literary examinations began to establish the following dating for the Priestly Code. If Leviticus 17—26 was older than Q but from the time of the Exile because of its similarities with Ezekiel, and if Q had passed through various editions before being incorporated into the Priestly Code, then a thoroughly post-exilic date was established for the emergence of the Priestly Code in its final form. This conclusion was hinted at in Wellhausen's examination of Numbers 1—10, 15—19 and 26—36,[25] but there was still to come Wellhausen's demonstration of the view that Deuteronomy was combined with the Jehovist work before the resultant JE + D was incorporated into the Priestly Code.

On Deuteronomy,[26] Wellhausen posited a first edition of the book (chs. 12—26), which was enlarged into two independent editions: (a) chs. 1—4, 12—26, 27; (b) chs. 5—11, 12—26, 28—30. These two editions were subsequently combined together into the JE + D work. Otherwise, Wellhausen argued strongly that the narrative parts of Deuteronomy were

---

[24] ibid., pp. 149–72.
[25] ibid., pp. 172–84.
[26] ibid., pp. 186–208.

entirely dependent upon JE, and knew nothing of the narrative sections of P.[27]

At the end of his literary investigations, Wellhausen had reached the today familiar formulation of the Documentary Hypothesis: JE, D and P in that order of composition. However, to state this result without qualification is grossly unfair to Wellhausen, and is the reason why the description here of the contents of the *Composition of the Hexateuch* has been as full as it is, if at the same time, inadequate. Wellhausen, the great advocate of the Documentary Hypothesis (as he has come to be viewed in the history of Old Testament criticism), in fact allowed value to the *supplementary* hypothesis in that he envisaged that both J and E had undergone supplementation, so that it was not J^1 and E^1 that had been combined into the JE work, but J^3 and E^3.[28] Q had similarly undergone supplementation. Wellhausen's view of the redaction process was an attempt to get away from the idea of a redactor as a mechanical fitter-together of materials in a scissors-and-paste sort of operation. The redactor was often an author, and as a result, it was often not possible to distinguish between J and E.

Wellhausen remained true to this very sophisticated view of the origin of the Pentateuchal sources, and it underlies his famous *History of Israel*. The only main respect in which he modified his views was with regard to material in the second half of Numbers and in Joshua, which he could not assign either to JE or to Q, but which stood somewhere between them.[29] Kuenen, in articles published between 1877 and 1884[30] addressed himself to some of these problems, and suggested that these passages were *supplements* to the tradition in the spirit of Q by someone who, however, was open to the outlook of JE + D. On the whole, Wellhausen was not unhappy with this further blow against the idea that the Hexateuch had arisen by the mechanical combination of sources.[31]

[27] ibid., p. 198: '. . . bei den Erzählungen, welche sowohl in JE als auch in Q vorhanden sind, befolgt das Deuteronomium in allen Fällen, wo man eine deutliche Differenz zwischen JE und Q constatiren kann, immer die Version von JE. Die Kundschafter gehn von Kades aus, nicht von der Wüste Pharan, sie gelangen bis nach Hebron, nicht bis beinah nach Hamath, Kaleb gehört zu ihnen, nicht aber Josua. Die Meuterer von Num. 16 sind die Rubeniten Dathan und Abiram, nicht Korah und die Leviten. Nach der Niederlassung im Ostjordanland hat das Volk es mit Moab und Ammon, aber nicht mit Midian zu tun . . .'

[28] ibid., p. 207.

[29] ibid., p. 208: 'In der zweiten Hälfte des Buches Numeri und im Buche Josua tritt ein Element auf, das unentschieden zwischen JE und Q schwebt und sich nicht recht bestimmen lässt.'

[30] The articles are listed by Wellhausen, ibid., p. 314, and appeared in the *Leidener Theologische Tijdschrift*.

[31] Wellhausen, ibid., p. 315, n1 reiterated what he had written in his *Text der Bücher Samuelis* (1871); 'Auf eine so mechanische Weise, wie man es sich jetzt im Gegensatz zu Ewald gewöhnlich vorstellt, sind überhaupt die geschichtlichen Bücher des Alten Testaments nicht entstanden. Auch im Pentateuch sind nicht zwei oder mehrere grosse geschichtliche Zusammenhänge, die den selben Gegenstand haben, ursprünglich unabhängig von einander

The articles on the 'composition of the Hexateuch' became the foundation for Wellhausen's great work, *The History of Israel*. This appeared in 1878 as the first of two intended volumes. However, since it dealt with the history of the cult and the history of the traditions, it was renamed *Prolegomena to the History of Israel* when it appeared in 1883 in its second edition. Wellhausen wrote a brief sketch of the history of Israel in 1880, and published it privately.[32] This resembled closely the article that appeared in 1881 in the ninth edition of the *Encyclopedia Britannica*.[33] His large *Israelite and Jewish History* appeared in 1894.[34]

In the *History/Prolegomena to the History of Israel*,[35] Wellhausen drew together many ideas that had been suggested by de Wette, Gramberg, George, Vatke and others, and presented them, in combination with his own literary view of the origin of the Hexateuch, in such brilliant fashion that his book has ever since marked a 'before' and 'after' in Old Testament criticism. He disposed of the historical reliability of Chronicles, and, freed of Chronicles,[36] he drew upon Samuel, Kings and the prophetic books to reconstruct the history of Israelite sacrifices and priesthood in a manner very reminiscent of Vatke and George. In describing how, before Josiah's reform, there was much freedom of worship and little priestly regulation, he reiterated, in effect, de Wette's dictum that, in this period, 'each meal [was] a sacrifice, each festive and important event a festival, and each prophet, king and father of a household was without further qualification a priest'.[37] Josiah's reform began the path to conformity, but it was the destruction of the Temple and the Exile that were really crucial. In Ezekiel one saw something of the movement towards the triumph of the priestly over the prophetic, and the Priestly Code and its back-projection of priestly religion to the time of Moses marked, together with Chronicles, the complete triumph of the priestly.[38]

---

geschrieben, so dass der spätere von dem früheren keine Notiz nimmt. Vielmehr an einen Kern, in welchem zum ersten male [*sic*] die bis dahin vereinzelten Geschichten an einander gefügt wurden, setzten sich teils kleinere Stücke an, teils wurde das Ganze im Zusammenhange neu bearbeitet . . .'

[32] It is reprinted in Julius Wellhausen, *Grundrisse zum Alten Testament*, ed. R. Smend, *TB* 27, Munich 1965, pp. 13–64.

[33] Art.: Israel, *Encyclopedia Britannica*, 9 (1881), pp. 396–431.

[34] *Israelitische und Jüdische Geschichte*, Berlin 1894.

[35] Reference is here made to *Prolegomena zur Geschichte Israels*, Berlin 1927[6], ET, *Prolegomena to the History of Israel*, Edinburgh 1885, repr. Cleveland 1957.

[36] *Prolegomena*, pp. 165–223; English pp. 171–227.

[37] See above p. 32, and *Prolegomena*, p. 74; English, p. 76.

[38] *Prolegomena*, pp. 419–20; English, p. 421: 'Ezechiel hat zuerst den Weg eingeschlagen, auf den die Zeit wies. Er ist das Mittelglied zwischen Prophetie und Gesetz . . . Von Natur ist er ein Priester, und sein eigenstes Verdienst ist, daß er die Seele der Prophetie eingeschlossen hat in den Körper eines auf den Tempel und den Kultus begründeten, unpolitischen Gemeinwesens.'

However, the *Prolegomena/History* does not deal only with sacrifices, festivals and priesthood. In the section on the history of tradition, Wellhausen brought forward further points in order to support his contention that P represented the last, developed phase of Israelite religion. On the question of mythological elements in myths, Wellhausen rejected the de Wettian (Friesian) view that myths were indications of *lateness*.[39] Wellhausen compared the mythological elements in J—appearance of angels, or of God 'in' human beings—with the demythologized state of the P narratives. For Wellhausen, the contrast demonstrated P's lateness and the early nature of J.

Again, it was clear to Wellhausen that behind the written sources J and E was oral tradition. This was not the case with P. The very summary and cryptic nature of P narrative made it clear that P was a summary of *written* narratives, and thus from a later period of Israel's history.[40]

The importance of Wellhausen's work up to 1878–83 (that is, including his articles on the composition of the Hexateuch) can be summarized as follows: (1) he argued on literary grounds, probably more effectively than anyone hitherto, for the post-exilic date of composition of the *Grundschrift* (P); (2) he reasserted a documentary hypothesis, for all that he allowed that documentary sources could be, and had been, subject to *supplementation*; (3) he established the order of composition JE, D, P for his three main sources, and he correlated these three sources with three main periods of Israelite cultic development: JE = period of the divided monarchy; D = seventh century and period of Josiah's reform; P = period of the return from the Exile and later. The strength, and originality of Wellhausen's work lay in the interlocking of the Pentateuchal sources and the periods of Israel's cultic and religious development. These results were not, in my opinion, the outcome of Hegelian philosophical influence. They are to be understood from within the stream of German critical scholarship of the nineteenth century. The importance of the articles on the composition of the Hexateuch cannot be overlooked. It was the literary-critical results that were presented there that were the foundation of Wellhausen's position, and anyone who wishes to try to refute him must begin there, and not with points taken from the *Prolegomena/History*.

The third part of Wellhausen's work on Old Testament criticism to be

---

[39] *Prolegomena*, p. 295; English, p. 296, where Wellhausen accepts that P. K. Buttmann, *Mythologus, oder gesammelte Abhandlungen über die Sagen des Alterthums*, 1, Berlin, 1828, pp. 121 ff, was correct over against de Wette on the greater age of the Jehovist. In the section beginning on p. 295 (English p. 296), Wellhausen argues that the Jahwist (J) contains many more mythological elements than the Priestly Code.

[40] *Prolegomena*, p. 334; English, p. 336: 'Was uns im Priestkodex geboten wird, ist die Quintessenz nicht der mündlichen, sondern der bereits schriftlich gewordenen Überlieferung. Und zwar ist die schriftliche Fixierung der Vorgeschichte, welche benutzt wird, das jehovistische Erzählungsbuch.'

mentioned here are the treatments of Israelite history mentioned above.[41] Of these, not a great deal needs to be said. For Wellhausen, the traditions about Abraham, Isaac and Jacob contained no historical information about the pre-Mosaic period, but served, among other things, to justify the cultic practices of the ninth–eighth centuries BC at various sanctuaries.[42] Wellhausen accepted that Moses had in some sense been the founder of Israelite religion, although no actual biblical evidence could be dated to his times.[43] The unity that the tribes that made up Israel possessed was not a unity imposed by the giver of a law or the founder of institutions. It was a 'natural' unity, founded upon kinship.[44] If Moses had given to the Israelites a unity, it was a unity based upon the slogan: Yahweh the God of Israel, Israel the people of Yahweh.[45] The crossing of the Red Sea was not impossible; more certain was the wandering across the desert to the land of Canaan.[46] After the occupation of the land, the people grew in size by assimilation of Canaanite elements. From the Philistine oppression to the rise of the monarchy and its aftermath, Wellhausen's history followed the lines which have become broadly familiar in critical histories of Israel.

Following the publication of Wellhausen's works up to 1878–83, a Wellhausen 'school' began to emerge, as scholars of roughly his own age accepted, promulgated, and enlarged upon the views which he had so brilliantly defended. Among the more significant supporters were Bernhard Duhm, whose book on the prophets (1875) had played its own part in

---

[41] See nn32—4 above.

[42] *Prolegomena*, pp. 29 ff, esp. pp. 31–2; English p. 32. 'Dies alles ist nur zu verstehn als eine Verklärung der Verhältnisse and Einrichtungen des Kultus, wie wir sie etwa in den ersten Jahrhunderten des geteilten Reiches antreffen. Was einer späteren Zeit anstössig und heidnisch erscheint, wird hier durch Jahve selbst und seine Lieblinge geweiht und autorisirt, die Höhen, die Malsteine (Masseboth), die Bäume, die Brunnen.'

[43] *Israelitische und Jüdische Geschichte*, p. 16: 'Das Gesetz reicht nicht von ferne an die mosaische Zeit heran. Wenn dem so ist, so gibt es keine direkten literarischen Quellen, aus denen der Mosaismus auch nur so zu erkennen wäre wie etwa die Lehre Jesu aus den Evangelien.' p. 27: 'ohne einen leitenden Geist kann die Volksbildung unter der Ägide Jahves nicht vor sich gegangen sein. Er war der Anfänger der Thora, die nach ihm von den Priestern fortgesetzt wurde. Er hat nichts 'Positives', ein für allemal Fertiges hinterlassen, kein Gesetz, keine Verfassung für alle Zukunft gegeben. Aber er hat die Anforderungen der Gegenwart in einer Weise befriedigt, daß die Gegenwart eine Zukunft haben konnte.' See further the illuminating work by R. Smend, *Das Mosebild von Heinrich Ewald bis Martin Noth*, BGBE 3, Tübingen 1959.

[44] *Israelitische und Jüdische Geschichte*, pp. 20 ff., esp. p. 20: 'Es wurde keine neue Verfassung durch Moses eingeführt, sondern die alte blieb . . . Sie gründet sich auf das Blut, es ist ein System von Familien, Sippen, Geschlechtern und Stämmen.'

[45] ibid., p. 23. See also the 1880 sketch (n32 above), p. 16.

[46] ibid., pp. 11 ff.

preparing the way for Wellhausen's synthesis,[47] Bernhard Stade,[48] of whose *History of Israel* Wellhausen wrote in a review that he could not criticize it without criticizing himself,[49] and Rudolf Smend, from 1889 working, like Wellhausen, in Göttingen.[50] In the 1830s, the positions of Gramberg, Vatke and George had made no headway. In 1888, R. Kittel could write of Wellhausen's views that they had set in motion a flood-tide of opinion that still flowed strongly.[51]

Probably one of the biggest differences between the 1830s and the 1880s was that, following Duhm and Wellhausen, a new generation of commentaries on the prophetic books was produced, which stressed the importance of the prophets in the development of Israelite religion. Also, by this time, the ranks had considerably thinned of those who wanted to treat the prophets as narrators of messianic forecasts. However, because of the large number of faculties in Germany, and the even larger number of professors and *Privatdozenten*, a wide range of opinion different from that of Wellhausen remained, and found expression. In the next paragraphs, four such alternative positions will be mentioned.

In a letter to his favourite pupil Wolf Wilhelm, Graf von Baudissin dated 25 May 1881, Delitzsch wrote that the cardinal question of Pentateuchal criticism was not the date of the composition of the Priestly Code, but its historical value:[52]

> If the historical account in P of things such as the Tent of Meeting, and the consecration of priests and Levites etc. are free didactic fiction, as opposed to tradition, then it is no longer of any interest when this pseudo-Isidor was written.

Baudissin, initially at any rate, took his mentor's advice to heart and in 1884

[47] Bernhard Duhm (1847–1928) studied in Göttingen under A. Ritschl, P. de Lagarde and H. Ewald. He was an *ausserordentlicher* Professor at Göttingen from 1877–89, and professor at Basel from 1889. He is best-known for his work on Isaiah 40—66, and the 'Suffering Servant' songs.

[48] Bernhard Stade (1848–1906) studied in Leipzig and Berlin, and was Professor at Giessen (1857–1906). He founded the *Zeitschrift für die alttestamentliche Wissenschaft*, in 1881. See R. Smend 'Bernhard Stade (1848–1906) Theologe' in H. G. Gundel and P. Moraw (eds.), *Giessener Gelehrte in der ersten Hälfte des 20. Jahrhunderts*, Lebensbilder aus Hessen, 2, Marburg 1982, pp. 913–24.

[49] See Smend, loc. cit., p. 918.

[50] Rudolf Smend (1851–1913) studied in Göttingen, Berlin and Bonn, and was professor in Basel (1881–9) and Göttingen (1889–1913).

[51] R. Kittel, *Geschichte der Hebräer*, 1, p. 43; English p. 47 (somewhat 'under-translated').

[52] Otto Eissfeldt and K. H. Rengstorf (eds.), *Briefwechsel zwischen Franz Delitzsch und Wolf Wilhelm, Graf Baudissin 1866–90*, Abhandlungen der Rheinisch-Westfälischen Akademie der Wissenschaft, 43, Opladen 1973, p. 470.

published a lecture entitled 'The present state of Old Testament scholarship'.[53] In the lecture, Baudissin accepted that P was published as a law book in the time of Ezra, but he refused to believe that the Exile and its aftermath could have occasioned the invention of the P rituals. He thus argued that P contained the pre-Exilic rituals of Jerusalem, which were *revived* and thus published after the Exile. Deuteronomy was not a law book produced by a priestly caste, but a much simpler law book based upon the practices of the cities of Israel and their high places. It was not to be seen as the linear predecessor of P, neither was it to be supposed that P and the law were the end-product of a development of Israelite religion that was initiated by the prophets. Prophetic, priestly and Deuteronomic religion were parallel developments. Baudissin warned against the temptation to see the development of Israelite religion in unilinear terms, a tendency which he saw as a hangover from the era of Hegelian influence.[54]

Baudissin's lecture did not attempt to oppose Wellhausen at the level of a detailed literary analysis of the Hexateuch. His was rather a position that owed its attractiveness to its very plausibility. The same can be said of the view found in 1888 in the first volume of Rudolf Kittel's *History of the Hebrews*, although Kittel's discussion is a good deal fuller, including a valuable survey of the origin of the so-called Graf–Wellhausen hypothesis. Like Baudissin, Kittel warned against the assumption that Israel's religion had developed unilinearly, he stressed the fundamental differences between the backgrounds of D and P, and he stressed the point that it would have been unlikely for there to be the large number of cultic innovations in the post-exilic era that the Graf–Wellhausen position supposed.

In his brief handling of the date of the Priestly Code, Kittel built upon a view that Wellhausen readily accepted, namely, that P had undergone various enlargements.[55] Kittel deployed this view in order to present a history of the composition of P that traced its earlier parts back to the tenth and ninth centuries, and its fundamental composition, including its narrative section, to the eighth century. Kittel criticized Wellhausen's disregard for Hezekiah's reform in the late eighth century, and saw that reform as a lower limit for the substantial composition of P. Later additions to P included Leviticus 17—26, and the final redaction of the Hexateuch occurred during the Exile.[56] In his reconstruction of the history of the Hebrews, Kittel was

---

[53] W. W. Graf von Baudissin, 'Der heutige Stand der alttestamentliche Wissenschaft' in G. Diegel, *Theologische Wissenschaft und pfarramtliche Praxis*, Giessen 1884, pp. 33–60. Baudissin (1847–1926) was professor in Strasbourg (1880–1), Marburg (1881–94) and Berlin (1894–1926). He was a leading expert in the comparative study of Semitic religions.

[54] Baudissin, p. 54.

[55] R. Kittel, *Geschichte der Hebräer*, pp. 96 ff; English, pp. 107 ff. Rudolf Kittel (1853–1929), who came from a Pietist background, and studied at Tübingen, was a professor at Breslau (1888–98) and Leipzig (1898–1929).

[56] ibid., p. 100; English, p. 111.

much more positive than Wellhausen as to what could be known about the Patriarchs and Moses,[57] and although he treated the books of Chronicles with reserve[58] and allowed that they had a discernible tendency, he also thought that they could be used on occasion to supplement the historical information in Samuel and Kings.

A year after the publication of the first volume of Kittel's *History*, there appeared the posthumous edition of Riehm's *Introduction to the Old Testament*, based upon lectures that he had delivered at Halle up to the time of his death in 1888.[59] If Baudissin and Kittel had touched only lightly on *literary* critical matters, the same could not be said of Riehm. In particular, he took issue with Wellhausen on one of the latter's most important points, namely, the different manner of combining together of J and E as opposed to the method of combining together of JE and P.[60] Riehm argued that the weaving together of J and E was not always as complete as Wellhausen implied. He did not dispute that there were occasions when it was virtually impossible to disentangle J and E; his point was that there were occasions when the identification of separable J and E material was relatively simple, for example in Genesis chs. 20—1; 40—2; 48. This fact allowed the very real possibility that J, E and the *Grundschrift* had been combined together on one and the same occasion. The fact that on occasions, it was impossible to separate J from E material was due to the great similarity in content between J and E, rather than proof of a separate redaction. Because the material in the *Grundschrift* was so different from that in J and E, the redactor could only attempt a mechanical rather than an artistic combining of the sources.

Riehm maintained that the *Grundschrift* came from the time of the early monarchy.[61] He did not believe that the exact method of the redaction of the Pentateuch could be proved conclusively, and he gave full, and fair, consideration to Wellhausen's views of the redaction process. Riehm's own preference was for the theory that J, E and the *Grundschrift* had been combined together, probably before the time of Hosea, and that the Deuteronomistic redaction had put the Pentateuch substantially into its extant form. However, if Wellhausen's view of the stages of redaction was correct, and the *Grundschrift* was combined with the JE + D work, this did not entail that the *Grundschrift* was late. JE + D would merely have been combined, in the time of Ezra, with an early pre-exilic priestly law code.[62]

---

[57] ibid., pp. 152 ff; English, pp. 168 ff.

[58] ibid., 2, pp. 197 ff; English, 2, pp. 213 ff.

[59] E. Riehm, *Einleitung in das Alte Testament*, 2 vols, Halle 1889. Riehm (1830–88) studied under Hupfeld in Halle, and succeeded to Hupfeld's chair in 1866, remaining in Halle until his death.

[60] Riehm, *Einleitung*, pp. 318 ff.

[61] ibid., p. 318.

[62] ibid., pp. 328–9.

Arguments very similar to those of Riehm were advanced by Dillmann in successive editions of his commentary on Genesis (1886[1]). What Wellhausen saw as different types and thus different stages of redaction as between J and E on the one hand, and JE and P on the other, Dillmann explained by the greater similarity between J and E, and the considerable difference of both from P.[63] The *Grundschrift*, although it had undergone enlargement in the exilic and post-exilic periods, belonged to the period of the Israelite monarchy.[64]

In critical circles in Germany, then, as the nineteenth century drew to a close, the *documentary* view of the origin of the Pentateuch had triumphed completely. Even conservative scholars, such as Delitzsch and König, had come to terms with a documentary approach. On the other hand, even the staunchest advocate of the documentary theory allowed that the sources had been supplemented, and thus it was not surprising that scholars, such as Karl Budde, began to divide the J source into J[1] and J[2].[65] The fundamental question that divided the critical scholars concerned the date of the *Grundschrift*. Did it originate from the period of the early monarchy or was it wholly post-exilic? The answer to this question provided the key to how the earliest history of Israel was to be regarded, especially the history of its cult and priesthood and the role of Moses. It also affected the interpretation of prophecy, and determined whether the prophets were to be seen in the context of a Mosaic theocracy, or as largely responsible for the growth in Israel of ethical monotheism.

As the century drew to a close, the Wellhausen 'school' began to become the predominant critical 'school'. In so doing, it helped to promote the development of the tendencies that were to become dominant in Old Testament scholarship in the first decades of the twentieth century.

The view of Israelite history, from de Wette to Wellhausen, that left a question mark over the period of the Patriarchs and of Moses, invited speculation about the pre-history of the Hebrews. Already in the early nineteenth century, scholars began to speculate about that pre-history on the basis of what was known about comparative religion. Wellhausen himself based his speculations upon the view that pre-Islamic bedouin traditions were the richest sources for knowledge of the religion and life of the earliest Hebrews.[66] But there were rival approaches, based upon the young science of Assyriology, and upon the so-called history of religions.

---

[63] Reference is here made to A. Dillmann, *Die Genesis*, *KEH* 1, Leipzig 1892[6], p. xix. Dillmann (1823–94) studied under Ewald, and was professor at Kiel (1860–4), Giessen (1864–9) and Berlin (1869–94).

[64] ibid., p. xi.

[65] K. Budde, *Die Biblische Urgeschichte*, Giessen 1883. Budde (1850–1935) was professor at Bonn (*ausserordentlicher*, 1879–89), Strasbourg (1889–1900) and Marburg (1900–21).

[66] See my *Anthropology and the Old Testament*, Oxford 1978, chs. 1–2.

The latter part of the nineteenth century saw the discovery of the history of Israel's great neighbours, Assyria and Babylon, saw the rise of the study of comparative mythology and its application to Old Testament studies, and saw a growing interest in the comparative study of literary forms.[67] In short, at the close of the nineteenth century, the study of the Old Testament had been put into the context of the study of the ancient world and of religion in general to an extent that had never been the case before.[68] Yet even in this respect, there was a circle that led back to de Wette and the early nineteenth century; for that scholar who had achieved the breakthrough which entailed that Old Testament studies could never again be the same had given lectures in Basel on the nature of religion.[69] He had been concerned with religion in general as part of the universal experience of mankind. He had tried to see how the Old Testament was a part of the religious heritage of mankind. Indeed, it was the discovery of what religion was to him that set in motion his own epoch-making contribution to Old Testament critical scholarship.

[67] See in addition to *Anthropology and the Old Testament*, my *Myth in Old Testament Interpretation*.

[68] See the excellent remarks in W. McKane, *Studies in the Patriarchal Narratives*, Edinburgh 1979, pp. 225 ff. This chapter contains a valuable account of the controversy between Wellhausen and Gunkel.

[69] *Ueber die Religion*.

20

England from 1880: the Triumph of Wellhausen

In 1880, the critical method still had only an apparently tenuous hold on English Old Testament scholarship.[1] By 1891, not only had the critical method begun to sweep all before it; indeed it had begun to do so in the form of an acceptance of the position of Wellhausen, albeit in a version congenial to English theology and philosophy. That it was remarkable that a position deriving from Wellhausen should have gained support will be appreciated when it is remembered that, prior to 1880, English critical scholarship had not at all welcomed any type of criticism that involved a radical reappraisal of the general outline of Israelite history as presented in the Old Testament itself.

The stages of the growth of the critical method in England in the years following 1880 can be plotted in more than one way. W. B. Glover, in his careful study of Old Testament criticism as it affected Evangelical Nonconformists, identifies the landmarks in terms of 1880, 1887 and 1890.[2] The procedure that will be followed in the present chapter will seek landmarks in terms of the development of the views of S. R. Driver.[3]

In November 1882, the death of E. B. Pusey brought to an end a tenure of the Regius Professorship of Hebrew at Oxford that had lasted for fifty-four years.[4] Driver was nominated to succeed Pusey, effectively beginning his work in the chair in October 1883.[5] Driver's position at the time of his appointment is best illustrated by an article published in 1882 in the *Journal*

[1] cf. W. B. Glover, *Evangelical Nonconformists and Higher Criticism in the 19th century* p. 36, who quotes Alfred Cave's opinion (1880) that 99% of biblical scholars in England, Scotland and America accepted the Mosaic authorship of the Pentateuch.

[2] Glover, pp. 157–62.

[3] The fullest exposition of Driver's development and views is to be found in Cheyne, *Founders of Old Testament Criticism*, pp. 248–372.

[4] Pusey died on 16 September 1882. See H. P. Liddon, *Life of E. B. Pusey*, p. 385.

[5] Samuel Rolles Driver (1846–1914), was educated at Winchester and at New College, Oxford, where he became a fellow from 1870 and tutor from 1875. In December 1881 he was ordained deacon in the Church of England. Because the holder of the Hebrew chair was required to be in priest's orders, his official appointment to the chair was made in January 1883, after Driver had been ordained to the priesthood. See J. W. Rogerson, 'Driver, Samuel Rolles (1846–1914)' in *TRE* 9, pp. 190–2.

of Philology and by a sermon preached before the University of Oxford on 21 October 1883. Of the two, the sermon was the more forthright, and was entitled 'Evolution compatible with Faith'.[6] It accepted that there were two creation accounts in Genesis each belonging to a different main document,[7] and it accepted that in some of their particulars, these accounts had not remained free from outside influence, especially that of Babylon.[8] However, Driver enunciated a very positive view of the inspiration and authority of the biblical accounts. Whatever the source of the materials employed by the biblical writers, and however the accounts might or might not relate to scientific views of the origin of the universe, they constituted an inspired narrative that taught that alike in its origin and in its growth, the universe was dependent upon God.[9] Although Scripture was amenable to criticism, at the level of the spiritual and moral truths which it taught, it was unassailable by criticism.

The 1882 article was a highly technical piece, displaying Driver's mastery of the Hebrew language, entitled 'On Some alleged linguistic Affinities of the Elohist'.[10] Basically, it examined an attempt by F. Giesebrecht to date the *Grundschrift* after the Exile on purely linguistic grounds. Driver's conclusion was that Giesebrecht's case was not proven, and his article contained many cogent points against Giesebrecht.[11] What is interesting about the article is that he shows how he was trying to come to terms with Wellhausen. At one point he rightly rejected one of Wellhausen's arguments;[12] but throughout the article he 'accepted Wellhausen's distinctions of sources', adding, 'without enquiring how far in particular cases it was justified'.[13] The aim of the article as a whole was not to try to disprove the view that the *Grundschrift* was written in or near the Exile; rather, Driver was simply investigating certain claims made upon linguistic grounds.

Granted the caution of his position in 1882–3, Driver's attitude was still

---

[6] It is reprinted in S. R. Driver, *Sermons on Subjects connected with the Old Testament*, London 1892, pp. 1–27.

[7] ibid., p. 1: 'These words [Gen. 2.7] are taken from the opening section of the two main documents, which have been interwoven with rare skill in our present Pentateuch, and which can be traced side by side to the close of the book of Joshua.'

[8] ibid., p. 3.

[9] ibid., p. 11: 'The object of that chapter is not to give an authoritative record of the history of the globe, but to show by, a series of representative pictures, that alike in its origin and in the stages through which it has passed it has been dependent upon the presence, and has given effect to the purposes, of Almighty God. Science, as such, cannot deny this. . . .'

[10] *Journal of Philology*, 11 (1882), pp. 201–35.

[11] Driver's remarks on the precarious nature of arguments about allegedly 'late' words are a good example of his sound and cautious judgement.

[12] op. cit., pp. 232–3, against Wellhausen's argument in *Geschichte Israels* p. 399 (*Prolegomena*, p. 386), that *rēšit* used temporally is an Aramaism.

[13] *Journal of Philology* 11, p. 233, n1.

worlds apart from that of his predecessor in the Oxford Hebrew chair. He was prepared to admit criticism and to consider the arguments of scholars who were vilified as dangerous rationalists by the orthodox. In a sermon preached in October 1885 on the ideals of the Prophets,[14] Driver, without committing himself or his hearers, 'to any theory of the growth of Hebrew historical literature',[15] nonetheless distinguished between the Priestly, the prophetic and the Deuteronomic streams of narrative in the Pentateuch. Two years later, in October 1887, in a sermon on the Hebrew Prophets,[16] we find him ascribing the 'inner progress' of the history of Israel to the activity of the prophets, the position first put so strikingly by Duhm in 1875. In 1891, with the publication of his *An Introduction to the Literature of the Old Testament*, Driver indicated his total acceptance of the Wellhausen position.[17] It was the most scholarly and most influential *Introduction* ever to be written by an Englishman, and it played no little part in advancing the critical cause in English Old Testament study.

We have traced, then, the growth of the critical method in England from 1880, using Driver as a sort of measuring-stick. What we have omitted is any reference to the fundamental importance of William Robertson Smith in this process. This will now be remedied.[18]

As has been noted above, Robertson Smith strictly falls outside the scope of the present book. He is to be seen in the context of the Free Church of Scotland in which he grew up and was educated, and in which he held a chair of Old Testament until his dismissal on the grounds of unorthodoxy in 1881. The present book is not the place to describe the influence of his great teacher A. B. Davidson,[19] nor to enquire into the politics of his

---

[14] In *Sermons on . . . the Old Testament*, pp. 50–71.

[15] ibid., p. 55.

[16] ibid., pp. 99–118.

[17] See also Driver's article in *Contemporary Review* 57 (1890), pp. 215ff; 'The Critical Study of the Old Testament'. The Wellhausen position is, apparently, outlined by Driver in *Critical Notes on the International Sunday School Lessons from the Pentateuch*, New York 1887 (not seen by me). The *Introduction to the Literature of the Old Testament*, Edinburgh 1891, appeared in 'The International Theological Library'.

[18] On Robertson Smith, see J. S. Black and G. Chrystal, *The Life of William Robertson Smith*, London 1912. A valuable list of his publications and of literature about him can be found in T. O. Beidelman, *W. Robertson Smith and the Sociological Study of Religion*, Chicago 1974. Smith (1846–94) studied in Aberdeen and Edinburgh, and was professor at the Free Church College, Aberdeen (1870–81), Lord Almoner Reader in Arabic, Cambridge (1883–9), University Librarian from 1886, and Sir Thomas Adams Professor of Arabic (1889–94). He was also a fellow of Christ's College from 1885.

[19] Andrew Bruce Davidson (1831–1902) was educated at Marischal College, Aberdeen, and New College, Edinburgh. He also studied under Ewald in Göttingen. From 1863 to his death he was a professor at New College, Edinburgh. Although a critical scholar, he did not enter into the controversy surrounding W. R. Smith's trial. A biographical sketch can be found in A. B. Davidson, *The Called of God*, Edinburgh 1902, pp. 1–58.

dismissal, and the part played in it by Principal Rainy.[20] Robertson Smith concerns us here on account of two books, published in 1881 and 1882, which presented the case for the critical study of the Old Testament, and for results that were deeply indebted to Wellhausen, but which did so in a manner which showed that there was nothing in this sort of criticism which was incompatible with Evangelical Christianity.[21] Indeed, this last sentence rather understates the case. One ought rather to say that for Robertson Smith's fervently-held Evangelical beliefs, a critical reading of the Old Testament in terms derived from Wellhausen was the only one which vindicated it as the Word of God. It is difficult to think of a book that has so profoundly combined critical insights with a type of Evangelical belief, as Robertson Smith's *The Old Testament in the Jewish Church*.

The importance of Robertson Smith's advocacy of a Wellhausenian position from an Evangelical standpoint cannot be over-estimated. It is true that the public lectures on which *The Old Testament in the Jewish Church* was based did not prevent his dismissal in May 1881. It will also be argued later in this chapter that the Anglican acceptance of Wellhausen rested on partially different theological grounds from those advocated by Robertson Smith. What the latter was doing, however, was meeting head on the objection that had been raised in Britain all through the nineteenth century against critical scholarship, namely, that it was rationalistic, and ultimately, a threat to the Christian faith.

Earlier chapters in this book have collected some of the verdicts passed upon the 'rationalism' of German criticism by orthodox English theologians. It has been noted, for example, in the case of Milman and the contributors to *Essays and Reviews*, that any mild inclination on the part of known liberals to the results of criticism could guarantee the concerted attacks of the orthodox. The cases of men such as Francis Newman, Samuel Davidson, and John William Colenso only seemed to prove the connection between criticism and unorthodoxy. Newman's penetrating work on the Hebrew monarchy was compromised by his *Phases of Faith*, Davidson moved closer to Unitarianism, and Colenso was a sort of universalist; and it was significant for the orthodox that Unitarians were always ready to accept and propagate critical views. Robertson Smith, in *The Old Testament in the Jewish Church* brought the whole issue of the relationship between criticism and faith to

[20] A list of material relating to the trial is provided by Beidelman, pp. 85–92. Robert Rainy was the Principal of the Free Church College in Aberdeen and is said to have sacrificed Smith in order to avoid the outlawing of criticism itself. See C. Simpson, *Life of Principal Rainy*, London 1909.

[21] W. Robertson Smith, *The Old Testament in the Jewish Church*, London 1881, 1892[2], to which reference is made; *The Prophets of Israel and their Place in History to the Close of the Eighth Century BC*, London 1882. These books represent public lectures given in Scotland at the time of Smith's trial.

the point where it was the traditionalists, not the liberals, who were called upon to show that they accepted the Old Testament as the Word of God in a realistic way.

Part of Robertson Smith's demonstration of his position depended upon the Old Testament text, and especially upon the divergences between the Hebrew and the Greek versions of Jeremiah and parts of 1 Samuel.[22] Robertson Smith argued that the Greek was, on the whole, superior to the Hebrew, although no fundamental tenet of faith was affected. The differences, however, showed that in considering the authorship of biblical books, attention had to be paid to ancient methods of compilation as witnessed by the evidence of the Hebrew and Greek versions, and that the argument could not be construed in terms of modern notions of authorship. The Jewish and Christian traditions about the authorship of biblical books could not be allowed to outweigh the internal evidence of the Bible itself. Biblical authorship was not different in kind from the editorial processes clearly evident in the Hebrew of Jeremiah, and thus, to ascribe parts of Isaiah or Zechariah to more than one prophet had nothing to do with the denial of inspiration or the supernatural.[23]

However, the real power of Robertson Smith's apologetic lay in his view of the nature of faith and of revelation. Here, he made it quite clear that for him, the heart of religion was a personal relationship with the living God. What God revealed was not doctrines, but himself. Faith was not intellectual assent, but trust and commitment. The purpose of the Bible was that its words should speak to the heart, through the agency of the Holy Spirit, so that the reader was brought to living faith in God.[24]

Viewed historically, the Old Testament was the record of how God had graciously dealt with the succeeding generations. It was a history of grace. From this, two things followed. First, revelation was gradual or progressive, in that God's encounter with each generation was in terms appropriate to the social and psychological situation of the generation. Second, and granting

---

[22] See *The Old Testament in the Jewish Church*, pp. 103–24.

[23] For the benefit of non-specialist readers it must be pointed out that the Greek version (translation) of Jeremiah is significantly shorter than the extant traditional Hebrew text. The latter has clearly expanded and elaborated a simpler *Vorlage*.

[24] See *The Old Testament in the Jewish Church*, p. 2: 'No tradition as to the worth of Scripture, no assurance transmitted from our fathers, or from any who in past time heard God's revealing voice, can make the revelation to which they bear witness a personal voice of God to us. The element of personal conviction, which lifts faith out of the region of probable evidence into the sphere of divine certainty, is given only by the Holy Spirit still bearing witness in and with the Word.'; cf. pp. 7–8, where Smith epitomizes Luther's teaching: 'The supreme value of the Bible does not live in the fact that it is the ultimate source of theology, but in the fact that it contains the whole message of God's love, that it is the personal message of that love *to me*, not doctrine but promise, not the display of God's metaphysical essence, but of his redeeming purpose . . .'

the first point, any exegesis of a text had to start from the concrete social, historical and psychological situation of the writer.[25]

This last point became a powerful weapon in Robertson Smith's treatment of those aspects of the Wellhausen position most likely to cause offence. In dealing with Chronicles, for example, he accepted that these books were unhistorical in their claim that the developed levitical system went back to the time of David. However, he shifted the focus away from the matter of historicity as conceived in modern terms, and instead sought to understand Chronicles in terms of the outlook of those who wrote it.[26] Again the apparent claim of certain parts of the Old Testament to be Mosaic when criticism judged that they were not was to be seen in the light of ancient beliefs in the authority of great religious figures; and Robertson Smith added the important argument that in the rabbinical period, no difficulty was found in regarding precepts that had been lately formulated, as part of the oral law delivered to Moses.[27]

The thrust of Robertson Smith's attempt to see criticism as a necessary part of theology lay, then, in his preference for a theology of experience over against dogmatic theologies that were intellectual systems. He believed profoundly that his was the position of the Lutheran Reformation.

A third factor that is implicit in *The Old Testament and the Jewish Church* and explicit in *The Prophets of Israel* (1882), was later to be expanded in his brilliant *Kinship and Marriage in Early Arabia* (1885) and *Lectures on the Religion of the Semites* (1889). This factor is the sociological factor, on the basis of which Robertson Smith believed that the earliest forms of Semitic, and thus Hebrew, religious life involved clans living in close fellowship with their clan god.[28] As I say, this is only implicit in the 1881 book, but it enabled Robertson Smith to give an account of the development of Israelite religion and sacrifice in Wellhausenian terms, but in harmony with his Evangelical beliefs. The key was the notion of 'access' to God, and Robertson Smith was able to contrast the awesome and developed levitical system with its access to God hedged about by the institutionalization of holiness, with a

---

[25] ibid., p. 99: 'There is a method in Revelation as much as in Nature, and the first law of that method, which no careful student of Scripture can fail to grasp, is that God's Revelation of himself is unfolded gradually, in constant contact with the needs of religious life. Every word of God is spoken for all time, but every word none the less was first spoken to a present necessity of God's people.'

[26] ibid., pp. 140–8. Robertson Smith states that the author of Chronicles can have had no knowledge of what conditions were like before the Exile, and that the books contain a mechanical conception of God's government of the world and of the speedy rewards or punishments that attend human actions.

[27] ibid., p. 313.

[28] See the discussion in my 'W. R. Smith: *Religion of the Semites*', *Expository Times* 90 (1979), pp. 288–33.

free access to God as described in the books of Samuel and Kings.[29] It was obvious that the latter view of access, and the spontaneous religion that accompanied it, was earlier than the levitical system. Yet Robertson Smith did not rush to make value judgements. The developed levitical system was as much an instance of the dispensation of grace in the Old Testament as was the religion of the earlier period. The levitical system was to be judged according to its time and place, that is, the exilic period, in which the Jews constituted a religious community centred upon the Jerusalem Temple. Although Robertson Smith could see the dangers of corrupted 'Judaism' or 'legalism', he had no place for the division of Old Testament religion into (good) pre-exilic religion and (bad) post-exilic religion.[30]

In *The Prophets of Israel* (1882) Robertson Smith addressed himself to the contribution made by the pre-exilic prophets to the development of Israelite religion. He placed the work of these prophets not in the context of the Mosaic theocracy, but in the context of general Semitic religion which the Israelites shared with their neighbours. It is here that we find the explicit references to early, Semitic religion, as evidenced, in particular, among 'primitive' peoples and pre-Islamic Arabs.

In the context of a form of religion in which access to God was simple and spontaneous, and in which it was easy to identify the God of Israel with a local Baal, the prophets shaped the religion of Israel by witnessing to the true nature of God. This did not mean that the prophets gave to Israel metaphysical doctrines about the nature of God. Rather, they witnessed to his character as a personal God, one actively involved in the historical fortunes of his people, the upholder of justice whose sovereignty gently weaned Israel away from supposing that he was there merely for the people's benefit and not vice versa.[31]

Thus, the brilliant speaking and writing of Robertson Smith made available in England as well as Scotland an apologetic for the critical method whose power and sincerity has scarcely, if ever, been matched. When, in 1885, an English translation of Wellhausen's *Prolegomena* was published, it was Robertson Smith who provided the introduction and who sought to ensure that the book would not be seen as an enemy of Christian faith.

Robertson Smith presented Wellhausen's *Prolegomena* as a book which could provide the historical key to the interpretation of the Old Testament,

---

[29] ibid., p. 248: 'Opportunity of access to Jehovah is near to every Israelite, and every occasion of life that calls on the individual, the clan, or the village, to look Godwards is a summons to the altar. In the family every feast was an eucharistic sacrifice.'

[30] ibid., p. 381.

[31] *The Prophets of Israel*, p. 70: 'The primary difference between the religion of Israel and that of the surrounding nations does not lie in the idea of a theocracy, or in a philosophy of the invisible world, or in the external forms of religious service, but in a personal difference between Jehovah and other gods.'

so that its 'wonderful literature' would become newly accessible to readers. The critical labours of generations of scholars had disclosed a false presupposition, with which the Old Testament had been constantly approached: that of supposing that Israel possessed the whole Pentateuchal law from the time of Moses. If the radical position of Wellhausen and many younger German scholars was accepted, that the law grew slowly, and that the prophets had transformed 'Old Israel' into something new, the true history of Israel could be recovered, and the providential hand of God could be seen anew in the process that led, through Judaism, to the gospel.[32]

From one point of view, Robertson Smith's advocacy of Wellhausen's results added little to what had been argued by liberal churchmen from Milman to Mozley. The idea of a progressive revelation or education had long been a key to the understanding of the Old Testament in liberal English circles, and Robertson Smith certainly argued for this, even if his primary concern was with each stage of religion as an example of living faith. Where he differed from the earlier liberals was in recasting progressive revelation, or the providential ordering of Israel's religious development, in terms of the Wellhausen as opposed to the Old Testament picture of Israel's history. What enabled him to adjust progressive revelation to the new critical picture, and what enabled many others to do the same from 1880 can best be described as 'the spirit of the age'.

From the 1870s, developmental or evolutionary ways of thinking made increasingly significant inroads into English intellectual thought. A neo-Hegelian school of philosophy, associated with names such as T. H. Green,[33] flourished in Oxford, while works such as E. B. Tylor's *Primitive Culture* (1871) and H. S. Maine's *Ancient Law* (1861) described the growth of human culture and institutions in developmental terms. In England in the 1880s, the time was ripe for the reception into Old Testament scholarship of the idea that the simpler was the earlier, and the more developed was the later. If this could be combined with a doctrine of divine providence, or progressive revelation, then the way was open *to that version of Old Testament criticism that was most amenable to presentation in developmental terms*—that of Wellhausen. It did not matter that Wellhausen himself was primarily a historian, and was urged by mainly inner-critical problems in the Pentateuch and historical books to his conclusions, and further, that he saw the Old Testament after the Exile as a process of *degeneration*. The important point was that the Wellhausen view fitted well into developmental thought, and if English critics shared Wellhausen's distaste for Israel's post-exilic form of cultic religion, they could always appeal to his observation that by becoming

[32] *Prolegomena to the History of Ancient Israel*, pp. v–x.
[33] Thomas Hill Green (1836–82), fellow of Balliol College, Oxford (1860–78), Whyte's Professor of Moral Philosophy (1878–82). See R. L. Nettleship, *Memoir of Thomas Hill Green*, London 1906.

encased in the hard shell of cult and legalism, the true religion of Israel had been protected against the heathenism of the post-exilic period.[34]

In the case of Robertson Smith, many more factors were at work in the formulation of his position than simply a developmentalist 'spirit of the age'. His contacts with Germany in his formative years,[35] and his deep admiration for scholars such as Richard Rothe, played an important part.[36] Nevertheless, his was the prophetic voice above all others that spoke out for the critical method.

Another scholar who must be mentioned briefly, and who is also significant as an important chronicler of the period is T. K. Cheyne.[37] Cheyne, like Robertson Smith, studied in Germany, and although at first he was an ardent follower of his teacher Ewald, he was one of the earliest English scholars to accept the post-exilic dating of the *Grundschrift*.[38] Prior to 1880, his work received little attention. In 1880, however, he adopted a more overtly Evangelical stance,[39] and for some years sought to show how criticism and faith could be reconciled and be mutually beneficial.[40] As one of the editors of the 'Theological Translation Fund Library' of Messrs Williams and Norgate, he was responsible for encouraging the translation of important German critical works. Some of his exegetical work on the prophetic books was hailed in Germany as well as Britain as being an outstanding contribution to scholarship.[41] Unfortunately, his brilliance seems to have been accompanied by an element of eccentricity which led him, from the turn of the century, to advocate increasingly absurd and fanciful critical theories.[42]

[34] See above, p. 265.

[35] In 1868, Smith visited Bonn; in 1869 he travelled to Göttingen to study Arabic.

[36] Richard Rothe (1799–1867) was professor at the *Predigerseminar* (theological seminary) in Wittenberg (1828–37), and a professor in Heidelberg (1837–67) apart from four years in Bonn. He combined deep religious convictions with an openness to studies which affected knowledge of the development and culture of mankind. There are numerous references to Rothe in Smith's lectures and essays. See, for example, the lecture 'Christianity and the Supernatural' in J. S. Black and G. Chrystal (eds.), *Lectures and Essays of William Robertson Smith*, London 1912, pp. 109–36.

[37] Thomas Kelly Cheyne (1841–1915), was a grandson of T. H. Horne, whose Introduction is discussed in chapter 13. He studied in Oxford, and in Göttingen under Ewald. He was a fellow of Balliol College from 1868, rector of Tendring (1880–5) and Oriel Professor at Oxford 1885–1908.

[38] According to A. S. Peake in *DNB* (1912–21) p. 119, Cheyne accepted what was then called the Grafian hypothesis in 1871.

[39] See Glover, *Evangelical Nonconformists and Higher Criticism*, p. 113.

[40] See his book *Aids to the Devout Study of Criticism*, London 1892.

[41] See the laudatory extracts from reviews on p. 447 of Robertson Smith's *The Prophets of Israel*, 1897[2], to which Cheyne wrote a preface.

[42] He was an advocate of the so-called North Arabian theory advanced by H. Winckler; see J. W. Rogerson, *Anthropology and the Old Testament*, p. 32. At the end of his life, he apparently embraced the Baha'i faith.

In England, as Robertson Smith in his Cambridge exile devoted his brilliant energies increasingly to Arabic and anthropological studies, it was S. R. Driver who became the leading advocate of a scholarly, cautious, yet totally committed Wellhausenian type of critical scholarship. Successive editions of his *Introduction* furthered the critical cause, while he became the British Old Testament editor of the International Critical Commentary, a scholarly series of the highest standards in which British and American scholars presented the critical method. Driver's own commentary on Deuteronomy in this series, published in 1895, indicated beyond all doubt the power of the critical school which had arisen in England.

Driver's theological position, if I understand it correctly, seems to have differed a little from that of Robertson Smith. Whereas Robertson Smith laid stress upon experiential knowledge of God, in which God revealed himself and not doctrines about himself, Driver seems to have seen revelation more in terms of information: information about the attributes of God and about his moral demands. If this is a correct presentation of Driver's position, then he conformed to the general Anglican position of the nineteenth century, which saw the Bible as divinely-communicated information. For the earliest liberals, the information concerned among other things the history of how God had established and guided the Jewish commonwealth. For Driver, who admitted the findings of science and of historical criticism, the information concerned the divine attributes, the lessons of human duty, and pointers to the coming of Christ.[43]

Driver distinguished between the *form* of revelation and its *content*. Criticism could not assail the latter; it was concerned only with the form of revelation, and its results enabled the scholar and his readers to arrive at an accurate view of exactly how God had revealed himself to his people. 'Criticism', he wrote, 'does not banish or destroy the inspiration of the Old Testament; it *presupposes* it'.[44]

Driver's view of Old Testament revelation as conveying *information* led, in some cases, to results which compare remarkably with the results of German criticism. Driver embraced a position which, while not directly attempting to reconcile the *details* of the early chapters of Genesis with scientific discoveries, nevertheless sought to reconcile with science and history the general drift of the biblical narrative. In his sermon, 'Evolution Compatible with Faith' (1883), he did not try to identify the 'days' of creation with geological eras. Nevertheless, he saw in the 'days' of creation 'a series of stages, each the embodiment of a Divine purpose, and the whole the realisation of a Divine plan'.[45] Again, in his Genesis commentary (1904),

[43] Driver, *Introduction*, 9th ed., p. ix. At this point, Driver is quoting from his introduction to the first edition (1891).
[44] ibid., p. xiii.
[45] *Sermons on . . . the Old Testament*, p. 23.

he interpreted the 'fall' of Genesis 3 in quasi-historical terms, in that he held the narrative to teach that at some point in the pre-history of mankind, a race or races had faced a moral choice, and had decided on the wrong choice.[46] These examples indicate that even with the adoption of the critical method in England, the English determination to see revelation primarily as information retained a strong grip on theological thinking, and led to the view that, in the Old Testament, divinely-inspired information was communicated which supplemented science and pre-history generally, if not in particular.

The publication, in 1889, of the famous set of essays entitled *Lux Mundi* indicated the acceptance of the critical method not only among leading Oxford Old Testament specialists, but also among Oxford churchmen who were 'servants of the Catholic Creed and Church, aiming only at interpreting the faith we have received'.[47] The essays are primarily concerned with 'the Religion of the Incarnation', but incidental references to the Old Testament show that the essayists had come to terms with the critical results of Old Testament study. Among authorities who are appealed to are to be found Kuenen, Ewald and Robertson Smith,[48] and it is acknowledged that for those who 'have learned to regard the Hebrew cosmology in a true light', the problems raised by the theory of the evolution of mankind have become far less pressing.[49]

The matter of Old Testament criticism is most explicitly dealt with in Gore's essay, 'The Holy Spirit and Inspiration', and in it, he faced the questions that had been the centre of controversy regarding the critical method in the nineteenth century. The first question concerned the general reliability of the picture of Israel's history as presented by a surface reading of the Old Testament. Gore maintained that there was 'a profound air of historical truthfulness' in the Old Testament traditions from the time of Abraham downward, and that the Church would continue to believe and to teach this general historical trustworthiness from the time of Abraham.[50] However, Gore allowed that 'very little of the early record can be securely traced to a period near the events', and he admitted the presence in the Old

[46] *The Book of Genesis*, London 1904, pp. 56–7: 'All that, as Christian theologians, we are called upon to believe is that a time arrived, when man's faculties were sufficiently developed for him to become conscious of a moral law, and that, having become conscious of it, he broke it.' Needless to say, this quasi-historicizing of Gen. 3 differs considerably from what is to be found in much critical German theology of the nineteenth century from Schleiermacher and de Wette onwards, in which the story of the 'fall' is essentially symbolical.
[47] C. Gore (ed.), *Lux Mundi. A Series of Studies in the Religion of the Incarnation*, London 1889. The quotation is from p. viii.
[48] ibid., pp. 34, 162, 171.
[49] ibid., p. 195.
[50] ibid., p. 352.

Testament of non-historical elements such as 'the attribution to first founders of what is really the remoter result of their institutions'.[51]

At this point, Gore turned to the results of historical criticism, which held that three stages in the growth of the law of worship were represented successively by 'the Book of the Covenant', the Book of Deuteronomy and the Priestly Code.[52] If this is how divine guidance had caused the law to develop, from simple ceremonies established by Moses to the fully-developed, levitical law, the attribution of the *whole* of the latter to Moses in the Old Testament was not 'untruthful', though it might be 'uncritical'. In any case, the symbolism of the final form of the levitical ordinances (as pointing to Christ) was not affected by the process by which the final form might have been reached.

In the case of Chronicles, Gore accepted that as sources for history, these books were less useful than Samuel and Kings. But in that Chronicles represented 'the version of history which had become current in the priestly schools', their version of the early monarchy was not 'conscious perversion' but 'unconscious idealization'.[53] Inspiration, as understood by Gore, did not rule out such 'idealization' although it was clearly incompatible with 'conscious deception or pious fraud'.

In *Lux Mundi* then, there is a readiness to accept critical Old Testament scholarship, even in its Wellhausenian form. This is because the critically-reconstructed history of Israel is accepted as an account of the actual process by which God guided his people. An important factor in *Lux Mundi* is the appeal to the Church Fathers, and the claim that the notion of progressive revelation is what the Fathers themselves taught.[54]

On the matter of post-exilic Judaism, the contributors took the view that in fully-developed Judaism, everything that was required for a universal religion was already present, waiting for the final revelation in Christ that would transform it from a particularist to a universal religion.[55] The fully-

---

[51] ibid., p. 352.

[52] ibid., p. 352. Gore's authority for this is Driver's 1887 *Critical Notes on . . . Sunday School Lessons*.

[53] ibid., p. 353.

[54] ibid., p. 329: 'It is the essence of the New Testament, as the religion of the Incarnation, to be final and catholic: on the other hand, it is of the essence of the Old Testament to be imperfect because it represents a gradual process of education by which man was lifted out of depths of sin and ignorance. That this is the case, and that in consequence the justification of the Old Testament method lies not in itself at any particular stage, but in its result taken as a whole, is a thought very familiar to modern Christians. But it is important to make plain that it was *a thought equally familiar to the Fathers of the Christian Church.*' (Italics mine.)

[55] ibid., p. 157: 'Perhaps if we performed the futile task of trying to imagine a world-religion, we should, with some generality of consent, define as its essentials three or four points which it is striking to find were fundamentals of the religion of Israel, and at that time of no other. . . . It needs no words to show how the religion of Israel in its full development

developed sacrificial system pointed, symbolically and typologically, to the work of Christ. The one note of criticism raised against critical scholarship concerned Cheyne's assertion that the record of Elijah and such narratives were not 'true to fact'.[56]

In Oxford, then, scholars such as Driver, Cheyne, Sanday, Burney, Gray and the contributors to *Lux Mundi* in their various ways, advocated the critical results of Wellhausen. Apart from Cheyne, they did so in a conservative fashion.[57]

The contribution of Cambridge to the growth of critical scholarship was no less important. In 1882, A. F. Kirkpatrick became Regius Professor of Hebrew at Cambridge.[58] He is best known today for his commentary on the Psalms in the *Cambridge Bible Commentary for Colleges and Schools*, a work of rare distinction in its combination of critical and devotional insights.[59] However, in 1891, the year of the appearance of Driver's *Introduction*, Kirkpatrick published a small book entitled *The Divine Library of the Old Testament*.[60] In it, he presented very broadly the results of critical scholarship, including, 'as the theory which is now most in favour', the view that the Priestly Code was the latest of the strands of the Pentateuch.[61] In some respects, the book is, initially at any rate, a much simplified version of Robertson Smith's *The Old Testament in the Jewish Church*.[62] Throughout, however, it insists that the Old Testament is the record of God's progressive revelation of himself to mankind, and that critical discovery of the complexities of the compilation of the record enhances, rather than diminishes, our understanding of divine providence.

An interesting feature of the book is its appeal to Westcott's commentary

---

not only taught these truths, but gave them the dignity and importance which belong to the cornerstones of a religion.'

[56] ibid., p. 345.

[57] This is not the place to enter into the opposition aroused by *Lux Mundi*, and especially Gore's essay on 'The Holy Spirit and Inspiration'. H. P. Liddon was particularly devastated to discover that at Pusey House, of which Gore was principal, critical ideas had been gaining acceptance. See his correspondence with Gore in J. O. Johnston (ed.), *Life and Letters of Henry Parry Liddon*, London 1904, pp. 362ff. The letters contain some interesting references to Old Testament scholars. For example, Liddon did not approve of Gore describing Driver as 'moderate and reasonable', and the word 'great' was begrudged to Delitzsch, in view of his eventual acceptance of a moderate type of criticism. See p. 376.

[58] Alexander Francis Kirkpatrick (1849–1940) studied at Trinity College, Cambridge. He was Regius Professor of Hebrew at Cambridge (1882–1903) and later, dean of Ely (1906–36).

[59] *Cambridge Bible Commentary for Colleges and Schools*, Psalms, Pt 1, 1892, Pts 2–3, 1895, Pts 4–5, 1912.

[60] A. F. Kirkpatrick, *The Divine Library of the Old Testament*, London 1891.

[61] ibid., p. 46.

[62] For example, it appeals to the differences between the Greek and Hebrew versions of Jeremiah. See p. 21.

on *The Epistle to the Hebrews* (1889), and to its concluding pages where Westcott defended, as taught by *The Epistle to the Hebrews*, the notion of progressive education.[63] These pages also have some salutary remarks to make about attitudes to critical scholarship. Westcott had written

> The Bible is the record, the inspired, authoritative record, of the divine education of the world. The Old Testament, as we receive it, is the record of the way in which God trained a people for the Christ *in many parts and in many modes*, the record which the Christ himself and his Apostles received and sanctioned. How the record was brought together, out of what materials, at what times, under what conditions, are questions of secondary importance. We shall spare no effort in the endeavour to answer them. Every result which can be surely established will teach us something of the manner of God's working, and of the manner in which he provides for our knowledge of it. At the same time we must remember that, here as elsewhere, his ways in the fulfilment of his counsel are, for the most part, not as our ways, but infinitely wider, larger, *and more varied.*[64]

In these words did a great Cambridge theologian show cautious support for Old Testament criticism, and Kirkpatrick was quick to use them to support his own work.

Other Cambridge scholars who can be mentioned in this period include J. J. S. Perowne (1823–1904), first general editor of the *Cambridge Bible Commentary* from 1872,[65] H. E. Ryle (1856–1925)[66] and W. E. Barnes (1859–1939).[67] The mention of the *Cambridge Bible Commentary* draws attention to a remarkable indication of how Old Testament studies were changing in England in the 1880s and 1890s. The earliest contributions to the series were by scholars who held to traditional views of biblical authorship. Thus, *Ecclesiastes* (1881) was treated by E. H. Plumptre,[68] and *Judges* (1884) by J. J. Lias.[69] 1884, however, saw the appearance of *Job* by

[63] ibid., p. 89.

[64] B. F. Westcott, *The Epistle to the Hebrews*, London 1889, pp. 493–4.

[65] Hulsean Professor of Divinity at Cambridge (1875–8), dean of Peterborough (1878–9), bishop of Worcester (1891–1904).

[66] Hulsean Professor (1887), bishop of Exeter (1901), bishop of Winchester (1903), dean of Westminster (1911). His *The Early Narratives of Genesis*, London 1892, took a critical position, while emphasizing the spiritual truths taught by the narratives.

[67] Lecturer in Hebrew at Clare College, Cambridge 1885–1901, Hulsean Professor of Divinity 1901–34.

[68] Edward Hayes Plumptre (1821–91) was Professor of Exegesis at King's College, London 1864–81, before becoming dean of Wells in 1881. His *Biblical Studies*, London 1869, rejected, for example, the Deutero-Isaiah theory, ascribing Isaiah 40—66 to 'the old age of Isaiah'. However, he allowed the legitimacy of criticism. See p. 209.

[69] J. J. Lias (1834–1923) was Professor of Modern Literature at Lampeter (1871–80), vicar of St. Edward's, Cambridge (1880–92), rector of East Bergholt (1892–1903) and chancellor of Llandaff Cathedral from 1903. His *Principles of Biblical Criticism*, London 1893, contains vigorous arguments against the Wellhausen position, and Driver's advocacy of it. See the conclusions regarding the Pentateuch at pp. 132–3.

A. B. Davidson, and notable commentaries by critical scholars included *Hosea* by Cheyne (1889), *Ezekiel* by A. B. Davidson (1892), *Ezra and Nehemiah* by Ryle (1893), *Isaiah 1—39* by Skinner (1896), *Joel and Amos* by S. R. Driver (1898 combined volume), *Chronicles* by W. E. Barnes (1899) and *Nahum, Habakkuk and Zechariah* by A. B. Davidson (1899). It is remarkable that a series designed for 'Colleges and Schools' should have begun to present the critical method from the mid-1880s.

In the last two decades of the nineteenth century in England, many writings supporting traditional views of biblical authorship and interpretation were still being published. A series of commentaries entitled *The Pulpit Commentary* appeared between 1882 and 1892, and although some of the contributors held critical views, some of the volumes were unashamedly traditional, albeit more friendly to critical results than would have been the case a decade earlier.[70] In the essay, 'The Authorship of the Pentateuch', by Thomas Whitelaw in the volume on Genesis (1881[4]), Mosaic authorship of the Pentateuch was defended. Yet it was conceded that written sources may have been used, and that there may have been a subsequent revision by Ezra. Objections to the acceptance of Mosaic authorship were considered fairly, and it was allowed that:

> ... an opinion which has secured the allegiance of authorities so eminent as Tuch, Knobel, Hupfeld, De Wette, Bohlen, Bleek, Delitzsch, Ewald, Graf, Kuenen, Wellhausen, and others, should have nothing in the shape of evidence to produce in its behalf is simply incredible.[71]

It was, for traditional English scholarship, a veritable step forward that such a roll call of critics, all German except for the Dutchman Kuenen, could be given as the prelude to a sober examination of arguments, rather than to a denunciation of impious rationalism.[72]

The tide was running strongly in favour of allowing that critical results could be combined with traditional theology, and, as the nineteenth century ended, the most substantial attempt of the period to effect the combination was carried out in R. L. Ottley's Bampton Lectures for 1897, published under the title *Aspects of the Old Testament*.[73]

Ottley was a High Churchman, a contributor to *Lux Mundi*, and a future

---

[70] H. M. D. Spence, J. S. Exell, *The Pulpit Commentary*, 36 vols., London 1882–92. Cheyne, for example, contributed to the volumes on Jeremiah.

[71] *The Pulpit Commentary*, Genesis, p. ii.

[72] It is possible only to mention briefly here the excellent series, *The Expositor's Bible*, ed. W. R. Nicoll (1887–96). The series and its editor, Sir William Robertson Nicoll are dealt with in Glover, *Evangelical Nonconformists and Higher Criticism*.

[73] R. L. Ottley, *Aspects of the Old Testament*, London 1897. R. L. Ottley (1856–1939) was vice-principal of Cuddesdon College, Oxford (1886–90), and later principal of Pusey House (1893–7), rector of Winterbourne Bassett (1897–1903), Regius Professor of Pastoral Theology at Oxford, from 1903. He was a contributor to *Lux Mundi* on Christian Ethics.

principal of Pusey House. His lectures very much echoed the tone of Gore's discussion of the Old Testament in *Lux Mundi*. Ottley's position was conservative, upholding a basic historicity of the Patriarchal narratives, and stressing the importance of Mosaism—which was not the same as the fully developed levitical law ascribed to Moses.

Frequent reference to Robertson Smith, including reference to the *Lectures on the Religion of the Semites*, enabled Ottley to present the Wellhausen view of the development of Israelite religion. Each stage, from the spontaneous nomadic stage with its free access to God, to the sombre stage of the ritual of the post-exilic period was seen as guided by God's providence. Each stage was fitted to enable Israel to cope with the demands of the situation in which the nation found itself, and the final form of the levitical system bore its typological references forward to the coming of Christ. Criticism not only enabled the true course of Israel's religious development (as the Wellhausen position was thought to be) to be recovered, it solved difficult questions. For example, why, if Moses established, under divine sanctions, such an elaborate system of ritual for the people, did they ignore it for centuries and constantly turn to the Baals? The acceptance of the view that the fully developed levitical system was a late phenomenon in Israel enabled sense to be made of the prophetic denunciations of idolatry and apostasy.[74]

At the end of the nineteenth century, German critical Old Testament scholarship had triumphed in England, albeit in a form adapted to Evangelical and Catholic versions of progressive revelation. The reconciliation of German and English scholarship was nowhere better summed up than by Ottley in his Bampton Lectures, when he wrote:

While however we allow that there was much which seemed to justify the uncompromising hostility with which Christian men of the last generation met the advance of criticism, we must in fairness acknowledge much fault on our own side: much slowness of heart, much want of faith and undue timidity, much unreasoning prejudice, much disproportioned and misdirected zeal, much unwillingness to take trouble, much readiness to explain away unwelcome facts, whereas 'explaining away is a process which has no place in historical inquiry.' We have failed to do justice to the laborious and patient thoroughness, the exact and profound erudition, the sagacious insight of the great scholars of Germany. We have seldom made due allowance for the immense difficulties of their self-imposed task, we have exaggerated the deficiencies of their method and the insecurity of its results. If however in the past suspicion and dislike have been carried too far, there are welcome indications that such a temper is gradually disappearing, and that Christians are learning to distinguish more accurately between what is essential and what is non-essential to their faith. And if it should be objected that we of this generation are unfaithful to the traditions of those

[74] *Aspects of the Old Testament*, p. 232.

venerated teachers in whose place we are allowed to stand, we can but reply that *wisdom is justified of all her children.* We whose training has been in many respects diverse from theirs, whose difficulties and responsibilities are altogether different, cannot fairly plead their example as an excuse for evading the task specially assigned to us, or for refusing to consider the claims of that which presents itself to us in the name of truth. It is not impatience, or love of novelty, or self-confidence, or a mere wish to be abreast of recent thought that has led to the changed attitude of younger men; it is the desire to follow humbly and honestly the guidance of the Spirit of Truth.[75]

[75] ibid., pp. 42–3.

Conclusion

The foregoing pages have demonstrated—if any demonstration was indeed necessary—that the critical method as practised in Old Testament scholarship today was born and developed in Protestant Germany, and that it was accepted in England only when the philosophical and theological conditions were right for acceptance. One reason for this has already been suggested: the vast difference in scale in theological activity between Germany and England for most of the nineteenth century. When the critical method was finally accepted in England, a fine school of Old Testament scholars emerged to be its champion. In addition to those named already, we can list George Buchanan Gray (1865–1923), tutor and later professor at Mansfield College, Oxford; Charles Fox Burney (1868–1925), lecturer in Hebrew at St John's College, Oxford, and later, Oriel Professor; John Skinner (1851–1925), a Scot who worked as professor in London from 1890, and later in Cambridge; Arthur Samuel Peake (1865–1929), tutor at Mansfield College, Oxford, and at the Hartley College, Manchester, and the first Rylands Professor of Biblical Criticism and Exegesis at Manchester. The list is far from complete, and omits great Scottish scholars such as George Adam Smith.

However, the emergence of this fine school of scholars did not result in what might be called a creative English (or Scottish or Welsh) school of Old Testament scholarship. It was Germany that led the way through the twentieth century. Form criticism and the comparative study of literary genres were pioneered in Germany by Gunkel and Gressmann. The attempt to regain some sort of historicity for the pre-Monarchic period by means of archaeological researches combined with painstaking tradition-criticism was pioneered by Albrecht Alt and Martin Noth. Indeed, from Noth came the classical statements of two of the most influential theories in twentieth-century Old Testament criticism: the amphictyony and the Deuteronomistic history.

It is true that other countries contributed significantly to Old Testament scholarship, and there is no intention here to overlook the distinguished work of scholars in the Scandinavian countries, Holland, Belgium, France, the United States and Palestine (later, Israel). There is also no desire to ignore the significant British results in the fields of textual criticism, comparative philology, Assyriology and archaeology. However, compared with

291

Germany, scholarly results in England in the historical-critical study of Old Testament literature were at the level of evaluation and mediation of results from elsewhere. One of the few distinctive contributions, that of the 'Myth and Ritual' school, was a synthesis of anthropological and Assyriological views as applied to the Old Testament.[1]

It is tempting to ask why, in comparison with England, German Old Testament scholarship continued to be far more innovative. In reply, one can hazard some guesses. First, the whole Protestant German theological tradition has been far more creative than in England, with a readiness to reinterpret theology around what is seen as its centre—justification by faith—in radical ways. There is a tradition of theological giants in whose shadows German Old Testament scholars worked: Schleiermacher, Rothe, Ritschl, Herrmann, Troeltsch, to name only a few. In England, the incarnation rather than justification has been the centre of theology, and for much of the present century, the incarnation was seen as the culmination of a process in history guided by God. Although this allowed the accommodation of the Wellhausen position, it did not encourage radical speculation.

This leads to the second point which is that, for whatever reason, there appears to be a strong empirical basis for English theology, probably derived from the empirical tradition of English philosophy. There is a strong desire to test and to evaluate evidence, but less willingness to enter the insecure realm of meddling with the evidence itself. If I may generalize from my own attitudes, English scholarship would prefer to say that it does not know, rather than build elaborate theories upon slender premises. Thus, English Old Testament study is in its natural environment when it finds itself testing and evaluating the theories of others. This, indeed, may be the greatest service that it can offer to Old Testament study generally.

However, there is no reason in general why England should not develop schools of creative Old Testament scholarship. It is true that the scale of theological studies in this country is still tiny, compared with Germany. Something like 750 university undergraduates begin theological studies in Britain each year. In Germany, a single university, such as Tübingen or Munich, probably has more theological students in its two faculties (Protestant and Catholic) than all the British universities combined. The present contraction of university education in Britain is, among other things, reducing the number of academic theological positions. Whatever the future pattern of Old Testament studies may be, here and elsewhere in

[1] See J. W. Rogerson, *Myth in Old Testament Interpretation*, pp. 66–84.

the world, they can only be helped by a greater self-awareness on the part of scholars of the history of their discipline. At the very least, this may reveal the absolute necessity of a partnership in scholarship between the innovative and the evaluative, tendencies long represented by German and English scholarship respectively.

Bibliography

Allgemeine Kirchenzeitung 1825, no. 138, 16 October 1825.
— 1825, no. 172, 15 December 1825.
— 1826, no. 15, 26 January 1826.
Anon., *Dr Davidson: his Heresies, Contradictions, and Plagiarisms.* London and Manchester 1857.
Arnold, Thomas, *Sermons.* London Vol. 1 1844[4], Vol. 2 1844[3].
— *Sermons Chiefly on the Interpretation of Scripture.* London 1845.
Ashton, Rosemary, *The German Idea. Four English Writers and the Reception of German Thought, 1800–60.* Cambridge 1980.
Astruc, J., *Conjectures sur les mémoires originaux dont il paroît que Moyse se servit pour composer le livre de la Genèse.* Brussels 1753.
Bachmann, J., *Ernst Wilhelm Hengstenberg. Sein Leben und Wirken,* 1–2, Gütersloh 1876–80, 3 (completed by T. Schmalenbach), 1892.
Baehring, B., *Bunsens Bibelwerk nach seiner Bedeutung für die Gegenwart beleuchtet.* Leipzig 1861.
Barnes, W. E., *Chronicles,* Cambridge Bible Commentary. Cambridge 1899.
Baudissin, W. W., Graf von, 'Der heutige Stand der alttestamentliche Wissenschaft' (bound up with G. Diegel, *Theologische Wissenschaft und pfarramtliche Praxis.* Giessen 1884, pp. 37–60).
Baumgartner, W., 'Eine alttestamentliche Forschungsgeschichte', *ThR* 25 (1959), pp. 93–110.
Baur, F. C., 'Ueber die ursprüngliche Bedeutung des Passahfestes und des Beschneidungsritus', *TZTh* 1 (1832), pp. 40–124.
Beidelman, T. O., *W. Robertson Smith and the Sociological Study of Religion.* Chicago 1974.
Benecke, H., *Wilhelm Vatke in seinem Leben und seinen Schriften.* Bonn 1883.
Beyreuther, E., *Die Erweckungsbewegung, Die Kirche in ihrer Geschichte* 4. Göttingen 1977[2].
Black, J. S. and Chrystal, G., *The Life of William Robertson Smith.* London 1912.
Bleek, F., 'Beitragen zu den Forschungen über den Pentateuch' *TSK* 1831, pp. 488–524.
— 'Einige aphoristische Beiträge zu den Untersuchungen über den Pentateuch', *BER* 1, 1822, pp. 1–19.
— *Einleitung in das Alte Testament,* ed. J. Bleek & A. Kamphausen. Berlin 1860.
— 'Ueber Verfasser und Zweck des Buches Daniel; Revision der in neuerer Zeit darüber geführten Untersuchungen' *TZS* 3, 1822, pp. 171–294.

Bohlen, P. von, *Die Genesis Historisch-Kritisch erläutert*. Königsberg 1835 (translation of parts of this in *Introduction to the Book of Genesis, with a Commentary on the Opening Portion*. London 1855).

Bolman, F. de W., Jr., *Schelling: the Ages of the World*, Columbia Studies in Philosophy 3. New York 1942.

Bonn, *150 Jahre Rheinische Friedrich-Wilhelms-Universität zu Bonn 1818–1968. Verzeichnis der Professoren und Dozenten*, ed. Otto Wenig. Bonn 1968.

Bonwetsch, G. N. (ed.), *Aus vierzig Jahren Deutscher Kirchengeschichte. Briefe an E. W. Hengstenberg, BFChTh* 22, 1 (1917).

Bornkamm, H., 'Die Theologische Fakultät Heidelberg' in *Ruperto-Carola. Aus der Geschichte der Universität Heidelberg und ihrer Fakultäten*. Heidelberg 1961, pp. 135–54.

Bradley, G. G. see R. E. Prothero.

Breslau, *Universität Breslau. Festschrift zur Feier des hundertjährigen Bestehens*, 1, *Geschichte der Universität Breslau 1811–1911*. Breslau 1911.

Brömse, M., *Studien zur 'Biblischen Theologie' Wilhelm Vatkes*. Diss., Kiel 1973.

Browne, E. M., *The Pentateuch and the Elohistic Psalms, in Reply to Bishop Colenso*. London and Cambridge 1863.

Budde, K., *Die Biblische Urgeschichte, Genesis 1—12.5 untersucht*. Giessen 1883.

Bunsen, C. C. J., *Ägyptens Stelle in der Weltgeschichte*, 1–3, Hamburg 1845, vols. 4–5, Gotha 1856–7. (ET, *Egypt's Place in Universal History: an Historical Introduction in Five Books*. London 1848–67).

— *Gott in der Geschichte oder der Fortschritt des Glaubens an eine sittliche Weltordnung*. 1–3, Leipzig, 1857–8. (ET, *God in History; or The Progress of Man's Faith in the Moral Order of the World*. London 1868–70).

— *Hippolytus und seine Zeit*, Leipzig, 1852–3. (ET, *Christianity and Mankind, their Beginnings and Prospects*. London 1854).

— *Vollständiges Bibelwerk für die Gemeinde* (completed by A. Kamphausen), 9 vols., Leipzig 1858–70.

Bunsen, Frances, *A Memoir of Baron Bunsen*, 2 vols., London 1868. (German trans. *Carl Josias Freiherr von Bunsen*, ed. F. Nippold, 3 vols., Leipzig 1868–71).

Burgon, J. W., *Lives of Twelve Good Men*. London 1888.

Burney, C. F., *Outlines of Old Testament Theology*. London 1899.

Buttmann, P. K., *Mythologus, oder gesammelte Abhandlungen über die Sagen des Alterthums*. 1, Berlin 1828.

Carpenter, J. E., *James Martineau, Theologian and Teacher. A Study of his Life and Thought*. London 1905.

— *The Bible in the Nineteenth Century*. London 1903.

Chadwick, Henry (ed.), *Lessing's Theological Writings*. London 1956.

Chadwick, O., *The Victorian Church*, 2 vols. London 1966–70.

Cheyne, T. K., *Aids to the Devout Study of Criticism*. London 1892.

— *Founders of Old Testament Criticism*. London 1893.

— *Hosea*, Cambridge Bible Commentary. Cambridge 1889.

Clarke, Adam, *The Holy Bible with a Commentary and Critical Notes*, 8 vols. London 1813 fol.

Clarke, J. B. B. (ed.), *An Account of the Infancy, Religious and Literary Life of Adam Clarke, LL.D., F.A.S.*, 3 vols. London 1833.

Cochlovius, J., *Bekenntnis und Einheit der Kirche im deutschen Protestantismus*, Die Lutherische Kirche, Geschichte und Gestalten, 3. Gütersloh 1980.

Colenso, J. W., *The Pentateuch and the Book of Joshua critically examined*, 7 parts. London 1862–79.

Cornish, F. W., *The English Church in the Nineteenth Century*, 2 vols. London 1910.

Courier, *Der Courier. Hallischer Zeitung für Stadt und Land*, Nr 251, 27 October 1842.

Cox, G. W., *The Life of John William Colenso, D.D., Bishop of Natal*, 2 vols. London 1888.

Critical Review 1795, Review of Eichhorn's *Urgeschichte*, pp. 549–50.

Critical Review 1798, Review of Nachtigall's *Gesänge Davids*, pp. 537–42.

Davidson, A. B., *Job*, Cambridge Bible Commentary. Cambridge 1884.

— *Ezekiel*, Cambridge Bible Commentary. Cambridge 1892.

— *The Called of God*. Edinburgh 1902.

Davidson, R. T. and Benham, W., *Life of Archibald Campbell Tait, Archbishop of Canterbury*, 2 vols., London 1891.

Davidson, Samuel, *Facts, Statements and Explanations*. London 1857.

— *An Introduction to the Old Testament*, 2 vols. London and Edinburgh 1862–3.

— *Sacred Hermeneutics Developed and Applied, including a History of Biblical Interpretation from the Earliest of the Fathers to the Reformation*. Edinburgh 1843.

— *The Text of the Old Testament Considered, with a Treatise on Sacred Interpretation and a brief Introduction to the Old Testament Books and the Apocrypha*. London 1856, 1859[2]. (This is the second vol. of T. H. Horne's *An Introduction to the Critical Study and Knowledge of the Holy Scriptures*, 10th edition.)

Davidson, S. (ed.), *The Autobiography and Diary of Samuel Davidson*. Edinburgh 1899.

Davies, T. Witton, *Heinrich Ewald, Orientalist and Theologian*. London 1903.

Delitzsch, Franz, *Die biblisch-prophetische Theologie, ihre Fortbildung durch Chr. A. Crusius und ihre neueste Entwicklung seit der Christologie Hengstenbergs*. Leipzig 1845.

— *Biblischer Commentar über den Prophet Jesaia*. Leipzig 1866 (ET, *Biblical Commentary on the Prophecies of Isaiah*. Edinburgh 1867).

— *Die Genesis ausgelegt von Franz Delitzsch*. Leipzig 1852.

— *Neuer Commentar über die Genesis*. Leipzig 1887 (ET, *New Commentary on Genesis*. Edinburgh 1888–9).

— *System der biblischen Psychologie*. Leipzig 1855, 1861[2] (ET, *System of Biblical Psychology*. Edinburgh 1875).

Dewar, E. H., *German Protestantism and the Right of Private Judgement in the Interpretation of Holy Scripture*. Oxford 1844.

Diegel, G., *Theologische Wissenschaft und pfarramtliche Praxis*. Giessen 1884.

Diestel, L., *Geschichte des Alten Testamentes in der christlichen Kirche*. Jena 1869, repr. Leipzig 1981.

Dillmann, A., *Die Genesis, KEH* 1. Leipzig 1892[6].

Distad, J. M., *Guessing at Truth, The Life of Julius Charles Hare (1795–1855)*. Shepherdstown 1979.

Dockhorn, K., *Deutscher Geist und angelsächsische Geistesgeschichte. Ein Versuch der Deutung ihres Verhältnisses*, Göttinger Bausteine zur Geschichtswissenschaft, 17. Göttingen, Frankfurt/M and Berlin 1954.

— *Der Deutsche Historismus in England. Ein Beitrag zur Englischen Geistesgeschichte des 19. Jahrhunderts*. Göttingen 1950.

D'Oyley, G., and Mant, R., *The Holy Bible with Notes Explanatory* . . . Oxford and London 1817.

Driver, S. R., *The Book of Genesis*, Westminster Commentaries. London 1904.

— *Critical Notes on the International Sunday School Lessons from the Pentateuch*. New York 1887.

— 'On some alleged Linguistic Affinities of the Elohist', *The Journal of Philology*, 11 (1882), pp. 201–36.

— *An Introduction to the Literature of the Old Testament*. Edinburgh 1891, 1913[9].

— *Sermons on Subjects connected with the Old Testament*. London 1892.

Duhm, B., *Die Theologie der Propheten als Grundlage für die innere Entwicklungsgeschichte der Israelitischen Religion*. Bonn 1875.

Dyson, A. O., 'Theological Legacies of the Enlightenment: England and Germany' in S. W. Sykes (ed.), *England and Germany. Studies in Theological Diplomacy*. Frankfurt/M and Bern 1982, pp. 45–62.

Ebel, W., *Catalogus professorum Gottingensium 1734–1962*. Göttingen 1962.

Eichhorn, J. G., *Einleitung ins Alte Testament*. Leipzig 1780–83, 1803[3], 1823–4[4].

Eissfeldt, O., Articles on Gesenius in *Kleine Schriften 2*. Tübingen 1963.

— 'Wilhelm Gesenius 1786–1842' in *250 Jahre Universität Halle. Streifzüge durch ihre Geschichte in Forschung und Lehre*. Halle (Saale) 1944, pp. 88–90.

Eissfeldt, O. and Rengstorff, K. H. (eds.), *Briefwechsel zwischen Franz Delitzsch und Wolf Wilhelm Graf Baudissin 1866–90*, Abhandlungen der Rheinisch-Westfälischen Akademie der Wissenschaften 43, Opladen 1973.

Ellicott, C. J., 'Scripture, and its Interpretation' in *Aids to Faith. A Series of Theological Essays*, ed. W. Thomson. London 1861.

Elliger, W., *150 Jahre Theologische Fakultät Berlin. Eine Darstellung ihrer Geschichte von 1810 bis 1960 als Beitrag zu ihrem Jubiläum*. Berlin 1960.

Engelhardt, R. von, *Die Deutsche Universität Dorpat in ihrer geistesgeschichtliche Bedeutung*. Munich 1933.

Ersch, J. S. and Gruber, J. G., *Allgemeine Encyclopädie der Wissenschaften und Künste*. Leipzig 1819– (not completed).

Essays and Reviews. London 1860, 1861[5].

Ewald, H., *Die Alterthümer des Volkes Israel.* Göttingen 1848 (ET, *The Antiquities of Israel.* London 1876).

— *Die Dichter des Alten Bundes.* Göttingen 1835–9, 1866–7[2].

— *Erklärung der grossen phönikischen Inschrift von Sidon.* Göttingen 1856.

— 'De feriorum hebraeorum origine ac ratione', *ZKM*, 1839, pp. 410ff.

— *Geschichte des Volkes Israel.* Göttingen 1843–59 (ET, *History of Israel.* London 1867–86).

— *Jahrbücher der biblischen Wissenschaft.* 1–12. Göttingen 1848–65.

— *Die Propheten des Alten Bundes.* Göttingen 1840–1, 1867–8[2] (ET, *The Prophets of the Old Testament.* London 1875–81).

— Review of George's *Die älteren Jüdischen Feste* in *GGA* 1836, pp. 678–80.

— Review of *Essays and Reviews* in *GGA* 1861 pp. 1161–80.

— Review of Colenso's *The Pentateuch and Joshua*, 1 in *GGA* 1863, pp. 26–39, 361–7, 372–6, 1062.

Flügge, B. G., *Die Weissagungen welche den Schriften des Propheten Zacharias beygebogen sind, übersetzt und critisch erläutert, nebst einigen Abhandlungen.* Hamburg 1784.

Frank, G., *Geschichte der Protestantischen Theologie*, 3, Von der deutschen Aufklärung bis zur Blütezeit des Rationalismus. Leipzig 1875.

Fries, J. F., *Neue oder anthropologische Kritik der Vernunft*, 3 vols. Heidelberg 1807, 1831[2], repr. Aachen 1967.

— *Wissen, Glaube und Ahndung*, Jena 1805; n. ed., ed. L. Nelson, Göttingen 1905.

— *Dialogues on Morality and Religion*, selected from *Julius und Evagoras.* Heidelberg 1822[2], Oxford 1982.

Fuller, R. C., *Dr Alexander Geddes. A Forerunner of Biblical Criticism*, Diss. Cambridge 1968; published in *HTIBS* 3. Sheffield 1984.

Geldbach, E. (ed.), *Der gelehrte Diplomat. Zum Wirken Christian Carl Josias Bunsens BZRGG* 21. Leiden 1980.

Gennrich, P., *Der Kampf um die Schrift in der deutschen evangelischen Kirche des neunzehnten Jahrhunderts.* Berlin 1898.

George, J. F. L., *Die älteren Jüdischen Feste mit einer Kritik der Gesetzgebung des Pentateuch.* Berlin 1835.

Gérold, C. T., *La Faculté de Théologie et le séminaire protestant de Strasbourg 1803–72.* Strasbourg and Paris 1923.

Gesenius, W., 'Abraham' in Ersch und Gruber's *Allgemeine Encyclopädie*, vol. 1.

— *Alttestamentlicher Dogmatik* (lecture notes taken by Hermann Schrader 1836–7). Ms Germ. Qu. 1509 in the Staatsbibliothek Preussischer Kulturbesitz, West Berlin (SBPK).

— *Biblische Archaeologie* (Schrader notes 1838–9) Ms Germ. Qu. 1508, in SBPK.

— *Einleitung ins Alte Testament* (Schrader notes 1836–7) Ms Germ. Qu. 1510, in SBPK.

— *Die Genesis* (Schrader notes 1838) Ms Germ. Qu. 1511, in SBPK.

— *Geschichte der hebräischen Sprache und Schrift.* Leipzig 1815, repr. Hildersheim 1973.

— *Hebräisch-deutsch Handwörterbuch über die Schriften des Alten Testaments*, 1–2. Leipzig 1810–12.

— *Kirchengeschichte* (Schrader's notes 1838) Ms Germ. Qu. 1515, in SBPK.

— *De Pentateucho Samaritano, ejusque indole et auctoritate.* Halle 1814.

— *Philologisch-kritischer und historischer Commentar über den Jesaia.* Leipzig 1820–1.

— *Die Psalmen* (lecture notes by C. Fr. Stolz, 1826–7 in the possession of Prof. R. Smend).

Gestrich, C., 'Deismus', *TRE* 8. Berlin 1981.

Giessen, *Die Universität Giessen von 1607 bis 1907. Beiträge zu ihrer Geschichte. Festschrift zur dritten Jahrhundertfeier.* Giessen 1907.

— *Ludwigs-Universität, Justus Liebig Hochschule 1607–1957. Festschrift zur 350-Jahrfeier.* Giessen 1957.

Glover, W. B., *Evangelical Nonconformists and Higher Criticism in the Nineteenth Century.* London 1954.

Goodwin, C. W., 'On the Mosaic Cosmogony' in *Essays and Reviews.* London 1860, pp. 207–253.

Gore, C. (ed.), *Lux Mundi. A Series of Studies in the Religion of the Incarnation.* London 1889.

Goulburn, E. M. (ed.), *Replies to Essays and Reviews.* Oxford and London 1862.

Graf, K. H., *Die geschichtlichen Bücher des Alten Testaments. Zwei historisch-kritischen Untersuchungen.* Leipzig 1866.

Gramberg, C. P. W., *Die Chronik nach ihrem geschichtlichen Charakter und ihrer Glaubwürdigkeit neu geprüft.* Halle 1823.

— *Kritische Geschichte der Religionsideen des alten Testaments.* 2 vols. Berlin 1829–30. 1, Hierarchie und Cultus; 2, Theocratie und Prophetismus.

— *Libri Geneseos secundum fontes rite dignoscendos adumbratio nova.* Leipzig 1828.

Grant, R. M., *A Short History of the Interpretation of the Bible*, new ed. London 1963.

Gröben, Ida, Gräfin von der, *Wissenschaft und der Bibel. Mit Beziehung auf Dr Bunsen: 'Hippolytus und seine Zeit . . .' und die Recension dieses Werkes in Dr Hengstenberg's Kirchenzeitung.* Stuttgart 1856.

Gross, K. D., *Die deutsch-englischen Beziehungen im Wirken Christian Carl Josias von Bunsens (1791–1860)*, Diss. Würtzburg 1965.

Gundel, H. G. and Moraw, P. (eds.), *Giessener Gelehrte in der ersten Hälfte des 20. Jahrhunderts.* Marburg 1982.

Günther, A., *Vorschule zur speculativen Theologie des positiven Christenthums, In Briefen*, 2 vols. Vienna 1828–9. 1, die Creationstheorie; 2, die Incarnationstheorie 1829.

Hagenbach, K. N., *Wilhelm Martin Leberecht de Wette. Eine akademische Gedächtnissrede.* Leipzig 1850.

Haight, G. S., *George Eliot, A Biography.* Oxford 1968.

Halle, *250 Jahre Universität Halle. Streifzüge durch ihre Geschichte in Forschung und Lehre*. Halle (Saale) 1944.

Hare, A. J. C., *The Life and Letters of Frances, Baroness Bunsen*. London 1879.

Hare, J. C., *Charges to the Clergy of the Archdeaconry of Lewes, delivered at the Ordinary Visitations in the Years 1843, 1845, 1846*. Cambridge 1856.

Haym, R., *Gesenius. Eine Erinnerung für seine Freunde*. Berlin 1842.

Hayner, P. C., *Reason and Existence. Schelling's Philosophy of History*. Leiden 1967.

Hegel, G. W. F., *Vorlesungen über die Philosophie der Religion*, Sämmtliche Werke, 15–16, repr. Stuttgart 1965.

— *Vorlesungen über die Geschichte der Philosophie*, 3, Sämmtliche Werke, 19. Stuttgart 1929.

Hengstenberg, E. W., *Beiträge zur Einleitung ins Alte Testament*, 3 vols. Berlin 1831–9 (ET, vols. 2–3, *Dissertations on the Genuineness of the Pentateuch*. Edinburgh 1847).

— *Christologie des Alten Testaments und Commentar über die Messianischen Weissagungen der Propheten*. Berlin 1829, 1856–7² (ET, *Christology of the Old Testament*. Edinburgh 1854–8).

— Review of *Hippolytus und seine Zeit* in *Evangelische Kirchenzeitung*, Oct.–Nov. 1853.

Henke, E. L. T., *Jakob Friedrich Fries. Aus seinem handschriftlichen Nachlasse dargestellt*. Leipzig 1867.

Herder, J. G., *Herders sämmtliche Werke*, ed. Bernhard Suphan, 33 vols. Berlin 1877–1913.

— vol. 10: *Briefe, das Studium der Theologie betreffend*.

— vols. 11 and 12: *Vom Geist der ebräischen Poesie*.

— vol. 14: *Ideen zur Geschichte der Philosophie der Menschheit* (ET of parts in *Reflections on the Philosophy of the History of Mankind*, reprint Chicago 1968).

Hermelinck, H. and Kaehler, S. A., *Die Philipps-Universität zu Marburg 1527–1927*. Marburg 1927.

Heussi, K., *Geschichte der Theologischen Fakultät zu Jena* (*Darstellungen zur Geschichte der Universität Jena*, 1, ed. Friedrich Schneider). Weimar 1954.

Hinchliff, P., *John William Colenso*. London 1964.

Hirsch, E., *Geschichte der neueren Evangelischen Theologie*, 5. Gütersloh 1954.

Hitzig, F., *Jesaja-Commentar*. Heidelberg 1833.

Höcker, Wilma, *Der Gesandte Bunsen als Vermittler zwischen Deutschland und England*, Göttinger Bausteine zur Geschichtswissenschaft 1. Göttingen 1951.

Hofmann, J. C. K., *Der Schriftbeweis*, 2 vols. Nordlingen 1852–6.

— *Weissagung und Erfüllung im alten und im neuen Testament*, 2 vols. Nördlingen 1841–44.

Horne, T. H., *An Introduction to the Critical Study and Knowledge of the Holy Scriptures*, 4 vols. London 1825⁵.

— *A Summary of the Evidence for the Genuineness, Authenticity, Uncorrupted*

Preservation and Inspiration of the Holy Scriptures (vol. 1 of the 10th edition of Horne's *Introduction to the Critical Study* . . .). London 1856.

Hornig, G., *Die Anfänge der historisch-kritischen Methode. Johann Salomo Semlers Schriftverständnis und seine Stellung zu Luther, FSThR* 8. Göttingen 1961.

Houtman, C., *Inleiding in de Pentateuch*. Kampen 1980.

Hübner, E., *Schrift und Theologie. Eine Untersuchung zur Theologie Joh. Chr. K. v. Hofmanns*. Munich 1956.

Hupfeld, H., 'Die heutige theosophische oder mythologische Theologie und Schrifterklärung', *DZCW* NF 4 (1861), pp. 269–92.

— *Die Quellen der Genesis und die Art ihrer Zusammensetzung*. Berlin 1853.

— *Ueber Begriff und Methode der sogenannten biblischen Einleitungen, nebst einer Uebersicht ihrer Geschichte und Literatur*. Marburg 1844.

Ilgen, K. D., *Die Urkunden des Jerusalemischen Tempelarchivs in ihrer Urgestalt als Beytrag zur Berichtigung der Geschichte der Religion und Politik*. Halle 1798.

Jenaer Allgemeine Literatur-Zeitung, February 1843, pp. 298–304.

Johnston, J. O., see Liddon, H. P.

Journal of Sacred Literature and Biblical Record, Review of von Bohlen's *Genesis*, 2, (1856), p. 469.

— Review of Kalisch on Genesis, 7 (1858), p. 258.

— Letter concerning Davidson's Resignation, 6 (1858), p. 388.

Jowett, B., 'On the Interpretation of Scripture' in *Essays and Reviews*. London 1860, pp. 330–433.

Kahnis, K. F. A., *Der innere Gang des deutschen Protestantismus seit Mitte des vorigen Jahrhunderts*. Leipzig 1854.

Kalisch, M. M., *A Historical and Critical Commentary on the Old Testament with a New Translation*. London, Exodus (1855), Genesis (1858), Leviticus (pt 1 1867, pt 2 1872).

Kamphausen, A., Review of Davidson's *Introduction to the Old Testament, TSK* 1863, p. 798.

Kant, I., *Kritik der Urteilskraft*, in Kants Werke, Akademie Textausgabe, 5. repr. Berlin 1968.

Kantzenbach, F. W., *Die Erlanger Theologie. Grundlinien ihrer Entwicklung im Rahmen der Geschichte der Theologischen Fakultät 1747–1877*. Munich 1960.

Kattenbusch, F., *Die deutsche evangelische Theologie seit Schleiermacher. 1, Das Jahrhundert von Schleiermacher bis nach dem Weltkrieg*. Giessen 1934.[6].

Kayser, A., *Das vorexilische Buch der Urgeschichte Israels und seine Erweiterungen*. Strasbourg 1874.

Keil, C. F., *Manual of Historico-Critical Introduction to the Canonical Scriptures of the Old Testament*, 1. Edinburgh 1869.

Kiel, *Professoren und Dozenten der Christian-Albrechts-Universität zu Kiel, 1665–1954*, Veröffentlichungen der Schleswig-Holsteinischen Universitätsgesellschaft NF 7, ed. Friedrich Volbehr and Richard Weyl. Kiel 1956.

Kirkpatrick, A. F., *Cambridge Bible Commentary for Colleges and Schools, Psalms*, 5 vols. Cambridge 1892–1912.

— *The Divine Library of the Old Testament.* London 1891.

Kirn, O., *Die Leipziger Theologische Fakultät in fünf Jahrhunderten (Festschrift zur Feier des 500 jährigen Bestehens der Universität Leipzig).* Leipzig 1909.

Kittel, R., *Geschichte der Hebräer*, 1–2. Gotha 1888–92. (ET, *History of the Hebrews.* London 1895–6).

Kneucker, J. J. (ed.), *Dr Ferdinand Hitzigs Vorlesungen ueber Biblische Theologie und Messianische Weissagungen des Alten Testaments.* Karlsruhe 1880.

Knight, Frida, *University Rebel. The Life of William Frend (1757–1841).* London 1971.

Knoodt, P., *Anton Günther. Eine Biographie.* Vienna 1881.

Koppe, J. B., *D. Robert Lowth's Jesaias übersetzt mit einer Einleitung und critischen philologischen und erläuternden Anmerkungen.* Leipzig 1780.

Kraus, H.-J., *Geschichte der historisch-kritischen Erforschung des Alten Testaments.* Neukirchen-Vluyn 1956, 1969[2], 1982[3].

Kuenen, A., *The Hexateuch.* London 1886.

— *The Religion of Israel to the Fall of the Jewish State*, 3 vols. London 1874–5.

Kuhn, T. S., *The Structure of Scientific Revolutions.* Chicago 1962, 1970[2].

Lachman, K. (ed.), see Lessing, G. E.

Leder, K., *Universität Altdorf. Zur Theologie der Aufklärung in Franken.* Nuremberg 1965.

Lenz, M., 'Zur Entlassung de Wettes' in *Philotesia. Paul Kleinert zum LXX Geburtstag dargebracht von Adolf Harnack u.a.* Berlin 1907, pp. 337–88.

— *Geschichte der königlichen Friedrich-Wilhelms-Universität zu Berlin.* 4 vols. Halle 1910–18 (vol. 2. 2, publ. 1918, the rest 1910).

Lepsius, R., *Letters from Egypt, Ethiopia, and the Peninsula of Sinai.* London 1853.

Lessing, G. E., *Gotthold Ephraim Lessings Sämmtliche Schriften* (ed. K. Lachman), bks 12, 13. Leipzig 1897[3].

Lias, J. J., *Principles of Biblical Criticism.* London 1893.

— *Judges*, Cambridge Bible Commentary. Cambridge 1884.

Liddon, H. P., *Life of Edward Bouverie Pusey.* London 1893–7.

— *Life and Letters of Henry Parry Liddon*, ed. J. O. Johnston. London 1904.

Loades, Ann L. and Gilley, S., 'Thomas Henry Huxley: The War between Science and Religion' in *JR* 61 (1981) pp. 285–308.

Locke, J., *The Reasonableness of Christianity as Delivered in the Scriptures* (1695), in *The Works of John Locke*, 7. London 1823.

— *Epistola de Tolerantia* (1689), ed. R. Kibansky. Oxford 1968.

Lowth, R., *Isaiah: A New Translation, with a Preliminary Dissertation and Notes, Critical, Philological, and Explanatory* (1799), n. ed. Glasgow 1822.

— *De sacra poesi hebraeorum.* Oxford 1753.

Lücke, F., 'Zur freundschaftlichen Erinnerungen an D. Wilhelm Martin Leberecht de Wette', in *TSK* 1850, pp. 497–535.

— W. M. L. de Wette, *Zur freundschaftlichen Errinnerung*. Hamburg 1850.

McCaul, A., 'The Mosaic Record of Creation' in *Aids to Faith. A Series of Theological Essays*, ed. W. Thomson. London 1861, pp. 189–238.

McClelland, Charles E., *State, Society and University in Germany 1700–1914*. Cambridge 1980.

McKane, W., *Studies in the Patriarchal Narratives*. Edinburgh 1979.

Maas, O., *Das Christentum in der Weltgeschichte. Theologische Vorstellungen bei Christian Karl Josias Bunsen*. Diss, Kiel 1968.

Mansel, H. L., *The Limits of Religious Thought*, Bampton Lectures 1858. London and Oxford 1859[3].

Marquardt, H., *Henry Crabb Robinson und seine deutschen Freunde. Brücke zwischen England und Deutschland im Zeitalter der Romantik*, 2 vols. Göttingen 1964–7.

Maurice, F. D., *The Kingdom of Christ*, 2 vols. London 1838, repr. London 1959.

— *Patriarchs and Lawgivers of the Old Testament*. London 1851.

— *The Prophets and Kings of the Old Testament*. London 1879[3].

Maurice, F., ed. *The Life of Frederick Denison Maurice*. London 1884.

Mensching, G., *Geschichte der Religionswissenschaft*. Bonn 1948.

Michaelis, J. D. *Commentaries on the Law of Moses*, ET, A. Smith. 4 vols. London 1814.

Milman, A., *Henry Hart Milman, D.D., Dean of St. Paul's. A Biographical Sketch*. London 1899.

Milman, H. H., *The History of the Jews*, London 1829–30, rev. edition 1863, repr. in Everyman series, London 1909.

Moore, J., *The Post-Darwinian Controversies*. Cambridge 1979.

Mozley, J. B., *Essays Historical and Theological*, 2. London 1878.

— *Letters of the Rev. J. B. Mozley, D.D.* London 1885.

— *Ruling Ideas in Early Ages and their relation to Old Testament Faith*, n. ed. London 1877.

Müller, F. M., *Chips from a German Workshop*, 3, Essays on Literature, Biography and Antiquities. London 1880.

Müller, K. O., *Prolegomena zu einer Wissenschaftlichen Mythologie*. Göttingen 1825, repr. Darmstadt 1970.

Nachtigall, J. C. K., *ps.* Othmar, Fragmente über die Allmählige Bildung der den Israeliten Heiligen Schriften in Henke's *Magazin für Religionsphilosophie, Exegese und Kirchengeschichte*, Helmstädt, 2 (1794), pp. 433 ff; 4 (1796), pp. 1–36, 329–370.

Nettleship, R. L., *Memoir of Thomas Hill Green*. London 1906.

Nicholas, T., *Dr Davidson's Removal from the Professorship of Biblical Literature in the Lancashire Independent College, Manchester, on account of alleged error in Doctrine*. London and Edinburgh 1860.

Niebuhr, B. G., *Römische Geschichte*, 1–2, Berlin 1811–12 (ET, by J. C. Hare and C. Thirlwall, *The History of Rome*, 1. London 1847[4]).

Nöldeke, T., 'Die s.g. Grundschrift des Pentateuchs' in *Untersuchungen zur Kritik des Alten Testaments*. Kiel 1869, pp. 1–144.

Oehler, G. F., *Prolegomena zur Theologie des Alten Testaments*. Stuttgart 1845.

Olshausen, J., *Die Psalmen erklärt, KEH*, Leipzig 1853.

Othmar, see Nachtigall, J. C. K.

Ottley, R. L., *Aspects of the Old Testament*, Bampton Lectures, 1897. London 1897.

Otto, R., *Kantisch-Fries'sche Religionsphilosophie und ihre Anwendung auf die Theologie. Zur Einleitung in die Glaubenslehre für Studenten der Theologie*. Tübingen 1909; (ET, E. B. Dicker, *The Philosophy of Religion based on Kant and Fries*. London 1931).

Otzen, Benedikt, *Studien über Deuterosachayra*, Acta Theologica Danica, 6. Copenhagen 1964.

Pauli, Sabine, 'Geschichte der theologischen Institut an der Universität Rostock' in *Wissenschaftliche Zeitschrift der Universität Rostock*, 17. Jahrgang 1968, pp. 309–65.

Perlitt, L., *Vatke und Wellhausen, BZAW* 94, Berlin 1965.

Perowne, J. J. S., and Stokes, L. (eds.), see Thirlwall, C.

Pfeiffer, R., *History of Classical Scholarship 1300–1850*. Oxford 1976.

Pfleiderer, Otto, *The Development of Theology in Germany since Kant, and its Progress in Great Britain since 1825*. London 1890.

Plummer, A., *The Church of England in the Eighteenth Century*. London 1910.

Plumptre, E. H., *Biblical Studies*. London 1869.

— *Ecclesiastes*, Cambridge Bible Commentary. Cambridge 1881.

Powell, Baden, 'On the Study of the Evidences of Christianity', in *Essays and Reviews*. London 1860, pp. 94–144.

Popper, K., 'Normal Science and its Dangers' Lavatos, I., and Musgrave, A. (eds.), *Criticism and the Growth of Knowledge*. Cambridge 1970.

Prickett, S., *Romanticism and Religion. The Tradition of Coleridge and Wordsworth in the Victorian Church*. Cambridge 1976.

Prothero, R. E., and Bradley, G. G., *The Life and Correspondence of Arthur Penrhyn Stanley, D.D. Late Dean of Westminster*. London 1893.

Pusey, E. B., *An Historical Enquiry into the Probable Causes of the Rationalist Character lately Predominant in the Theology of Germany*. London 1828.

Reill, H. P., *The German Enlightenment and the Rise of Historicism*. Berkeley 1975.

Reuss, E., *Die Geschichte der Heiligen Schriften, Alten Testament*. Braunschweig 1881.

— 'Die wissenschaftliche Theologie unter den französischen Protestanten 1831–42' in *TSK* 1844, pp. 262–98.

Reventlow, Henning Graf, 'Das Arsenal der Bibelkritik des Reimarus: Die Auslegung der Bibel, insbesondere des Alten Testaments, bei den englischen Deisten' in *Hermann Samuel Reimarus 1694–1768. Ein bekannter Unbekannter der Aufklärung*. Göttingen 1973.

— *Bibelautorität und Geist der Moderne. Die Bedeutung des Bibelverständnisses für die*

Geistesgeschichte und politische Entwicklung in England von der Reformation bis zur Aufklärung, FKDG 30. Göttingen 1980.

Riehm, E., Appreciation of Umbreit in *TSK* 1862, pp. 479–511.

— *Einleitung in das Alte Testament*, 2 vols. Halle 1889–90.

— D. *Hermann Hupfeld. Lebens- und Charakterbild eines deutschen Professors.* Halle 1867.

Ritschl, O., *Die Evangelisch-Theologische Fakultät zu Bonn in dem ersten Jahrhundert ihrer Geschichte*, 1819–1919. Bonn 1919.

Robinson, J. A. T., *Honest to God.* London 1963.

Rogerson, J. W., *Anthropology and the Old Testament.* Oxford 1978.

— *Myth in Old Testament Interpretation, BZAW* 134. Berlin 1974.

— 'Philosophy and the Rise of Biblical Criticism: England and Germany' in S. W. Sykes (ed.), *England and Germany. Studies in Theological Diplomacy.* Frankfurt/M and Bern 1982, pp. 63–79.

— 'Progressive Revelation: its History and its Value as a key to Old Testament Interpretation,' *Epworth Review*, 9 (1982), pp. 73–86.

— 'W. R. Smith: *Religion of the Semites,*' *ET* 90, 1979. pp. 228–33.

Rogerson, J. W. and McKay, J. W., *Psalms*, Cambridge Bible Commentary, 3 vols. Cambridge 1977.

Rorison, G., 'The Creative Week' in *Replies to Essays and Reviews*, London 1862, pp. 277–346.

Rose, Henry John, *The Law of Moses, viewed in connexion with the History and Character of the Jews with a Defence of Joshua against Professor Leo of Berlin* (Hulsean Lectures 1833). Cambridge 1834.

— 'Bunsen, the Critical School and Dr Williams' in *Replies to Essays and Reviews.* London 1862, pp. 55–134.

Rose, Hugh James, *The State of the Protestant Religion in Germany.* Cambridge 1825.

Rosenmüller, E. F. C., *Scholia in Vetus Testamentum*, Partis Tertiae, Jesajae Vaticania Complectentis, Sectio Secunda. Leipzig 1793.

Rostock, *Geschichte der Universität Rostock 1419–1969.* Rostock 1969.

Rowley, H. H., 'The Unity of the Book of Daniel' in *The Servant of the Lord and other Essays on the Old Testament.* Oxford 1965[2].

Rudolph, K., *Die Religionsgeschichte an der Leipziger Universität und die Entwicklung der Religionswissenshaft*, Sitzungsberichte der Sächsischen Akademie der Wissenschaften zu Leipzig. Phil.-hist. Klasse, Band 107, Heft 1. Berlin 1962.

Ruprecht, Eberhard, *Die Auslegungsgeschichte zu den sogennanten Gottesknechtlieder im Buch Deuterojesaia unter methodischen Geschichtspunkten bis zu Bernhard Duhm.* Diss. Heidelberg 1972.

Ryle, H. E., *The Early Narratives of Genesis.* London 1892.

— *Ezra and Nehemiah*, Cambridge Bible Commentary. Cambridge 1893.

Sadler, T., *Diary, Reminiscences and Correspondence of Henry Crabb Robinson*, London 1872[2].

Sandford, E. G., *Memoirs of Archbishop Temple*. London 1906.

Schenkel, D., *W. M. L. de Wette und die Bedeutung seine Theologie für unsere Zeit.* Schaffhausen 1849.

Schleiermacher, F., *Der christliche Glaube nach den Grundsätzen der evangelischen Kirche im Zusammenhange dargestellt*. Berlin 1821f.

Schmidt-Clausen, K., *Vorweggenommene Einheit. Die Gründung des Bistums Jerusalem im Jahre 1841, AGTL* 15. Berlin and Hamburg 1965.

Schrader, W., *Geschichte der Friedrichs-Universität zu Halle*, 2 vols. Berlin 1894.

Schröter, M. (ed.) *Schellings Werke*, Sechster Ergänzungsband. Munich 1954.

Selle, G. von, *Die Georg-August-Universität zu Göttingen 1737–1937*. Göttingen 1937.

Senft, C., *Wahrhaftigkeit und Wahrheit. Die Theologie des 19. Jahrhunderts zwischen Orthodoxie und Aufklärung, BHTh* 22. Tübingen 1956.

Shaffer, Elinor S., *'Kubla Khan' and the Fall of Jerusalem. The Mythological School in Biblical Criticism and Secular Literature 1770–1880*. Cambridge 1975.

Sieveking, G., *Memoir and Letters of Francis W. Newman*. London 1909.

Simpson, C., *Life of Principal Rainy*. London 1909.

Skinner, J., *Isaiah 1–39*, Cambridge Bible Commentary. Cambridge 1896.

Smend, R., 'De Wette und das Verhältnis zwischen historischer Bibelkritik und philosophischem System im 19. Jahrhundert', *ThLZ* 14, 1958, pp. 107–19.

— 'Friedrich Bleek 1793–1859' in *150 Jahre Rheinische Friedrich-Wilhelms-Universität zu Bonn 1818–1968*. Bonn 1968, pp. 31–41.

— *Das Mosebild von Heinrich Ewald bis Martin Noth, BGBE* 3. Tübingen 1959.

— 'Julius Wellhausen (1844–1918)' in *Theologen des Protestantismus im 19. und 20. Jahrhundert*, 1. Stuttgart 1978, pp. 166–80.

— 'Wellhausen in Greifswald', *ZThK* 78 (1981), pp. 141–76.

— 'Wellhausen und das Judentum', *ZThK* 79 (1982), pp. 249–82.

— *Wilhelm Martin Leberecht de Wettes Arbeit am Alten und am Neuen Testament.* Basel 1958.

Smiles, S., *A Publisher and his Friends. Memoir and Correspondence of the late John Murray*, 2. London 1891.

Smith, J. Pye, *The Scripture Testimony to the Messiah*. London 1847[4].

Smith, W. R., *The Old Testament in the Jewish Church*. London 1892[2].

— *The Prophets of Israel and their Place in History to the Close of the Eighth Century BC*. London 1882.

Spence, H. M. D., and Exell, J. S., *The Pulpit Commentary*. London 1882–92.

Staehelin, E., *Dewettiana. Forschungen und Texte zu Wilhelm Martin Leberecht de Wettes Leben und Werk*. Studien zur Geschichte der Wissenschaften in Basel, 2. Basel 1956.

Stähelin, J. J., *Kritische Untersuchungen über den Pentateuch, die Bücher Josua, Richter, Samuels und der Könige*. Berlin 1843.

Stähelin, R., *W. M. L. de Wette nach seiner theologischen Wirksamkeit und Bedeutung geschildert*. Basel 1880.

Stanley, A. P., *Lectures on the History of the Jewish Church*. London 1865[3].

— *Sinai and Palestine in Connection with their History*. London 1856.

Steck, K. G., *Die Idee der Heilsgeschichte:* Hofmann, Schlatter, Cullmann, *TS* 56, 1959.

Steffens, H., *Von der falschen Theologie und dem Wahren Glauben. Eine Stimme aus der Gemeinde*. Breslau 1823.

Steinmann, Jean, *Richard Simon et les origines de l'exégèse biblique*. Bruges 1960.

Stephan, H. and Schmidt, M., *Geschichte der deutschen evangelischen Theologie seit dem deutschen Idealismus*. Berlin 1960.

Storr, V. F., *The Development of English Theology in the Nineteenth Century, 1800–60*. London 1913.

Suphan, B., see Herder, J. G.

Sykes, S. W., 'Germany and England: An attempt at Theological Diplomacy' in *England and Germany. Studies in Theological Diplomacy*, ed. S. W. Sykes. Frankfurt/M and Bern 1982, pp. 146–70.

Taylor, C., *Hegel*. Cambridge 1975.

Temple, F., 'The Education of the World' in *Essays and Reviews*. London 1860, pp. 1–49.

Thirlwall, C., *Letters Literary and Theological of Connop Thirlwall*, ed. J. J. S. Perowne and L. Stokes. London, 1881.

Thöllden, G. A., *Neuen Nekrolog der Deutschen*. 27, Jahrgang 1849, Weimar 1851.

Tholuck, August (F. A. G.), *Einige Apologetische Winke für das Studium des alten Testaments*. Berlin 1821 (ET, *Hints on the Importance of the Study of the Old Testament*. Edinburgh 1833).

— *Die Lehre von der Sünde und vom Versöhner, oder die wahre Weihe des Zweiflers*, Hamburg 1823 (ET, *Guido and Julius. The Doctrine of Sin and the Propitiator*. London 1836).

— *Geschichte des Rationalismus: 1, Geschichte des Pietismus und des ersten Stadiums der Aufklärung*. Berlin 1865.

Thompson, R. J., *Moses and the Law in a Century of Criticism since Graf, SVT* 19. Leiden 1970.

Thomson, W., (ed.), *Aids to Faith. A Series of Theological Essays*. London 1861.

Toland, J., *Tetradymus, containing Hodegus, Clidophorus, Hypatia and Mangoneutes*. London 1720.

Twesten, D., *August Twesten nach Tagebüchern und Briefen*, von C. J. Georg Heinrici. Berlin 1889.

Ullmann, C., Obituary of Umbreit in *TSK* 1862, pp. 435–79.

Umbreit, F. W. K. 'Ist Jesus Christus in den Psalmen?' in *TSK* 1840, pp. 697–708.

— Review of K. F. C. W. Bähr, *Symbolik des Mosaischen Kultus*, 2 vols. Heidelberg 1837–9, in *TSK* 1843, pp. 144–92.

— 'Vorwort zu Christologischen Beitragen' in *TSK* 1830, pp. 1–24.

— Review of Hitzig's Commentary on Isaiah in *TSK* 1834, pp. 653–74, 947–59.

Vater, Johann Severin, *Commentar über den Pentateuch, mit Einleitungen zu den einzelnen Abschnitten, der Eingeschalteten Uebersetzung von Dr. Alexander Geddes's Merkwürdigeren Critischen und Exegetischen Anmerkungen und einer Abhandlung über Moses und die Verfasser des Pentateuchs*, 3 vols. Halle, 1802–5.

Vatke, W., *Die biblische Theologie wissenschaftlich dargestellt*, 1, *Die Religion des Alten Testamentes*. Berlin 1835.

Volck, W. (ed.) *Theologische Briefe der Professoren Delitzsch und v. Hofmann*. Leipzig 1891.

Vries, S. J. de, *Bible and Theology in the Netherlands*. Wageningen 1968.

Waardenburg, S., *Classical Approaches to the Study of Religion*, 2. The Hague and Paris 1974.

Wagner, S., *Franz Delitzsch, Leben und Werk, BEvTh* 80. Munich 1978.

Wapler, P., *Johannes v. Hoffman. Ein Beitrag zur Geschichte der theologischen Grundprobleme der kirchlichen und der politischen Bewegungen im 19. Jahrhundert.* Leipzig 1914.

Wellhausen, J., *Die Composition des Hexateuchs und der Historischen Bücher des Alten Testaments.* 1889.

— *Grundrisse zum Alten Testament*, ed. R. Smend, *TB* 27. Munich 1965.

— *Israelitische und Jüdische Geschichte*. Berlin 1894.

— *Geschichte Israels*, 1. Berlin 1878.

— *Heinrich Ewald* repr. in *Grundrisse zum Alten Testament*, ed. R. Smend. Munich 1965.

— *Prolegomena zur Geschichte Israels*. Berlin 1883 (ET, *Prolegomena to the History of Ancient Israel*. Edinburgh 1885).

Wendebourg, E-W., 'Die heilsgeschichtliche Theologie J. Chr. K. von Hofman's in ihrem Verhältnis zur romantischen Weltanschauung' in *ZThK*. 52, 1955.

Westcott, B. F., *The Epistle to the Hebrews*. London 1889.

Weth, G., *Die Heilsgeschichte. Ihr universeller und ihr individueller Sinn in der offenbarungsgeschichtlichen Theologie des 19. Jahrhunderts, FGLP.* 4. 2. Munich 1931.

Wette, W. M. L. de, *Auffoderung zum Studium der Hebräischen Sprache und Litteratur*, Jena and Leipzig. 1805.

— *Beiträge zur Einleitung in das Alte Testament*, 2 vols. Halle 1806–7. 1, Kritischer Versuch über die Glaubwürdigkeit der Bücher der Chronik, mit Hinsicht auf die Geschichte der Mosaischen Bücher und Gesetzgebung; Ein Nachtrag zu den Vaterschen Untersuchungen über den Pentateuch; 2, Kritik der Mosaischen Geschichte; repr. Darmstadt 1971.

— 'Beytrag zur Characteristik des Hebraismus' in Daub, C. and Creuzer, F. (eds.), *Studien* 3. 2. Heidelberg 1807.

— *Biblische Dogmatik Alten und Neuen Testaments*. Berlin 1831[3].

— *Die biblische Geschichte als Geschichte der Offenbarung Gottes*. Berlin 1846.

— *Commentar über die Psalmen*. Heidelberg 1811, 1823[2], 1829[3].

— 'De morte Jesu Christi expiatoria commentatio' in *Opuscula Theologica*. Berlin 1830 pp. 1–148.

— *Dissertatio critica qua a prioribus Deuteronomium Pentateuchi libris diversum, alius cuiusdam recentioris auctoris opus esse monstratur 1805*, repr. in *Opuscula Theologica*. Berlin 1830, pp. 151–68.

— *Eine Idee über das Studium der Theologie*, ed. A. Stieren. Leipzig 1850.

— *Lehrbuch der historisch-kritischen Einleitung in die Bibel Alten und Neuen Testaments*, Berlin 1817, 1822[2].

— *Die Religion, ihr Wesen und ihre Erscheinungsformen und ihren Einfluss auf das Leben*. Berlin 1827.

— Review of Vatke's *Biblische Theologie*, von Bohlen's *Genesis* and George's *Jüdische Feste* in *TSK* 1836, pp. 953–81.

— *Theodor, oder des Zweiflers Weihe*. Weimar 1828[2].

— *Ueber die erbauliche Erklärung der Psalmen. Eine Beilage zum Commentar über dieselben*. Heidelberg 1836.

— *Ueber Religion und Theologie. Erläuterungen zu seinem Lehrbuche der Dogmatik*. Berlin 1815.

Whitelaw, T., 'The Authorship of the Pentateuch' in *Genesis* (The Pulpit Commentary). London 1881[4].

Wiegand, Adelbert Friedrich Julius, *W. M. L. de Wette (1780–1849), Eine Säkularschrift*. Erfurt 1879.

Willey, B., *The Eighteenth Century Background*. Harmondsworth 1962.

Willi, Thomas, *Die Chronik als Auslebung, FRLANT* 106. Göttingen 1972.

Williams, R., 'Bunsen's Biblical Researches' in *Essays and Reviews*. London 1861[5].

Witte, L., *Das Leben Tholucks*. Bielefeld and Leipzig 1884.

Wordsworth, C., 'On the Interpretation of Scripture' in *Replies to Essays and Reviews*. London 1862, pp. 409–500.

Index of Biblical References

Genesis—Numbers
33, 42, 52, 199, 225, 228, 230, 242, 257

Genesis
17, 58, 67, 112, 133, 175, 176, 177, 180, 211, 212, 216, 237, 243, 252, 257, 262, 271, 282
1—11 19, 20, 76, 176, 225, 226, 260, 261
1—9 210
1—3 214, 239n6
1 155, 160, 181, 183, 215–16, 218, 227
1.1—2.4 46, 94, 262
1.1 231
1.2 113
1.16 181
1.24 181
1.27 183
2—3 18, 95, 155, 198
2 183
2.2 56
2.4b—3.24 261
2.5–9 46
2.7 118, 183, 274n7
2.21–3 183
3 70, 85, 95, 135, 181, 227, 283
3.1ff 181
3.1 181
3.15 109, 120
4.1–15 261
4.16–24 261
4.25ff 261
5.29 261
6—10 261
6.19–21 183
7.2 183
7.6–9 225
7.7–10 225n26
7.19 226

9.18–27 95
10—11 94
10 226, 228
10.1–7 230
10.8–19 226n27
10.13–32 230
10.16–18a 261
10.21 226n27
10.24–30 226n27
10.25 94
11 56, 210
11.1–9 261
11.9 56
11.31 183
12—50 54
12—16 261
12 186
12.1 183
12.6 149
12.10–20 261
13.10 204
14 95, 98
14.14 89
15 95
19.31–8 95
20—2 261
20—1 270
20 185
20.29–31 94
21.22–32 94
22 185, 231
25.19—28.22 261
25.26 56
26 186
26.1–33 99n19, 261
26.28–31 94
26.34 204
27—36 261
27 95
27.41–5 203
27.46—28.9 203
28.9 204
30 54

30.25–43 204
31.4–48 204
31.19 54
31.44–54 94
32.29 56
37 20, 21, 95
39—47 95
39.1 21
40—2 270
48 270
49 52, 56, 94, 230

Exodus
33, 42, 58, 59, 60, 62, 64–8, 89, 133, 177, 180, 198, 230–1, 236n57, 242–3, 257
1.15—2.22 95
3.14 224
3.15 95
4.18 94
6.2–3 182, 224
6.2 88
9.6 183
9.20 183
12—13 67
12 88
12.1–3 95
12.6–8 95
12.14–20 67
12.35 222
12.37–8 221
12.37 221
12.40 125, 178
13 77
14.19 151
14.21–9 25
15.1–18 94
18 94
18.1—19.28 95
19—24 77, 112
20.1–17 94
20.23—23.19 94

21—3 68
21 68
23.11 68
23.24 59
24 94
25—9 262–3
25 262
30—1 263
32—4 77, 95
32 88
34.12–17 59
35—40 94
35—9 263
38.26 221

Leviticus
   58–9, 62, 64–6, 68, 97,
   133, 177, 180, 195,
   236n57, 242–4, 257
1.20 94
6.1–11 244
6.8–18 244
6.12–16 244
6.17—7.7 244
6.19–23 244
6.24—7.7 244
9 262–3
10.1–5 263
10.12–15 263
11—15 263
12.6–8 222
16 67, 127, 263
17—26 263, 269
17.1–9 263
18—27 230
18—20 231
19—26 263
19—25 263
19.29 259
23 94
24.1–9 263
25 68
25.1—26.2 94
26 32, 52, 55, 230–1
46 94

Numbers
   62, 64, 66, 68, 94, 95, 133,
   177, 180, 231, 236n57,
   257, 264n29
1—10 263
1.20–43 221

1.46 221
3.43 222
15—19 263
16 56, 58–9, 264n27
21.14 94, 149
21.20 94
22—4 56
24.17 199
24.19 199
26—36 263

Deuteronomy
   31, 33, 34n27, 35, 39, 42–
   3, 46n77, 52, 59, 62, 64–8,
   89, 95–6, 113, 177, 195,
   199, 200, 207, 224–5, 231,
   244, 260, 263, 269, 284
1—4 231, 263
5—26 231
5—11 263
5.26 231
5.28 231
11—27 149
12—26 263
15 68
16 88, 231
17.14–20 225
18.5ff 66
23.12–14 223
27 263
27—30 95
27—8 35
27.2–8 59
28 52, 231, 263
29–30 231
33 52, 96
34.1 89
34.6 149

Joshua
   31, 59, 61–2, 94, 96, 98,
   149, 182, 195, 221, 223,
   230–2, 257, 264n29,
   274n7
1.1–9 183
1.10–18 183
2.1–24 183
3—11 183
4.9 149
5.9 149
7.26 149
8.30–5 59, 240

10.13 94
12—21 183
17.14–18 94
22 183
23—4 183
24 54

Judges
   32, 58, 61, 74, 88–9, 94,
   96, 149, 200, 286
1 61
5.20 242n23
17—18 96
18.29 89
19—21 96

Ruth
   58, 94, 149

Samuel
   22, 29, 30–1, 52, 58–9, 61,
   75n23, 94, 96, 97, 149,
   174, 183, 201, 205,
   264n31, 265, 270, 279,
   284

1 Samuel
   96, 230, 277
1 96
13—14 96, 194
13.19ff 193
14.44ff 194
16 183, 187
16.1–13 183
16.14–23 183
17 183, 187
18.1–9 183
18.10–30 183
21 32
23—30 96
23.9 61n50
24 96
26 96

2 Samuel
   22, 30, 32, 230
1.18 94
11—12 30
21—4 97
24 22
24.1 30
24.6 89
24.24 194n70

Kings
22, 29, 30–2, 52, 59, 75, 75n23, 88–9, 94, 96–7, 149, 174, 183, 201, 205, 239, 265, 270, 279, 284

1 Kings
22, 29, 30, 62, 96, 231
2 96
3—4 30
6.1 125
11 62
12.31 76
17.4 56
22 76

2 Kings
60, 62, 258
11.4–12 31
18—19 187
22—3 59
22 31
22.4 66
22.8 66, 149
23 149
25 97
25.27–30 96

Chronicles
22, 29, 32, 34, 36, 42, 48, 52, 55, 58–9, 62, 75n23, 94, 96, 97, 149, 166, 174, 183, 194, 201, 205–6, 224, 230, 239, 243, 257–8, 265, 278, 284

1 Chronicles
2 224
12 205
20.1–3 30
20.3 183
21 22
21.25 194n70
22 205
23—6 205
27 194

2 Chronicles
1.3 30
1.4 31
23.1–11 31

Ezra
31, 59, 94, 97, 231, 239, 270, 287

Nehemiah
31, 59, 94, 97, 287
6.17–19 32

Esther
59

Job
41–2, 47, 59, 127, 137, 149, 248n54, 286
12—13 46
32—42 123
38 46
38.4–7 113

Psalms
31, 41–3, 45–6, 53, 56, 102, 160, 165, 190, 224, 248n54
1—72 127
1—41 224
1—2 134
2 45, 56n28, 57, 165
9 160
10 160
14 224
15 45
18 160
19 160
20 45, 56n28, 57
21 45, 56n28, 57
22 137n35
23 45
24 45, 56n28, 160
26 57
37 45
39 160
40 160
42—80 224
42 160
43 160
45 45, 56n28
51 160
52 224
53 224
54 224
56 224
57 160, 224

63 224
68 45, 224
72 45, 56n28, 57
73—150 134
73—106 127
73 45
78 45, 56n28, 57
81 45
87 45
104 46
105 45, 56n28, 57
106 45, 56n28, 57
107—50 127
110 45, 56n28, 57
114 45, 56n28
122 56n28, 57
132 56n28
132.8–9 160
132.13–18 160
134 45
135 45

Proverbs
59
8.22–31 46

Ecclesiastes
41–2, 47, 59, 134, 137, 286

Song of Songs
59, 134, 137

Isaiah
50, 77, 81n10, 87, 112–13, 134, 200, 213, 257, 260, 277
1—39 287
1—35 58
1—33 128
1—12 128
7.14 127, 165, 213
9.1–7 127
13 113
13.1—14.23 128
14 113
14.24—20 128
21 113
21.1–10 128
24—7 128
21.11—23 128

23—7 113
24—7 23
28—33 128
34—5 113, 128
40—66 23, 59, 128, 268 n47,
   286 n68
40—55 81, 113
42.1-7 23
49.1-9 23
50.4-10 23
52—3 173
52.12—53 176
52.13—53.12 23
53 114, 137 n35, 213

Jeremiah
   24, 52, 59, 75 n23, 134,
   177, 225, 231, 277,
   285 n62
1.5 118
7.22 239
7.25 31
50—1 60

Lamentations
   59, 128

Matthew
27.9-10 24

John
8.56 247 n52

Romans
7 85

Ezekiel
   59, 62 n60, 75 n23, 230–1,
   263, 265, 287
44.9 66

Daniel
   6 n8, 24, 48, 59, 134, 152,
   200–1, 213
1.1—2.3 24
2.4—6.28 24
2.4b—7.28 24
3—6 24
7—12 24

Hosea
   58, 88–9, 259, 260, 270,
   287
1.3 259

Joel
   58, 123, 149, 287
2.3 204

Amos
   58, 88–9, 287
5.15–16 72
5.25 239
5.26 135

Epistles, Pauline
   216

Ephesians
2.3 119

Hebrews
   190, 286

Jonah
   59, 149

Micah
   58

Nahum
   58, 287

Habakkuk
   287

Zephaniah
   58

Haggai
   59

Zechariah
   23, 48, 59, 213, 257, 277,
   287
1—8 24
9—14 23–4
10.10–11 24
11—13 24

Malachi
   59, 149

2 Peter
1–14 119

Revelation
13.8 118

Index of Modern Authors

Alt, A.   92, 291
Altenstein, K. Freiherr von   69
Arnold, T.   159n, 162, 188–92, 209, 218, 245–6
Arnoldi, A.J.   16, 131
Ashton, R.   159n
Astruc, J.   19, 35n
Auberlen, E.   6n

Bachmann, J.   44n, 51nn, 85nn, 86nn, 89, 110n
Baehring, B.   124n
Bahrdt, F.   217n
Barnes, W.E.   286–7
Barth, K.   7
Baudissin, W.W. Graf   112n, 268–9
Bauer, G.L.   23n, 56, 172–3
Baumgarten, M.   89, 111n, 117
Baumgarten, S.J.   167, 173
Bayle, P.   153
Beck, J.T.   173
Beddoes, T.   159
Beidelman, T.O.   275n
Belsham, T.   159, 164–5
Benecke, H.   69n
Benham, W.   209n
Bertholdt, L.   174
Beyreuther, E.   79n
Black, J.S.   275n, 281n
Bleek, F.   8, 103, 130–1, 139, 202, 208, 221, 228n, 233n, 287
Bleek, W.   221
Bohlen, P. von   63n, 133n, 172, 175–7, 200, 239, 251, 287
Bornkamm, H.   15n
Brömse, M.   69n, 70n, 72n, 79n
Browne, E.H.   234n
Bucer, M.   148n
Buckland, W.   214
Budde, K.   271
Bunsen, C.C.J.   102, 121–9, 140, 162, 177, 179, 188,

212–13, 217–18, 233n, 252
Bunsen, F.   122n, 124nn, 125n, 164
Burgon, J.W.   166nn, 173n
Burney, C.F.   285, 291
Butler, J.   153, 246n
Buttmann, P.K.   266n

Carpenter, J.E.   192n
Cave, A.   273n
Chadwick, O.   209n, 213, 221n, 234n
Chalmers, T.   214
Cheyne, T.K.   1–2, 5, 36n, 91n, 111n, 121, 130n, 131n, 134n, 154n, 233, 242, 248n, 273n, 281, 285, 287
Chrystal, G.   275n, 281n
Church, R.W.   245
Clarke, A.   180–2
Clarke, J.B.B.   180n, 182n
Cochlovius, J.   79n, 80nn, 86n, 111n
Colenso, J.W.   7–8, 114n, 158, 176, 179–80, 192, 194, 216, 219, 220–37, 239–40, 245, 252–3, 259n, 276
Coleridge, S.T.   159, 161
Collins, A.   152
Conybeare, W.J.   198
Cornish, F.W.   209n
Corrodi, H.   24
Cox, G.W.   220n, 221n, 233n, 234n, 235n
Creighton, M.   244n

Darwin, C.   11, 253
Davidson, A.B.   248, 275, 287
Davidson, R.T.   209n
Davidson, S.   5, 170–3, 197–208, 221, 252, 276
Davies, T.W.   91n
Delitzsch, F.   80, 83n, 87, 89, 90, 102, 103, 104–5, 107,

111–20, 137, 139, 217, 268, 287
Dewar, E.H.   169–70, 226–7
Diestel, L.   1, 4, 50, 58n, 91n, 105n, 121, 131n, 148n, 220n, 242
Dillmann, A.   271
Dockhorn, K.   7, 8
Döderlein, J.C.   23nn, 121, 161n, 165
D'Oyley, G.   184n
Driver, S.R.   20, 225n, 232, 273–5, 282–5, 286nn, 287
Duff, A.   121, 242
Duhm, B.   23, 260, 267–8
Dyer, G.   159
Dyson, A.O.   16n

Eichhorn, J.G.   15, 17, 18, 19–22, 23, 24, 29–30, 32, 35, 56, 92, 123n, 131, 136–7, 138, 155–6, 159n, 160, 162, 164–5, 167–8, 171–2, 174, 184
Eissfeldt, O.   50n, 53n
Eliot, G. (Evans, M.A.)   250
Ellicott, C.J.   216–17
Elliger, W.   15n, 83n, 84n, 85n, 130n
Ernesti, J.A.   173
Ewald, H.   1, 5, 6n, 8, 51, 69, 83n, 91–103, 113, 121, 123–4, 125, 128–9, 132, 133n, 134, 139–40, 156, 165, 177, 179, 193, 208, 209n, 217–18, 220, 221n, 223, 226, 228n, 232n, 233n, 238–40, 248, 268n, 271n, 281, 283, 287

Fichte, J.G.   53, 140
Flügge, B.G.   24
Franck, G.   16n
Frend, W.   159
Fries, J.F.   28n, 36, 37–9, 41–4, 46, 47n, 48n, 85, 132, 140, 161, 168

314

Fulda, F.V.   29
Fuller, R.C.   154n, 155nn, 156nn

Gabler, J.P.   15, 17, 18, 56, 159–60, 166, 172
Geddes, A.   154–6, 159n
Geldbach, E.   122n
George, J.F.L.   4, 63–8, 83n, 90, 92, 128, 130, 172, 175, 242–3, 258, 265, 268
Gérold, C.T.   259n
Gestrich, C.   147n, 148n, 150n
Giesebrecht, F.   274
Goethe, J.W.   140
Gesenius, W.   50–7, 63, 69, 71n, 72, 81n, 83–4, 89, 102–3, 123n, 132, 134, 139, 165, 166, 174–5, 183n, 251
Gilley, S.   253n
Glover, W.B.   248n, 273, 281n, 287n
Goodwin, C.W.   209, 214–16, 253
Gore, C.   283–5
Goulburn, E.M.   209n
Graf, H.K.   230, 258–9, 287
Gramberg, K.P.W.   4, 57–65, 71n, 72, 92, 128, 139, 166, 174, 201, 242, 243n, 265, 268
Grant, R.M.   148n
Gray, G.B.   285, 291
Gray, R.   221, 235–6
Green, T.H.   280
Gregory, G.   160n
Gressmann, H.   291
Griesbach, J.J.   34n, 161
Gross, K.D.   122nn
Günther, A.   114–17
Gunkel, H.   272n, 291

Havernick, H.A.C.   79, 89, 176, 200, 213, 221–2
Haight, G.S.   250n
Hare, A.J.C.   122n
Hare, F.G.   163
Hare, J.C.   122, 162–4, 188
Hartmann, J.M.   132
Haym, R.   50n, 51
Hayner, P.C.   107n
Heber, R.   198
Hegel, G.W.F.   6, 53, 64, 69–71, 104–7, 140
Henke, E.L.T.   37n
Hengstenberg, E.W.   4, 8, 44n, 79–83, 85–9, 103, 104,

109–10, 111n, 112n, 113, 129, 134, 137n, 139, 176, 179, 199–201, 213, 217, 220–1, 247n
Henley, S.   160n, 161n
Herder, J.G.   16n, 17, 26–7, 123n, 131, 140
Herrmann, W.   292
Heyne, C.G.   17
Hezel, W.F.   16
Hinchliff, P.   220n, 233n, 234n
Hincks, T.D.   207
Hirsch, E.   16n, 18n
Hitzig, F.   103, 113, 132, 134–6, 139–40, 193, 217
Hobbes, T.   53, 148–50
Höcker, W.   122n
Hofmann, J.C.K.   48, 80, 83n, 87, 89, 90, 102, 104–11, 114, 116–20, 127, 217
Holland, H.S.   244n
Horne, T.H.   129, 139, 182–4, 185n, 187, 197, 201–2, 281n
Hornig, G.   16n, 17nn
Hübner, E.   104n, 108n, 110n
Hume, D.   53
Hupfeld, H.   8, 102, 111nn, 130, 131–4, 139, 179, 200, 203, 207–8, 217, 225–6, 228–9, 261, 270n, 287

Ilgen, K.D.   20–1, 35
Illingworth, J.R.   244n

Jacobi, F.H.   132, 170
Jahn, J.   171, 173–4
Jowett, B.   209, 216–18, 247
Justi, L.J.C.   23n

Kahnis, K.F.A.   80n
Kalisch, M.M.   242–4, 252
Kamphausen, A.   203
Kant, I.   16n, 18, 38, 42, 53, 85, 161n, 166, 170–1
Kattenbusch, F.   104n
Kayser, A.   259–60
Keil, C.F.   79, 89, 199–201, 203–6
Kirkpatrick, A.F.   285–6
Kittel, R.   258n, 259n, 268–70
Kitto, J.   179
Kleinert, A.F.   89
Knight, F.   159nn
Knobel, A.   233n, 287
Knoodt, P.   114nn
Koppe, J.B.   23

Kotzebue, A.   44
Kraus, H.-J.   2, 50, 51n, 70n, 91n, 105n, 112n, 121, 148n, 154n, 220n, 242
Kück, H.   92n
Kuenen, A.   221, 230, 233, 248, 258, 259n, 260, 264, 283, 287
Kuhn, T.S.   2, 3, 10n
Kurtz, J.H.   8, 111n, 220, 222

Lagarde, P. de   268n
Lenz, M.   15n, 44n, 63n, 83n, 85n, 86n, 89n, 90
Lepsius, K.R.   125, 178
Lessing, G.E.   9, 25, 209n
Lias, J.J.   286
Liddon, H.P.   167n, 209n, 273n, 285n
Lindsey, T.   159
Loades, A.L.   253n
Locke, J.   150–1
Lowth, R.   22, 153–4
Lücke, F.   44n, 136, 164, 170
Luther, M.   86, 277n
Lyell, C.   226

Maas, O.   122n, 124n
Maine, H.S.   280
Mant, R.   184n
Marquardt, H.   161nn
Maurice, F.D.   6, 163, 188–92, 194, 209, 220, 221n, 234–5, 241n
McCaul, A.   215, 227n
McClelland, C.E.   15n
McKane, W.   272n
McKay, J.W.   224n
Mensching, G.   136n
Michaelis, J.D.   9, 16, 24, 153, 156, 162–3, 165, 167–9, 184, 222n, 240n, 244, 246n
Milman, A.   184n
Milman, H.H.   184–8, 238, 244, 250, 276, 280
Moberly, R.C.   244n
Moore, J.   253n
Morgan, T.   152–3
Movers, F.K.   201
Mozley, J.B.   244–7, 280
Müller, F.M.   122n
Müller, K.O.   92
Murray, J.   184

Nachtigall, J.C.K. (Otmar)   29, 31, 160

Neander, J.A.W.   69, 86, 130, 172, 208
Newman, F.W.   192–6, 239–40, 276
Newman, J.H.   192, 239n, 240n, 245
Nicholas, T.   201n
Nicoll, A.   4
Nicoll, W.R.   287n
Niebuhr, B.G.   92, 97, 124, 140, 164, 188
Nippold, F.   122n
Nöldeke, T.   258–9
Noth, M.   92, 97, 177, 291

Oehler, G.F.   82, 89, 139
Olshausen, J.   134n, 173
Ottley, R.L.   287–9
Otto, R.   38n
Otzen, B.   23n, 24n

Paley, W.   153
Paulus, H.E.G.   16, 23n, 121, 159, 161, 164, 167, 171, 173
Peake, A.S.   281n, 291
Perlitt, L.   69n
Perowne, J.J.S.   286
Pfeiffer, R.   92n
Pfleiderer, O.   6
Phillipi, F.A.   110n
Picton, J.A.   197n, 201nn
Plummer, A.   148n, 153n
Plumptre, H.E.   286
Popper, K.   3
Powell, B.   121n
Pratt, J.   214
Priestley, J.   159
Pusey, E.B.   4, 6n, 165, 167–9, 239n, 240n, 242n, 245, 251, 273

Rainy, R.   276
Rambach, J.J.   173
Ranke, L. von   104–6, 140
Reimarus, H.S.   9, 25, 100n, 223
Reuss, E.   259
Reventlow, H. Graf   9, 10, 147n, 148nn, 150n, 151nn, 152n, 153n
Richard of St Victor   186
Riehm, E.   131n, 132nn, 136n, 258n, 270
Ritschl, A.   268n, 292
Ritschl, O.   15n, 130n, 131n
Robinson, H.C.   159n, 161-2

Robinson, J.A.T.   158
Rogerson, J.W.   17n, 33n, 64n, 91n, 172n, 188n, 224n, 271n, 273n, 278n, 281n
Rorison, G.   215
Rose, Henry J.   173–5, 213
Rose, Hugh J.   165–7
Rosenmüller, E.F.K.   23, 121, 138, 161n, 165, 174
Rosenmüller, J.G.   15
Rothe, R.   281, 292
Rowley, H.H.   24n
Ruprecht, E.   23n
Ryle, H.E.   286

Sadler, T.   159n, 162n, 164n
Sand, K.L.   4, 44
Sanday, W.   285
Schelling, F.J.   53, 107–8, 124, 128, 140
Schiller, F.   140
Schleiermacher, F.D.E.   36, 44nn, 63–4, 69, 104, 117n, 130, 132, 136, 164, 167n, 170, 173, 283n, 292
Schmidt, M.   105n
Schmidt-Clausen, K.   122n
Schrader, W.   50n, 51n, 83n
Schultz, F.W.   89
Schuster, C.G.   23n
Scott, T.   198
Selle, G. von   92n
Semler, J.S.   9, 16, 17, 153, 166, 168–9, 171–3, 217n
Senft, C.   105n
Shaffer, E.S.   159n
Sieveking, G.   192n
Simon, R.   16, 18
Simonis, J.   161n
Skinner, J.   287, 291
Smend, R. (1851–1913)   260n, 268
Smend, R.   28n, 36n, 46nn, 64n, 130nn, 131n, 260n, 267n, 268nn
Smith, A.   162nn
Smith, G.A.   291
Smith, J. Pye   164–5, 176n, 198
Smith, W.R.   5, 232, 248, 275–84, 288
Spener, A.   167
Spinoza, B.   16, 18, 107n
Staehelin, E.   11n, 28n, 36n
Stähelin, J.J.   85, 200
Staeudlin, K.F.A.   16

Stanley, A.P.   8, 184n, 238–42, 253
Steck, K.G.   105n
Steffens, H.   80n, 86
Steinmann, J.   16n
Stephan, H.   105n
Stieren, A.   37
Storr, V.F.   187n
Strauss, D.F.   63, 69, 102, 133n, 170n, 172, 250n
Sykes, S.W.   6n, 8, 9

Tait, A.C.   209n
Taylor, C.   71n
Temple, F.   8, 209–12
Thirlwall, C.   122, 162–3, 166, 188
Thöllden, G.A.   36n
Tholuck, F.A.G.   16n, 79, 83–5, 86, 89n, 150, 172, 176, 190, 208
Thompson, R.J.   69n
Thrupp, J.S.   6n
Tindal, M.   9
Toland, J.   151–2
Tregelles, S.P.   202
Troeltsch, E.   7, 292
Tuch, F.   133n, 139, 172, 200, 226
Twesten, A.   44n
Tylor, E.B.   280

Ullmann, C.   136
Umbreit, F.W.K.   123n, 134, 136–7, 140, 165

Vater, J.S.   15, 28, 29, 34n, 35, 52, 64, 83, 88, 133n, 156, 172, 200
Vatke, W.   69–79, 83n, 88, 90–3, 102, 113, 128, 140, 175, 239, 258, 259n, 265
Vries, S. de   259n

Wagner, S.   89n, 111nn, 114n, 115, 117n
Wapler, P.   104n, 110n
Wegscheider, J.A.F.   51, 84, 121, 132
Wellhausen, J.   2, 4, 11, 20, 50, 64, 67–8, 91, 93n, 97, 102–3, 232, 243, 252, 257–8, 259n, 260–71, 273–6, 278–85, 286n, 287–8, 292
Wendebourg, E.-W.   105nn, 106n
Westcott, B.F.   285–6
Weth, G.   104n

Wette, W.M.L. de   1, 4, 8, 11, 22, 28–49, 52–65, 71–3, 78, 81, 83n, 84, 85–8, 91–3, 101–3, 106n, 113, 121, 128, 130–4, 136, 137n, 139–40, 151, 156, 161, 164–70, 173–7, 190, 192, 200, 208, 230, 239, 243n, 258, 265–6, 271–2, 283n, 287

Whately, R.   198

Whitelaw, T.   287

Wiegand, A.   11, 28n, 37n, 161n

Willey, B.   158n

Willi, T.   22nn

Williams, R.   121, 209, 212–13, 218

Wordsworth, C.   217, 247

Index of Subjects and Biblical Names

Aaron 55, 61–2, 66, 75, 88, 101, 113, 222
Abimelech 94
Abraham (Abram) 54, 56, 60, 94, 98–9, 125, 178, 185–6, 213, 228, 240, 267, 283
Accommodation 17, 170–2
Achilles 98
Adonijah 30
Agamemnon 98
Ahasuerus 116
Ahndung, Ahnung 38–40, 42–3, 140
Ammon, Ammonites 56, 74, 95, 98, 193
Amphictyony 291
Angels 76, 266
Apis 61
Aries 77
Ark of the Covenant 29 n4, 32–3, 60, 101, 160
Ark, Noah's 182, 226–7
Assyria 76, 272
Astarte 74–5, 195
Atonement 81, 110, 114, 119
Augsburg Confession 79–81, 86–7
Azazel 67, 77, 101, 127

Baal 55, 74–5, 195
Babylon 76–7, 128, 190, 272, 274
Baruch 128
Bathsheba 30

Calvinism 7, 80, 192
Canaan 55, 61 n47, 98–9, 185
Canaanites 55, 95, 267
Cherdolaomer 185
Comparative religion 63, 71–2, 135–6
Conquest of Canaan 61
Creation 107–8, 113–15
  biblical account of 181, 183, 198, 211–12, 214–16, 227, 262, 272, 282

Croesus 128
Cyrus 55, 128

Dan 89
David 29–33, 60, 74–6, 96, 101, 125, 155, 187, 193 n64, 194, 224
Day of Atonement 67, 77, 101
Deism 9–10, 16, 147, 149–53, 158, 223
Demythologizing 151–2, 266
Documentary hypothesis
  see Pentateuch
Dogmatics, Old Testament 46–7, 53–4

Edom 30, 56, 99, 128, 225
Edward VI 148
Egypt 47, 48, 61, 67, 77, 122, 125, 135, 178, 185–6, 190
  plagues of 186
Egyptology 54n, 122, 177–8
Eleazar 113, 200, 222
Elegy 41
Elijah 55–6, 62, 76, 187
Elisha 55, 76
Elizabeth I 148
Elohist writer(s) or source(s) 19–21, 112, 133, 199, 207, 223, 225, 228–30, 230–3, 257, 259, 261–4, 266, 270–1
  laws vs. narratives 133, 231–2
  see also Grundschrift
Elohistic Psalter 224
El Shaddai 99, 135
Enlightenment, the 10, 79–80
Epic period 65
Esau 98–9
Evolution, theory of 253, 274, 282
Exodus from Egypt, numbers involved 25, 100, 176, 182, 221–2, 240

'Fall' of mankind 70, 108, 110–11, 119, 160, 181, 198, 227, 283
Form criticism 291

Gibeon, sun standing still at 187, 240–1
Goliath 187
Greece 48, 193
Grundschrift of the Pentateuch 133, 257–63, 266, 270–1, 274, 281
  laws vs. narratives 133, 233, 258–9
  see also Elohist

Hagar 98
'Hallischer Streit' 1830 51, 84
Hebrew religion vs. 'Judaism' 46, 48–9, 78, 140, 212, 241
Hebron 98
Hegelianism 9, 11, 51, 64, 70–1, 83, 106–7, 140, 249, 280
Henry VIII 148
Heilsgeschichte 48–9, 108–11, 116
Hezekiah 33, 62, 127, 148, 155, 269
Hilkiah 149, 195
History of science 2–3
History, prophetic nature of 109–11, 116
  providential ordering of 93, 124–5, 128–9, 140, 164, 178, 187–8, 234, 280
Hobab 152
Hyksos 99, 125, 178

Immortality 47
Inspiration, plenary 168–9
Isaac 56, 94, 98, 185–6, 267
Isaiah 87
Ishmael 98

Israelite religion, stages of 54–
  5, 58–9, 65, 72–8, 98–101,
  126, 185–7, 241, 284
Ithamar 222

Jacob 60, 94, 98–9, 125, 186,
  267
Jahwist
  see Yahwist
Jehovist (redactor of J and E)
  261–2
Jephthah 187
Jeremiah 213, 225, 231
Jeroboam 75–6, 88
Jochebed 223
Jonathan 96
Jordan, crossing of 187
Joseph 99
Joshua 113, 200, 223, 240
Josiah 31, 34–5, 55, 62, 65,
  76–8, 95–6, 148, 149, 177,
  194–5, 225, 226–65
Judaism:
  as a 'degeneration' 46n77,
  47–9, 53, 55, 65, 140, 279
  Hegel's view of 70–1
Judges, period of 55, 74, 187

Kantianism 37–8, 140, 166,
  170–1

Laban 94
Laish 89
Law, book of, discovered in
  Josiah's reign 31, 34–5,
  59–60, 65, 77, 95, 177,
  194–5
O.T., Christian obligation
  to 150–1, 163
Levi, tribe of 60, 75, 101
Levites 31–2, 61–2, 65–6, 75,
  77, 101, 230, 239, 241
Levitical religion 29–30, 55,
  65, 76, 87, 97, 175, 177,
  236, 241, 243, 278–9, 284,
  288
Liberal Anglicans 122, 162–4,
  188–92, 212, 234–5, 282
Lot 98, 185
Lutheranism 7, 16, 79–80, 86,
  129, 138
Lux Mundi 283–5, 287
Lyric poetry or period 42–3, 65

Maccabean Psalms 128, 134
Manasseh 225
Melchizedek 61
Merneptah 178
Messiah 47–8, 62, 81, 86

Messianic prophecies 23, 109–
  10, 111n20, 127, 134, 165,
  189, 199
Micaiah ben Imlah 76
Moab 56, 95, 98, 128
Moloch 195
Moses 21, 29, 33, 47n83, 52,
  55, 60, 67, 73–4, 77–8, 87–
  8, 94, 99–101, 112–13,
  125, 135, 149, 152, 155,
  177, 186, 199–200, 213,
  223, 228, 267, 271, 284
  law of 26, 55, 112, 186,
  194–5, 267n43
  religion of 29, 33, 55, 60,
  73, 125
Myth(s) 38, 41n53, 56, 92,
  266
Mythical interpretation 17,
  29, 33, 155, 160, 166, 170–
  2, 198, 252
Mythology 38, 47

Nazirites 55, 74
Neologism 16–18, 79, 138,
  155, 174, 249, 252

O.T. Scholarship, English vs.
  German 5–8, 123
Orthodoxy, confessional 79–
  80, 82–3, 89–90, 104, 138,
  249–50
  British, and critical
  problems 180–3, 198,
  251–2
Oxford Movement 245, 247,
  251, 283, 287–8

Paradigm shifts 3, 260
Passover 67, 77, 88, 101
Pentateuch, date of language
  of 52, 228
  dates of laws of 68, 131
  time of writing of 31–2,
  34–5, 52, 64–5, 89, 94–7,
  128, 149, 155, 177, 199–
  200, 257
  Mosaic authorship of 8, 21,
  87, 180, 199, 287
  documentary hypothesis
  19–22, 67, 133, 199, 223,
  226, 264, 266
  fragmentary hypothesis 35,
  64, 155–6
  supplementary hypothesis
  127, 133, 226, 261, 266
Persia 48, 55, 77–8, 116, 135
Pharisees 78, 212

Philistines 193, 267
Philosophy 6, 8, 85n, 249–50,
  292
  speculative idealism 44,
  107–8, 115–16, 249
Phoenicia 55
Pietism 16, 104, 166–7, 170,
  173
Plagiarism, S. Davidson's
  alleged 202–6
Priestly writer or source 64,
  260, 262–3, 265–6, 268–
  71
  see also Elohist *and*
  Grundschrift
Priests and priestly religion
  60, 62, 65, 75, 97, 177,
  241, 265
Progressive education or
  revelation 26, 187–9,
  191, 209–12, 216, 219,
  242, 246–7, 277, 284–5
Prophecy 126–7, 189–90,
  260, 275, 279
Prophets, prophetic
  religion 74, 76, 126, 150,
  241
Prussia 44, 80, 89, 92, 122,
  131
Psalms, form or type criticism
  of 41, 44, 45–6, 56–7
Psychology, biblical 117–20

'Q' (book of the four covenants)
  260–4

Rationalism 9, 16n3, 18, 39,
  51, 79, 82–3, 90, 111n20,
  136, 158, 165, 168, 170,
  172–3, 184, 201, 249, 252,
  276, 287
Reformation, the 9, 79, 81,
  278
Reviews, German works in
  British journals 160–1,
  178–9
Revival movement
  (*Erweckungs-
  bewegung*) 79, 139
Rome 48, 92, 164, 188

Sabbath 101
Sacrifice in the O.T., history
  of 29, 31, 33–4, 61–3, 74,
  100–1, 231, 239, 241, 243–
  4, 265, 278
Sadducees 78, 212

320 Index of Subjects and Biblical Names

Samaritan Pentateuch 31–2, 53, 87, 155
Samaritans 32
Samson 55, 75
Samuel 55, 74, 187, 193–4, 223–4, 240
Sanctuary, central vs. many 32, 34–5, 61, 65
Sarah (Sarai) 185
Satan 30, 77, 101, 118, 127
Saturn 72–3, 135
Saul 74–5, 96, 187, 193–4, 240
Sennacherib 187
Servant Songs in Isaiah 40–55 23
Social anthropology 4, 292
Sodom and Gomorrah 185
Solomon 29, 31, 35, 55, 62, 74–5, 94, 101, 116, 224
Structuralism 4
Sublimity 41–2, 70
Sun god 74–6
Supranaturalism 16n3, 18, 39, 79, 249
Syria 95

Temple, Jerusalem 62, 74, 76–8, 160
Ten commandments 33
Tent of meeting 29n4, 30, 60, 65, 268
Theocracy 60, 62, 65, 73, 77, 271
Tragedy 41
Translations, German to English 162–4, 175–8, 248, 281

Ulysses 98
Union, Church union in Germany 79–80, 86

Unitarianism 153, 158–9, 161–2, 164, 166, 207–8, 250, 276
Universities, English 138, 292
German 15, 138–9, 142–4, 292
University,
Aberdeen 275nn18–19
Altdorf 15
Basel 44, 85–6, 139, 268nn47 & 50, 272
Berlin 4, 15, 36n35, 44, 69, 81, 83, 86–7, 90, 104, 130, 136, 139, 164n35, 268nn48 & 50, 269n53
Bonn 15, 85, 130–1, 139, 268n50
Breslau 15, 89, 269n55
Cambridge 138, 159, 220, 249, 275n18, 282, 285, 286, 291
Dorpat (Tartu) 15, 89, 138–9
Dublin, Trinity College 138
Duisburg 15
Durham 138
Edinburgh 275nn18–19
Erfurt 15
Erlangen 15, 89, 104–5, 112, 139
Frankfurt an der Oder 15
Giessen 16, 268n48
Göttingen 15, 92, 122, 134, 136, 139, 159, 260nn9–10, 268nn47 & 50, 275n19, 281nn35 & 37
Greifswald 4, 64, 260n10
Halle 15, 51, 57, 83–4, 132, 134, 139, 208, 260n10, 270

Heidelberg 15, 37n35, 134, 136, 139, 281n36
Helmstedt 15
Jena 15, 36–7, 44, 139
Kiel 117n48, 130, 258n4
Königsberg 15, 89, 139
Leipzig 16, 89, 111–12, 139, 268n48, 269n55
London, King's College 138, 215–16, 286

Manchester (incl. Owens College) 138, 291
Marburg 16, 122, 131–2, 139, 260n10, 269n53
Oxford 4, 138, 193, 238n1, 249, 273, 281n37, 285, 287, 291
Prague 114
Rinteln 15
Rostock 89, 112, 117n48
Strasbourg 138, 258nn2 & 4, 259n8, 269n53
Tübingen 89, 92, 139, 269n55
Vienna 114, 136
Würzburg 16
Zürich 138–9
Uriah 30

Yahweh and Elohim not criteria for sources 88
Yahweh, name introduced in time of David 223–4
Yahwist writer or source 19–20, 133, 199–200, 207, 229–30, 257, 261–4, 266, 270–1

Zadok 75
Zoroastrianism 55